China Insights

This book series collects and presents cutting-edge studies on various issues that have emerged during the process of China's social and economic transformation, and promotes a comprehensive understanding of the economic, political, cultural and religious aspects of contemporary China. It brings together academic endeavors by contemporary Chinese researchers in various social science and related fields that record, interpret and analyze social phenomena that are unique to Chinese society, its reforms and rapid transition. This series offers a key English-language resource for researchers and students in China studies and related subjects, as well as for general interest readers looking to better grasp today's China. The book series is a cooperation project between Springer and China Social Science Press of China.

More information about this series at http://www.springer.com/series/13591

Yang Li · Xiaojing Zhang

China's National Balance Sheet

Theories, Methods and Risk Assessment

中国社会科学出版社
CHINA SOCIAL SCIENCES PRESS

Springer

Yang Li
Chinese Academy of Social Sciences
Beijing
China

Xiaojing Zhang
Chinese Academy of Social Sciences
Beijing
China

Translated by Yili Fu

ISSN 2363-7579 ISSN 2363-7587 (electronic)
China Insights
ISBN 978-981-10-4384-0 ISBN 978-981-10-4385-7 (eBook)
DOI 10.1007/978-981-10-4385-7

Jointly published with China Social Sciences Press, Beijing, China.

The print edition is not for sale in China Mainland. Customers from China Mainland please order the print book from: China Social Sciences Press.

Library of Congress Control Number: 2017937912

Printed on acid-free paper

This Springer imprint is published by Springer Nature
The registered company is Springer Nature Singapore Pte Ltd.
The registered company address is: 152 Beach Road, #21-01/04 Gateway East, Singapore 189721, Singapore

Preface

In 2012, the three research teams led respectively by Dr. Cao Yuanzheng, chief economist at the Bank of China, Dr. Ma Jun, Deutsche Bank's chief economist for Greater China, and I carried out research on China's sovereign balance sheet almost simultaneously and have published the lengthy analysis reports successively. In the Chinese research community, it is rare for several research teams to invariably study a boring topic that is purely "monarchy trickery". That is because, since the end of 2011, due to the debt problems of the Chinese local government financing platform and the slight downturn of the Chinese economy, pessimistic views about the prospects of China from many foreign research institutions and investment banks have resurfaced; some international statistical rating organizations even downgraded China's sovereign rating. Chinese economists can't just sit back and do nothing about this. We are duty-bound to prepare China's sovereign balance sheet (especially the government balance sheet), carry out in-depth analysis of the origins, current status, characteristics and development prospects of the government debts at all levels in China and assess the sovereign debt risks.

Balance sheet was originally an indispensable basic tool for enterprises to perform scientific management. Based on accrual accounting, a balance sheet or statement of financial position is a summary of a series of carefully designed financial balances. From the perspective of liabilities, a balance sheet reflects a company's total liabilities and their structure at a specific point in time and reveals the amount, urgency and solvency pressure of its current and future debts; from the perspective of assets, a balance sheet reflects a company's total assets and their structure at a specific point in time and reveals its economic resources, resource distribution and profitability. Based on its liabilities and assets, we can assess the performance of a company, analyze its financial flexibility and safety and measure its solvency and operational stability.

In the mid-twentieth century, the U.S. economist Goldsmith tried to introduce the unique analysis function of balance sheet into state governance (see Goldsmith and Lipsey 1963; Goldsmith 1982) and prepared the sectoral and aggregate national balance sheets on a trial basis. Later, the developed economies followed suit one after another. So far, most of the OECD member countries have published their financial balance sheets excluding physical assets.

It was after the Latin American debt crisis in the 1990s that the world had a different face for the national balance sheet due to its important role in state governance and even economic analysis. Unlike the past crises, the Latin American crisis was mainly caused by excessive borrowing, thus showing the typical characteristics of a debt crisis. Therefore, balance sheet as an analysis framework that can accurately portray a country's a debt risks and assess its solvency has naturally won the favor of the international community.

After balance sheet, as a mainstream analysis tool, was introduced, a series of new achievements were quickly made. Among them, what was particularly fresh and new was the reinterpretation of the past crises, especially the interpretation of some special phenomena during the spread and recovery of a crisis. In this regard, the research findings of Richard C. Koo, chief economist of Nomura Research Institute in Japan, were most famous (Richard C. Koo 2008). In his view, mainstream economics missed the point in explanation of the causes for the Great Depression and Japan's "two lost decades" since the 1990s. He believes that the currency demanders rather than the suppliers should be blamed for the crisis. Japan's "Great Recession" that began in 1990 was a "balance sheet recession". It was triggered by a collapse in land and stock prices, which caused Japanese firms that had excessively expanded their businesses to have negative equity, meaning their assets were worth less than their liabilities. Therefore, even though companies were still operating, they had been caught in a situation of technical insolvency. The point was, in such case, most companies shifted their business objective from "profit maximization" to "debt minimization". That is, while reducing or even stopping lending, companies opted to pay down their debts from their own cash flows, or you may say, did their upmost to "repair their balance sheets". If many companies were pursuing this "debt minimization" measure, the whole society would form a "fallacy of composition" in which companies did not attend to business or investment, but specialized in paying debts, so even though banks were willing to provide loans, no company would borrow money from them. The credit crunch of the whole society would thus form. The crisis recovery process would therefore slow down.

The "once-in-a-blue-moon" global economic crisis demonstrates once again the charm of asset and liability analysis. The crisis was also triggered by operation or consumption on borrowings of residents, businesses and governments in developed countries and high leverage operation of financial institutions. Therefore, to recover from the crisis, "deleveraging" is apparently a necessary condition. However, deleveraging involves at least two issues. First, deleveraging needs plenty of savings and huge capital investment; while the savings rate can not be raised arbitrarily and it is more difficult to find funds. Second, deleveraging as a major path of economic recovery will lead to a comprehensive "balance sheet repair" process. In this process, after economies obtained additional funds, they will opt to enrich the capital, reduce debts and "repair" their balance sheets rather than engaged in normal economic activities the monetary authorities want to produce, such as consumption, production and investment. Thus, injecting liquidity into the economy will on the contrary produce stagnant consumption, sluggish investment and credit market contraction in a long period of time.

An incredible case occurred in the U.S. Although in the past few years, the Fed and the Treasury have created dollars to such an extent that the U.S. and even the world were awash with liquidity, the U.S. credit markets were still in decline, so the Fed continued to expand its quantitative easing program, and its assets and liabilities have increased unprecedentedly by three times.

It is particularly worth mentioning that China has actually felt the impact of assets and liabilities this time. On the one hand, corporate and governmental debts continued to rise and have reached the level of severity that might be cashed in on by persons with ulterior motives; on the other hand, money and credit supply expanded significantly, but the real economy still thought it "difficult and costly to get loans". These complex problems need to be addressed quickly. To prepare China's national balance sheet, we must first of all have a "clear idea in mind", which is apparently the basis and prerequisite for addressing all the problems.

The research group of the Chinese Academy of Social Sciences (CASS) for "Research on China's National Balance Sheet" published its first findings in 2012. At that time, we had completed the preparation of China's Sovereign Balance Sheet (2000–2010), and the major findings were published on Issue 6–7 of *Economic Research Journal* in 2012. Li Yang, Zhang Xiaojing, Chang Yan, Tang Duo Duo, Li Cheng: China's Sovereign Balance Sheet and Risk Assessment (Vol. 1 and 1), Issue 6–7 of *Economic Research Journal* in 2012. The research findings of the research group have been repeatedly cited by the IMF (IMF 2013), the Research Bureau of the People's Bank of China and some well-known domestic and foreign investment banks. In addition, the research paper in English on China's sovereign balance sheet has been included in the monograph published by the IMF[1]. In September 2012, the research group held the International Seminar on Chin's National Balance Sheet Analysis, and more than 60 well-known experts and scholars from, the People's Bank of China, the National Bureau of Statistics, the World Bank, the IMF and related fields attended the seminar. Experts naturally showered praise, but they also raised poignant suggestions on further improvement and promotion. The book was written with reference to these suggestions.

The book fully updated the data on the basis of the research findings in 2012 and added the contents and analysis of China's national balance sheet.

The book's key findings can be summarized as follows:

1. In 2011, China's net national assets (non-financial assets plus net external assets) was over 300 trillion yuan.
   China's national balance sheet expanded rapidly in 2007–2011: China's total assets increased from 284.7 to 546.5 trillion yuan; its total liabilities increased

[1]Li Yang, Zhang Xiaojing, 2013, "China's Sovereign Balance Sheet and Implications for Financial Stability", in China's Road to Greater Financial Stability: Some Policy Perspectives, edited by Udaibir S. Das, Jonathan Fiechter, and Tao Sun, the IMF Press

from 118.9 to 242 trillion yuan; and its net assets increased from 165.8 to 304.5 trillion yuan. These three indicators nearly doubled in the five years, with a growth rate higher than the growth rate of the nominal GDP over the same period.

China's overall liability-asset ratio, i.e. ratio of total liabilities to total assets, shows an upward trend as a whole, especially in the two years of 2009–2010 with more serious impact of the financial crisis. It fell slightly later in 2011, but was still much higher than the level in 2007. This structural change shows an increased reliance on debt financing in the formation of national assets and consequently higher debt risks.

2. The increase of China's net national assets was continuously less than the year's GDP, indicating that not all the GDP has been transformed into real cumulative wealth. In other words, a fairly large part in our GDP output is invalid. This is because the GDP indicator has some congenital defects: some invalid investment (corresponding to the excess capacity) or even activities that destroy resources and environment are included in the GDP, so these parts should be excluded in wealth formation. Taking 2010 for example, the gap between the increase of net assets and GDP was up to 7.5 trillion yuan, accounting for 18.7% of GDP. Although we cannot assert that this 7.5 trillion yuan has been wasted or lost, but it at least shows that there is some serious problem with the quality of this year's GDP.
3. The inventory to total assets (ITA) ratio has surged in recent years, showing that the overcapacity problem is very serious. There are always two explanations for inventory and its changes: this may reflect the expectation of an enterprise for the economic recovery (which is mostly reflected as positive inventory replenishment or can be understood as a positive inventory increase), or may be related to the current widespread overcapacity in China (which is mostly reflected as passive inventory accumulation or can be interpreted as negative inventory increase). We tend to believe that the later cause, namely overcapacity, may be a major factor for the surge in the ITA ratio. We should remain highly vigilant about this.
4. If the assets of sovereign sector (or government sector in a broad sense, including the central government, local governments, state-owned non-financial enterprises, administrative institutions, the central bank, and state-owned financial enterprises) are worth more than their liabilities, their net assets will be positive. This suggests that in a long period of time, China is unlikely to suffer a sovereign debt crisis.

China's sovereign debts and assets showed an upward trend during 2000–2011. On the part of sovereign assets, the state-owned assets and reserve assets of non-financial enterprises saw fastest growth. On the part of sovereign debts, the debts of the governments (both central and local) and state-owned enterprises and the contingent debts from disposal of non-performing assets grew rapidly. Since in the past 12 years, China's sovereign assets have increased sharper than its sovereign debts, the net worth of China's sovereign assets has been growing.

In 2011, based on the wide-scope rough estimate, the net worth of Chin's sovereign assets was 87 trillion yuan. But given that the state-owned assets of administrative institutions are highly illiquid (because they have to perform the government functions) and the right to use land and resource assets is also highly illiquid and can not be transferred in whole (in fact, the land transfer fees are recently only 2~3 trillion yuan a year), therefore the net worth of narrow-scope sovereign assets is 21.6 trillion yuan.

5. In 2012, the total debt of the central government and local governments was nearly 28 trillion yuan, accounting for 53% of GDP. China's total debt, including government debt, as well as the debt of financial institutions, non-financial businesses and households, amounted to 111.6 trillion yuan, accounting for 215% of GDP. This means that the leverage ratio of the whole society is very high. To create a long-term stable environment for economic development, deleveraging is inevitable.

   Sectorally, as of the end of 2012, the leverage rate of the corporate sector (ratio of corporate debt to GDP) was up to 113%, more than the threshold of 90% of the OECD countries, which needs to arouse our sharp vigilance. These indicators topped the list of all statistical countries. This is a distinctive feature of the Chinese debt structure. This is closely related to China's economic development pattern and the characteristics of the financial sector focusing on indirect financing.

   The balance of loans of the household sector was 16.1 trillion yuan (including consumer loans of 10.4 trillion yuan and business loans of 5.7 trillion yuan), accounting for 31% of GDP.

   The debt balance of the non-financial corporate sector was 72.12 trillion yuan, accounting for 139% of GDP. Given that the debt of the non-financial corporate sector includes to a considerable extent the debt of the government-backed entities of the local government financing platform, it is necessary to exclude the debt of the local government financing platform to prevent overlapping, and the debt balance of the non-financial corporate sector thus obtained was 58.67 trillion yuan, accounting for 113% of GDP.

   The total debt of central government and local governments, i.e. total government debt, was 27.7 trillion yuan by the end of 1012, accounting for 53% of GDP.

   If only the balance of the bonds issued by the financial sector was regarded as financial sector debt, then the total bond balance of f the financial institutions was 9.13 trillion yuan by the end of 2012, accounting for 18% of GDP.

   By adding up the debts of the above four sectors, we can obtain the overall debt scale of the Chinese economy, which is 111.6 trillion yuan, and the leverage rate of the whole society is 215%.

   Aggregately, China's total debt remains at a relatively mild and controllable moderate level, lower than most developed economies, but higher than all the other BRIC countries (excluding South Africa). However, given that China's debt level has increased rapidly in recent years, we should be highly vigilant about this. If the debt of local governments or the sovereign debt in a wide scope is taken into account, China's government (sovereign) debt will be much greater and the overall debt level will also be much higher. In this regard, we must not sit by idly and remain indifferent.

6. After entering the new century, China's national and sovereign balance sheets have been showing a rapid expansion momentum. Among them, on the part of assets, external assets, infrastructures, and residential real estate assets accumulated rapidly and constitute the dominant factor for expansion of assets. This records the historical process of China's accelerated industrialization and urbanization under the export-oriented development strategies. On the part of liabilities, the debt level of the governments, state-owned enterprises and other sovereign sectors are expanding at a rate higher than that of the private sector. This highlights the institutional feature that the government plays the leading role in economic activities.
7. The near-term risks of the national balance sheet are mainly reflected in real estate credit, local debt, and non-performing loans and other aspects, while the long-term risks are more concentrated in foreign assets, corporate debt, social security bad debt and other aspects. Regardless of what kind of risks they are, these risks are closely related to the economic current development pattern and structure. Therefore the best way to cope with and fend off the risks is to change the development pattern and adjust the economic structure to achieve healthy, high-efficient, high-quality and sustainable growth.
8. If the current old-age insurance system continues to operate, the old-age insurance system for employees of enterprises will face fund shortage by 2023; the cumulative balance will be fully exhausted by 2029; the cumulative shortage of pension for workers will account for 91% of GDP that year by 2050. In addition, China's total expenditure on pensions (including the old-age insurance for workers and residents) will account for 11.85% of GDP by 2050, which is roughly consistent with the current level of some European countries with high social welfare.

We have also analyzed the impact of some policy measures and pension systems on the sustainability of the old-age insurance under various scenarios. We found that raising the retirement age and the age to receive basic pension can significantly reduce the extent of pension shortage. In addition, improving the return rate of investment from old-age insurance premiums can also help reduce pension shortage, though with limited effects. Maintaining a high pension substitution rate will significantly improve the potential pension debt level. We prefer the action to raise retirement age and the age to receive basic pension and suggest increasing the return rate of investment and maintaining a high pension substitution rate.

Undoubtedly, we can provide financial subsidies to the old-age insurance by using the dividends of state-owned assets or returns from sale of state-own assets, raising taxes or issuing bonds, which is a viable option to solve or alleviate the pension shortage problem.

The Decision of the Central Committee of the Communist Party of China on Some Major Issues Concerning Comprehensively Deepening the Reform adopted at the third Plenary Session of the 18th CPC Central Committee clearly stated that we should establish a unified national accounting system and formulate the national and local balance sheets. It is rare in today's world to promote research and preparation of the national balance sheet at the highest national level. This fully demonstrates the Chinese government's determination and wisdom "to promote the modernization of the state governance system and governance capacity".

As scholars of the highest social science research institute established by the State, we will respond to the call of the third Plenary Session of the 18th CPC Central Committee and continue to carry out research and preparation of the national balance sheet so as to make our due contribution to improving and developing the socialist system with Chinese characteristics and promoting the modernization of China's national governance system and capacity.

Beijing, China — Yang Li

Contents

List of Figures

List of Tables

Part I
General Report

Chapter 1
Introduction

1.1 Research Background

Debt crises have become the indispensable essential elements in modern economic crises. The most appropriate tool for analyzing a country's debt situation is the balance sheet of the country. Therefore, in order to reveal the root causes of a crisis, analyze its spread process and find the solutions, investigation on the assets and liabilities of the country where the crisis occurred as well as their dynamic equilibriums is sorely needed. Based on such an understanding, more and more researchers tend to regard the economic crises since the 1980s as the "balance sheet shocks", and also because of this, the analytical framework of balance sheets has been employed in recent years to address various macroeconomic issues, especially business cycles.

In the above practical and theoretical background, when local financing platforms in China began to see a wave of debt problems, there was concern over China's sovereign debt risks and pessimistic views about the economic development prospects of China resurfaced. Faced with these challenges, it is of great importance to formulate China's national balance sheet, especially a government balance sheet, and analyze the sources, status quo, and future prospects of China's debts.

The national balance sheet identifies the "real financial position" of an entire country through a well-designed theoretical framework and a series of data processing methodologies. Based on this framework, it reveals the relationships between major economic activities of economic entities and draws the outline of a country's economic operation mechanism. This framework is useful in accurately capturing a country's economic health and forecasting the sources and intensity of possible shocks. During financial crises in particular, the national balance sheet can offer references for policy discussions. Furthermore, as a stock indicator instead of flow indicator such as gross domestic product (GDP), the national balance sheet enables us to reveal the cumulative effect of a country's economic growth over

Y. Li and X. Zhang, *China's National Balance Sheet*, China Insights,
DOI 10.1007/978-981-10-4385-7_1

time. With the help of a deeper analysis on a sector's asset-liability structure and its changing trends as well as the relevance with other sectors, we may also be able to interpret the structural and institutional characteristics of a country's economy so as to identify problems in the transformation of its development pattern and reveal the future trend of economic development.

Although the analysis methods for stock indicators such as balance sheet only aroused extensive attention in recent years, preparation and study of national balance sheet has a long history in the field of academic research. As early as in 1936, American scholars proposed applying corporate balance sheet preparation techniques to the national economy (Dickinson and Eakin 1936). As a sophisticated accounting framework, national balance sheet accounting emerged in the 1960s. Goldsmith et al. started the pioneering task of formulating sectoral and aggregate national balance sheets of the United States for a number of years from the early 20th century to 1980 (see Goldsmith and Lipsey 1963; Goldsmith 1982). Revell (1966) tentatively compiled the UK's national balance sheets for 1957–1961. Since 1975, the UK's national balance sheets have been officially published (see Holder 1998). Canada started to prepare its national balance sheet calculated at book and market values in 1990. So far, most OECD member states have published financial balance sheets that do not covers physical assets at least.

China started late in studying and compiling its national balance sheets. Although the National Bureau of Statistics (NBS) published two versions of *Methodology for the Compilation of China's Balance Sheet* in 1997 and 2007 respectively, China's official balance sheets are still in the stage of tentative draft and no data have been officially released to the public. So far, the balance sheets may only be an intermediate reference indicator or intermediate product of national economic accounting. The almost blank situation in this area makes it all the more urgent and challenging to draft not only a national balance sheet, but especially a sovereign balance sheet for China.

It should be noted that, over a long period of time, balance sheet has entered people's sights only as a statistical method under the overall framework of national economic statistical accounting. Since the large-scale financial crises broke out in Latin America and Asia in the 1990s, there have been increasingly animated discussions on this approach. There is a strong tendency following these discussions to evolve from pure statistical accounting to a standard approach for macroeconomic analysis. The studies of the theories and policies such as Balance Sheet Approach and Balance Sheet Recession have become common practice in recent years, clearly showing the development momentum of this kind of theories. What is particularly worth noting is that just in the three years from 2003 to 2005, the IMF has published more than 30 reports on analysis of national balance sheet and greatly promoted the development of relevant studies (see Mathisen and Pellechio 2006). After the global financial tsunami began in 2007, this analytical framework received extensive attention and recognition from academia, governments and international institutions. Some Chinese scholars also conducted preliminary analyses on China's economic issues using this approach (Yi 2008; Li 2009).

In general, in the academic innovation wave of discussions on financial crises in recent years, major progress has been made in researches applying national and sectoral balance sheets. For example, Allen et al. (2002) noted that the characteristics and advantages of the balance sheet approach (BSA) lie in that the four major financial risks can be clearly defined using the BSA: maturity mismatch, currency mismatch, capital structure mismatch and deficient solvency.[1] Analyses on these four risks are critical to unraveling the root cause and transmission mechanism of crises, reactions of micro-level economic entities to crises and the development of countermeasure policies. In addition to macro-level analyses, balance sheet studies are further conducted in the following three areas. First, the relationship between the capital structure of a sector (country) and financial stability as well as currency crises, are addressed (Allen et al. 2002; Hou 2006). Second, the sharing and contagion of inter-sector financial risks are studied (Gray et al. 2007; Hou 2006). Third, the country case studies on debts, capital structure and financial stability are conducted (Haim and Levy 2007, Israel; Mathisen and Pellechio 2006, South Africa; Lima et al. 2006, Columbia; Rosenberg et al. 2005, the Emerging Markets).

The *Decision of the CCCPC on Some Major Issues Concerning Comprehensively Deepening the Reform* adopted at the 3rd Plenary Session of 18th CPC National Congress that was recently concluded clearly stated the strategic task of "accelerating the establishment of a unified national economic accounting system and preparing the national and local balance sheets". To promote the research and preparation of national balance sheet at the highest state level is rare in today's world. It fully demonstrates the Chinese government's determination and wisdom "to promote the modernization of the national governance systems and governance capacity".

This book aims to study and prepare China's aggregate balance sheet and the balance sheets for residents, non-financial corporations, financial institutions, the central bank, the central and local governments, the external sector and other sectors. It has fully considered the periodic, institutional and structural characteristics of economic development in the process of China's market reform, systematically analyzed the features and tracks of scale expansion and structural adjustment of China's economy, comprehensively evaluated the short- and long-term operation characteristics of the Chinese economy and objectively assessed the debt situation in China's economic development and its inherent financial risks. It should be noted that, given the limitation of data and possible controversies of estimation methodologies, we dare not overestimate the quality and systematic integrity of the data provided in this book. The task we set for ourselves is: to provide a series of scalable, amendable, extendable and inclusive estimation methods and analytical framework for China's balance sheets; to preliminarily analyze China's national and sectoral balance sheets based on scientifically estimating various types of data carefully collected; to try to use this analytical

[1]Among them, the first three mismatches, i.e. maturity mismatch, currency mismatch and capital structure mismatch, can be generally called balance sheet mismatch.

framework to examine from a new perspective the major issues China is currently facing, such as development sustainability, government restructuring, local debts, welfare reform, and openness and stability of the financial system; and to explore the countermeasures and programs for institutional reform.

1.2 Structure of the Book

Part I is the general report of research on China's national balance sheet and consists of 7 chapters. Chapter 1 is the introduction, which introduces research background and general theoretical framework; Chap. 2 focuses on the preparation and analysis of China's national balance sheet, including constituent items, accounting principles, estimation methods, data sources, sizes and structures, dynamic changes and other contents; Chap. 3 shifts to the studies of the balance sheets of the sovereign sector, i.e. government departments in a broad sense, and mainly discussed the structure and characteristics of the sovereign sector and its relationship with the private sector and its special status and role in China's economic structure etc.; Chap. 4 further analyzed assets, liabilities and other economic stock indicators by combining them with GDP, fiscal revenue and expenditure and other flow indicators, explored the overall level of China's national debts and the whole society leverage ratio and carried out scenario analysis of the future evolution track of debts with the help of the theoretical model; Chap. 5 analyzed from a more macro perspective the mechanism through which China's balance sheet has expanded under the background of China's economic growth and structural transformation and particularly highlights the impact of the special mechanism of China's economic system on assets and liability expansion and the logical connections between macroeconomic performance and balance sheet; Chap. 6 explored the risk level and accumulation path of China's national balance sheet and sectoral balance sheet and mainly revealed the severity, causes and potential changes of balance sheet risks and inter-departmental risk contagion; Chap. 7 systematically summarized the research findings of this book, drew the basic conclusions and proposed the appropriate policy recommendations.

Part II gives the details of the preparation of the balance sheets of residents, non-financial corporations, financial institutions as well as the central bank, the central government, local governments, the external sector and other sub-sectors. On this basis, combined with the historical track and future tasks of market-oriented reform and economic and social restructuring, Part II carried out forward-looking analysis of scale, structure and trends of respective assets and liabilities.

Part III brings together the special studies in the fields closely associated with the national and sectoral balance sheets, including China's implicit pension debt and its transition dynamics, research on residential real estate market, comparison of wealth of citizens of China and the US, estimate of value of land and resources, international experience associated with national balance sheet and comparative analysis, balance sheet methods, financial crises and so on.

1.3 Some Explanations

The national balance sheet research group of the Chinese Academy of Social Sciences (CASS) was founded in 2011. The head of the research group is Li Yang, a member of the Academic Divisions of CASS and vice president of CASS, and the deputy head is researcher Zhang Xiaojing, academic secretary (the level of deputy bureau director) of the Academic Division of Economics of CASS. The first findings were achieved in 2012. At that time, it had already completed the preparation of China's sovereign balance sheet (2000–2010), and the main findings were published in Issue 6 and 7 of *Economic Research* in 2013.[2] In September 2012, the group held the International Symposium on Analysis of China's National Balance Sheet, and more than 60 well-known experts and scholars from the People's Bank of China, the National Bureau of Statistics, the World Bank, the International Monetary Fund and the related fields attended the symposium. The experts not only spoke highly of the findings, but also put forward suggestions on further improvement and expansion. The research findings of the research group were repeatedly cited by IMF (2013), the Research Bureau of the People's Bank of China and some well-known domestic and foreign investment banks. In addition, the English version of paper for research on China's sovereign balance sheet has been included in the monograph published by IMF.[3]

This book has comprehensively updated the data based on the research findings in 2012 and added the preparation and analysis of China's national balance sheet. It should be noted that due to the limitation of data available, the latest data in this book about the national balance sheet as well as the balance sheets of the sovereign sector, residents, financial institutions, the central government, local governments and other sectors were updated to 2011; non-financial corporations, the central bank, the external sector as well as debt level, leverage ratio and other indicators were updated to 2012. In addition, according to the characteristics of data and study objects, this book has made a traceback of the related indicators in different time periods (for example, the time span for whole society leverage ratio analysis is from 1996 to 2012) so as to better reflect the changing trend of variables.

The authors of this book are as follows: Chaps. 1–7 General Report (Li Yang, Zhang Xiaojing, Chang Xin, Tang Duoduo and Li Cheng), Chaps. 8, 16–18 (Li Cheng), Chaps. 9 and 14 (Wang Jia), Chap. 10 (Zhang Lei), Chap. 11 (Chen Changbing), Chap. 12 (Wang Hongju), Chap. 13 (Chang Xin), Chap. 15 (Liu Xueliang), and Chap. 19 (Sun Tao). Li Yang and Zhang Xiaojing are responsible for designing the framework of this book and its proofreading. The book was finalized by Li Yang.

---

[2]Li Yang, Zhang Xiaojing, Chang Xin, Tong Duoduo and Li Cheng (2012), "China's Sovereign Balance Sheet and Its Risk Assessment" (Vol. 1 and 2), "Economic Research", Issue 6 and 7, 2012.

[3]Li Yang, Zhang Xiaojing, 2013, "China's sovereign balance sheet and implications for financial stability", in *China's Road to Greater Financial Stability: Some Policy Perspectives*, edited by Udaibir S. Das, Jonathan Fiechter, and Tao Sun. The IMF Press.

Chapter 2
China's National Balance Sheet: Preparation and Analysis

2.1 Basic Framework

A national balance sheet aims to study a country's overall economic stocks. According to the System of National Accounts (SNA2008) jointly developed by the UN, IMF, OECD and the European Commission, the balance sheet of a country includes six major sectors: non-financial corporations, financial corporations (including the central bank),[1] general government (including the governments at all levels, social security funds and non-profit organizations controlled by the governments), residents (also called households), non-profit organizations serving households (NPISHs),[2] and the non-household sector (i.e. the external sector).

Based on the relevant international standards and the related description of NBS (2007), we have compiled the simple framework of national balance sheet suitable for China's national conditions (see Table 2.1). In the table, the main columns cover assets, liabilities and their difference, and the auxiliary column covers various sectors of the national economy and their aggregates.

The basic logic relationship of balance sheet can be broadly summarized as follows:

$$\text{Total assets} = \text{liabilities} + \text{net assets} \tag{2.1}$$

$$\text{Total assets} = \text{non-financial assets} + \text{financial assets} \tag{2.2}$$

---

[1]The central bank was also included in the government sector by some scholars, such as Allen et al. (2002).

[2]They refer to non-government-controlled organizations that serve households free of charges or charging only nominal fees, including professional associations, religious organizations, charities and research institutes.

Y. Li and X. Zhang, *China's National Balance Sheet*, China Insights,
DOI 10.1007/978-981-10-4385-7_2

Table 2.1 Framework of national balance sheet

	Non-financial corporations	Financial institutions	Governments	Households	Total of domestic sectors	External sector	Total
Non-financial assets							
Fixed assets							
Inventory							
Other non-financial assets (land, intangible assets, deferred assets and other assets)							
Financial assets/liabilities							
(I) Domestic financial assets/liabilities							
Currencies and deposits							
Loans							
Stocks and other equities							
Debt securities							
Insurance reserves							
Other receivables/payables							
(II) External financial assets/liabilities							
Direct investment							
Security investment							
Other investments							
(III) Reserve assets							
Gold reserves and special drawing right							
Foreign exchange reserves							
Difference between assets and liabilities (net asset)							

As liabilities are financial liabilities[3] and the financial claims in the national balance sheet (of a country) and the financial liabilities (of the other country) are mirror images, they occur simultaneously and are equal in size and opposite in direction. That is, on a global scale (or in all economies), financial assets = financial liabilities, so we can combine (2.1) and (2.2) to obtain:

$$\text{Net assets} = \text{non-financial assets} \tag{2.3}$$

To make Eq. (2.3) tenable, the premise is to include the external sector. To include the external sector is, on the one hand, to meet the need for accounting balance, and on the other hand, it will make sense to study the external sector only if we regard the global economy as an international organization on the whole as the United Nations or the IMF does (in Table 2.1, the global economy is regarded as the study object). As far as individual economies are concerned, the aggregate of the domestic sectors has a real sense, so the two columns of external sector and aggregate can be ignored.

Going a step further, financial assets/liabilities include three items: item (I) is domestic financial assets/liabilities, and item (II) and (III) are actually International Investment Position (IIP) as we usually refer to. Because domestic financial assets = domestic financial liabilities (that is the assets and liabilities in item (I) are fully offset), then the total net financial assets of the domestic sectors are equal to the sum of item (II) and (III) and also equal to net IIP, so there exists:

$$\begin{aligned}\text{Net assets of the domestic sectors} &= \text{non-financial assets} \\ &\quad + \text{net financial assets of the domestic sectors} \\ &= \text{non-financial assets} + \text{net IIP}\end{aligned} \tag{2.4}$$

Comparing (2.3) and (2.4), we can find that, when specifically studying an economy, the consolidated balance sheet tends to lose a lot of useful information. Therefore, SNA2008 takes a reserved attitude towards the consolidation of balance sheets.

The sectoral division, subject categories, aggregation methods for national balance sheets and some accounting equations given above constitute the theoretical basis for the preparation of balance sheet.

[3]As the debtor-creditor relationship does not exist for non-financial assets, they only reflect the asset side of the holder, i.e. the user, but are not reflected in the liability side, i.e. the originator. Thus, the liability side of balance sheet only includes financial liabilities.

2.2 Preparation of National Balance Sheet

According to the analytical framework described above, in this chapter, we have tentatively prepared China's national balance sheets of 2007–2011 using publicly available data and relevant theoretical assumptions and estimation methods.

The asset side of national balance sheet includes the two major items of non-financial assets and financial assets. Non-financial assets include residents' real estate and automobiles, rural productive fixed assets, cooperate fixed assets, inventories, cooperate intangible assets and business reputation, administrative institutions' fixed assets, public institutions' intangible assets and government-owned resource assets (land); financial assets include currencies, deposits, loans, bonds, stocks, securities investment fund shares, clients' margins of securities companies, insurance reserves, settlement funds, transactions of financial institutions, reserves, cash holdings, lending of the central bank, other items (net), foreign direct investment, other external claims and obligations, and international reserve assets.

The liabilities side includes currencies, deposits, loans, bonds, stocks, securities investment fund shares, clients' margins of securities companies, insurance reserves, settlement funds, transactions of financial institutions, reserves, cash holdings, lending of the central bank, other items (net), foreign direct investment, other external claims and obligations, international payment errors and omissions and other items. By definition, liabilities refer only to financial liabilities, without physical counterparts. The difference between assets and liabilities is net assets, which corresponds to the owner's equity or capital in the financial statements of enterprises.

Here are some explanations about the estimates: (1) non-financial assets mainly include the relevant assets of the subsectors such as households, non-financial corporations and governments. (2) The basic method to estimate financial assets and financial liabilities is to add up the flow data of the following years on the basis of the stock of funds accounts of a base year. Based on this idea, in this study, we added up the data of the domestic sectors in the flow of funds accounts (financial transactions) of the following years published by the National Bureau of Statistics (NBS) on the basis of the research on China's national financial assets and liabilities in 1998 conducted by NBS (Department of National Accounts, NBS 2003).[4] We did not use the sectoral accumulation method because it is difficult to ensure complete correspondence and matching between assets and liabilities through direct accumulation as there may be differences in the estimation methods and data sources of various sectors. (3) As the stock of funds accounts in 1998 did not include the items such as securities investment fund shares, clients' margins of securities companies, settlement funds, transactions of financial institutions,

[4]In fact, the Survey and Statistics Department of the People's Bank of China has completed the preparation of the financial stock of funds accounts for 2004 and 2005. If the data are available, the estimates may be more accurate.

reserves, cash holdings, lending of the central bank, and international payment errors and omissions, we added up only the flow data of the previous years (the data of the flow of funds accounts published by NBS from 1992). (4) Given that the 1998 stock of funds accounts and the flow of funds accounts of the previous years were not entirely consistent in items, when determining the base year data, necessary adjustment was made for the two items of "Other Items (Net)" and "Other External Claims and Obligations".

According to the above estimation method, Table 2.2 lists China's national balance sheets of 2007–2011.

2.3 National Balance Sheet Analysis

2.3.1 Total Size

(1) The national balance sheet has expanded significantly, with net assets of more than 300 trillion yuan

As shown in Table 2.2, during 2007–2011, China's national balance sheet expanded sharply: the total assets increased from 284.7 to 546.5 trillion yuan (see Fig. 2.1); the total liabilities increased from 118.9 to 242 trillion yuan (see Fig. 2.2); and the net assets increased from 165.8 to 304.5 trillion yuan (see Fig. 2.3). The three indicators almost doubled in five years, and their growth rates were all faster than the growth rate of nominal GDP in the same period.

(2) The increase in net assets was continuously lower than GDP, showing that not all of the GDPs will form a real accumulation of wealth.

To put it simply, the relationship between a country's GDP and net assets is a flow-stock relationship. On the assumption of an ease policy, a country's stock of wealth (i.e. net assets) is obtained by adding up the flows of GDP of various years. Of course, as the two statistical indicators are different in coverage, the total flow of GDP is not exactly equal to the stock of wealth in most cases.

To find the sum of the flows of GDP, the stock of wealth in the base year is needed. To avoid this hard nut, we have chosen to compare the increase in net assets with GDP. As shown in Fig. 2.4, the increase in net assets of each year during 2008–2011 calculated based on the national balance sheet is closer to the GDP of the year. However, when studying further, we will find that the increase in net assets is continuously less than the GDP of the year. Apart from the possible aforementioned statistical reasons, this has also revealed a more important message: although the growth rate of GDP each year is high, not all of GDPs will form a real accumulation of wealth. This is because the GDP indicator is flawed, some invalid investment (leading to excess capacity) and even the activities destroying resources and environment are included in GDP, so these should be deducted from the wealth.

Table 2.2 China's national balance sheet: 2007–2011 (unit: 1 billion yuan)

Item\Year	2007	2008	2009	2010	2011
Non-financial assets	**158,311.0**	**185,944.5**	**213,630.2**	**244,233.6**	**288,550.7**
Residents' real estate	56,700.3	57,816.8	73,911.3	80,902.3	96,287.5
Residents' automobiles	2357.6	2811.8	3512.3	4463.7	5445.8
Rural productive fixed assets	1488.4	1589.7	1727	1819.1	2708.3
Corporate fixed assets	39,852.0	50,929.3	55,091.7	61,461.5	68,962.5
Inventories	13,878.4	17,844.8	21,131.9	28,699.8	36,697.1
Other corporate non-financial assets	8438.2	13,070.6	14,324.6	16,636.9	19,871.4
Administrative institutions' fixed assets	4304	4759	5293	5868.2	6528
Public institutions' intangible assets	20	24.2	31.2	44.9	48
Government-owned resource assets (land)	31,272.1	37,098.4	38,607.1	44,337.1	52,002.2
Financial assets	**126,386.6**	**150,754.3**	**187,107.8**	**224,414.2**	**257,961.3**
Currencies	2924.426	3310.926	3691.226	4302.926	4882.126
Deposits	39,226.35	47,387.05	61,327.05	74,705.05	86,127.05
Loans	30,036.24	36,107.74	48,219.74	57,942.44	67,518.84
Bonds	13,007.52	15,686.22	18,144.82	20,966.52	22,586.02
Stocks	8476.147	8763.147	9498.447	10,442.547	10,942.747
Securities investment fund shares	810.7	1142.7	1023.8	993.4	1219.2
Clients' margin of securities companies	1267.2	733.2	1352.1	1116.7	470.1
Insurance reserves	2971.87	3829.57	4708.67	5339.16	6073.96
Settlement funds	−213.162	−213.162	−213.162	−213.162	−213.162
Transactions of financial institutions	3049.717	2630.017	2765.417	2997.317	3228.117
Reserves	5672.43	7782.43	8933.13	12,259.23	15,874.63
Cash holdings	235.953	240.953	280.953	356.053	463.253
Lending of the central bank	−808.923	−857.423	−1016.32	−969.417	−1042.12

(continued)

Table 2.2 (continued)

Item\Year	2007	2008	2009	2010	2011
Other items (net)	3098.759	4055.959	5455.059	7394.559	10,069.86
Foreign direct investment	717.878	1089.478	1389.378	1796.568	2117.668
Other external claims and obligations	3865.634	4105.734	3866.134	4109.534	4262.534
International reserve assets	12,047.903	14,959.803	17,681.403	20,874.803	23,380.503
Total assets	**284,697.6**	**336,698.8**	**400,738**	**468,647.8**	**546,512**
Financial liabilities	**118,945.77**	**140,234.37**	**174,534.98**	**209,742.8**	**241,967.2**
Currencies	3037.58	3448.78	3853.38	4504.12	5120.32
Deposits	39,599.05	47,788.15	61,734.15	74,800.15	86,142.15
Loans	30,090.44	35,878.94	47,687.94	57,292.44	66,851.64
Bonds	13,168.07	15,846.77	18,305.37	21,127.07	22,746.57
Stocks	9315.481	9654.681	10,351.281	11,450.581	11,992.181
Securities investment fund shares	810.7	1144.3	1023.7	992.9	1221.1
Clients' margin of securities companies	1267.2	733.2	1360.4	1123.1	472
Insurance reserves	2971.969	3829.669	4708.769	5339.259	6074.059
Settlement funds	−223.405	−223.405	−223.405	−223.405	−223.405
Transactions of financial institutions	3280.677	2760.077	3292.877	4299.377	4718.177
Reserves	5423.763	7533.763	8684.463	12,010.56	15,625.96
Cash holdings	713.392	718.392	759.992	831.391	935.591
Lending of The Central Bank	−1273.86	−1322.36	−1481.26	−1434.36	−1507.06
Other items (net)	2578.101	3535.301	4934.401	6873.901	9549.201
Foreign direct investment	6454.98	7482.08	8016.18	9269.08	10,691.48
Other external claims and obligations	2478.447	2354.247	2752.447	3116.347	3412.847
BOP errors and omissions	−746.812	−928.212	−1225.71	−1629.71	−1855.61
Net financial assets	**7440.83**	**10,519.93**	**12,572.82**	**14,671.4**	**15,994.1**
Net assets	**165,751.83**	**196,464.43**	**226,203.02**	**258,905**	**304,544.8**

Taking 2010 for example, the difference between the increase in net assets and GDP is up to 7.5 trillion yuan, accounting for 18.7% of GDP. Although 7.5 trillion yuan may not be all wasted or lost, this at least shows the quality of the year's GDP is highly questionable.

The above analysis fully reveals the importance of balance sheet analysis. That is, wealth as a stock indicator can be used to measure the quality of GDP growth and whether there is something wrong with the development mode.

2.3.2 *Structure*

The balance sheet provides two groups of meaningful data. The analysis of the relationship between different assets and different liabilities and between assets and liabilities may lead to a number of important conclusions reflecting the national economic structure. Based on these conclusions, coupled with other data and analysis, we can better plan our development direction and path.

In all structural data, we pay particular attention to the country's overall debt ratio, financial interrelation ratio, inventory percentage in total assets and changing trends of net financial assets.

(1) China's overall debt to assets ratio is generally showing an upward trend and the quality and efficiency of economic operation is low.

Figure 2.5 shows that China's overall debt to assets ratio, i.e. the ratio of total liabilities to total assets, is generally showing an upward trend. Especially during 2009–2010, a period seriously affected by the global financial crisis, China's overall debt to assets ratio saw a comparatively sharp increase, and later, despite a slight drop in 2011, it was far higher than the level in 2007. This structural change shows that in the formation of national assets, reliance on debt financing has increased, thus causing an increase in debt risks. More importantly, during this period, China's net asset expansion was generally slower the rate of expansion of total assets and total liabilities. This unequivocally tells us that: the wealth accumulation effects of

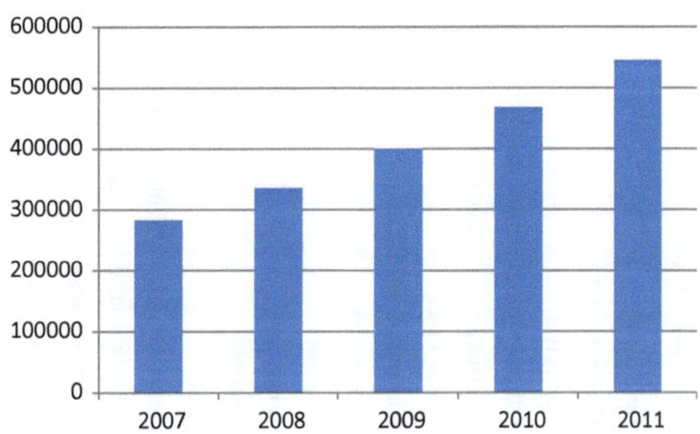

Fig. 2.1 China's total assets: 2007–2011 (unit: 1 billion yuan). *Source* Estimates of the research group

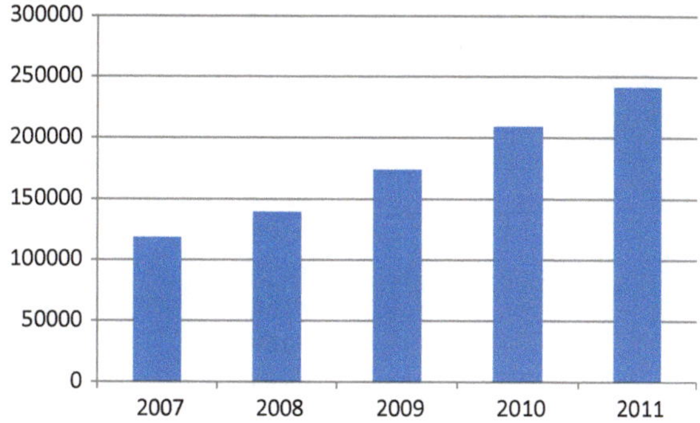

Fig. 2.2 China's total liabilities: 2007–2011 (unit: 1 billion yuan). *Source* Estimates of the research group

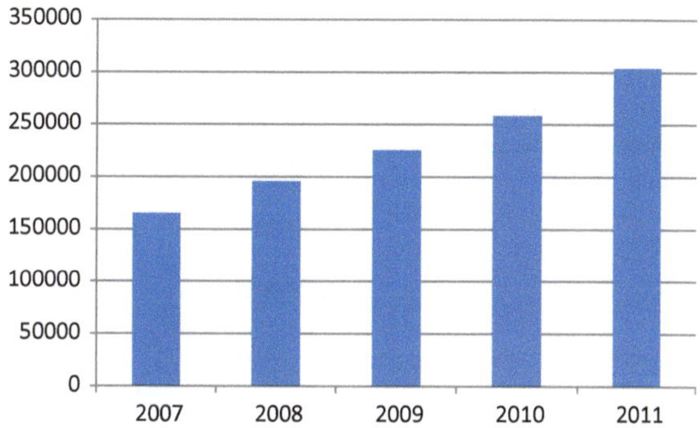

Fig. 2.3 China's total net assets during 2007–2011 (unit: 1 billion yuan). *Source* Estimates of the research group

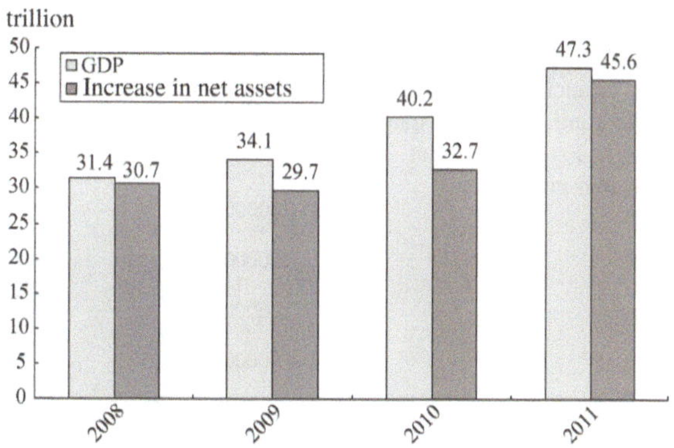

Fig. 2.4 Changes in GDP and the increase in net assets (unit: 1 trillion yuan)

economic growth in China are weak, and the low quality and efficiency as a traditional problem has not been essentially addressed.

(2) "Financial interrelation ratio" is still at a low level

During the investigation period, the size of China's financial assets and non-financial assets expanded rapidly (see Figs. 2.6 and 2.7). As the size of financial assets expanded at a faster rate, China's financial interrelation ratio had increased. This dynamic trend is similar to the development paths of other countries.

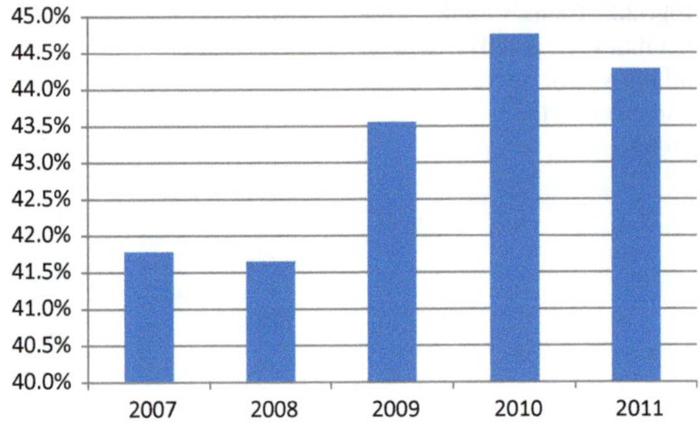

Fig. 2.5 Changes in China's debt to assets ratio: 2007–2011 (unit: %). *Source* Estimates of the research group

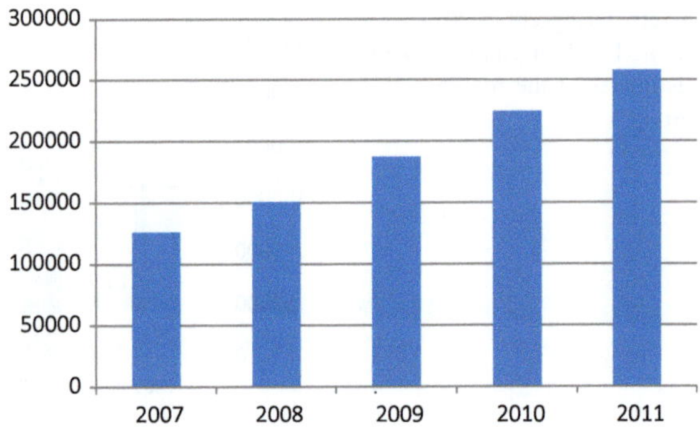

Fig. 2.6 China's total financial assets: 2007–2011 (unit: 1 billion yuan). *Source* Estimates of the research group

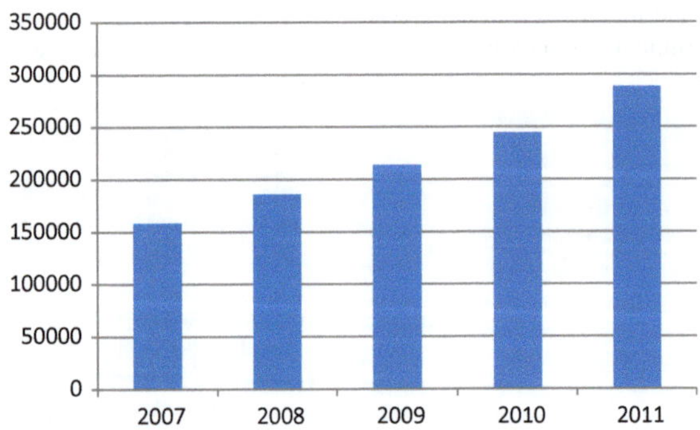

Fig. 2.7 China's total non-financial assets: 2007–2011 (unit: 1 billion yuan). *Source* Estimates of the research group

Financial interrelation ratio (FIR) was proposed by the American economist Goldsmith and Lipsey (1963). It refers to the ratio of a country's financial assets to real assets, and it is used to measure the extent of financialization of a country's economy.[5] Goldsmith's first study was completed in 1969, covering a financial

[5]Here, Goldsmith's concept is not very rigorous. For example, financial assets include financial assets and foreign assets, in which financial assets also include the financial assets in the financial

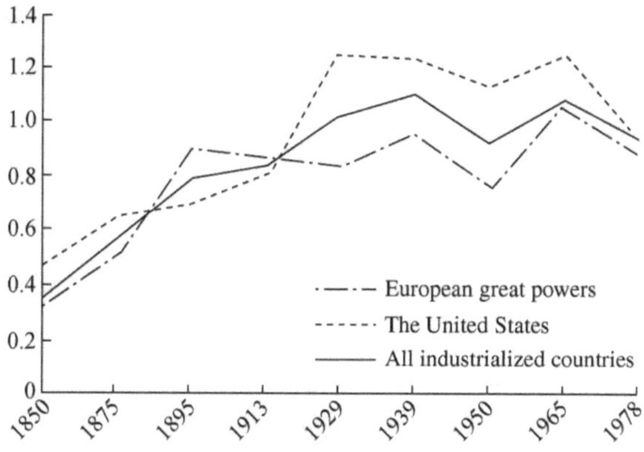

Fig. 2.8 Changes of FIR in industrialized countries (1850–1978). *Sources* Goldsmith (1985) and Tables 4–6

development history of 100 years (1860–1963) of 35 countries (Goldsmith 1969); the second study was completed in 1985 (Goldsmith 1985), covering a financial development history of nearly 200 years' (1688–1978) of 20 countries.

Figure 2.8 shows that in the industrialized countries that were studied, FIR was in a rising trend on the whole. In general, it rose from about 0.4 in 1850 to 0.8 or so at the end of the nineteenth century and reached and even exceeded 1 in the 1920s before the Great Depression. Since then, FIR continued to rise, but hit the bottom during the World War II and then rose again. Based on the data in Table 2.3, the FIR of the UK, as an established developed country, has always been the highest in the world and continued to rise in recent years and even reached above 4 in 2011. This fully demonstrates the characteristics of the UK as one of the world's largest offshore financial markets and the world's largest financial centers. China's FIR rose from 0.80 to 0.92 in the study period (later declined slightly), equivalent only to the level of the US before the Great Depression and lower than the general level of the US after the World War II (Goldsmith and Lipsey 1963; Carlson 1991). This to some extent shows that the financial deepening in China is still at a low level, and the financial development potential is still huge.

FIR, as an indicator reflecting the level of financial development, also provides a unique perspective for depicting the structural characteristics of a country's economy. As shown in Table 2.3, the countries where the real economy sectors (especially manufacturing) were well-developed, such as Germany and Japan, had a relatively low FIR. This reflects the fact that they emphasized the accumulation of non-financial assets (such as plants, equipments and intangible assets etc.), demonstrating their position as a global manufacturing power. In contrast, the UK had a relatively higher FIR, reflecting that the financial industry was a pillar

(Footnote 5 continued)

sector. As a result, while selecting the variables, banks' assets and liabilities are included, and in many cases, the businesses between banks were not mutually offset.

Table 2.3 Comparison of FIRs of different countries: 2007–2011

Country\year	2007	2008	2009	2010	2011
China	0.80	0.81	0.88	0.92	0.89
Japan	2.07	1.92	2.01	2.05	–
Germany	1.75	1.68	1.69	1.71	1.65
The UK	3.14	4.56	3.91	3.90	4.12
Canada	2.19	2.07	2.18	2.23	2.18

Source Estimates of the research group

industry in the UK's economic structure and showing the fact that it was an international financial center.

By comparing China's relatively low FIR and rapid increase of M2/GDP ratio in the same period, we can also find some shortcomings of China's financial structure. First, the relatively low FIR reflects that China's financial system was not yet mature, and especially the development of direct financing was seriously lagging behind; second, FIR was relatively low but the M2/GDP ratio increased rapidly. The opposite trend of the two financial indicators shows that the proportion of direct financing was overly low, the funds needed in economic activities rely heavily on credit creation in the banking system; third, the low FIR reflects that there was a larger proportion of fixed capital formation in China, resulting in decrease in money circulation speed, and this requires issuing a large amount of money to make up the deficit.

(3) A sharp increase of percentage of inventories in total assets and increasingly serious excess capacity

Among the total assets, non-financial assets mainly reflecting wealth accumulation in the real economy increased from 158.3 to 288.6 trillion yuan (Fig. 2.7), among which "inventories", "other non-financial assets of enterprises", residents' automobiles" and other subjects expanded most significantly. Among them, the phenomenon of surge of "inventories" is more complicated. This may reflect enterprises' expectations for economic recovery (mostly presented as positive restocking, which can be understood as positive inventory increase) or may also be related to the ubiquitous serious overcapacity in today's China (mostly presented as passive accumulation of inventories, which can be understood as negative inventory increase). We tend to believe that the later cause, i.e. overcapacity, may be a major factor for the surge in the proportion of inventories. The increase in the proportion of "other non-financial assets of enterprises" largely reflects the greater importance of intellectual property rights and other intangible assets and the rise in the value hierarchy of Chinese enterprises. The increase in the proportion "residents' automobiles" indicates the rapid accumulation of residents' wealth.

(4) The changes in net financial assets and net IIP were broadly consistent

Table 2.2 shows that China's net financial assets increased from 7.4 trillion yuan in 2007 to nearly 16 trillion yuan in 2011. Over the same period, China's net IIP increased from $1.2 trillion to $1.7 trillion (see Table 14.1). By converting based on the exchange rate, the difference between the two items is not extremely great, and their changing trends are consistent. According to the previously mentioned equations:

$$
\begin{aligned}
\text{Net assets of the domestic sectors} &= \text{non-financial assets} \\
&\quad + \text{net financial assets of the domestic sectors} \\
&= \text{non-financial assets} + \text{net IIP}
\end{aligned}
$$

It can be concluded that the net financial assets of the domestic sectors are equal to the net IIP. That is, if the national balance sheet (particularly financial assets and financial liabilities) is prepared in a reasonable manner and the data are reliable, then the net financial assets will be equal to the net IIP theoretically. In fact, due to the imperfectness of the existing statistical data system and comparatively low data quality as well as the difficulty in the availability of data, the estimation results are not completely accurate, so the net financial assets are not fully consistent with the net IIP. By comparing the data above, the magnitudes of the two are basically consistent and their overall changing trends also are basically the same. This confirms that the preparation of the national balance sheet is generally reliable.

Chapter 3
Preparation and Analysis of China's Sovereign Balance Sheet

After studying China's overall assets and liabilities, this chapter discusses the sovereign sector. The latter can also be called "the general government", including the central government, local governments, state-owned non-financial corporations, administrative institutions, the central bank and state-owned financial enterprises. Given that the government and the public economy play a special role in China's economic development and institutional transformation, a separate analysis of the assets that are owned or can be directly used by the sovereign sector and the corresponding debt obligations and wealth accumulation has an irreplaceable significance in revealing the characteristics of China's economic and social systems and mechanisms, evaluating the economic resource allocation efficiency of the public sector, revealing the financial pressure and debt risks, depicting the debtor-creditor relationship and risk association between the public and private sectors, analyzing the track of transforming from the "construction-oriented government" to the "service-oriented government" and improving the state governance and capacity.

3.1 Data Sources and Estimation Methods

Due to limitation in the availability of data, to prepare China's sovereign balance sheet in the calendar years from 2000 to 2011, we have made full use of the existing statistical data and carried come up with a large number of estimated data that can not be directly acquired based on the relevant economic theories. In the paragraphs below, we will make an explanation on the data sources and estimation methods for the components of sovereign assets and liabilities respectively.

Y. Li and X. Zhang, *China's National Balance Sheet*, China Insights,
DOI 10.1007/978-981-10-4385-7_3

3.1.1 Operating State-Owned Assets

Operating state-owned assets include state-owned assets of non-financial corporations and financial corporations. Among them, the (total) state-owned assets of non-financial corporations are obtained by adding up the total state-owned assets and liabilities of state-owned corporations (the data are from *Finance Yearbook of China* of the relevant year). It should be noted that the total amount of state-owned assets of state-owned corporations here is actually a concept of state-owned equity. Apart from the state-owned equity, the total owner's equity (i.e. total net assets) of state-owned corporations also include the equity of other owners (such as the equity of foreign, Hong Kong, Macao and Taiwan-funded enterprises, collective enterprises or individual owners in joint-venture, cooperative and joint-stock state-owned corporations). Only the state-owned equity in state-owned corporations from which the equity of other owners as mentioned above has been deducted can be really disposed and used by the government. Of course, from a dynamic point of view, non-performing assets of state-owned corporations generated during operation should also be deducted from the state-owned equity. In other words, the actual amount of assets that can be used by the government to pay off its debts may be smaller than the size of the existing state-owned equity.

The data on state-owned assets of financial corporations in operating state-owned assets are estimated according to the relevant data of the Ministry of Finance and *Finance Yearbook of China*. Among them, the data of 2009–2011 on state-owned assets of central and local financial corporations are obtained by adding up the data in the balance sheets of the relevant central and local financial corporations. It should be noted that, as the equity of other state-owned legal persons in the central financial corporations has been largely reflected in the state-owned assets of non-financial corporations, we have excluded it and obtained the state-owned assets of the Ministry of Finance (including Central Huijin Investment Ltd.) (the equity in 2011 was not excluded due to lack of the relevant data). A part of state-owned assets of local financial corporations have also been reflected in the balance sheets of non-financial state-owned corporations (based on the research experience, a large part of state-owned assets of local financial corporations belong to the legal persons of state-owned corporations), but due to lack of further data, it is impossible to estimate the share of non-financial state-owned corporations in the state-owned assets of local financial corporations, so it is impossible to exclude these assets.

As the data of 2000–2008 can not be acquired directly through calculation, we have come up with the estimates. The core step is to acquire the data on the owner's equity of the financial industry based on the data released by the Ministry of Finance and *Finance Yearbook of China*. According to the mean value of the data of 2009 and 2010, the equity of central and local financial corporations accounted for 56 and 44% respectively, the state-owned assets belonging to the Ministry of Finance accounted for 60% of the owner's equity of the central financial corporations, and 40% of the owner's equity of local financial corporations was state-owned assets. Based on the research experience, this proportion remained largely stable in recent years. On the basis of the previous estimates on owner's equity, we have calculated the state-owned assets of central and local financial corporations in accordance with this proportion and then added them up to obtain the state-owned assets of the financial industry.

Adding the above-mentioned state-owned equities and the financial bonds of the policy banks, we can obtain the (total) state-owned assets of the financial industry.

3.1.2 Non-operating State-Owned Assets

Non-operating state-owned assets, namely state-owned assets of administrative institutions, are from *Accounting Yearbook of China* of the relevant years.

3.1.3 Government-Owned Resource Assets

For this subject, we focus on estimating the value of land and resources. Here, we have made reference to the research ideas of the World Bank (2006). The basic method is to regard the present total value of land and resources (excluding oil, gas and mineral resources) as the sum of present discounted value of the net output from land and resources (i.e. total receipts less costs or resource rents) in a certain period in future. Due to the limitation in availability of data, we have not calculated separately the incomes of different categories of resources such as arable lands, grasslands and forests, but replaced it by the general term of "total output value of agriculture, forestry, animal husbandry and fishery" and used the rental rate of 40%. See the relevant contents in Part 3 of this book for the detailed estimation methods.

3.1.4 External Sovereign Assets

The data of 2004–2011 on reserve asset assets as external sovereign assets are directly from the IIP, and the data of 2000–2003 were calculated according to the international investment position (IIP) of 2004 and balance of international payments (BIP) of the relevant years. We then converted the data in US dollars into the data in RMB according to the reference exchange rate of RMB (period average). It should be noted that the reserve assets held by the central bank were mainly from the trade surplus of the domestic private sector, foreign direct investment in China, other forms of international capital flows (such as hot money inflows) and other channels. Based on the strict balance sheet accounting principles, the reserves are obtained by the central bank through incurring debts (issuing the equivalent RMB), but here we did not completely set out from the perspective of accounting and thus did not equivalently include the liability side into the corresponding liabilities while including the asset side into reserve assets. This is mainly based on the consideration in the following 3 aspects:

(1) The preparation method. In our view, the so-called sovereign balance sheet mainly consists of three parts: the governments, state-owned corporations (enterprises) and institutions, and the central bank, which means the governments have a claim on the assets of these sectors and should assume the responsibilities for liabilities. Therefore, the ideal approach for constructing the sovereign balance sheet is to first construct 3 sub-statements and then consolidate them. If based on the method of consolidating the sub statements, foreign exchange reserves as the assets of the central bank will directly be included in sovereign assets when consolidating. Likewise, the corresponding money issued by the central bank and other liabilities of the central bank have are also included into the sovereign liabilities. However, in specific operations, due to the difficulties in data availability and in deducting the overlapped portions when consolidating and adding up and other aspects, we adopted a more viable approach, i.e. overall construction based on the definition. Based on the overall construction approach, we set out from the perspective of the government and sorted out the assets that can be used and the liabilities that should be borne separately and then used the net worth to illustrate the "real financial position" of the government. Then, the one-to-one relationship between assets and liabilities of these sub-sectors was broken and some off-balance-sheet items were also introduced into the balance sheet items. For example, there was no liability side corresponding to foreign exchange reserves, and some contingent liabilities were included into the balance sheet but there was no corresponding asset side.[1] From the current situation, we believe that the conclusions drawn by the overall construction approach may be more reliable and more compliant with the reality. In fact, the adding of the data of sub-sectors, due to the difficulties in availability of data and in excluding the overlapped portions during adding up as mentioned above, the results may be more unreliable. Moreover, we believe that the overall construction approach has unique advantages because it helps bluntly cut into the topics concerned by people. For example, some contingent debts and implicit debts have no specific corresponding asset side, but the government does bear the "final" responsibility.
(2) Purposes of preparation. In the *Public Sector Debt Statistics-Guide for Compilers and Users* issued by IMF, currencies and deposits are a part of debts or liabilities, among which currencies are the central bank's liabilities, and deposits are mainly the liabilities of commercial banks. According to this definition, when preparing the sovereign balance sheet, currencies as liabilities of the central bank and deposits as liabilities of state-owned commercial banks

[1]For example, the Meeting of the G20 Finance Ministers and Central Bank Governors had specifically adopted a motion on the issue of data missing, which pointed out that in some sectoral balance sheets there is often only the asset side, but there is no the liability side (such as the financial management of the household sector), or vice versa.

(even including all commercial banks, when taking into account the problem of contingent liabilities caused by implicit guarantee) should be included into the sovereign liability side. But here we would like to point out that the main purpose for preparing the sovereign balance sheet is to assess the risks of the sovereign sector, especially external risks. In practice, when a country is exposed to external shocks, foreign exchange reserves will fully exert its positive effects, while the negative impact of the corresponding domestic currencies and deposits is basically non-existent. Therefore, when considering the sovereign debts, we have excluded currencies and deposits.

(3) The nature of the central bank's liabilities. On the surface, the central bank belongs to the public sector, so the central bank's liabilities should also constitute the sovereign liabilities. But in fact, the central bank's liabilities are different from sovereign liabilities in general sense in nature. For public debts in general sense, the government usually bears the responsibility to repay with "real money". But there is no explicit creditor for the money issued by the central bank as its liabilities, and there is no hard constraint on debt repayment. More importantly, in a growing economy, the central bank that is performing its duties correctly must print more money to keep pace with the economic growth: if the money printed is more than what is needed by economic growth, this will lead to inflation, but if the money printed is less than what is needed by economic growth, this will lead to deflation. Nevertheless, the increase in money supply listed in the liability side of the balance sheet of the central bank will only lead to sovereign risks when a sovereign country is bankrupt. That is why the government needs not worry about the currency issuance constraint of the debit side when using its foreign exchange reserves. This is a distinctive characteristic of credit currency system. We certainly do not advocate unlimited expansion of liabilities by the central bank, which will result potential inflationary pressures, but we must understand and remember the fact that the central bank's assets and liabilities can not be regarded as equal to the assets and liabilities of an ordinary economic entity. In other words, as the central bank's liabilities has a bearing on macroeconomic performance, all relevant analysis can only proceed from the logic of macroeconomic operation, and the evaluation from the microscopic perspective may lead to deviations.

3.1.5 State-Owned Assets of National Social Security Fund

The data are from CEIC and the relevant annual financial statements of the National Council for Social Security Fund.

3.1.6 Governments' Deposits at the Central Bank

The data are from the balance sheets of the monetary authorities.

3.1.7 Central Government Debts

The data on the outstanding internal debt of the central government for 2000–2004 is from CEIC; those for 2005–2011 are from *Statistical Yearbook of China* (the outstanding internal debt of the central government has been officially released since 2006 when government debt balance management was implemented). The data on sovereign external debt owed by the central government are from the State Administration of Foreign Exchange. Based on the definition of broad-scope external debt we will discuss below, the data for 2000 is the total external debt owed by the relevant ministries and commissions under the State Council, domestic banks and non-bank financial institutions and foreign-sino joint ventures; the data for 2001 is the total external debt owed by the relevant ministries and commissions under the State Council, domestic banks and non-bank financial institutions, foreign financial institutions and foreign-sino joint ventures; the data of 2002–2005 is the total external debt owed by the relevant ministries and commissions under the State Council, domestic banks, non-bank financial institutions and Sino-foreign joint ventures; the data for 2006–2011 is the total external debt owed by the relevant ministries and commissions under the State Council, Sino-foreign joint venture banks and foreign-sino joint venture enterprises. We have then converted the data in US dollars to the data in RMB according to the average RMB exchange rate of all the years.

3.1.8 "Quasi-Government Bonds"

Quasi-government bonds refer to the covered bonds issued by the government departments and policy institutions. Here we have mainly studied the financial bonds issued by policy banks (the data are from CEIC).

3.1.9 Local Government Debts

The data for 2011 have combined the data of the National Audit Office, China Banking Regulatory Commission (CBRC), Weekly Statistics on China's Bond Market and China Trustee Association; the data for 2010 have combined the data of the National Audit Office and China Banking Regulatory Commission; the data for

2000–2009 were calculated based on the changes in the growth rate of outstanding local government debt in the *Results of National Audit of Local Government Debts* issued by the National Audit Office in June 2011.

3.1.10 Debts of State-Owned Enterprises

The data in this section are from *Finance Yearbook* of *China* for the relevant years. It should be noted that local state-owned enterprises to a large extent include the local government financing platforms as government-backed entities. Therefore, in consolidating the statements, we made the necessary adjustments to prevent overlapping. Specifically, the debt data of local government financing platforms have been deducted from the debt data of state-owned enterprises for 2011.

3.1.11 Contingent Liabilities Existing as Financial Non-performing Assets or Their Transformation Forms

First, the non-performing assets of banks. The data sources and calculation methods for all the years are as follows: the data for 2000 and 2001 are the non-performing assets of the four state-owned commercial banks, the data for 2000 were obtained by adding up the non-performing assets of the annual statements of the banks (where ABC's non-performing asset ratio is not reflected in the annual statements, so it was calculated based on the change range of non-performing asset ratio during 2006–2000); The data for 2001 were calculated based on the relevant data in the *Monetary Policy Implementation Report in 2002* issued by the People's Bank of China and the report on the work of CBRC for the first half of 2003; the data for 2002 and 2003 are the non-performing assets of major banking financial institutions, including state-owned commercial banks, policy banks and joint-stock commercial banks; the data for 2004 are the non-performing assets of the major commercial banks, including state-owned commercial banks and joint-stock commercial banks; the data for 2005–2011 are the non-performing assets of commercial banks, including state-owned commercial banks, joint-stock commercial banks, urban commercial banks, rural commercial banks and foreign banks; the data for 2002–2011 are from CBRC.

Second, the contingent liabilities arising from the disposal of the banks' non-performing assets. This is roughly divided into several periods: the data for 2000–2003 reflect the acceptance of stripped non-performing assets of Industrial and Commercial Bank of China, Agricultural Bank of China, Bank of China, China Construction Bank and China Development Bank through issuing bonds by the four asset management companies and re-lending by the People's Bank of China in the late 1990s. The data for 2004 mainly reflect the commercial stripping of doubtful and loss loans of Bank of China, China Construction Bank and Bank of Communications as well as the writeoff of loss assets of Bank of China and China Construction Bank; They also include the equal swap of the non-performing assets of Bank of China and China Construction Bank by the People's Bank of China by means of bank bill. The data for 2005–2007 reflect the commercial stripping of doubtful and loss loans of Industrial and Commercial Bank of China and Bank of Shanghai and asset losses of central bank bills and re-lending of rural credit cooperatives as well as the case of re-lending of the central bank. The data for 2008–2011 reflect the non-performing assets (including doubtful loans, loss loans and non-credit assets) stripped through equal swap by interest-free re-lending of the People's Bank of China and the "condominium fund" jointly established by the Agricultural Bank of China and the Ministry of Finance.

3.1.12 *Social Security's Funding Gap Dominated by Implicit Pension Debt*

The data in this section are our estimates (see Part 3 for details).

3.2 Analysis of Sovereign Assets

3.2.1 *Operating State-Owned Assets*

Operating state-owned assets are assets in respect of which the state, as the contributor, invests resources into production and operation so as to obtain profits. According to the business nature of enterprise, these state-owned assets are equal to the state-owned assets of non-financial corporations plus the state-owned assets of financial corporations.

The state-owned assets of non-financial corporations account for a large proportion of operating state-owned assets in China. By the end of 2011, the state-owned assets of the central non-financial corporations (including the corporations under the supervision of the State-owned Assets Supervision and Administration Commission of the State Council and the corporations directly under the central authorities) amounted to 10.4 trillion yuan, and the state-owned assets of local non-financial corporations amounted to 11.3 trillion yuan. The state-owned assets of non-financial corporations totaled 21.7 trillion yuan. Coupled with the total liabilities of state-owned corporations, the total state-owned assets of non-financial corporations amounted to 70.3 trillion yuan.

The state-owned assets of financial corporations mainly refer to all forms of investment of the state in financial corporations and the equities formed by the investment as well as all other equities legally recognized to be owned by the state. According to our estimates, the state-owned assets of central financial corporations in 2011 amounted to 3.2 trillion yuan; the state-owned assets of local financial corporations amounted to 1.4 trillion yuan; the state-owned assets of the entire financial sector in China amounted to 4.6 trillion yuan. Coupled with the financial bonds of the policy banks, the state-owned assets of financial corporation totaled 11.1 trillion yuan.

3.2.2 Non-operating State-Owned Assets

Non-operating state-owned assets refer to the state-owned (public) properties occupied by administrative institutions and public institutions. As the support for the government to fulfill its functions in public administration and public affairs, this part of assets are the components of a country's sovereignty assets. As far as China is concerned, given the scale and characteristics of the government, this part of assets take an important position in the state's sovereign assets. As of the end of 2011, the total state-owned assets of administrative institutions in the whole country reached 8.8 trillion yuan. From the internal structure of assets, fixed assets accounted for a considerable proportion. In 2011, the fixed assets of administrative institutions and public institutions accounted for 45.3 and 39.4% of total assets. This to some extent explains the illiquidity of non-operating state-owned assets. In the meanwhile, as this part of assets is for specific use, its market either does not exist or is underdeveloped, and its net realizable value may be less than the book value or the appraised value (Zhang 2006). Therefore, when analyzing the financial risks and roughly calculating debt repayment resources, we should pay attention to this particularity of non-operating assets of administrative institutions.

3.2.3 Government-Owned Resource Assets

Government-owned resource assets mainly refer to economic resources that shall be owned by the state according to the laws, including state-owned land, forests, minerals, rivers and oceans. According to the method described above, we estimated that the total value of China's land resources was 15.9 trillion yuan in 2000 (current price). As the reference, the World Bank (2006) estimated the total value of land and resources of China in 2000 at $2.16 trillion according to the categories of forest resources, non-timber forest resources, arable land, pastures and protected areas separately, roughly equivalent to to 17.8 trillion yuan based on the exchange rate in that year, with no significant difference between them. Based on the same approach, we estimated the total value of land and resources in 2011 at 52 trillion yuan.

The Constitution of the People's Republic of China provides that: "Land in the cities is owned by the state. Land in the rural and suburban areas is owned by collectives except for those portions which belong to the state in accordance with the law; house sites and privately farmed plots of cropland and hilly land are also owned by collectives." This means that land owned by collectives does not belong to state-owned assets. But changing through the legal processes, land acquisition or expropriation, we can change collectively owned land into to urban land which also falls into the category of state-owned resource assets. Therefore, state-owned land and resources with estimated value of 52 trillion yuan can be regarded as the maximum value of state-owned land and resource assets.

Of course, the liquidation form of China's resource assets is rather special. As the ownership is not allowed to sell and only the right to development and use can be transferred, the revenue of resource assets is mainly reflected in the income from the fees for transfer of the right to the use of state-owned land and included in the government's public revenue system. Taking 2011 for example, the fees for assignment of the right to the use of state-owned land reached 3.1 trillion yuan, accounting for 75.6% of government-managed funds revenue.

3.2.4 *External Sovereign Assets*

As shown by the IIP, China's external assets mainly include four categories: outward FDIs, portfolio investment, other investments and reserve assets. The reserve assets in the IIP held by the government are mainly external sovereign assets. The size of China's reserve assests rose from $618.6 billion in 2004 to $3255.8 billion in 2011, showing a rapid accumulation of external sovereign assets.

3.2.5 *State-Owned Assets of National Social Security Fund (NSSF)*

NSSF is the national strategic reserve fund centralized and held by the central government. It consists of the capital allocated by the central government, the capital and equity assets derived from reduction or transfer of state-owned shares and so on. By the end of 2011, NSSF's equity capital was valued at 772.765 billion yuan. In addition, the personal account fund and its investment proceeds under the management of the National Council for Social Security Fund as entrusted by the trial provinces (autonomous regions and municipalities) for personal accounts, i.e. the equity capital of personal accounts fund, was valued at 65.793 billion yuan. The sum of the two portions is the total equity capital of the fund under the management of the National Council for Social Security Fund, which amount to 838.558 billion yuan. It should be noted that, overlapped accounting may exist between the national social security fund as state-owned assets and the aforementioned state-owned assets of non-financial and financial corporations. The process of reduction or transfer of state-owned shares involves only the adjustment of the department that performs the functions of the investor. That is, the investor is adjusted from the State-owned Assets Supervision and Administration Commission of the State Council (SASAC) or the Ministry of Finance to the National Council for Social Security Fund, and the aforementioned state-owned assets of non-financial and financial corporations have not been substantively transferred. Overlapped calculation may occur in NSSF's statistics of this portion of assets.

3.2.6 Government Deposits at the Central Bank

The Law of the People's Republic of China on the People's Bank of China provides that the People's Bank of China shall manage the "State treasury". This requires the financial departments at all levels to deposit their general budgetary and fund budgetary capital into the treasury single account of the People's Bank of China. Treasury deposits include central treasury deposits and local treasury deposits. Treasury deposits and other public finance-cash in bank (various fiscal budget fund deposits at commercial banks not included in treasury deposits and part of special fund deposits designated by the Ministry of Finance to be deposited at commercial banks, as bank deposits reflected in the asset item of administrative institutions) together constitute public finance-cash in bank. It is a kind of fiscal assets managed and allocated by the financial departments at various levels on behalf of the governments at the corresponding levels. As of the end of 2011, government deposits at the central bank amounted to 2.3 trillion yuan.

We estimated and added up the above categories of sovereign assets and obtained China's sovereign assets and their configuration in 2000–2011 (see Fig. 3.1). As shown in the figure, relatively speaking, the state-owned assets of non-financial corporations and reserve assets increased most rapidly.

3.3 Analysis of Sovereign Liabilities

3.3.1 Central Government Debts (Internal and External Debts)

As of the end of 2011, the outstanding internal debt of the central government was 7141.08 billion yuan; the balance of sovereign external debt owed by the ministries and commissions under the State Council was $37.37 billion, equivalent to 241.37 billion yuan calculated based on the average exchange rate in 2011. In the meanwhile, the balance of external debt owed by Sino-foreign financial institutions,

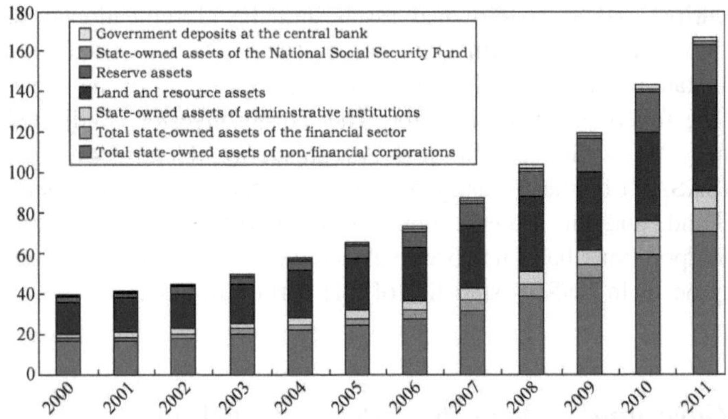

Fig. 3.1 Size and structure of China's sovereign assets (unit: 1 trillion yuan). *Source* Estimates of the research group

Sino-foreign joint ventures and other private sectors was $408.29 billion, equivalent to 2637.06 billion yuan. Under normal circumstances, the external debt of the private sector should be repaid by the relevant entities, but once they are unable to make ends meet, and the external debt also ultimately needs be repaid by the central government. Therefore, we believe that it is necessary to include them into the statistics of sovereign external debt. In this way, the total outstanding external debt was $445.66 billion, equivalent to 2878.43 billion yuan.

3.3.2 *"Quasi-Government Bonds"*

Although bond issuance by policy banks is market behavior (the size and pricing of bonds issued by them are determined based on their own credit worthiness, and the funds raised are also for market-oriented use), but rely on the state's credit. Therefore, if the risk control is inadequate or losses or devaluation occur due to domestic and international economic and financial shocks, this portion of debts may ultimately translate into sovereign debts, so these debts should be regarded the contingent liabilities of the public sector. In 2011, the balance of financial bonds of policy amounted to 6.5 trillion yuan.

3.3.3 *Local Government Debts*

Local government debts mainly consist of two parts. One part is the debt of local government financing platforms that has aroused wide concern in recent years. The second part is the local government debt of Non financing Platform Companies.

The borrowers mainly include local government departments and agencies, fund subsidy public institutions, public utility institutions and other entities.

First, we will analyze the three major ways of financing of LGFPCs. First, bank loans. According to CBRC's statistics, as of the end of 2010, the balance of the loans borrowed by LGFPCs nationwide was 9.09 trillion yuan, accounting for 19.16% of all RMB loans. Since 2011, due to the strict control by regulatory authorities, the loan growth of local government financing platforms (LGFPs) has basically stalled, so by the end of 2011, the balance of the loans in this part was still 9.1 trillion yuan. Second, urban construction investment corporation bonds (including corporate bonds, medium-term notes and short-term financing bonds etc.). This kind of bonds is nominally corporate bonds, but in essence are quasi government bonds, similar to municipal bonds abroad. According to the statistics of bond market, as of the end of 2011, the balance of urban construction investment corporation bonds was about 1.3 trillion yuan. Third, infrastructure trust and other shadow banking channels. According to the major business data of trust companies released by China Trustee Association, as of the end of December 2011, the total trust loans invested in infrastructure projects amounted to 1.02 trillion yuan. Adding up the figures of the above the three categories, as of the end of 2011, the debt balance of LGFPs was 11.42 trillion yuan.

Then, we will introduce the local government debt outside LGFPCs. The debtors are local government departments and agencies, public institutions receiving financial subsidies, public utility institutions and other entities. According to the *Results of National Audit of Local Government Debt* released by the National Audit Office in June 2011, as of the end of 2010, this portion of debt amounted to 5746.423 billion yuan. According to the *Audit Results of the Debts Held by 36 Local Governments* released by the National Audit Office in June 2013, the outstanding government debt grew by 12.94% during 2010–2012, with a projected annual growth rate of 6.27%. Assuming that the outstanding local government debt outside LGFPCs also grew at the same rate, then by the end of 2011, this portion of debt stock was 6.11 trillion yuan.

The above two portions of local government debt together were close to 17.53 trillion yuan.

3.3.4 Debts of State-Owned Enterprises

Theoretically, state-owned enterprises are corporate and market entities that enjoy full management authority and assume sole responsibility for their profits and losses, so they should take on their own debts. However, from the perspective of investors, there is an inseparable link between the government and state-owned enterprises. From a legal perspective, when state-owned enterprises are unable to repay their debts, the governments have to take the responsibility for repaying their debts according to their contribution proportion. Furthermore, from the perspective of social stability, the government will also provide a bailout to state-owned enterprises and assume the role of the final payer. Therefore, we can reasonably regard the debt of state-owned enterprises as contingent government debt.

As of the end of 2011, the total liabilities of state-owned enterprises nationwide amounted to 48.6 trillion yuan, of which the liabilities owed by the central state-owned enterprises amounted to 24.7 trillion yuan and the liabilities owed by local state-owned enterprises amounted to 23.9 trillion yuan. In the central state-owned enterprises, the liabilities of the central management enterprise amounted to 17.3 trillion yuan, and those of the central department management enterprises amounted to 7.4 trillion yuan (including the liabilities of 2.41 trillion yuan owed by the Ministry of Railways that have aroused wide concern in the society). As mentioned earlier, the liability data of local state-owned enterprises and LGFPs were overlapped, we have excluded them in processing.

3.3.5 Contingent Liabilities Existing as Financial Non-performing Assets and Their Transformation Forms

This portion of liabilities mainly include non-performing assets of banks and other financial institutions (such as securities and insurance companies) and contingent liabilities arising from disposal of non-performing assets of banks. With regard to the existing non-performing assets of commercial banks, in 2011, the five tiers of non-performing loans of commercial banks totaled 427.87 billion yuan. Of course, in non-performing loans, except for loss loans, a certain proportion of substandard and doubtful loans can be recovered, so the actual size of non-performing assets is smaller.

Banks can dispose non-performing assets in many ways, including stripping and writing-off non-performing assets, capital injection, issuing special government bonds, central bank bills and re-lending and attracting financial investors. But no matter how non-performing assets are disposed, they have just changed in form and have by no means disappeared (for example, the non-performing assets of commercial banks have been changed into the non-performing subloans of the central bank). Therefore, a part of the non-performing assets of banks still exist as sovereign liabilities, and the other part are converted into other forms of contingent liabilities. Since 1999, the disposed contingent liabilities and contingent liabilities were about 4.2 trillion yuan, included the non-performing assets stripped from the four state-owned commercial banks and China Development Bank, the stripped doubtful and loss non-performing assets and the written-off loss assets arising from the joint-stock reform and financial restructuring of the four state-owned commercial banks during 2003–2008, and the central bank's re-lending asset losses.

3.3.6 *Social Security's Funding Gap Dominated by Implicit Pension Debt*

Here we mainly take into consideration the social security's funding gap dominated by implicit pension debt. It specially refers to the implicit pension debt burden left over from the transition from the old pension system to the new system (so here it is the estimation based on narrow scope). For the size of implicit pension debt, a lot of research estimates have been made by a number of domestic and international institutions, such as the Social Security Institute under the former Ministry of Labor, the World Bank, the former Offer for Institutional Reform under the State Council, and the Research Institute of Fiscal Science under the Ministry of Finance. The estimated results range from about 1 to 6 trillion yuan. However, the definitions of implicit pension debt adopted by the research institutes are not exactly the same, and due to the difference in calculation method and time point, the results are also significantly different. This research group has also calculated the implicit pension debt over the years arising from the transition of the pension system. The results show that in 2011, the narrow-scope implicit pension debt stock (retaining the transition costs) was about 3.5 trillion yuan.

We have estimated and added up the estimates of the above categories of sovereign liabilities and obtained China's sovereign liabilities and their structure during 2000–2011 (see Fig. 3.2). As shown in the figure, compared with other debt items, government debt (central and local), debt of state-owned enterprises and contingent liabilities arising from disposing non-performing assets grew rapidly.

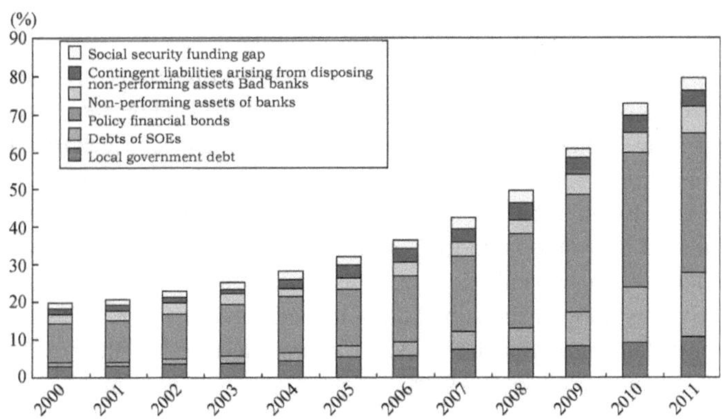

Fig. 3.2 Size and structure of China's sovereign liabilities (unit: 1 trillion yuan). *Source* Estimates of the research group

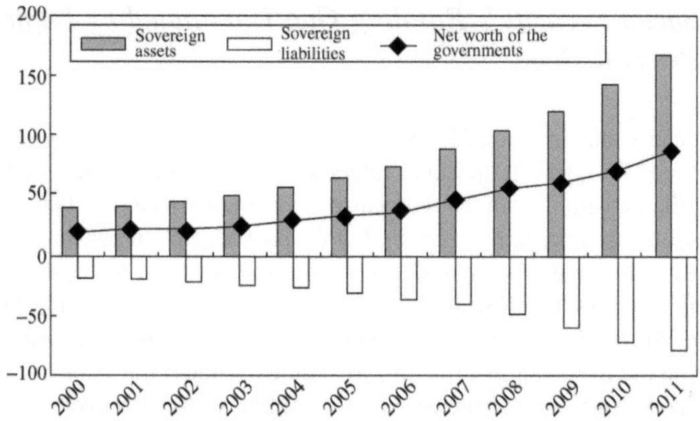

Fig. 3.3 Amount and structure of China's sovereign assets/liabilities (unit: 1 trillion yuan). *Source* Estimates of the research group

3.4 Sovereign Balance Sheets

Adding up sovereign assets and sovereign liabilities, we will get China's sovereign assets and liabilities of various years and the net government (or sovereign) assets. Figure 3.3 reflects the changes in sovereign assets, sovereign liabilities and net government assets during 2000–2011. It shows that in the 12 years, China's sovereign assets and sovereign liabilities were expanding, while the increase in sovereign assets was higher than that in sovereign liabilities. Accordingly, the size of net government assets in China was constantly growing.

Based on the above sovereign assets and sovereign liabilities, we can prepare China's sovereign balance sheet for 2000–2011. The following is the analysis using the sovereign balance sheet for 2011 as an example.

As shown in Table 3.1, calculated on a broad-scope basis, the net worth of China's sovereign assets stood at 87 trillion yuan in 2011. However, given the poor liquidity of state-owned assets of administrative institutions (because they should perform government functions) and the impossibility of realizing one-time transfer of all the rights to use land and resource assets (in fact, the fees for transfer of the right to use land only amounted to 2–3 trillion yuan per year in recent years),[2] then based on narrow-scope statistics, i.e. after deducting the state-owned assets of administrative institutions and substituting the land and resource assets of 52 trillion yuan by the fees of land transfer of 3.1 trillion yuan in 2011, the sovereign assets will decrease from 166.3 to 108.6 trillion yuan. As a result, China's net sovereign assets calculated based on the narrow-scope method stood at 21.6 trillion yuan.

[2]If the land transfer system is adjusted in future and the land leasehold system is replaced by the land yearly-rent system (one-time charge of land transfer fees for several decades is replaced by charge of land rent or land use fees per year), then the income from land and resource assets will be further reduced.

Table 3.1 China's sovereign assets and liabilities in 2011 (unit: 1 trillion yuan)

Assets		Liabilities and net government assets	
Government deposits at the central bank	2.3	Internal debt of the central government	7.1
Reserve assets	21	External sovereign debts	2.9
State-owned land and resource assets	52	Non financial platform companies	6.11
State-owned assets of administrative institutions	8.8	Debts of LGFPs	11.42
Total state-owned assets of non-financial corporations	70.3	Total liabilities of non-financial state-owned corporations (excluding the debts of financial platform of local governments)	37.18
Total state-owned assets of the financial sector	11.1	Financial bonds of policy banks	6.5
		Non-performing assets of banks	0.4
		Contingent liabilities arising from disposal of banks' non-performing assets	4.2
State-owned assets of national social security fund	0.8	Implicit pension debt	3.5
Total assets	166.3	Total liabilities	79.31
		Net government assets	86.99

Source Estimates of the research group

Calculated based on the narrow or broad-scope method, China's net sovereign assets were positive, which was an indisputable fact. This suggests that on the whole, the Chinese government has enough sovereign assets to cover its sovereign debts. Therefore, in a fairly long period of time, the likelihood of a sovereign debt crisis in China is extremely low, but the contingent liability risks including the pension gap should arouse our attention.

It should be noted that whether the net assets are positive or not will be somewhat helpful in judging the healthiness of the current balance sheet, but should not serve as the main indicator for judging whether there is any debt risk. Under normal circumstances, positive net assets are a necessary condition, but not a sufficient condition, for nonappearance of a debt crisis. As to whether there is any debt risk, this depends not only on whether the net assets are positive, but also on the liquidity of assets and the asset-liability duration matching. For land and resource assets of administrative institutions with certain limitation on liquidity, if we include them into the balance sheet, this is often unlikely to increase the government's solvency.

Therefore, for the debt risks of a state or its sovereign or even other sectors, we should not simply judge solely from the perspective of net assets, but should investigate from different dimensions. Therefore, in this study, we have paid special attention to the following points: first, we have not only carried out assessment at the macro level so as to examine the risk of solvency. In the meanwhile, we have also carried out assessment at the structural level, with emphasis on balance sheet mismatch risk (including currency mismatch, maturity mismatch and capital structure mismatch) and the corresponding liquidity risks.

Second, we have not only carried out investigation at the static level and assessed the healthiness of the current balance sheet. In addition; we have also examined the sustainability of sovereign debt from a dynamic perspective and analyzed the prospects of changes in government debt balance.

In addition, we have not only examined the risks of the assets and liabilities of all sectors constituting the sovereign balance sheet but also taken into consideration the risk transfer among all sectors, especially the possibility that the explicit debt of the private sector may be translated into the contingent sovereign debt in certain conditions. We have examined the overall debt level and leverage rate of all sectors and assessed the overall risks of the economy.

Finally, we have also fully considered the liquidity of assets of the administrative institutions and land and resource assets and carried out narrow-scope statistics. Specifically, on the one hand, we have realized that the liquidity of assets of the administrative institutions is relatively low, so they were deducted. On the other hand, we have also realized that the liquidation form of land and resource assets is special. That is, only the right to development and use can be transferred, the ownership can not be sold, and one-time transfer of the right to use is also impossible, so the income from transfer of annual use right (income from land transfer) is the replacement value of land resource assets. Meanwhile, we have also estimated the possible adjustment of the land transfer system in the future, and the possible reform direction is to transform the land leasehold system into the land rent system. That is, we can transform the one-off charge of land transfer fee for decades into the charge of land rent fee (land use fee) on an annual basis. We believe that in such case the income from land and resource assets may be further reduced each year.

Chapter 4
Research on Total Debt Level and Whole Society Leverage Ratio

The previous chapter focuses on the preparation and analysis of the sovereign balance sheet, but given the risk transfer between various sectors, examining the overall debt level and leverage ratio of various sectors (not limited to the public sector) is helpful to understand the overall risks of an economy, especially helpful to make a holistic judgment for the size of contingent liabilities that may arise. This provides a broader background support for the later assessment of balance sheet risks. To this end, this chapter will further expand the balance sheet and thus study the relationship between China's overall debts and the debts to all sectors and its GDP flow from the perspective of total debt level and whole society leverage ratio by international comparison so as to more comprehensively and directly reveal the debt pressure and level of relevant subjects.

4.1 Debt and Leverage Ratio Analysis Framework

Here we first need to clarify that the "liability" in the previous balance sheet has changed to "debt" here, and they are not different expressions of identical concepts. The report recently published by IMF (2011) gives a detailed definition and classification of debt. First, debt is liability presented in the form of debt instrument, so debt is only a portion of liability. Debt instruments are divided into six categories: special drawing rights (SDRs), currencies and deposits, debt securities, loans, insurance, pensions and standardized security arrangements and other payables. Second, except for net worth of assets, investment fund shares, financial derivatives and employee stock options, all liabilities can be regarded as debts. Third, according to the specific legal, institutional and practical arrangements, there are other definitions of debt. Therefore, it is necessary to clarify the relevant definitions from the perspective of debt instruments included. A general understanding of the definition of debt in a narrow sense includes only: currencies and deposits, debt securities and loans. Fourth, debt securities are negotiable financial instruments as

Y. Li and X. Zhang, *China's National Balance Sheet*, China Insights,
DOI 10.1007/978-981-10-4385-7_4

debt obligations and generally have clear repayment arrangements, including the following nine categories: bills, banker's acceptance bills, commercial paper, negotiable certificate of deposit, bonds, negotiable loans, non-dividend-paying preference shares, asset-backed securities and secured debts, and similar tools of financial market transactions.

Given the characteristics of China's financial system and the availability of data, we adopted the definition of debt in a narrow sense in this study, i.e. only taking into consideration currencies and deposits, debt securities and loans. Currencies are the central bank's liabilities, deposits are primarily the liabilities of commercial banks, and both are also a major part of money supply in China. The main purpose of debt analysis to assess the debt leverage ratio risk, while currencies and deposits do not constitute major risks or have less risks in the financial sector, so we have excluded currencies and deposits even in calculating the debts of the financial sector in accordance with the established practice. According to the definition by IMF (2011), standard debt securities include 9 categories, such as promissory notes, commercial paper, bonds and transferrable loans, and they mainly include bonds in China, with little or no stock of other debt instruments. Therefore, China's debts can be roughly divided into two categories, namely bonds and loans, among which loans make up a large proportion. Undoubtedly, bonds have grown rapidly in the past ten years and more (see Fig. 4.1).

Generally speaking, the total debt is the sum of the debts of the three sectors of households, corporations and government (Cecchetti et al. 2011). Some scholars have also included the debts of the financial sector (MGI 2010, 2012). Here, based on MGI's studies, we have added up the debts of the four broad sectors of households, corporations, general government and financial institutions (the following section introduces the relevant estimates in details). Figure 4.2 and Table 4.1 show the ratios of China's total debt and the debts of various sectors to its GDP during 1996–2012. Although the ratio of China's total debt to its GDP remained a rising trend (it declined slightly during 2003–2008, and there is a deleveraging process), but the whole society leverage ratio increased rapidly after the outbreak of the Asian financial crisis in 1997, the IT bubble burst in 2000 and the outbreak of the international financial crisis in 2008. The impact of a crisis on increase of total debt is evident.

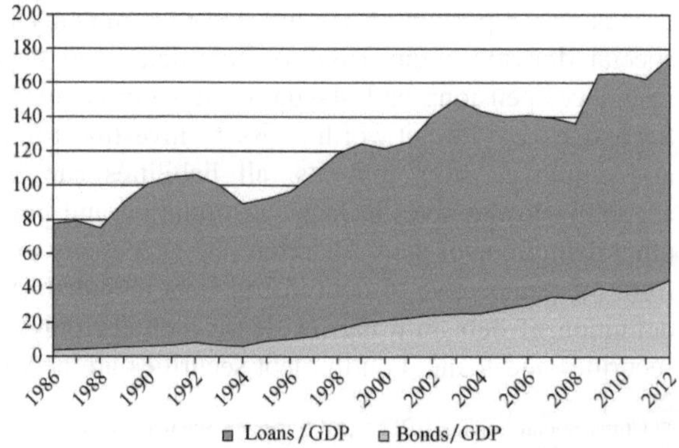

Fig. 4.1 China's loan/GDP ratio and bond/GDP ratio. *Source* CEIC. The data for 2012 are estimates of the research group based on in accordance with the balance of corporate sector bonds, government bonds and policy financial bonds

Fig. 4.2 Ratios of the debts of various sectors to GDP in China. *Source* Estimates of the research group

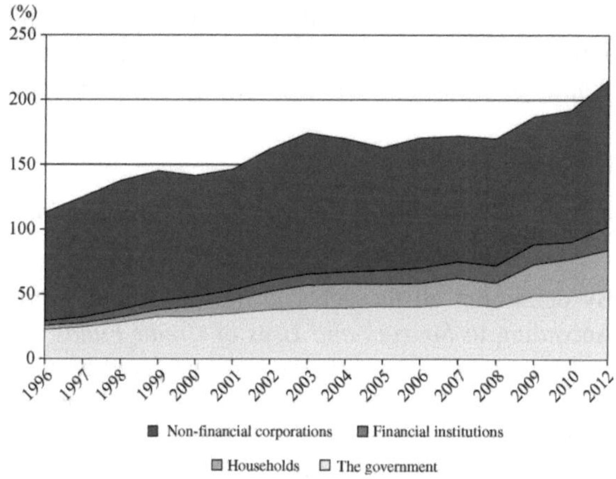

Table 4.1 Ratios of the debts of various sectors to GDP in China (unit: %)

Sector/year	Government	Households	Financial institutions	Non-financial corporations	Total
1996	23	3	4	84	113
1997	25	3	5	93	125
1998	28	4	6	99	138
1999	33	5	7	100	145
2000	33	7	7	94	142
2001	35	10	8	93	147
2002	38	14	8	102	162
2003	39	18	9	109	174
2004	40	18	9	103	170
2005	41	17	11	95	163
2006	40	18	12	100	171
2007	43	19	13	97	172
2008	41	18	13	98	170
2009	49	24	15	99	187
2010	49	28	13	101	192
2012	53	31	18	113	215

Source The same as above

4.2 Estimation of the Debts of Various Sectors in China

The estimates in this section are roughly based on the MGI framework, but based on our understanding of the characteristics of China, there are two adjustments and expansion here: first, in addition to loans and bond financing, the debts of non-financial corporations have also included the financing of "shadow banking" which has expanded rapidly in recent years; second, unlike the general handling approach of the developed countries, the government debts here are divided into central government debts and local government debts.

4.2.1 Household Sector Leverage Ratio

By definition, all the debts in the household sector are loans rather than bonds. According to *Sources and Uses of Credit Funds of Financial Institutions in RMB and Foreign Currency (by Sectors)* prepared by the People's Bank of China, as of the end of 2012, the outstanding balance on loans in the household sector was 16.1 trillion yuan (in which consumer loans amounted to 10.4 trillion yuan and business loans.7 billion yuan), accounting for 31% of the GDP. It should be noted that it is almost a common practice to include business loans into the household sector rather than the corporation sector. For example, this practice was adopted in the household sector's balance sheets compiled by the People's Bank of China, and Japan, Canada and other countries have also consolidated the balance sheets of households and non-corporate sector (see the relevant contents in Part II and III of this book).

4.2.2 Leverage Ratio of Non-financial Corporate Sector

The total amount of funds acquired by the non-financial corporate sector from the financial system can be estimated by three levels within the framework of total amount of social financing.

At the first level, the non-financial corporate sector gains financial support through traditional loan channels. According to *Sources and Uses of Credit Funds of Financial Institutions in RMB and Foreign Currency (by Sectors)* prepared by the People's Bank of China, as of the end of 2012, non-financial corporations and other sectors received loans worth 49.78 trillion yuan.

At the second level, the non-financial corporate sector raises funds directly from the financial market through debt instruments, mainly including corporate bonds, short-term financing bonds, medium-term notes and corporate bonds and the like. According to the statistics of the bond market, as of the end of 2012, the balance of non-financial corporate bonds was 7.29 trillion yuan.

At the third level, the non-financial corporate sector raises funds through credit intermediation activities outside the banking sector, mainly including trust loans, entrusted loans, banker's acceptance bills and other forms. According to the business data of leading trust companies released by China Trustee Association, as of the end of December 2012, the balance of trust loans was 3 trillion yuan. According to the cumulative flow of *Aggregate Financing to the Real Economy* released by the People's Bank of China, as of the end of 2012, the balance of entrusted loans was 5.75 trillion yuan. According to *China Monetary Policy Report*

(Quarter Four, 2012) released by the People's Bank of China, as of the end of 2012, the balance of unexpired bank acceptance bills was 8.3 trillion yuan, the ending balance of discount was 2 trillion yuan, and the balance of undiscounted bank acceptance bills was 6.3 trillion yuan. Adding up the figures of the above three items, the amount of money lent by the entire financial system to the non-financial corporate sector through quasi shadow banking channels was 15.05 trillion yuan.

Adding up the aggregate financing at the above three levels, we have obtained the outstanding debt of the non-financial corporate sector at the end of 2012, which was 72.12 trillion yuan, accounting for 139% of the GDP. It should be noted that the estimated debt of the non-financial corporate sector here includes to a considerable extent the debt of LGFPs as entities with government background. To prevent overlapping, it is necessary to deduct the estimated size of the debt of LGFPs, and the outstanding debt of non-financial corporate sector thus obtained was 58.67 trillion yuan, accounting for 113% of the GDP.

4.2.3 Leverage Ratio of Government Sector

First, the central government debts. According to the data of *National Government Final Accounts* released by the Ministry of Finance, as of the end of 2012, the outstanding balance of central government debt t was 7.76 trillion yuan, of which the outstanding internal debt was 7.67 trillion yuan and that of external debt 0.08 trillion yuan.

Second, the local government debts. According to the aforementioned ideas, local debts mainly consist of two parts: first, the debt of local government financial platforms (LGFPs) that has aroused widespread concern in recent years; second, the local government debt of non financial platform companies (NFPCs). The debtors are local government departments and agencies, public institutions receiving financial subsidies, public utility institutions and other entities.

LGFPCs mainly borrow money through three means. First, bank loans. According to CBRC's statistics, as of the end of 2012, the balance of loans borrowed by LGFPs nationwide was 9.3 trillion yuan. Second, issuing urban construction investment corporation bonds (including corporate bonds, medium-term notes and short-term financing bonds etc.). According to Wind's statistics, as of December 31, 2012, the balance of unexpired urban construction investment corporation bonds was about 2.5 trillion yuan. Third, infrastructure trust and other shadow banking channels. According to the major business data of trust companies released by China Trustee Association, by the end of December 2012, the total trust loans invested in infrastructure projects amounted to 1.65 trillion yuan. The sum of the above the three categories is the outstanding debt owed by local government financing platforms by the end of 2012, which was 13.45 trillion yuan.

With regard to the local government debt of non finacial platform companies, according to the *Results of National Audit of Local Government Debts* issued by the National Audit Office in June 2011, as of the end of 2010, this portion of debt amounted to 5.75 trillion yuan. Meanwhile, according to the *Audit Results of the Debts Held by 36 Local Governments* released by the National Audit Office in June 2013, the outstanding government debt grew by 12.94% during 2010–2012. Assuming that the outstanding local government debt of non finacial platform companies also grew at the same rate, then by the end of 2012, this portion of debt stock would be 6.49 trillion yuan. The sum of above two portions is the local government debt, which amounted to 19.94 trillion yuan.

Adding up the debts of the central government and local governments, we obtained the total government debt of 27.7 trillion yuan, accounting for 53% of the GDP.

4.2.4 Leverage Ratio of Financial Institutions

The main purpose of estimating the leverage ratio of financial institutions is to assess the risks, while currencies and deposits do not constitute major risks or have less risks in the financial sector, so we have excluded currencies and deposits from the debt of the financial sector in accordance with the established practice and only regard the balance of bonds issued by financial institutions as the debt of the financial sector. By the end of 2012, the balance of financial bonds issued by the policy banks (mainly CDB) was 7.86 trillion yuan, and the balance of bonds issued by other financial institutions was 1.27 trillion yuan. The sum of the two portions is the total balance of bonds issued by financial institutions, which was 9.13 trillion yuan, accounting for 18% of the GDP.

Adding up the figures of these four sectors, the total debt of China's economy stood at 111.6 trillion yuan and the whole society leverage ratio is 215%.

4.2.5 Expansion Scenarios

On the basis of the above estimates, two expansion scenarios can also be taken into consideration: first, to investigate the debts arising from the fiduciary relationship between the entities in the real economy, especially private financing. According to a survey carried out by the People's Bank of China in mid 2011, the total private financing was 3.38 trillion yuan, equivalent to 5.8% of all bank loans. Assuming that the share remains unchanged, the total amount of private financing was roughly estimated at 3.9 trillion yuan at the end of 2012, accounting for 7.5% of the GDP.

Another expansion scenario is to investigate the debt owed by the external sector. According to the data of the State Administration of Foreign Exchange, as of the end of 2012, the external debt owed by the ministries and commissions under the State Council (excluding external government loans), the external debt owed by Sino-foreign joint venture enterprises and the external debt owed by Sino-foreign joint venture financial institutions was $36.614 billion, $152.118 and $256.602

billion respectively, totaling $445.334 billion, equivalent to 2.81 trillion yuan according to the average exchange rate at that time, accounting for 5.4% of the GDP.

If the above two expansion scenarios are taken into account, the total debt of the Chinese economy will rise to 118.3 trillion yuan, and the whole society leverage ratio will reach 228%.

4.3 A Comparative Study of International Debt Levels

The above figures can produce a large amount of meaningful analysis results. Due to space limitations, this section will only interpret and judge China's total level of debt and whole society leverage ratio from the international comparative perspective.

China's total level of debt was lower than that of most developed economies, but higher than other BRIC countries (excluding South Africa). As shown in Table 4.2, in 2011, the total debt-to-GDP ratio of Japan and the UK had exceeded 500%, that of Spain, France, Italy and South Korea was more than 300%, and that of the US, Germany and Canada was relatively low, but still more than 270%. Among the BRICS countries, in 2010, the total debt-to-GDP ratio of Brazil and India was 148 and 122% respectively, and that of Russia was only 72% (MGI 2012), lower than China's 215% in 2012. By comparison, China's total debt-to-GDP ratio (or the whole society leverage ratio) was still at a relatively modest level, and China's level of debt was still in a mild, controllable range. However, given that China's level of

Table 4.2 Comparison between debt structure and total leverage ratio of China and the developed economies (ratio to GDP, %)

	Ratio of household debts	Ratio of non-financial corporate debts	Ratio of financial corporate debts	Ratio of government debts	Ratio of total debt
Japan	67	99	120	226	512
The United Kingdom	98	109	219	81	507
Spain	82	134	76	71	363
France	48	111	97	90	346
Italy	45	82	76	111	314
South Korea	81	107	93	33	314
The United States	87	72	40	80	279
Germany	60	49	87	83	279
Australia	105	59	91	21	276
Canada	91	53	63	69	276
China	31	113	18	53	215

Note The data of China are estimates by the research group for 2012; other data are from MGI (2012) for the second quarter of 2011 (only the data of Italy are for the first quarter of 2011)

debt has increased rapidly in recent years, we should stay vigilant for this. If the local debt or wider-scope sovereign debt is taken into account, China's government (sovereign) debt will be much greater, and its overall level of debt will have a substantial increase. In this regard, we should not sit by idly and remain indifferent.

From a structural perspective, Table 4.2 shows that non-financial corporate debt took an extremely high proportion, topping the list of all statistical countries. This is a distinctive feature of China's debt structure. This is closely related to the characteristics of China's economic development and financial system. Historically, the assets and liabilities of enterprises in China had experienced a significant transition and change. Prior to and at the beginning of reform and opening up, the investments of enterprises were from the financial budget arrangements. Although current funds were provided by banks ostensibly, they were not loans, but fixed quotas given by the financial budget, the banks were responsible for arranging and only played the role of a cashier. Therefore, the corporate debt at that time was almost zero. The reforms of substitution of tax payment for profit delivery and "allocation of funds replaced by loan grants" starting during 1985–1983 changed this situation. The substitution of tax payment for profit delivery was a major move to reform the profit distribution relationship between the state and state-owned enterprises, in which the income tax was introduced into the area of profit distribution of state-owned enterprises and state-owned enterprises should pay taxes instead of turning over their profits to the state and can keep all their after-tax profits. As a result, the financial departments no longer needed to allocate funds to the enterprises for their investments, which were replaced by bank loans. This is called "allocation of funds replaced by loan grants". This reform measure had a significant impact on state-owned enterprises' assets and liabilities. At the beginning of the reform, 62% of all fixed asset investment in state-owned entities was supported by financial capital, the other part was supported by the enterprises' own capital, with less than 2% from the financial institutions, However, in 2000, the governments' financial capital's support in investment in fixed assets of enterprises accounted for only 10%, bank loans accounted for 25% of funding needs, and the enterprises' own funds took the most important position. As the government gradually withdrew from its position as source of self funds of enterprises, the corporate debts began soaring. The debt to assets ratio of (state-owned) industrial enterprises increased from 11% in 1978 to 45% in 1988 and to around 70% in the 1990s. Considering the risks from a high debt to assets ratio, the government adopted a series of measures, including: (1) the banks started the commercialization reform during 1994–1995 and were no longer willing to grant loans to the enterprises with poor management; (2) the tax reform in 1994 specified the tax obligations of enterprises, and enterprises no longer needed to turn over all of their profits and could keep portion of the profits to increase their net worth automatically; (3) after the stock exchange had been established, enterprises can raise funds through equity financing, thereby reducing their debt to assets ratio; after the implementation of bankruptcy and restructuring of enterprises, enterprises with a high debt to assets ratio were phased out, resulting in decline of the overall debt to assets ratio; (4) the high debt to assets ratio of industrial state-owned enterprises declined in 2000 because of the debt-to-equity swap, and the corporate debts of 460 billion became equities. After these measures were adopted, the debt to assets ratio of enterprises has gradually declined and tended to be stable in the new century. Since 2000, the debt to assets ratio of enterprises has basically maintained at about 57–58%. Although by comparing with enterprises worldwide, Chinese enterprises have a moderate debt to assets ratio (on the whole, the nonfinancial corporations in the US and South Korea have a lower debt to assets ratio than those in China, while the nonfinancial corporations in Britain, Japan and Canada have a higher debt to assets ratio than those in China), but in 2012, the corporate sector leverage ratio (the proportion of corporate debts to GDP) reached 113%, higher than the threshold of 90% of the OECD countries, for which should remain highly vigilant.

So far, China's financial structure remains the characteristics that indirect financing plays a leading role, and most of the financial resources are allocated through bank intermediaries. This financial structure decides the high debt to assets ratio of Chinese enterprises. In a period of steady economic growth, bank loans constitute the main source of corporate debts and have the advantages of low costs and low risks, but if the economy fluctuate violently, especially if the economic growth rate is showing a decline trend, then quite a large part of corporate debts may form non-performing assets and thus detriment the healthiness of balance sheets of enterprises and banks.

Unlike China, the household debts of the US, the government debts of Japan and the financial institution debts of the UK were very high.

The household debts of the US accounted for 87% of its GDP and 31.2% of its total debt, higher than the ratios of the debts of the other three sectors, highlighting the feature of debt-based consumption or deficit spending.[1]

Japan's government debt to GDP ratio was as high as 226%, accounting for 44% of its total debt, and the debts of the other three sectors are relatively small. This is because, after the bubble economy burst, the Japanese economy remained sluggish, and the government had to repeatedly use the fiscal policy to stimulate the economy, leading to heavy debts. However, comparing with other countries, China's government debts as shown in Table 4.2 are somewhat misleading. This is because, in some developed economies, the central government are responsible for the debts at the local level, and if the local debts are too large, the local governments cal apply for bankruptcy, so local government debt are not included in government debts. This is why IMF's government debt statistics generally excludes local debts. But China's situation is completely different, the central government is in fact the last guarantor and even the redeemer of local government debts, so China's government debts listed in Table 4.1 include both central debts (accounting for 15% of the GDP) and local debts (accounting for 38% of the GDP).

The UK's characteristic was that the debts of financial institutions took a large proportion, accounting for up to 219% of the GDP and 43% of the total debt. This is

[1]The household sector leverage ratios of Australia and Canada were actually even higher than that of the United States, while the United States was often more likely to become the compared object.

because the UK is in fact the global financial and business center (the governor of the Bank of England once pointed out that the whole UK is the world's largest offshore financial center), and many foreign companies have set up their branch offices in the UK to carry out related businesses, and their assets and liabilities are included in statistics as the UK's enterprises. As these enterprises are mostly financial corporations, the UK's financial sector debts are relatively high. Some more extreme examples are Iceland and Ireland, and both were committed to building themselves into the international financial center before the crisis. Iceland's total debt to GDP ratio once increased to a staggering 1189%, in which the debt to GDP of the financial sector was up to 580%. Ireland's total debt to GDP also once reached more than 700%, in which the debt to GDP of the financial sector was up to 421%.

So far, there is no conclusive evidence showing what the best level of debt to GDP ratio is. However, it is confirmed that the rising debts will lead to higher debt-paying pressure and continuous accumulation of risks. Here, there is a threshold value, and the mounting debt beyond it will more harm than good and may lead to a financial and economic crisis. Cecchetti et al. (2011) made estimation based on the capital flow data of 18 OECD countries during 1980–2010 and came to the conclusion that the threshold value of government sector and household sector debt is 85% (debt/GDP), and that of corporate sector debt is 90% (debt/GDP). In this context, China's corporate sector debt to GDP reached 113% in 2012, which is obviously not good news.

The issue is complicated because due to the various sectors of the national economy are closely related and mutually influence, the change in the debt of one sector will affect the debt of other sectors. Here, there exist extremely complicated situation. MGI's study for the Japanese situation (MGI 2010) gave a disturbing example. The total debt to GDP ratio of the Japanese enterprises was 148% in 1995 and then declined to 125% in 2000 and further reduced to 91% in 2005, a decline of 57% in the decade. However, on the other hand, the debt to GDP ratio of the Japanese government rose sharply: from 84% in 1995 to 131% in 2000 and further to 180% in 2005, an increase of 96% in the decade. Thus, it seems that there is some relationship between the decline of corporate debt and the increase of government debt, but it is necessary to further study what is the relationship mechanism. However, this phenomenon has also revealed that while studying a country's national balance sheet, total amount analysis and sectoral analysis should be closely combined because there may be relationship of "increase in one sector but decrease in another sector" between the assets and liabilities of various sectors. In view of this, in Part II of this book, we will separately study the balance sheets of various sectors of the national economy so as to more thoroughly and comprehensively reveal the characteristics and risks of China's economy from the balance sheet perspective.

Chapter 5
Expansion of Balance Sheet with Chinese Characteristics

Since entering the new century, China's national and sovereign balance sheets have been showing a rapidly expanding trend. On the asset side, foreign assets, infrastructure and residential real estate assets have accumulated rapidly, becoming the dominant factor for asset expansion. This has recorded the historical process of China's rapid industrialization and urbanization under the export-oriented development strategy. On the liability side, the total liabilities of the sovereign sectors such as the governments at all levels and state-owned enterprises is expanding at a rate higher than that of the private sector. This highlights the institutional characteristics that the government plays the leading role in economic activities.

5.1 Asset Formation in Structural Change

5.1.1 Export-Oriented Industrialization and Accumulation of Foreign Assets

China's rapid industrialization has led to the formation of a large amount of industrial fixed assets and a huge trade surplus under the export-oriented economy, thus leading to the accumulation of huge foreign assets. This is a distinctive characteristic of China's asset accumulation, particularly accumulation of sovereign assets.

China's industrialization has been a long process. Since the 1990s, especially after entering the new century, industrialization has been gathering pace, and the manufacturing sector has been expanding rapidly. This can be proved in the data of UNIDO. From the perspective of growth rate of value added in the manufacturing sector, the real annual growth rate of value added in China's manufacturing sector was 11.11% during 2000–2005. In the same period, it was only 8.85% for the entire Asian region and only 6.7% throughout the developing countries. During 2005–2009, the

Y. Li and X. Zhang, *China's National Balance Sheet*, China Insights,
DOI 10.1007/978-981-10-4385-7_5

real annual growth rate of value added in China's manufacturing sector further increased to 12.25%, which was 2.92 and 4.89% higher than that of Asia and the developing countries respectively. Then from the perspective of percentage of manufacturing value added to GDP, the value added in China's manufacturing sector accounted for 32.12% of its GDP in 2000, 9.52 and 12.32% higher than that of the Asian countries and the developing countries respectively. In 2005, China's percentage of manufacturing value added to GDP increased to 34.11%, which was 9.68 and 13.16% higher than that of the Asian countries and the developing countries respectively. In 2009, China's percentage of manufacturing value added to GDP further increased to 35.7%, and the gap between China and the two reference systems reached 9.66 and 14.05% respectively.

The rise of China's manufacturing sector is closely related to its implementation of the opening-up strategy. In the context of economic globalization, China has actively joined the global division of labor, and by virtue of its unique factor endowment and corresponding comparative advantages, China has attracted the labor-intensive processing and assembling sectors in the global manufacturing chain and quickly established its position as the important global manufacturing base focusing on processing.[1] At the beginning of reform and opening up, China's manufacturing sector accounted for less than 4% of the value added in the global manufacturing sector. Since the late 1990s, especially after its accession to the WTO, the position of China's manufacturing sector in the world has increased rapidly. According to World Bank's World Development Indicators (WDI), the value added of China's manufacturing sector grew from 7.6% in 2001 to 18.1% in 2009, making China the world's second largest manufacturer after the United States (the value added in the US's manufacturing sector accounted for 18.8% of the world's value added in 2009). In 2010, the value added in China's manufacturing sector reported a lower proportion but still accounted for 17.6%, representing a narrowed gap with the US's global share (the added value in the US's manufacturing sector accounted for 18.2% of the world's value added in 2010), making China a veritable large manufacturer. The rising global position of China's manufacturing sector has resulted in a significant increase in goods trade surplus. During 2000–2007, China's goods trade surplus to GDP ratio soared from 2 to 7.6% (see Fig. 5.1). Since 2008, under the impact of the global financial crisis, the external sectors of all the countries have generally shrunk, and China's goods trade surplus to GDP ratio has also gradually declined.

Trade surplus continued to increase, resulting in the rapid accumulation of China's foreign assets, which is mainly reflected in rapid increase of reserve assets, particularly official reserve assets in the IIP. Since 2006, China has been the country with fastest-growing official foreign exchange reserves in the world and became the world's first country with official foreign exchange reserves of more than $3 trillion.

---

[1]The proportion of processing trade to exports maintained above 50% for a long time, but with the outbreak of the international financial crisis in 2008, the proportion of processing trade fell to less than 50%, while the proportion of general trade to exports increased.

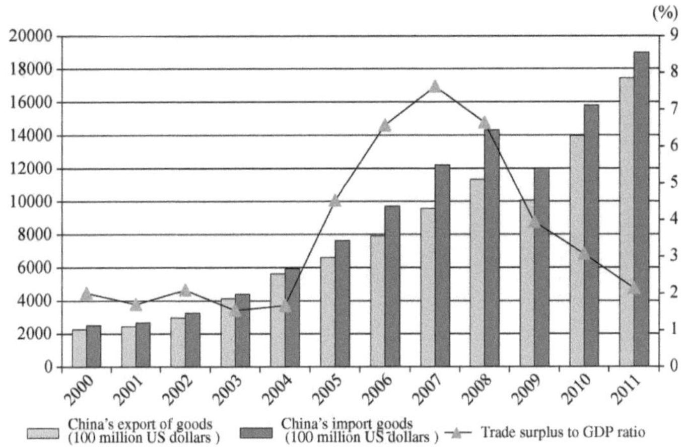

Fig. 5.1 China's import and export of goods and trade surplus to GDP ratio. *Source* The National Bureau of Statistics

Coupled with gold reserves, SDR and reserve position in the IMF, China's total official reserve assets reached $3255.8 billion at the end of 2011. China's foreign exchange reserves accounted for about 70% of its total foreign assets (Table 5.1), and the rapid growth of foreign exchange reserves has naturally led to the rapid expansion of China's foreign assets. From the perspective of international comparison, China ranks second by the ratio of foreign exchange reserves to total assets in the emerging market countries, next only to India (see Fig. 5.2). As the ratio of foreign exchange reserves to total assets of the emerging market countries is significantly higher than that of the developed countries, this also means that the ratio of foreign exchange reserves to total assets of China is in a relatively prominent position in the global comparison.

Under China's current foreign exchange management system, the newly-added foreign exchange assets were mainly included into the central bank's balance sheet

Table 5.1 Changes in China's reserve assets and total foreign assets

	Reserve assets (100 million US dollars)	Total external assets (100 million US dollars)	Proportion of reserve assets (%)
2004	6186	9291	66.6
2005	8257	12,233	67.5
2006	10,808	16,905	63.9
2007	15,473	24,162	64
2008	19,662	29,567	66.5
2009	24,513	34,571	70.9
2010	29,142	41,260	70.6
2011	32,558	47,345	68.8

Source The IIPs for these years

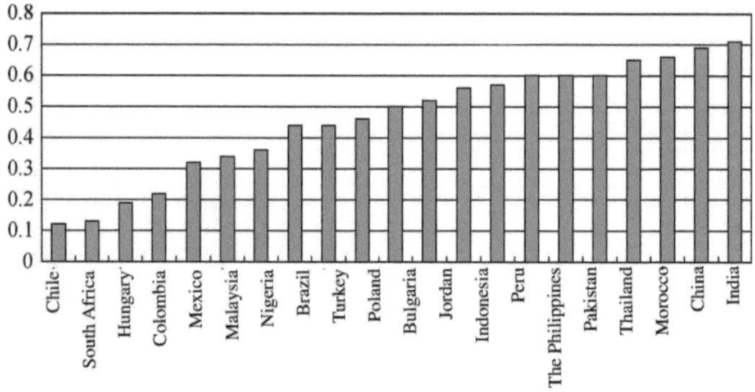

Fig. 5.2 The ratio of foreign exchange reserves to total assets of the emerging market countries in 2010. *Data sources* Lane and Milesi-Ferretti (2007) databases

and caused a significant increase of funds outstanding for foreign exchange in the central bank. This dynamic trend can be clearly seen on the asset mix of the central bank's balance sheet. Unlike other major central banks in the world, foreign exchange reserve assets constitute the main part of the assets of the People's Bank of China. Since the new century, the proportion of funds outstanding for foreign exchange has not only ranked first for a long time but is showing a constantly rising trend. In 2000, it accounted for less than 60% of the central bank's assets, and in 2011, it increased to nearly 83% (see Table 5.2). In 2010, the ratio of foreign exchange reserve assets to total assets of the People's Bank of China reached 1.3, 8.1, 2 and 1.2 times of that of the central banks of the United States, Britain, Japan and Europe respectively. The rapid expansion of foreign exchange reserve assets has led to the rapid expansion of the assets of China's central bank and made the People's Bank of China the world's largest central bank in 2006.[2] As of the end of 2011, the total assets of the People's Bank of China was up to 28.1 trillion yuan, accounting for 59% of the GDP. The amount of assets of China's central bank was 1.6 and 1.5 times of that of the Federal Reserve and the European Central Bank. The ratio of assets to GDP of China's central bank was 4 and 3 times of that of the Federal Reserve and the European Central Bank respectively (Sun Tao 2011).

5.1.2 Accumulation of Infrastructure Assets

Since entering the new century, China's urbanization drive has accelerated. During 2000–2011, the proportion of urban population to total population increased from

[2]The People's Bank of China overtook the central banks of the United States, Europe and Japan in June 2004, September 2005 and January 2006 respectively and became the central bank with largest assets in the world.

Table 5.2 Asset items of the balance sheets of China's central bank in recent years (unit: %)

Time	Foreign assets	Foreign exchange	Gold reserves	Other foreign assets	Claims on government	Claims on other depository corporations	Claims on other financial corporations	Claims on non-financial sector	Other assets
2000	61.09	59.94	0.33	0.83	2.79	12.24	12.76	0.06	11.05
2001	66.71	65.61	0.26	0.84	2.22	5.07	17.07	0.05	8.88
2002	73.8	68.09	0.2	5.51	9.65	4.65	7.67	0.04	4.2
2003	78.49	72.25	0.16	6.08	7.82	4.07	5.72	0.02	3.88
2004	81.45	76.98	0.29	4.18	6.88	3.15	5.07	0.02	3.43
2005	81.67	77.26	0.29	4.12	6.8	3.1	5.01	0.02	3.4
2006	81.79	77.41	0.29	4.09	6.74	3.1	4.97	0.02	3.38
2007	81.38	77.22	0.28	3.87	6.62	3.65	4.88	0.02	3.46
2008	81.64	77.55	0.28	3.81	6.51	3.63	4.8	0.02	3.41
2009	81.59	77.57	0.28	3.74	6.47	3.66	4.77	0.02	3.49
2010	83.09	79.75	0.26	3.08	5.95	3.66	4.37	0.01	2.93
2011	84.67	82.71	0.24	1.72	5.48	3.65	3.79	0.01	2.41

Source The balance sheets for the years of the monetary authorities

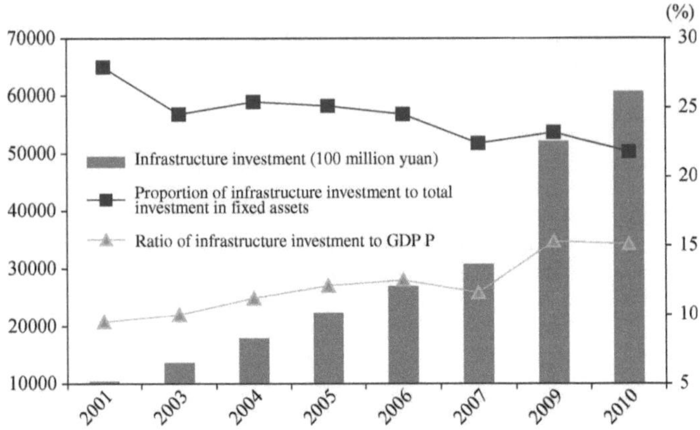

Fig. 5.3 Changes in scale of infrastructure investment and its proportions. *Source* The relevant of *Statistical Yearbook of China*

36.22 to 51.3%, an average annual increase of 1.37%, and an average annual increase of 0.44% over the period of 1990–1999. The acceleration of urbanization has resulted in rapid expansion of infrastructure and real estate assets.

First, the expansion of infrastructure. With the advancement of urbanization, China has invested a large sum of money in electric power, transportation, communications, municipal utilities (water supply and drainage, piped gas and heat supply etc.) and other fields of infrastructure. It is estimated that (see Fig. 5.3), in 2001, China's urban infrastructure investment stood at 1039.177 billion yuan and significantly increased to 6070.54 billion yuan in 2010, an increase of 4.84 times.[3] After deflating the fixed asset investment price index, the real growth was still up to 3.57 times, with an average annual growth of 18.4%. Especially since 2009, driven by China's huge investment stimulus plans, investment in infrastructure has been growing rapidly. The expansion of investment in the railway sector was particularly significant, with a growth rate of 63.5% in 2009, a new high in recent years. During the 11th Five-Year Period, the investment in railway infrastructure amounted to 1.98 trillion yuan, 6.3 times of that in the 10th Five-Year Period.

Since the beginning of this century, the proportion of infrastructure investment to total investment in fixed assets in China has remained at above 20%. The proportion of infrastructure investment to GDP is showing a rising trend on the whole

[3]We have added up the following categories of data on investment in fixed assets given by "Statistical Yearbook of China": electric power, gas and water production and supply, transportation, postal services, telecommunications and other information transmission services, and public facilities management (including urban public transportation, rail transportation, urban roads, drainage and sewage treatment and other municipal utilities, waste treatment and other environmental health industries, and landscaping etc.). The tax threshold for investment in fixed assets was substantially adjusted in 2011, the data have poor comparability with those of the previous years, so here we have only used the data for 2010 and before.

(see Fig. 5.3) and reached above 15% in 2009 and 2010. This proportion is far more than the policy recommendation of the ratio of economic infrastructure investment to GDP of no less than 5% given by the World Bank in *World Development Report 1994: Infrastructure for Development* (The World Bank 1994).

Long-term and heavy investment has led to a rapid increase in the level of China's infrastructure. Since the beginning of the new century, China's electricity generation and consumption has increased by 1.7 times, its highway mileage has increased by 3.5 times, its telephone and Internet penetration rate has increased by 67 and 30%, its water and gas penetration rate has increased by 33 and 47%, and its central heating area has increased by three times. By the end of 2010, China ranked first in the world by the scale of power grid, ranked second for 15 consecutive years by installed power generation capacity, ranked second by highway operation mileage and electrified railway operation mileage and ranked first by high-speed railway operation mileage as well as fixed telephone and mobile phone users. China has remained in the first place in the world by the number of Internet users and Internet broadband users since it jumped to the first place in 2008.

Comparing the main indicators representing the level of infrastructure development worldwide, we can get a more profound and intuitive impression on the accomplishments China has made in infrastructure construction since the beginning of the new century. As shown in Table 5.3, China's indicators are not only higher than those of middle-income countries but are most higher than the world averages in the main infrastructure areas such as electricity consumption, road density, quality of port infrastructure, number of subscribers of Internet service and number of telephone lines per 100 persons.[4]

5.1.3 Accumulation of Real Estate Assets

Since the housing monetarization reform in China started and the urbanization drive accelerated, China's residential housing assets have quickly accumulated. Accordingly, the risks of the real estate market have also risen sharply, and the balance sheets of the three sectors of residents, banks and government have been linked through the real estate credit channel to form potential systemic risks.

[4]It should be noted that, in the current investment and financing system, private capital can hardly enter the infrastructure sectors, especially the sectors managed by the central government, and the phenomenon of state-owned capital as "one single-large shareholder" still exists. Especially in the railway sector where there is no a clear line between the functions of the government and enterprises, there was only a very small amount of private capital (based on the statistics in 2010, the privately held part only accounted for 2% of the fixed assets investment in railway transportation). This means that a large amount of infrastructure assets accumulated in the acceleration of urbanization have actually constituted an important part of state-owned operating assets. This has also to a certain extent explained the cause for rapid increase of non-financial state-owned assets we've discovered in the process of preparation of sovereign balance sheets.

Table 5.3 International comparison of the level of infrastructure development

	Power consumption (kWh per person, 2011)	Road density (km, 2010)	Quality of port infrastructure (score, 2012)	Number of subscribers of Internet service	Number of telephone lines per 100 persons (2012)
China	3298	41.8	4.4	42.3	20.6
The World	3044.4	27.8 (2008)	4.3	35.6	17.3 (2011)
Middle-income countries	1816.3	28.4 (2008)	3.8	29.8	12.6 (2011)

Source The World Bank's World Development Indicators (WDI) database

Note (1) road density refers to the ratio of total length of a country's road network to its land area. The road network includes all domestic roads: expressways, highways, trunk roads or national roads, secondary or regional roads, and other urban or rural roads. (2) the data on the quality of port infrastructure are from the Survey of Corporate Executives jointly conducted by the World Economic Forum and the relevant research institutions, which aims to measure their feelings for the port facilities in their own countries. The questionnaire responses were aggregated using the weighted average of the industry. The data of the recent year were combined with those of the previous year to create a two-year moving average. The scores range from 1 (port infrastructure is very underdeveloped) to 7 (according to international standards, port infrastructure is well developed and efficient)

In this study, we have made use of the data of the survey on urban and rural residents conduced by NBS and other related depreciation assumptions to estimate the value of urban and rural housing assets (for the process in details, see Part 3 of this book).

5.2 Liabilities Formed Under the Catch-up and Surpassing System

In China's rapid growth in the past 30 years, the government has been playing a leading role. Under the development mode decided by the catch-up and surpassing system, on the one hand, the government is directly involved in economic activities, thus forming a large amount of government debts in explicit sense, especially government debts at the local level. On the other hand, due to the government's indirect intervention in economic activities or provision of implicit guarantees, the non-performing loans of state-owned enterprises and state-owned commercial banks as well as the pension fund gap have become implicit government liabilities. The absolute and relative size of liabilities of the private sector, particularly the household sector, is still small, but real estate-related mortgage credit risks should arouse our attention.

5.2.1 Growth Priority Strategy Under the Catch-up and Surpassing System

So far, in China's performance appraisal system and political incentive structure, economic growth and fiscal revenue growth are most important. Therefore, economic development has become the center of all local work. In recent years, with the promotion of scientific outlook on development, some indicators measuring social development and sustainable development are beginning to be incorporated into the system for appraising and evaluating the performance of local officials. However, as economic development is of "overriding importance", the above positive changes are still insufficient to shake the core position of GDP in the entire appraisal system.

The local governments' strong preference for growth can be clearly seen in the GDP growth targets set in the 12th Five-Year plans of various regions (Table 5.4). The expected average annual GDP growth target set by the National 12th Five-Year Plan is 7%, but the GDP growth targets set by all provinces have all exceeded this minimum limit. Except for Beijing, Shanghai and a few other economically developed provinces (municipalities) that have set a single-digit economic growth target, most provinces have set the economic growth target at more than 10%. On average, the expected annual growth rate of GDP set by 31 provinces (autonomous regions

Table 5.4 Annual growth rate of GDP in the 11th and 12th Five-Year plans of various regions

	11th Five-Year plan (%)	12th Five-Year plan
Beijing	9	8%
Tianjin	12	12%
Hebei	Around 11	8.5%
Shanghai	9	8%
江苏 Jiangsu	Above 10	Around 10%
Zhejiang	Around 9	Around 8%
Fujian	Above 9	Above 10%, strive to be doubled
Shandong	Around 10	Around 9%
Guangdong	Above 9	Above 8%
Hainan	Above 9	Above 10%
Liaoning	Around 11	11%
Jilin	Above 12	Above 12%
Heilongjiang	Above 10	Above 12%, to be doubled in 5 years
Shanxi	10	13%, to be doubled in 5 years
Anhui	Above 10	Above 10%, strive to be doubled
Jiangxi	11	Above 11%, strive to be doubled
Henan	Around 10	Above 9%
Hubei	Above 10	Above 10%
Hunan	Above 10	Above 10%
Inner Mongolia	Above 13	Above 12%
Guangxi	Above 10	10%, strive to be doubled
Chongqing	10	12.5%, to be doubled in 5 years
Sichuan	Around 9	Around 12%
Guizhou	10	Above 12%, to be doubled in 5 years
Yunnan	Above 8.5	Above 10%, strive to be doubled
Tibet	12	Above 12%
Shaanxi	Around 11	Above 12%
Gansu	10	Above 12%
Qinghai	Above 10	12%, to be doubled in 5 years
Ningxia	Above 10	12%, to be doubled in 5 years
Xinjiang	9	Above 10%

Sources The 11th and 12th Five-Year plans of various regions

and municipalities) reached about 10.5%. Among them, some provinces even proposed to double their GDPs and even their GDPs per capita during the 12th Five-Year Plan Period, which means an average annual economic growth rate of close to 15% or higher. In contrast, in the 11th Five-Year period, the GDP growth rate set by the state was 7.5%, but it was increased to 10% at the local level, with the latter being 30% higher than the former. From the perspective of the gap between the growth targets set by the central and local governments, it further expanded in the 12th Five-Year Plan compared with the 11th Five-Year Plan. This shows that, since the central government advocated the scientific outlook on development, the local governments' preference for GDP has not diminished.

5.2.2 Construction-Oriented Government and Local Government Debt Expansion

The catch-up and surpassing system highlighting economic growth has created the typical "construction-oriented" and "investment-oriented" government. The governments at all levels assume a lot of economic functions and have input plenty of financial resources and efforts into the field of production and operation, which is the main characteristics of construction-oriented and investment-oriented government.[5] According to the IMF's *Government Finance Statistics Yearbook* 2008, we have compared the fiscal expenditure structures of the governments of the relevant countries based on functional classifications (we selected the data for 2007 with a view to excluding the distorting effect of the government's deep involvement in economic affairs on the fiscal expenditure structures in the financial crisis as an abnormal event). As shown in Table 5.5, compared with the developed economies or the emerging and developing economies, or compared with the transition economies or the government-led traditional East Asian economies, the expenditure of the Chinese government in economic affairs took a high proportion. In all the countries with data available, China is the country with the highest proportion of economic expenditures except Bhutan, around 13% higher than that of the second highest country.

At the central level, the Chinese government's economic expenditure was not very high compared with the relevant countries (see Table 5.6), so the characteristics of the so-called construction-oriented government is mainly reflected at the local level. This characteristic is reflected in the changes in the relationship of administrative subordination of urban fixed asset investment projects. The data show that, after entering the new century, the growth of local projects were significantly higher than that of the central projects (see Fig. 5.4). This has led to the increasing proportion of local projects, which exceeded 80% in 2002 and was over

[5]Theoretically, China has been regarding "constructive" as the main feature distinguishing a socialist country and its government from a capitalist country and its government. Accordingly, investment takes precedence over consumption, and production takes precedence over life. This is regarded as the guide line in various fields. Judging from the state budget, constructive expenditure has always constituted a major item of the spending of the Chinese government. In recent years, with the popularization of the concept of "people orientation" and the proposal of increasing the proportion of consumption in GDP, the feature of "construction precedence" in China's economy has just slowly subsided. In the last century, China's financial sector began to propose the goal of building "public finance", in which an important change direction is to reduce investment (constructive) expenditure and increased public consumption expenditure.

Table 5.5 Comparison between the fiscal expenditure structures between the governments of China and some other countries in 2007 (unit: %)

	General public affairs	National defense	Public order and security	Economic affairs	Environmental protection	Housing and community living facilities	Health	Culture, entertainment and religious affairs	Education	Social security
China	18.2	5.24	4.98	37.68	3.21	0.44	2.51	1.27	9.32	17.15
The United States	13.47	11.54	5.71	9.98	–	1.85	21.06	0.87	16.93	18.59
Germany	13.61	2.41	3.51	7.23	1.1	1.93	14.01	1.36	9.09	45.75
France	13.28	3.39	2.41	5.36	1.66	3.62	13.72	2.9	11.24	42.41
Italy	15.98	3.14	3.89	10.23	1.83	2.16	12.75	3.05	11.22	35.93
Japan	12.91	2.59	3.89	10.55	3.55	1.81	19.6	0.43	10.74	33.93
Singapore	12.37	27.99	6.24	9.81	–	12.19	6.04	0.48	20.82	4.07
Poland	12.58	3.89	4.72	10.15	1.4	1.7	10.62	2.64	12.72	39.57
Ukraine	7.66	3.04	5.25	13.54	0.66	2	9.05	1.9	14.01	42.89

Source The IMF's *Government Finance Statistics Yearbook* 2008

Table 5.6 Comparison between the fiscal expenditure structures of the central governments of China and some other countries in 2007 (unit: %)

	General public affairs	National defense	Public order and security	Economic affairs	Environmental protection	Housing and community living facilities	Health	Culture, entertainment and religious affairs	Education	Social security
China	60.49	11.37	1.82	19.67	0.03	0.27	0.16	0.32	1.22	4.65
The United States	13.4	19.96	1.53	5.91	–	1.95	25.18	0.15	2.39	29.54
Germany	14.56	3.68	0.5	5.37	0.06	0.71	20.35	0.15	0.59	54.03
Italy	19.98	3.52	4.08	6.39	0.4	0.5	13.54	0.83	10.9	39.87
South Korea	24.02	11.33	5.48	17.63	–	4.42	0.99	1.01	15.36	20.73
Singapore	12.37	27.99	6.24	9.81	–	12.19	6.04	0.48	20.82	4.07
Poland	13.88	4.63	5.29	6.8	0.21	0.42	11.58	0.9	11.48	44.82
Ukraine	23.52	3.65	6.24	11.58	0.58	0.59	3.1	0.84	5.81	44.08
Chile	7.71	6.51	7.02	14.3	0.32	1.49	15.94	0.71	17.24	28.76
Mexico	38.36	3.04	2.72	8.11	–	6.92	4.95	0.56	24.73	20.12

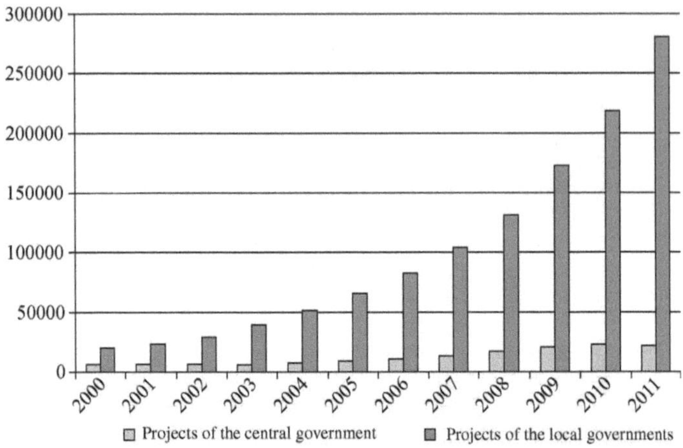

Fig. 5.4 Changes in urban fixed asset investment by relationship of administrative subordination (100 million yuan). Source: *Statistical Yearbook of China 2012*

92% in 2011. This suggests that local investment takes a dominant position, which constitutes an important trend in the area of investment in China in recent years.

On the one hand, the local governments assume many economic development functions, and on the other hand, institutional funding sources that can be used by them are in serious shortage, so the local governments have to support their ambitious investment plans through a large amount of non-standard liabilities. "LGFPs" thus emerged and soon saw rapid development.[6] According to the data of the National Audit Office, as of the end of 2010, the governments at provincial, municipal and county levels had set up 6576 financing platform companies nationwide, including 165 at the provincial level, 1648 at the municipal level and 4763 at the county level. From the perspective of these companies' business scopes, 3234 companies are mainly engaged in financing government construction projects, 1173 companies are engaged in financing and investing in construction of government projects, and 2169 companies are simultaneously engaged in other business activities.

LGFPCs raise funds mainly through two means.[7] First, bank loans. In the massive credit expansion in 2008 and 2009, LGFPs were once important financing

[6]The mismatch between routine power and financial power (mainly inadequate financial power) is a problem the local governments in China should always face. Therefore, the local governments always bypass the central government's regulations and make every endeavor to "hunting the ministries" for money. Keenly finding and seizing all new funding sources has become an important economic behavior of the local governments. Before the "financing platforms" became popular in 2009, "packaged loans", "land finance" and the like have become important financing channels and means of local governments.

[7]In addition, they also include the forms of financing such as "credit-government cooperation" and "bank-government cooperation". But due to incomplete data available, the amount of money raised through local government financing platform companies is still unclear.

entities. According to the statistics of CBRC, as of the end of 2009, the outstanding balance of loans of LGFPs was 7.38 trillion yuan, accounting for 20.4% of the outstanding balance of conventional loans. Among them, the new loans of LGFPs in 2009 were about 3.05 trillion yuan, accounting for 34.5% of all new conventional loans. Second, urban construction investment corporation bonds (including corporate bonds, medium-term notes and short-term financing bonds etc.). According to the statistics of the bond market, as of the end of June 2010, the outstanding balance of urban construction investment corporation bonds amounted to 488.25 billion yuan.

Loans and bonds issued have formed local government debts. The data of the National Audit Office show that by the end of 2010, the outstanding debt owed by LGFPs was 4971.068 billion yuan, accounting for 46.38% of the outstanding local government debt, including: 3137.529 billion yuan worth of debt that will be repaid by government fiscal revenue, 814.371 billion yuan worth of debt for which local governments issued official guarantees and 1019.168 trillion yuan worth of other related debts, accounting for 63.12, 16.38 and 20.50% respectively. From the hierarchy view, the debt at provincial level amounted to 882.667 billion yuan, that at the municipal level 2684.575 billion yuan and that at the county level 1403.826 billion yuan, accounting for 17.76, 54 and 28.24% respectively.

From the perspective of investment direction of local government debt capital nationwide as of the end of 2010 the (part has already been spent) (see Fig. 5.5), the debt capital was mainly invested in the following three areas: utility construction, transportation and land purchase and storage, totally accounting for 72%. These are all directly related to urban infrastructure construction. This fact further reveals that: acceleration of urbanization is the main engine for China's current and future economic growth. Therefore, investment in urban infrastructure constitutes the main content of the current and future investment in China, and the local governments are the main entities of such investments.

It is noteworthy that recently there is a trend that LGFPs are transforming into non-bank financing. In fact, the regulatory authorities carried out special screening of loans borrowed by LGFPs in mid-2010, the rapid expansion momentum of local government debts was once curbed, and the loans borrowed by basically ceased to

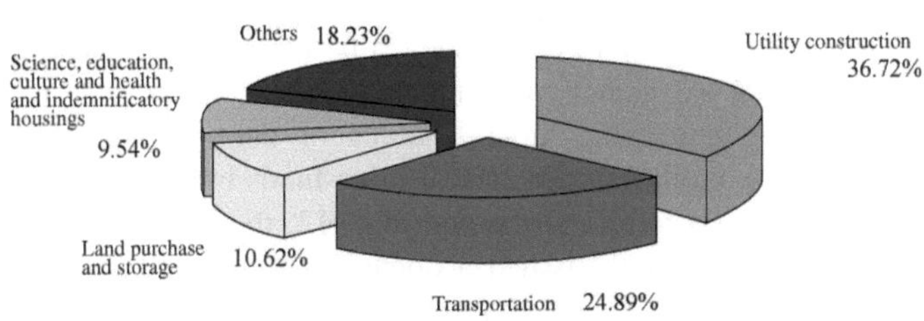

Fig. 5.5 Investment direction of local government debt capital nationwide as of the end of 2010. Source: *Results of National Audit of Local Government Debts* issued by the National Audit Office in June 2011

grow. Since 2012, the economic growth has slowed down, and investment in infrastructure construction nationwide has been increased to ensure "steady growth". In this context, LGFPs that assume the primary task of infrastructure construction had increasingly stronger funding needs. Meanwhile, the growth of local public financial revenue declined, the fees for land transfer reduced, LGFPs entered the peak period of debt repayment, and there were a large amount of maturing bank loans. All these factors increased the financing needs of LGFPs. Thus, after experiencing a brief silence, local government debts rebounded in 2011 the 2012. After the traditional bank credit financing channels were tightened, more and more LGFPs changed the existing financing modes and raised funds through urban construction investment bond, loan in trust and other non-banking modes.

From the perspective of bond financing, in the 3 years between 2009 and 2011, the amount of urban construction investment bonds issued remained largely stable. Since 2012, with changes in the macroeconomic environment and the bond issuing conditions became loose, urban construction investment bonds saw rapid growth, with the amount of bonds issued in the whole year reaching 1.27 trillion yuan, the amount of bonds maturing in the year reaching 99.7 billion yuan, a net increase of 1.17 trillion yuan, a year-on-year increase of 189%.

In the meanwhile, the off-balance sheet businesses represented by "shadow banking" were booming, a large amount of bank capital were flowing into LGFPs in convert forms through trust, fund, financial leasing and other channels. "Shadow banking" is gradually developing into a major alternative local financing solution under credit squeeze. From the perspective of trust financing, trust funds investing in basic industries only increased by 20.93 billion yuan in 2011 and 755.1 billion yuan in 2012, among which a single trust scheme was worth 615 billion yuan. In 2011, the balance of trust-government funds reduced by 102.64 billion yuan but increased by 247.87 billion yuan in 2012. This shows that more and more trust companies have shifted their core businesses gradually to the field of local government financing.

By rough estimation, in 2012, the debt owed by LGFPs increased by about 1.9 trillion yuan, of which 1.17 trillion yuan was raised through issuing urban construction investment bonds and 755.1 billion yuan through the trust scheme. As of the end of 2012, the debt owed by LGFPs probably had increased to 12–13 trillion yuan.

The local debt structure and risks tended to be more complicated, and particularly, illegal financing has gained momentum, such as constructing public welfare projects illegally by borrowing large amounts of debts though raising funds, build-transfer ("BT") or other means and injecting funds into or offering guarantees to LGFPCs illegally. Therefore, at the end of 2012, the Ministry of Finance and other three departments jointly issued a document to strengthen once again the regulation on the conduct of local government financing. This regulation covers the majority of the financing channels and focuses on regulating the local governments' "land financing" modes and screening the shadow banking businesses that are expanding disorderly. Meanwhile, the National Development and Reform Commission also strengthened corporate debt risk prevention in mid-December

2012 and specified and detailed the assets-liability ratio criteria of corporate issuers. In March 2013, CBRC issued a document to regulate the wealth management funds of commercial banks that are invested in the business of "non-standardized debt assets" directly or indirectly through non-bank financial institutions and asset trading platforms, which acturally also involves the rectification of LGFPs.

It is still doubtful whether these regulatory constraints for the debts of LGFPs can fundamentally solve the potential growth pressure of local debt. First, under the current macroeconomic situation, due to the uncertainty in external demands and weak consumer demands, sluggish investment in manufacturing and the likelihood of real estate investment being affected by the regulatory policies, infrastructure investment will continue to play an important role in ensuring steady growth. Based on the plans of various regions, in 2013, nearly 20 provinces set their fixed asset investment growth targets at 20% and above, and some provinces even set their targets at 30%. In this context, the new regulation opinions are likely stimulate the local governments' new circumvent impulse and continue looking for alternative financing and variant financing options.

So far, the management of the debts of LGFPs has been focusing on limitation and constraint. Such countermeasure giving top priority to "blocking" can hardly solve the debt risks of LGFPs fundamentally. After blocking the crooked roads, we also need to blaze the right road. According to the *Decision* adopted at the 3rd Plenary Session of the 18th Central Committee of the Communist Party of China, "we should establish a transparent and procedure-based investment and financing mechanism for urban development, allow local governments to expand the channels of financing for urban development by issuing bonds and other means, allow private capital to participate in urban infrastructure investment and operation by franchise and other means, and study the possibility of setting up policy financial institutions for developing urban infrastructure and housing". The direction has been clearly identified, and we hope that the spirit of the *Decision* will be implemented in the coming years.

5.2.3 Implicit Government Guarantees and Contingent Liabilities

For China's success in the past 30 years, the governments have played an important role. This role is reflected not only in their direct involvement in economic construction as investors, but also in their providing a large number of implicit guarantees to microcosmic subjects to support the development of state-owned enterprises and state-owned financial institutions. Meanwhile, the governments have also borne enormous market-oriented economic restructuring costs.

The implicit guarantees of state-owned enterprises mainly take three forms as follows: (1) implicit guarantees for losses on account of state-owned enterprises. Under the traditional planned economy, the state finance provided subsidies for all the losses of state-owned enterprises. Since the reform of "allocation of funds replaced by loan grants" starting in 1985, the subsidies provided by the central finance to cover enterprise losses of state-owned enterprises (the income that should be turned over to the finance but had actually not turned over) declined on the whole, but the losses of state-owned enterprises (losses after receiving subsidies) had increased year by year. These losses basically existed in the form of losses on account. This means that the central finance deficit actually provided implicit guarantees for the losses on account of state-owned enterprises. (2) Guarantees for the debt of state-owned enterprises. This typical case is the sorting out of "chain debts" in the 1990s. (3) Guarantees for loans of state-owned enterprises in arrears from the state-owned banks, which in fact were implicit guarantees of the government for the financial industry because these non-performing loans would ultimately be borne by the central government.

In addition to the above-mentioned disposal (including write-off and stripping etc.) of non-performing assets, the implicit guarantees of the government for the financial industry was also reflected in improving the banks' capital adequacy ratio by issuing bonds or directly injecting financial funds as well as finally providing bank deposit insurance.[8]

An important implicit guarantee provided by the Chinese government is to bear the major reform and restructuring costs. Among them, the deficit of social security fund is most serious. Under the traditional system, China has been implementing the policies characterized by "low wage, low consumption and high accumulation". During 1952–1978, the average money wage of workers grew from 445 to 615 yuan,[9] an increase of 38.2%, while the prices rose by 21.5% (the retail price index rose from 82.3 in 1952 to 100 in 1978). Taking into account the inflation rate, wages actually grew by 16.7%, an average annual increase of only 0.6%. But the accumulation rate grew from 21.4% in 1952 to 36.5% in 1978 and was even as high as 40% in some years.[10] Such distribution pattern made state-owned enterprises unable to accumulate social security funds for their workers, thus accumulating a large amount of historical debts. These historical debts were formed as a result of the government's long-term implementation of the high accumulation policies of "draining the pond to get all the fishes" in the past, so there is ample reason to include them in contingent liabilities of government.

[8]Providing implicit guarantee from the government for the financial sector is not a phenomenon unique to China, and it is also very common in mature market economies.

[9]The data are from "China Compendium of Statistics 1949–2004", Department of Comprehensive Statistics, NBS (2005).

[10]The data are from "Statistical Yearbook of China" in 1981.

Chapter 6
Balance Sheet Risk Assessment

6.1 General Framework for Balance Sheet Risk Assessment

A country's balance sheet risks can be analyzed and assessed from the three levels: intra-sector, inter-sector and long-term macroeconomic operation performance.

First, intra-sector risks. They refer to internal commercial and financial risks in all sectors such as balance sheet mismatches and accumulation of contingent debt. Among them, balance sheet mismatches include three aspects: (1) currency mismatch: when the income and expenditure activities of a stakeholder (a sovereign state, bank, non-financial enterprise or a household) are dominated in different currencies, due to the different currency structures of its assets and liabilities, "currency mismatch" will occur when the net worth or net income (or both) of its equity are very sensitive to changes in the exchange rate. From the stock perspective, currency mismatch refers to the sensitivity of a balance sheet (i.e. net worth) to changes in the exchange rate. From the flow perspective, it refers to the sensitivity of an income statement (net income) to changes in the exchange rate. The more sensitive the net worth/net income to changes in the exchange rate, the greater the currency mismatch. (2) Maturity mismatch: the mismatch between the maturity structures of assets and liabilities, which is mainly represented as "short-term borrowing for long-term use", leading to the need of a stakeholder to frequently enter the market to bridge the liquidity gap. (3) Capital structure mismatch: when a stakeholder is overly reliant on rigid debt financing, while the proportion of capital or equity is too low in the financing structure, the phenomenon of a high debt to equity ratio or leverage ratio will occur. In essence, the risks arising from the above three mismatches are liquidity risks.

Second, inter-sectoral contagious risks (systemic risks). They refers to the "contagious" risks arising from correlation and business contact between different sectors of the national economy in assets, liabilities, equity and other items. The study mainly focuses on clarifying the possible paths for inter-sectoral debt

Y. Li and X. Zhang, *China's National Balance Sheet*, China Insights,
DOI 10.1007/978-981-10-4385-7_6

repayment and risk absorption and the relationship between changes in ownership of assets and liabilities. By channel, this mechanism can be divided into two kinds: direct contagion and indirect contagion by other sectors (mainly financial institutions). By direction, it can be divided into two kinds: the "bottom-up" contagion from the private sector to the public (sovereign) sector and the "top down" contagion from the public (sovereign) sector to the private sector. As an example, the following figure (Fig. 6.1) shows a simplified mechanism for the risk contagion from non-financial corporations, financial institutions and households to the government sector.

Third, mid- and long-term dynamic risks. On the basis of combining the stock and flow methods, it mainly refer to the dynamic structure of assets and liabilities of equity entities, including the issues of leverage ratio, solvency and debt sustainability. As a large country opening up to the outside world that is concurrently under institutional restructuring, transformation of economic development pattern and periodic promotion of economic development, China is currently facing a number of special long-term dynamic risks. These risks mainly from the transformation of economic growth path (such as structural economic slowdown), government restructuring, an aging population, social welfare improvement, financial openness (such as internationalization of RMB) and other changes in internal and external factors of economic and social development. All these changes will be reflected on the balance sheet. Obviously, this is the scope of balance sheet risks in broad sense that needs comprehensive macro-level analysis of various types of structures. This issue will be discussed in the next chapter independently.

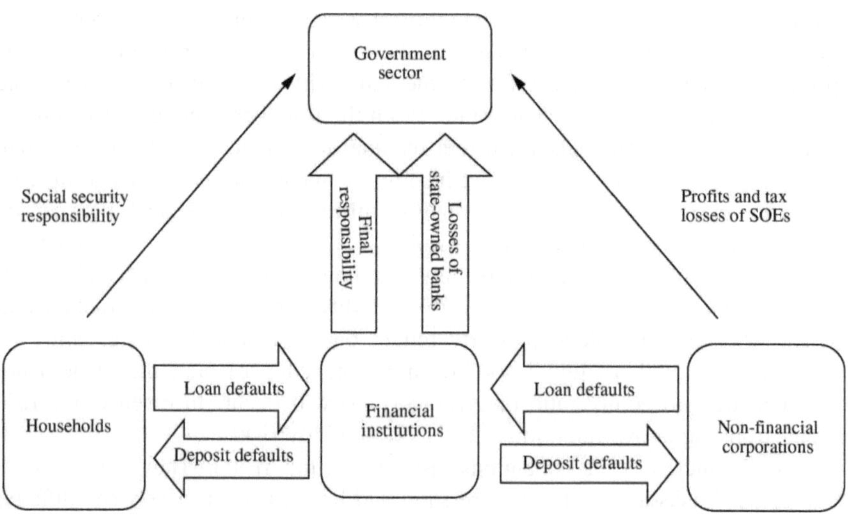

Fig. 6.1 Inter-sectoral risk contagion mechanism

6.2 National Balance Sheet Mismatches and Contingent Liability Risks

6.2.1 Term of Balance Sheet and Capital Structure Mismatch Risks

As mentioned above, balance sheet mismatches mainly include currency mismatch, maturity mismatch and capital structure mismatch. Here we will discuss the latter two mismatches and then discussed currency mismatch and associated RMB internationalization in the next subsection.

First, maturity mismatch risks. China is now in the process of accelerated urbanization. Urbanization requires huge investments. Compared to industrialization, investments in urbanization are not only huge in amount, but also involve a longer period. Under the condition of slow development of the capital market and imperfect long-term funding system, the commercial banks' existing risk of "short-term borrowing for long-term use" is more serious. Such is also the case for the local governments. They undertake huge investments in urban infrastructure. These investments have a long cycle and slow effects, and it still takes 5–10 years for even the projects with stable and good return prospects to generate cash flow. However, the sources of funds to support these projects are mainly land transfer fees, tax revenues, bonds issued by the central government on behalf of the local governments and some mid- and short-term capital borrowed by LGFPs. This has led to serious mismatches between debt maturity and cash flow distribution of projects. Although these mismatches generally will not produce "solvency risks", it will give rise to some "liquidity risks".

Second, capital structure mismatch risks. By international comparison, we found that the debt of China's non-financial corporate sector accounted for 62.4% of its total debt, 30–40% higher than that of other countries (Fig. 6.2). This highlights the chronic problems of China's bank-led financial system focusing on debt financing. Undoubtedly, due to such capital structure mismatch, the debt and leverage ratio of China's non-financial corporations is at a level very likely to trigger a crisis.

6.2.2 Currency Mismatch Risks and RMB Internationalization

With regard to currency mismatch risks, at the end of 2012, China's foreign assets stood at $5174.9 billion, and its external liabilities $ 3438.5 billion, with net IIP of up to $ 1736.4 billion. As China's foreign currency assets were greater than its foreign currency liabilities, the main problem China is facing is currency mismatch on credit. This is greatly different from currency mismatch on debt the countries most seriously affected by the Asian financial crisis were facing. In the currency structure of China's assets denominated in foreign currency, about 60–70% are U.S. dollar-denominated

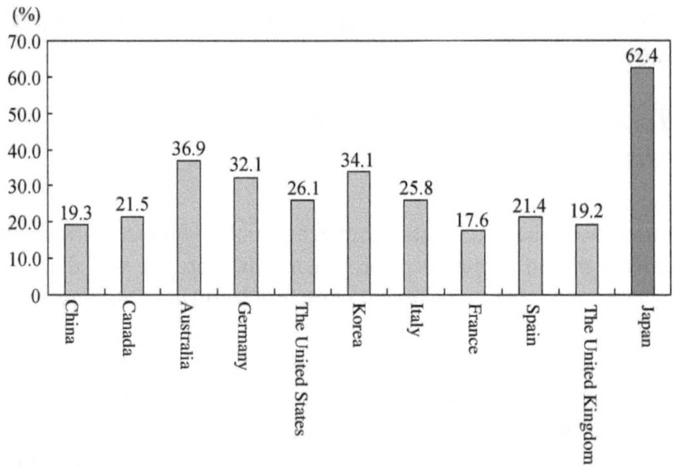

Fig. 6.2 International comparison of non-financial corporate debt to total debt ratios. *Sources* China's Data are from the estimates of the research group and other data are from MGI (2012)

assets, 20–25% are euro-dominated assets, and the rest are sterling-denominated and yen-denominated assets. From July 2005 when China started a new round of reform of the formation mechanism of the RMB exchange rate to the end of 2012, the RMB exchange rate against the US Dollar appreciated nearly 32% cumulatively, and due to such change, China's foreign assets suffered huge book losses (the so-called "floating loss" in the industry). If RMB continues to appreciate in the future, such losses on assets will still be inevitable.

In 2012, some new changes appeared in China's balance of international payments, which brought some new challenges to the currency structure of the Central Bank's Balance Sheet: the "double surplus" pattern lasting for 13 years (1999–2011) had changed into the new pattern of "current account surplus and capital and financial account deficit". China saw a deficit on its capital and financial account mainly because it experienced large-scale net capital outflows in the form of non-direct investment, especially the net outflow of $260 billion under other investment items. Among them, the net worth of foreign assets under other investment items (including foreign loans, foreign borrowing and lending, deferred receipt for export and advance payment for import etc.) increased by $231.6 billion, and the external liabilities under other investment items (including trade finance and foreign deposits etc.) decreased by $28.4 billion.

The increase in domestic investors' use of foreign assets and the decrease in their liabilities is closely related to the differentiated expectation on RMB exchange rate fluctuations. Under the background that RMB exchange rate is gradually approaching a reasonable and equilibrium level, the currency would be more likely to experience two-way fluctuation instead of the unilateral appreciation, and enterprises, households and other private sectors have adjusted their financial operations accordingly from the previous "converting assets to RMB-denominated assets and liabilities to foreign-currency denominated liabilities" to "converting assets to foreign-currency denominated assets and liabilities to RMB-denominated liabilities" or achieved an equilibrium in assets and liabilities denominated in foreign currencies. From the perspective of domestic enterprises and individuals' willingness to settle and sell foreign exchanges, their willingness to settle foreign exchanges is weak, while their willingness to hold and purchase foreign exchanges is strong. The exchange settlement of the non-banking sector declined by 2% in 2012, up 19% compared with 2011, and the forex settlement and sale surplus was $110.6 billion, down 70% compared with 2011, only equivalent to 22% of the historical highest surplus in 2007.

With the change in the pattern of balance of international payments, especially with the change in the willingness of domestic institutions and individuals for foreign exchange settlement and sale and the substantial increase in foreign assets held by them, China has started to change from "foreign exchange held by the state" to "foreign exchange held by the people". In 2012, the growth of reserve assets slowed down significantly. Excluding the influence of changes in non-trading values such as exchange rate and prices, the reserve assets increased by $96.6 billion, down 75% compared with 2011, the lowest increase level in nearly a decade since 2002. The reserve assets to GDP ratio was 1.2%, down 4.1% compared with 2011. Among them, the foreign currency reserve assets increased by $ 98.7 billion, with a less increment of $ 286.1 billion compared with 2011, lower than the average annual increase of $435.1 billion during 2007–2011. From the IIP perspective, at the end of 2012, the proportion of reserve assets to external financial assets had decreased to 65%, the lowest level since 2008. In the increment of external financial assets in 2012, the contribution rate of reserve assets dropped to 30%, far lower than the average annual contribution rate of above 60% during the 2005–2011.

Undoubtedly, the changes in the pattern of balance of international payments has changed the direction of the central bank's balance sheet currency mismatch risks, and through the investment of foreign currency assets and diversification of holding risks to enterprises and residents, the pressure that the state has to centrally bear the risks has eased. But in the meanwhile, such change has also brought huge structural impact on the central bank's balance sheet. Due to the sharp shrinkage of the size of "double surplus" in the balance of international payments (the surplus in the balance of international payments totaled $176.3 billion in 2012, much lower than the average annual surplus of $455.2 billion during 2007–2011), the central bank was under less pressure to intervene the foreign exchange market, and there was a substantial decline in net purchases of foreign currency and the amount of base money supply generated through exchange purchase channels. In 2012, the balance of funds outstanding for foreign exchange of the central bank was only 428.12 billion yuan, the lowest since 2003, a significant decrease especially when compared with an annual increase of 2–3 trillion yuan during The proportion of increment of funds outstanding for foreign exchange to base currency increment was only 0.16 in 2013, the lowest level since entering the new century, significantly lower than the average level of more than 200% during 2004–2005 and 100% during 2006–2009.

It is also noteworthy that in recent years, the RMB internationalization process has also affected balance sheet currency mismatch in many aspect. In this regard, some people believe that: the internationalization of the RMB will not reduce the balance sheet currency mismatch risk, but will exacerbate this risk. The logic behind it is: after RMB cross-border trade settlement started, RMB was mostly used to settle import trade transactions (80–90% of trade transactions settled in RMB are import trade transactions). In the import trade settlement process, if domestic enterprises pay for imported goods with RMB instead of a foreign currency, the demand for foreign exchange purchases will decline correspondingly. As supply continues to exceed demand in the foreign exchange market, the declining demand for foreign exchanges has further aggravated the oversupply. To stabilize the exchange rate, the monetary authority has to buy more foreign exchanges. The increase in foreign exchange reserve assets has exacerbated the risk of currency mismatch.

In our opinions, as currency mismatch risk refers to "the high sensitivity of net worth or net income(or both) of equity to changes in exchange rate", it always exists and is "original sin" of non-reserve currency countries. Therefore, RMB internationalization is nothing more than a possible change in the direction of currency mismatch risk or just a new form of expression, which needs to be studied and dynamically analyzed by stages. First, in the initial period of time after RMB cross-border trade settlement started in 2009, import trade settled in RMB was indeed greater than export trade settled in RMB. As RMB is mostly used for oversea payment, cross-border RMB revenue is much smaller than expenditure, resulting a net cross-border RMB outflow. According to *Monitoring Report on China's Cross-Border Capital Flows* released by the State Administration of Foreign Exchange, from October 2009 to August 2011, the average monthly cross-border RMB inflow/outflow ratio was 1: 2.6. In 2010, the cross-border RMB income/expenditure ratio was 1: 5.3, and in the first eight months of 2011, the ratio was 1: 2.2. The net cross-border RMB outflow is equivalent to domestic purchase of foreign exchange, which will reduce the demand for purchase of foreign exchange and result in an increase in foreign exchange reserves and thereby increase the risk of currency mismatch on credit.

But it is noteworthy that, after entering the fourth quarter of 2011, RMB settlement for export of goods started to exceed RMB settlement for import of goods, and the phenomenon that cross-border RMB income was greater than expenditure under trade in goods started to appear, leading to a net inflow of cross-border RMB. During September to December 2011, the average monthly cross-border RMB inflow/outflow ratio was 1.4: 1. As exports were settled in RMB instead of the original foreign exchange, the sources of foreign exchange reduced accordingly and the foreign currency assets of the monetary authorities increased, thus reducing the risk of currency mismatch.

In 2012, as the pilot scheme for RMB qualified foreign institutional investors (RQFII) was introduced, offshore RMB backflow channels were broadened and the net inflows under capital and financial accounts have increased. The cumulative inward remittance by overseas institutions under the RQFII scheme was 56 billion yuan in the whole year, and the net inward remittance was 3.0 billion, with a net inward remittance of 53 billion yuan. Especially since the second half of 2012, with the launch of RQFII-ETF product, net capital inflows under the RQFII scheme saw a significant increase, and this was reflected as an increase in capital inflows for securities investment under capital and financial accounts. In the case of net cross-border RMB expenditure being replaced by net income (particularly under capital and financial accounts), this has objectively reduced onshore exchange settlement and slowed the accumulation of foreign assets. This also helps to reduce the risk of currency mismatch.

6.2.3 Contingent Liability Risk 1: Credit Risk

In addition to balance sheet mismatches, the macroeconomic sector is also facing the contingent liability risk. In China, the problem is centrally reflected in the two types of risks the sovereign sector is exposed to, i.e. real estate credit risk and social security's funding gap risk.

First, the real estate credit risk. The real estate mortgage loans are mainly presented as assets or claims in the financial sector, but given the dominant position of state-owned banks in the financial system and the implicit guarantee provided by the government for the financial sector, the risk will eventually be partially borne by the government, so in essence, it also belongs to the contingent liability of the sovereign sector. Historically, the bad debts of commercial banks in China were once disposed by means of recapitalization of government funding and stripped bad debts being replaced by re-lending by the central bank. These methods have shifted the risks from the banking sector to the government sector and ultimately formed the national sovereign risk.

China's real estate credit risk exposure measured by the proportion of real estate development loans and housing mortgage loans to total loans of banks has never exceeded 20%. As far as the international standards are concerned, this level is not high. Meanwhile, China's current loan-to-value ratio is less than 70% on average. Therefore, the leverage ratio of housing mortgage loan of the household sector still remains at a low level. According to the non-performing loans of commercial banks by industry disclosed by CBRC, the non-performing loans ratios of the real estate sector and individual housing mortgage loans were 1.26 and 0.37% respectively, which are not too high compared with the non-performing loan ratio in other industries or projects. Therefore, we believe that the exposure of the risk of real estate loans of the banking sector is still within the controllable range.

Although the direct risk exposure of bank loans to the real estate sector is small, indirect risks should arouse our attention. First, in the loan business in China's banking sector, mortgage loans account for a large proportion. 30–45% of the loans provided by Industrial and Commercial Bank of China, Agricultural Bank of China, Bank of China, China Construction Bank and Bank of Communications are mortgage loans, especially real estate mortgage loans. Apart from home mortgage loans and developer mortgage loans, real estate mortgage loans also mainly include loans of LGFPs in which the rights to use the land of state-owned enterprises were used as mortgages, other infrastructure investment and industrial investment mortgage loans. If real estate prices decline sharply, the value of mortgages will shrink accordingly, and once the debtor is in default, the banking sector will suffer huge losses.[1] In the meanwhile, as the forward and backward industries of the real estate sector are highly correlated and occupy an important position in the national economy, once the prices of the real estate sector decline sharply, this will inevitably impact a large number of related industries and cause chain adverse effects on the asset quality of the banking system. In addition, the LGFPs are also highly correlated with the real estate sector. In the case of limited cash flow of the bank-funded projects, the debt repayment is greatly dependent on the land transfer revenue. The audit results of the National Audit Office showed that, by the end of 2010, in the outstanding balance of debt that will be repaid by local government fiscal revenue (6710.951 billion yuan), the outstanding balance of debt with land transfer income as the sources of repayment fund amounted to 2547.351 billion yuan, accounting for 38%, involving a total of 12 provincial-level governments, 307 city-level governments and 1131 county-level governments. If the real estate industry encounters difficulties and affects the amount of land transfer revenue, the quality of loans of LGFPs will be adversely affected.

In practice, the necessary condition for the transfer of the above-mentioned indirect risk into the real risk and thus concentrated outbreak is the sharp adjustment of real estate prices. Its sufficient condition depends on the ratio of housing values to GDP and resident income. If ratios of housing values/GDP and housing values/residents' disposable income are high, the sharp adjustment in real estate prices is likely to lead to a real estate market crisis and further trigger an extensive economic crisis.

Through a comparative study with the major developed countries, we find that China's housing values to GDP ratio is still at a low level. In this regard, the overall risk of the Chinese real estate market is still controllable. However, the ratio of housing values to residents' disposable income is relatively high in China, indicating that the market can hardly achieve sustain development. This is because, on the one hand, the ratio of residents' income to GDP, as the denominator, in China is much lower than the average level of 60% of the developed countries, and this situation should be reserved urgently; on the other hand, China's urban housing prices, as the molecular, may have increased too fast under the background of accelerating urbanization.

---

[1]Kiyotaki and Moore (2002) divided the balance sheet risk contagion mechanisms into direct and indirect channels. Among them, indirect contagion channel is to change the values of loan mortgages through changing the market prices of assets. Kiyotaki and Moore particularly pointed out that, as the Japanese companies tend to use their fixed assets (such as real estate) as mortgages when borrowing money from banks, the indirect contagion effect is particularly evident. Given that China's banking sector's dependence on real estate mortgage loans, the indirect contagion mechanism of balance sheet should arouse our attention.

6.2.4 Contingent Liability Risk 2: Social Security's Funding Gap

Another contingent liability risk is social security's funding gap. The sovereign debt crises in Europe, the United States and other developed economies in recent years show that the funding gap of the social security system, especially that of the pension system is the major inducing factor for an extensive economic crisis. So faced with the dual challenges of institutional transition and an aging population, China must attach great importance to the social security's funding gap, especially the pension system's funding gap.

With regard to the challenge posed by the institutional transition, the reform of the basic old-age insurance system for enterprise employees starting in China in 1995 has determined the principle of combining social pooling with individual accounts. The Guofa No. 26 document issued in 1997 further confirmed this hybrid model and announced the transition from the fully PAYG system to a partially funded one. Then, in theory, a portion of the pensions paid by in-service employees should be deposited into their personal saving accounts rather than be used for the PAYG pension payment. But in reality, the model of "social pooling plus personal accounts" in which the PAYG system and the funded system coexsit was transited from the previous fully PAYG system, while the previous personal accounts had no accumulated money, and especially for "the old men" who had no personal accounts and the "middle-age person" who had little money in their personal accounts in the past, the funding gap for pension payments will appear. This is the so-called transition costs incurred in the pension system transition.

In quite a long time in the past, who should bear the costs incurred in the transition has not been completely solved. When the traditional PAYG system was transited into the one combining social pooling with personal accounts, China failed to adopt a special method to handle the transition costs, but expected to gradually eliminate the costs through increasing the contribution rate of enterprises, expanding the pension coverage and combining social pooling with personal accounts (Song et al. 2000; Jia et al. 2007). Transition costs and "empty personal accounts" were closely linked, and as no measure was taken to address the funding gap, the old-age insurance administration departments had to divert funds from personal accounts to ensure the payment of pensions for retired workers, which led to the emptiness of the personal accounts of in-service employees under the new payment system and the degeneration of the nominal system of social pooling plus personal accounts into a de facto PAYG system.

As mentioned above, many domestic and foreign institutions have estimated China's total implicit pension debt, but the definitions of implicit pension debt in the studies are not entirely consistent, and due to the great differences in its calculation methods and points of time, the results are significantly different. The research group has also estimated the implicit pension debt formed as a result of transition over the years. As shown in Fig. 6.3, the annual pension transition cost of enterprises was 100–400 billion yuan (at current prices) during 2000–2050, and the

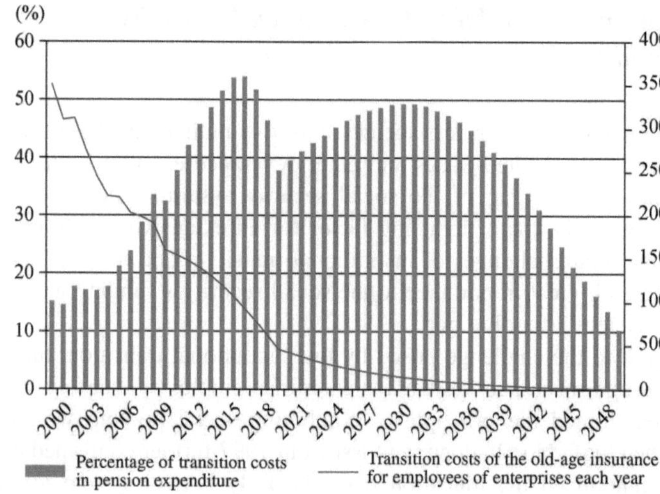

Fig. 6.3 Transition costs of the old-age insurance for employees of enterprises. *Sources* estimates of the research group

transition costs even accounted for nearly 50% of pension expenses of enterprise in 2000.[2] During 2000–2011, the cumulative transition costs of pension insurance of enterprises reached 1.84 trillion. As mentioned above, the funding gap arising from the transition costs was mainly filled through diverting the funds from personal accounts, but according to *China Pension Development Report (2012)*, as of the end of 2011, the empty amount of the personal accounts in the basic old-age insurance system for urban residents and workers reached 2.2 trillion yuan, much greater than the cumulative transition costs we calculated. This is partially because there were also the transition costs incurred during 1996–1999. Assuming that the transition costs in the four year are equal to the level in 2000, then they exactly amount to 2.24 trillion yuan. The stock of transition costs was 3.47 trillion yuan in 2011, accounting for up to 7.33% of the GDP.[3]

However, as the transition costs were focused on "the old men" and "the middle men", the percentage of transition costs in pension expenditure is bound to decline rapidly over time. In the future, what is more worrying is the pension fund pressure caused by an aging population.

With regard to the challenges posed by an aging population, the current structure of China's population is undergoing fundamental changes, and the problem of population aging is increasingly serious. The data of the 6th nationwide population

[2]This is partly because this only existed for the elderly, but the elderly had no personal account accumulation, so a considerable part of transition costs existed in the form pension fund and were paid by misappropriation of the funds in personal accounts.

[3]That is the transition costs still needs to be paid in the future. The transition costs incurred have already been reflected in the empty personal accounts of old-age insurance.

census show that: the total population of Mainland China is 1.34 billion people, including 222 million children aged 0–14, accounting for 16.6%, down 6.29% compared with the 2000 census; the total elderly population aged 60 and above is 178 million, accounting for 13.26%, up 2.93% over the 2000 census. Meanwhile, according to the report of NBS, the working-age population in China begun to decline in 2012, the proportion of working-age population aged 15–59 in China declined for the first time, and the absolute number of working-age population also reduced by 3.45 million. These data reveal three important messages: first, the "low birth rate" phenomenon in China's current total population structure is very serious, and the data of the 6th census show that China's current total fertility rate is 1.188, making China one of the countries with the lowest fertility rates in the world; second, the rate of population aging significantly exceeded the previous population projections and planning; third, the turning point of China's working-age population has also emerged, and the demographic bonus will gradually subside. This means that, on the one hand, the acceleration of population aging and rapid increase of the elderly population will lead to more pension spending, and on the other hand, the decrease of the working-age population and low birth rate will slow down and even reduce the old-age insurance fund income in future. This shows that China's old-age insurance system will face more serious problems in financial sustainability in the future.

Either institutional transition or population aging will lead to the funding gap in pension payments and contingent debts. In fact, an unbalance or a funding gap between the income and expenditure of old-age insurance fund has occurred in some regions. According to the statistics of the Ministry of Human Resources and Social Security, excluding the 195.4 billion yuan of financial subsidies, a total of 15 provinces were unable to strike a balance between income and expenditure in the old-age insurance system for enterprise employees, and the gap amounted to 67.9 billion yuan. This means that the potential financial risk of the old-age insurance system for enterprise employees in China is showing some explicit signs and has reached the extent of relying on financial subsidies. Therefore, the pension funding gap is being actually transformed into one of the root causes of government liabilities.

In the previous paragraphs, we have mainly discussed the problems of the old-age insurance system for enterprise employees. In the meanwhile, to achieve the goal of full coverage of old-age insurance, workers in informal employment including both urban and rural residents are also gradually being covered by the social insurance, and this needs more direct financial subsidies.[4] Therefore, the urban and rural residents that are not included in the old-age insurance system for workers are taken into consideration, the total full-scope social old-age insurance debt and the government's repayment responsibility will be much greater.

[4]This is because the basic part of the pension fund entirely relies on government subsidies, without the corresponding contribution income. Personal contributions are theoretically only used for accumulation of pension funds in personal accounts and pension payment.

We have estimated and forecast the income and expenditure of the old-age insurance system each year during 2010–2050 in the section for special study of implicit pension debts. The results show that, if we continue to implement the existing old-age insurance system and does not adjust the retirement age or carry out other reforms, the basic old-age insurance system nationwide will be unable to strike a balance between income and expenditure and there will be a funding gap, and the accumulated surplus of the old-age insurance fund should be used. By the end of 2029, the accumulated surplus will be used up, and it is necessary to find new sources of income to guarantee the payment of pensions. Assuming that, once the surplus is used up and the funding gap appears, government subsidies will be needed to fill the gap, then the government subsidy expenditure over the years during 2010–2050 discounted to 2011 will reach 46.5 trillion yuan, accounting for 98% of the GDP.[5] If the old-age insurance that has widely covered urban and rural residents is taken into consideration, the implicit debts of the government will reach 6.08 trillion yuan, and the proportion of implicit pension debt to GDP will further expand to 111% in 2011. By the end of 2050, the ratio of China's total pension expenditure of the whole society (including the old-age insurance for workers and residents) to GDP will reach 11.85%, a result close to the current level of some European states with high welfare (see Table 6.1). Presently, the ratio of China's total pension expenditure of the whole society to GDP is less than 3%.

Note: the data in the table for other countries except China are from OECD Factbook 2013 in 2009. The data for China are our estimates. In the table, there are two pension expenditure to GDP ratios. Ratio 1 is the public sector pension expenditure to GDP ratio. Public sector pension expenditure refers to the expenditure of statutory (mandatory) pensions that are operated by the social security funds of the government or managed by the government and for which the government bears the direct responsibility to repay. In this study, the estimate on China belongs to the first ratio. Ratio 2 is the private sector pension expenditure to GDP ratio. Private sector pension expenditure refers to the expenditure of pensions that are operated and managed by commercial insurance agencies and for which the government does not bear the direct responsibility to repay, such as annuity.

It is noteworthy that the above discussion is limited only to the old-age insurance. In addition, China's medical insurance and unemployment insurance etc. also face the problem of inadequate investment, which is also in urgent need to improve and requires enormous capital accumulation. In short, the contingent debt risk of the government, as the final payer of social security's funding gap, especially the potential debt burden arising from the pension funding gap, has become a serious problem, which should arouse our close attention.

[5]As such, compared to the institutional transition costs in 2011 calculated above, the change in population structure will have greater impact on the pension gap: the implicit debt arising from the institutional transition accounts for 7.5% of the total implicit debt of the old-age insurance for workers, while the implicit debt caused by the population aging accounts for 92.5% of total implicit debt of the old-age insurance for workers.

Table 6.1 Pension expenditure to GDP ratios of major developed countries and regions in the world (unit:%)

Country	Ratio 1	Ratio 2	Country	Ratio 1	Ratio 2
Italy	15.4	0.2	OECD	7.8	2.2
France	13.7	0.4	Luxembourg	7.7	0.1
Austria	13.5	0.2	The United States	6.8	2.9
Greece	13.0	0.0	The United Kingdom	6.2	3.2
Portugal	12.3	1.0	Norway	5.4	–
Poland	11.8	0.0	The Netherlands	5.1	3.9
Germany	11.3	0.3	Israel	5.0	1.7
Japan	10.2	–	New Zealand	4.7	1.9
Belgium	10.0	3.3	Canada	4.5	2.7
Finland	9.9	0.7	Australia	3.5	4.6
Hungary	9.9	0.2	South Korea	2.1	1.1
Spain	9.3	0.6	Mexico	1.3	0.3
Czech	8.3	0.4	China 2010	2.7	–
Sweden	8.2	1.3	China 2050	11.9	–

6.3 Inter-sectoral Debt Clearing and Risk Transfer

Taking the disposal of non-performing loans of banks for example, we will analyze the correlation and transfer of balance sheet risks among non-financial corporations, financial institutions and governments. For the contagion mechanism, refer to the above Fig. 6.1.

As the Chinese government has huge sovereign assets (more than 166 trillion in 2011), the debt clearing process will generally not lead to greater debt risks. Historically, China has once used foreign currency assets to bail out financial institutions and effectively solved the disposal and re-capitalization of huge non-performing assets of financial institutions. China has also ever used the proceeds from reduction of state-owned shares to replenish the social security fund and accumulate substantial strategic reserves for the social security system. China has also mitigated the debt risk of LGFPs through the sale of state-owned land and/or sale of local state-owned assets. Compared with the developed economies and most emerging economies in the world, China is showing great superiority in its huge sovereign assets, positive government equities and ability to strike a balance among various kinds of social accounts in the form of "moving mountains to fill seas".

The Chinese government issued 270 billion yuan worth of special government bonds in 1998 to supplement the capital of state-owned commercial banks (namely ICBC, ABC, BOC and CCB). In 1999, four financial asset management companies were established, and the non-performing assets of nearly 1.4 trillion yuan were stripped from the four banks and shifted to the asset management companies in 1999–2000. During 2003–2005, the bad loans of BOC, CCB and ICBC were stripped again, and Central Huijin Investment Ltd. injected capital into BOC and

CCB respectively in 2003 and into ICBC in 2005 to facilitate their shareholding reform and create the conditions for their listing. In March 2006, the weighted average recovery rate of the above-mentioned non-performing assets of the four asset management companies of Huarong, Great Wall, Orient Fund and Cinda was less than a quarter, with the actual loss of around 1 trillion yuan. Coupled with more than 500 billion yuan non-performing assets stripped in the restructuring of BOC, CCB and ICBC in 2003–2005, the costs of non-performing assets stripped in this stage alone reached more than 1.5 trillion yuan. This did not include a substantial amount of written-off assets and capital injected into the banks. In 2008, the stripped non-performing assets of ABC (including 217.323 billion yuan of doubtful loans, 549.445 billion yuan of loss loans and 48.927 billion yuan of non-credit assets) amounted to 815.695 billion yuan. For the above-mentioned non-performing assets, ABC's 150.602 billion yuan of non-performing assets were swapped equally by the interest-free loan provided by the People's Bank of China on December 31, 2007, and the remaining 665.093 billion yuan formed the receivables to be collected from the Ministry of Finance, and the interest was calculated at an annual percentage rate of 3.3% for the unpaid balance since January 1, 2008. ABC and the Ministry of Finance has jointly established a "condominium fund" to repay to ABC the principal and the corresponding interest of the receivables to be collected from the Ministry of Finance in 15 years. The fund sources of the condominium fund include the distributed cash dividends turned over by ABC to the Ministry of Finance, the corporate income tax paid ABC to the central government, the fund recovered from disposal of non-performing assets minus the recovery expenses, the proceeds from reduction of the shares of ABC by the Ministry of Finance and so on. All the rights related to the transfer of assets should be enjoyed by the Ministry of Finance, and all the risks should be borne by the Ministry of Finance. Unlike other state-owned banks, ABC's disposal of non-performing assets was entrusted to be carried out by ABC itself. The Ministry of Finance entrusted ABC to set up a special asset disposal organization to be responsible for collection. This is mainly because ABC's non-performing assets have the feature of "large in number, small in amount and wide distribution" and the traditional asset management company model is not suitable for the disposal of these non-performing assets.

The disposal of non-performing assets in China also involves the costs of reform of rural credit cooperatives and the capital injected in the restructuring of securities companies (these funds basically come from the Securities Investor Protection Fund and the re-lending of the central bank, among which the equity capital of the Securities Investor Protection Fund and the capital prepaid are from financial contribution and relending by the central bank).[6]

---

[6]In 2005, China established the Securities Investor Protection Fund, which is wholly-owned by the State Council. The Ministry of Finance invested 6.3 billion yuan as its registered capital and capital stock, and the Bank contributed 61.7 billion as advance fund (which should be refunded to the central bank in future).

China's major banks were wholly owned by the government before the reform and are still controlled by the state after the joint-stock reform. By the end of 2010, in the ownership structure of the entire banking sector in China, state-owned shares accounted for 53.85%, state-owned legal person shares accounted for 6.81% and non-state-owned shares accounted for 39.34%. Among them, in the ownership structure of the five major banks of ICBC, ABC, BOC, CCB and BCM, state-owned shares accounted for 68.19%, state-owned legal person shares accounted for 1.36% and non-state-owned shares accounted for 30.45%. In the ownership structure of the 12 nationwide joint-stock banks, state-owned shares accounted for 3.60%, state-owned legal person shares accounted for 25.93% and non-state-owned shares accounted for 70.47%. Based on such a property right relationship, the Chinese government has forced the banks to provide a large number of non-commercial loans over the years. These loans have become the major sources of non-performing assets in the banking sector in China. As the governor of the People's Bank of China (2004) Zhou Xiaochuan put it, on the whole, roughly 30% of enormous non-performing assets of the banking sector formed in the 1990s and before were from direct executive orders and administrative intervention of the governments at all levels, 30% were mainly resulted from the support to the state-owned enterprises, roughly 10% were from the local administrative environment and administrative environment of law enforcement, and about 10% were from the state-led industrial restructuring, including positively "closing down, suspending operation, merging with others or shifting to different line of production". In addition, approximately 20% of the non-performing assets were from the banks' poor management, including the mechanism-related problem. In such case, it is undoubtedly logical that the government used the resources under its control to dispose the non-performing assets of state-owned banks. Similarly, as the Chinese government is the sole major shareholder of China's banking sector, the government's injection of capital into the banks is inevitable.

Disposal of banks' nonperforming assets takes many forms, including stripping of bad debts, write-off of bad assets, capital injection, issuing special government bonds, issuing central bank bills, granting loans to swap non-performing assets and attracting external financial investors. After the disposal moves, the banks' non-performing asset rate decreased rapidly, but a considerable part of the non-performing asset stock had not disappeared and was just shifted between departments. The non-performing assets of the commercial banks were changed into the relending of the central bank or the liabilities of the Ministry of Finance, resulting in reduction of sovereign assets accordingly. The time series analysis for sovereign debts we have made previously shows that the banks' non-performing assets decreased from 2173.1 billion yuan in 2000 to 433.6 billion yuan in 2010, and in the meanwhile, the contingent liabilities arising from disposal of non-performing assets increased from 1.4 trillion yuan in 2000 to 4.2 trillion yuan in 2010. There is an obvious decrease-increase relationship between them.

6.4 Dynamic Trend and Sustainability of Sovereign Debt

In this section, taking the sovereign sector as an example, we will identify the dynamic trend of balance sheet risks and their determinants with the scenario analysis method under the premise of assuming several fundamental economic variables. In a sense, this is a useful trial in combining the balance sheet approach with the traditional macroeconomic analysis.

As mentioned above, after a systemic economic and financial crisis occurs, one of the most serious challenges to the government or sovereign sector is how to reduce the public debt. First, it should be stated clearly that in a modern economy, the government is a macroeconomic stabilizer and regulator, so its deleveraging process will lag far behind that of the private sector. That is to say, only after the deleveraging process of the private sector has basically ended and the economy begins to recover will the government have the environment, leisure time and conditions to reduce its own debt. Second, as Reinhart and Sbrancia (2011) put it, under the relatively stable and moderate inflation scenario, financial repression is the most effective means for the government to reduce its debt. In the following paragraphs, we will further demonstrate that a macro environment accompanied by steady growth, moderate inflation and low interest rates is more conducive to reduction of public debt, while the opposite environment will worsen the public debt problems.

Supposing that the government debt to GDP ratio is Z (i.e. the outstanding balance of government debt Z/GDP), this ratio is mainly determined by four variables, namely policy deficit rate (*f*, that is basic deficit, which refers to the difference between autonomous financial expenditure minus debt interest payments *E* and financial revenue *T*), inflation rate (π), economic growth rate (n) and interest rate (i). The changes in the balance of government debt are decided by policy deficit and interest expense:

$$\frac{dZ(t)}{dt} = -[T(t) - E(t) - Z(t)i(t)] \tag{1}$$

The equation above means that the increase in financial revenue will reduce the balance of government debt, and autonomous financial expenditure and interest expense will increase the debt balance. Let *Y* be actual output and *P* be the price level, thus:

$$\frac{dz(t)}{dt} = \frac{d[Z(t)/GDP(t)]}{dt} = \left\{\frac{dZ(t)}{GDP(t)} - \frac{Z(t)}{GDP(t)}\left[\frac{dY(t)}{Y(t)} + \frac{dP(t)}{P(t)}\right]\right\} \Big/ dt$$

Substitute Eq. (1) and $\frac{dY(t)}{Y(t)} = n(t)$, $\frac{dP(t)}{P(t)} = \pi(t)$, $\frac{E(t)-T(t)}{GDP(t)} = f(t)$, $\frac{Z(t)}{GDP(t)} = z(t)$ into the above equation, we can obtain that at any time t, the change of government debt (or public debt) burden ratio is determined by:

$$\frac{dz(t)}{dt} = f(t) - z(t)[n(t) + \pi(t) - i(t)] \tag{2}$$

Assuming that the other four variables are constants, the equation above is a first-order differential equation. By solving the Eq. (2), we can explore the path of debt burden ratio and carry out dynamic comparison analysis by changing the values of parameters. The solution of Eq. (2) is as follows:

$$z(t) = \frac{f}{n + \pi - i} + ce^{-(n+\pi-i)t} \tag{3}$$

In the equation, c is an arbitrary constant. This result is consistent with the result given by Yu (2000).

The basic meaning of Eq. (3) is that, when the policy deficit rate, growth rate, inflation rate and government bond interest rate maintain a stable relationship, the government debt burden ratio will tend to converge to a particular stable level over time. In Eq. (3), the value of $n + \pi - i$ is very important. First of all, a key condition for z to eventually keep stable is $n + \pi - i > 0$. That is to say, the nominal growth rate $(n + \pi)$ is greater than the nominal interest rate, or the actual growth rate is greater than the actual interest rate $(i - \pi)$. Otherwise, the government debt burden ratio will increase sharply. Secondly, the size of $n + \pi - i$ determines the convergence rate of national debt burden ratio. Obviously, the larger the difference between the growth rate and interest rate, the greater the convergence rate of z towards a stable level, and vice versa. Finally, the size of $n + \pi - i$ determines the level of sustainable policy deficit rate. $f/(n + \pi - i)$ represents the final equilibrium value of z. If the reasonable equilibrium value is identified, then the size of $n + \pi - i$ actually determines the space of policy deficit. Obviously, the larger the difference between the growth rate and interest rate, the greater the policy deficit space. For example, if the reasonable level of government debt burden ratio is 60%, then a 1% difference between growth rate and interest rate means that the policy deficit rate should be no greater than 0.6%, and a 3% difference between growth rate and interest rate means that the policy deficit rate should be no greater than 1.8%.

The Eqs. (1), (2) and (3) discussed above are a differential equation system, we can use the corresponding differential equation system to simulate the policy scenario (Yu 2000 also conducted a similar operation, but, unfortunately, the paper did not take into consideration the interest rate during simulation). Supposing the expression mode of the variables are unchanged, place the time t on the local label to express a discrete time, then the evolutionary path of government debt ratio $z_t = Z_t/Y_tP_t$ will be determined by the following differential equation system.

$$Z_t - Z_{t-1} = iZ_{t-1} + Y_tP_tf \tag{4}$$

$$Y_t = Y_0(1 + n)^t \tag{5}$$

$$P_t = P_0(1+\pi)^t \quad (6)$$

In the equation, f, π, n and i are constants, we can explore the path of z_t through different assignments. As highlighted above, the value of $n+\pi-i$ is most critical, and it determines whether the government debt burden ratio is converging or diverging, the convergence speed and the operating space of policy deficit. In the following paragraphs, we will set six scenarios for China to specifically illustrate this. Table 6.2 lists the initial values of various scenarios and the assignments of associated parameters and Table 6.3 gives the corresponding simulation results.

In Scenario 1, due to economic stagnation, $n+\pi-i$ is less than zero, so the national debt burden ratio takes a divergent path and grows by about 60% in 20 year with an annual growth rate of about 3%. If the conditions remain unchanged, such deterioration will continue until the debt finally collapses and massive default and an economic turmoil occur.

Scenario 2 and 3 compare the different convergence rates under different values. Both have the same initial conditions, i.e. a high debt burden ratio of 200% and the deficit policy rate of 2%. In Scenario 2, the difference between growth rate and interest rate is 6%. Under this condition, the government debt burden ratio will decrease by more than a half in 20 years and ultimately reach 91%. In Scenario 3, the difference between growth rate and interest rate is 2%. Under this condition, the public debt ratio will decrease by only 30% in 20 years and still remain at a high level of 169%. Reinhart and Sbrancia (2011) pointed out that in 1945 and 1980, the debt cut by the US and the UK each year accounted for 3–4% of the GDP on average, and this figure reached 5% in Australia and Italy. Such intense deleveraging is close to the case set in Scenario 2.

Scenario 4 and 5 compare the final equilibrium value differences arising from different policy deficit rates. The other conditions of the two scenarios are the same, but the policy deficit rate is 3% and the equilibrium government debt burden ratio is 50% in Scenario 4, while the policy deficit rate is 6% and the equilibrium government debt ratio is 100% in Scenario 5. If starting from zero debt, the debt burden ratio of the latter is almost twice of the former every year since then. Scenario 4 will

Table 6.2 Initial values of the scenarios and the assignments of related parameters

	Scenario 1 (%)	Scenario 2 (%)	Scenario 3 (%)	Scenario 4 (%)	Scenario 5 (%)	Scenario 6 (%)
Initial value (z_0)	60	200	200	0	0	40
Policy deficit rate (f)	2	2	2	3	6	3
Inflation rate (π)	2	3	2	3	3	3
Economic growth rate (n)	0	8	4	8	8	6
Interest rate (i)	3	5	4	5	5	5
$n+\pi-i$	−1	6	2	6	6	4

Table 6.3 Scenario simulation of government debt burden ratio evolution path

Year	Scenario 1 (%)	Scenario 2 (%)	Scenario 3 (%)	Scenario 4 (%)	Scenario 5 (%)	Scenario 6 (%)
2011	60	200	200	0	0	40
2012	63	191	198	3	6	41
2013	65	182	196	6	12	43
2014	68	174	194	9	17	44
2015	71	166	193	11	22	46
2016	73	159	191	13	27	47
2017	76	152	189	16	31	48
2018	79	145	187	18	36	49
2019	81	139	186	20	40	50
2020	84	133	184	22	43	51
2021	87	128	182	23	47	52
2022	90	123	181	25	50	53
2023	93	118	179	27	53	54
2024	96	113	178	28	56	55
2025	99	109	176	30	59	56
2026	102	105	175	31	62	57
2027	105	101	173	32	64	58
2028	108	97	172	33	67	59
2029	111	94	171	35	69	59
2030	114	91	169	36	71	60

eventually keep stable at 50%, and Scenario 5 will keep stable at 100%. The comparative meaning of Scenario 4 and 5 is clear. Good macroeconomic environment and fiscal austerity will enable government debts to keep stable at an appropriate level, otherwise a dangerous high debt level will appear, just like many developed economies.

Finally, Scenario 6 is a simulation of China's national debt burden ratio. Supposing China's government debt burden ratio was 40% in 2011 and the average economic growth rate in the coming two decades is 6%, the inflation rate is 3%, the interest rate is 5% and the policy deficit 3%, then China's government debt burden ratio will rise slowly and reach 60% in 2030 and will eventually keep stale at 75% [i.e. $f/(n+\pi-i)$].

The above simulative analysis shows that the evolution path of government debt to GDP ratio mainly depends on the difference between growth rate and interest rate. First, only when the growth rate is greater than the interest rate will the proportion of bonds converge, otherwise it will undergo explosive growth. Second, the greater the difference between growth rate and interest rate, the faster the stable level of government debt ratio will converge. Finally, the difference between growth rate and interest rate also determines the sustainable fiscal deficit level. From China's macro environment, as long as the difference between growth rate and interest rate can maintain at a high level, the government's own debts are not highly risky, and the government debt to GDP ratio will keep at a relatively stable level. Therefore, a long-term high rate of economic growth is a powerful weapon to cope with sovereign debt risks.

Based on the above analysis, as far as China is concerned, the near-term risks of national balance sheet mainly lie in real estate credit, local debt, banks' bad loans and so on, while the long-term risks are more concentrated in foreign assets, corporate debt, social security debts and so on. As shown in the exposition above, each kind of risks are closely related to the current mode of development and economic structure. Therefore, the best way to cope with or resolve the risks is to change the development mode and adjust the economic structure to realize healthy and sustainable economic growth. In other words, only by ensuring an adequate income flow in future can the debt stock problem be ultimately addressed. This view will be further expounded below. In addition, while changing the development mode at the macro level, more positive moves in micro-level policy design should also be taken. For example, in the real estate market, local government debt, social security transition and other aspects, deep-seated contradictions and problems such as market and government relationship are universally exposed in the existing regulatory policies and institutional arrangements. Obviously, enormous risk thus accumulated and hidden not only pose a threat to the smooth operation of macroeconomic system, but also test the wisdom and courage of decision makers.

Chapter 7
Basic Conclusions and Policy Suggestions

7.1 Basic Conclusions

This book comes to the following basic conclusions through the preparation, analysis of China's national and sectoral balance sheets:

First, China's national balance sheet showed a rapid expanding trend in 2007–2011. Rapidly accumulated foreign assets, infrastructure and real estate assets were the dominant factors for the expansion of non-financial assets. This has recorded the historical process of China's accelerated industrialization and urbanization under the export-oriented development strategy. But in the meanwhile, the rapid growth of financial assets and the increase in financial correlation ratio reflect the fact of financial deepening in this period. On the liability side, the liabilities of the governments at all levels and state-owned enterprises were expanding more rapidly than those of the private sector, showing the institutional characteristics of government-led economic activities or a "construction-oriented" or "investment-oriented" government. Liabilities accumulated more rapidly than assets, leading to the increase in China's overall debt to assets ratio and decrease in the relative size of net assets. This phenomenon indicates that the reliance on debt is strengthened and debt risks are rising in the financing structure, which can also be interpreted as an inadequate contribution of economic growth to actual accumulation of wealth, low economic efficiency and quality of development.

Second, the balance sheets of China's sovereign sector, including the central and local governments, the central bank and state-owned enterprises also showed a significantly expanding trend during 2000–2011. Among them, the net sovereign assets were always positive and showing an upward trend, indicating that the government had enough sovereign assets to cover its sovereign debts. Therefore, the financial position of the governments were generally healthy and sustainable, and the likelihood of occurrence of a sovereign debt crisis similar to the European debt crisis is very small. However, as the old development mode is continuing, the sovereign sector has accumulated huge contingent liabilities through a variety of

Y. Li and X. Zhang, *China's National Balance Sheet*, China Insights,
DOI 10.1007/978-981-10-4385-7_7

explicit and implicit guarantees. Particularly, real estate credit, local debts, mid- and long-term foreign allocation of assets, corporate debts, social security debts and other risks need to arouse close attention. Furthermore, our simulative analysis shows that the evolution path of government debts to GDP ratio mainly depends on the difference between economic growth rate and interest rate. Therefore, maintaining a sustainable economic growth is essential to cope with the sovereign debt risks.

Third, the analysis of the overall debt level and the whole society leverage ratio (i.e. total debt/GDP ratio) shows that: China's whole society leverage ratio is higher than those of the BRIC countries, but far lower than the major developed economies and it is mild and in a controllable range on the whole. However, in recent years, the leverage ratio has increased rapidly, which must rouse our attention. The sectoral analysis shows that: corporate debt ratio (to GDP) is relatively higher, becoming a distinctive feature of China's balance sheet. In 2011, the ratio reached 113%, higher than the threshold value of 90% of the OECD countries, and we should maintain keen vigilance for this; the debt ratio of the household sector was relatively lower, and from the perspective of dynamic trend in the future, the liabilities of this sector may have greater room for growth; the net worth of the government sector was high, but based on the international experience, as the economy entered a period of rapid development and the level of public services is improving, the total level of government debt will increase and even a change from positive into negative net worth may appear, so it is necessary to plan ahead.

7.2 Policy Suggestions

Through the research on national and sectoral balance sheets, we believe that promoting the transformation of development mode should be an essential measure to realize continual accumulation of national wealth and coordinated development of economic sectors and to cope with balance sheet risks.

First, to reduce the currency mismatch risk in the balance sheet of foreign assets, we should strive to expand domestic demands, reduce reliance on external demands and ease the accumulation of foreign assets. In addition, we should encourage "foreign exchange held by the people", promote direct investment in foreign countries and promote RMB internationalization. More importantly, under the situation that currency mismatch on credit, we should more actively and initiatively make use of the sovereign wealth fund mechanism to reduce the risk of currency mismatch.

Second, we should reduce the government's intervention on microeconomic activities, strengthen the market's decisive role in resource allocation and reduce the risk of government's contingent liabilities. Government dominance has played an important role in the catch-up and surpassing system, but it has led to more sovereign or contingent liabilities than the mature market economies. The basic path to reduce the risk of contingent liabilities is to reduce the government's intervention on microeconomic activities, further promote market-oriented reform and government transformation so as to change implicit contingent liabilities into explicit direct liabilities and identify and diversify the debtors.

Third, we should promote the transformation from debt financing to equity financing, reduce the whole society deleverage ratio and ease the capital structure mismatch risk of enterprises. China's financial system is dominated by banks. Mobilization, gathering and distribution of savings are mainly achieved through the banking system. Reliance on the funds provided by the banking system has not only aggravated the capital structure mismatch risk of balance sheets of enterprises but also increased the whole society leverage ratio. Therefore, in China's financial development in the future, we should earnestly implement the *Decision* of the 3rd Plenary Session of 18th CPC Central Committee, strive to "improve the multi-layer capital market system, promote reform toward a registration-based stock-issuing system, promote equity financing through diverse channels, develop and regulate the bond market, and increase the proportion of direct financing", and promote China's financial structure to transform from debt financing to equity financing.

Fourth, we should adjust the pattern of income distribution and deepen the strategic adjustment of the layout of the state-owned economy to cope with the social security's fund gap risk. We may consider further expanding the scale of budget income from state-owned capital operation, including: further expanding the number of state-owned enterprises that should turn over their profits to the state, and apart from the enterprises under the control of the central authorities, local state-owned enterprises, railways and other monopoly industries not under the control of SASAC and state-owned financial enterprises should also give capital dividends, and in the meanwhile, more profits of state-owned enterprises should be turned over to the state and the dividend ratio should be adjusted dynamically.[1] On this basis, the increase of state-owned capital operating income subsidies to social security. In addition, the state-owned shares should be further reduced to enrich the social security reserve funds. We should transfer part of the state-owned shares in the domestic stock exchanges to social security funds. On this basis, we can reduce discretionarily gradually the state-owned shares of non-listed state-owned enterprises and holding groups of listed companies and listed state-owned shares not issued in a secondary offering and transfer the proceeds to social security funds on the premise of ensuring the control over state-owned economy.

Fifth, we should prevent and mitigate real estate credit risks.

To prevent and mitigate real estate credit risks, the key is to promote the housing prices to return to reasonable levels. Therefore, we should focus on reforming the land and taxation systems.

---

[1]In the operating budgetary income of central state-owned capital in 2010, transferred to finance spending on social security of 10 billion yuan, accounting for the central enterprises accounted for only 0.1% of net profit. There are four billion yuan in 2011 was transferred to government for the proportion of social security expenditure, the central enterprises accounted for net profit of only 0.4%.

The core of the land system reform is to clearly define the roles of the government, gradually weaken the role of the government as land trader and direct operator and strengthen its role as service provider and regulator. On the one hand, we should change administrative compulsory transactions to voluntary market transactions, and the government should no longer directly get involved in the transaction of land resources by force, but should allow direct negotiations and transactions between the existing land users and the potential demanders according to law and on a voluntary and compensatory basis. The government should only serve as a third party and be responsible for developing the trading rules, supervise the transaction behaviors, provide transaction services and maintain a good trading environment and order.

On the other hand, the government system can be separated from the state-owned land asset management and operation systems, and a separate state-owned land asset management system (similar to the SASAC for land) can perform all the functions and obtain the proceeds from resource transactions as the resource owner, while the government only get relevant tax revenue generated during resource transaction. The government should also no longer directly undertake the business activities for state-owned land assets, while the state-owned land asset operation system (similar to a state-owned land asset management company) should be authorized to exclusively undertake the business activities for state-owned land assets. Under such suboptimal arrangement of monopoly operation of resources, the role of the government as a regulator should be strengthened, and pricing and seeking exorbitant profits by monopoly should be prevented through price regulation. Where necessary and feasible, a number of state-owned land operation companies can be established and a market pattern of moderate competition can be formed to avoid extremely high monopoly prices.

Through the reform of the above transaction systems and their "double-separation", the channel through which the government makes use of its monopoly right to operate land resources to seek benefits can be cut off fundamentally to avoid jacking up the housing prices due to institutional distortion.

The key of tax reform lies in weakening local governments' reliance on land finance (mainly in production and trading links) and cutting off the direct interest relationship between local governments and jacking up the prices. To this end, we should not only adjust the fiscal relationship between the central and local governments but also reconstruct the related real estate tax system and regulate land transfer fee management. Those tax types with distinctive regional characteristics in tax sources, lower mobility and stricter information requirements, less spillover and suitable for local control can be established as major local tax types. Particularly, the existing fiscal revenue system related to land and housings should be adjusted, and one-off land rents and tax in terms of development and sale should be integrated into a unified real estate tax or property tax. We can explore to levy a unified "property tax" in terms of real estate possession with the value of real estate as tax base to serve as a stable source of local finance and improve local financial self-sufficiency. On this basis, we can transform the short-term local land finance behavior into the long-term behavior. That is, we can transform from putting too much efforts to city operation to striving to provide public services.[2] Meanwhile, after the property tax is launched, we can also increase the cost of housing possession and suppress the existing huge investment needs. While launching the property tax, to curb local governments' impulse to undertake land marketing activities, we can also consider transforming the land leasehold system into the land rent system. That is, we can transform the one-off charge of land transfer fee for decades into the charge of land rent fee (land use fee) on an annual basis. This will also to some extent play a certain role in adjusting land and housing prices.

Sixth, we should properly solve the local government debt problem.

To solve the local government debt problem, the key is to control debt increment and reduce debt stock through institutional factors. This mainly involves the reform in three aspects:

(1) Reforming the functions of government. To curb the impulse of local governments to borrow money and control the corresponding debt risks, it is necessary to transform the function of the government from a "economic-development-oriented government" to a "service-oriented government" and truly implement the Decision of the 3rd Plenary Session of the 18th CPC Central Committee: "we must greatly reduce the government's role in the direct allocation of resources, and promote resources allocation according to market rules, market prices and market competition, so as to maximize the benefits and optimize the efficiency. The main responsibility and role of the government is to maintain the stability of the macro-economy, strengthen and improve public services, safeguard fair competition, strengthen oversight of the market, maintain market order, promote sustainable development and common prosperity, and intervene in situations where market failure occurs". To achieve such transformation, an essential part is to reform and improve the performance appraisal system, effectively weaken the tendency of the evaluating political achievements merely by the economic growth rate and gradually raise the level of concern over the quality and efficiency of economic growth and social development, resource conservation and environmental protection beyond economic development. In addition to improving the top–down appraisal mechanism for the appraisal of the government at a lower level by the government at a higher level, we should actively introduce the bottom–up appraisal mechanism in which citizens participate. This is the key to correct the behaviors of local governments.
(2) Reforming the investment and financing system. To alleviate the financial pressure, we should change the situation of local government-led investment in infrastructure and promote the transition of the role of local government from

[2]This is equivalent to some sort of "voting with their feet" mechanism (threat of exit of liquidity factor). That is, residents' selection of public services by changing their place of residence can affect the value of real estate, which in turn have a substantial impact on the property tax based on the values of local real estate. Therefore, local governments have an incentive to improve public services.

the first investor to the last investor and from the investor to the investment supervisor. That is, their investment scope should be limited mainly to the non-profit and public welfare fields where private capital is unwilling to enter and they should in principle no longer invest in profitable business areas. For quasi-public welfare projects with stable operating income and non-public welfare projects with promising market prospects, we should ease the restrictions on market admittance for private capital to achieve commercial operation as soon as possible. By transferring the ownership or operation right to social forces, we can achieve the transfer of government risks to market risks.

(3) Reforming the tax system. We should try to change the situation of asymmetric decentralization of expenditure responsibilities and revenue power and local governments' overly dependence on transfer payments and various financing platforms and adjust local governments' financing pressure and distorted behavior styles arising there from. We should re-divide the administrative powers and expenditure responsibilities of governments at all levels based on the new needs of socialist market economy. In this regard, the key is still to implement the Decision of the 3rd Plenary Session of the 18th CPC Central Committee and straighten out the fiscal relations between governments at all levels as soon as possible.

Part II
Sectoral Analysis

Chapter 8
Household Balance Sheet

8.1 Introduction

In the *Methodology for the Compilation of China's Balance Sheet* issued by NBS (2007), "the household sector" is defined as a collection of "permanent resident households", including urban permanent resident households, rural permanent resident households and urban and rural "self-employed laborers".[1] The estimate and analysis in this section will be carried out on the basis of this concept.

It should be noted that, as a core sector of the national economy, the level and structure of assets and liabilities of households is directly related to a series of key issues, such as accumulation of wealth, income allocation, consumption, investment and macro-financial risks. Especially with the acceleration of urbanization and economic and social structure changes in recent years, household wealth and financial risks have accumulated rapidly, further highlighting the importance of the sector. However, as the relevant official data have not been released, there are few academic research papers on the balance sheets of the household sector. Undoubtedly, some scholars and institutions have carried out analysis using some partial estimates. For example, in terms of use of micro-data, Shi et al. (2000) and Renwei (2007) have studied the wealth distribution of Chinese residents based on the data of the household surveys carried out by the Institute of Economics, Chinese Academy of Social Sciences, in 1995 and 2002; Yunwen et al. have carried out statistical analysis of income and wealth distribution of urban and rural residents based on the data of the door-to-door household survey in Aldo Apartments Center; China Household Finance Survey and Research Center of Southwestern University of Finance and Economics (2012) has comprehensively studied the assets and liabilities of Chinese urban and rural residents and their distribution characteristics

[1]The term of household sector in China is similar to the definition of household sector in the Canadian national balance sheet, which includes individuals and unincorporated business units. But in the official statistics of the United States and Britain, households and non-profit organizations are combined into one sector.

Y. Li and X. Zhang, *China's National Balance Sheet*, China Insights,
DOI 10.1007/978-981-10-4385-7_8

and presented the results in its *China Household Finance Survey Report*. In terms of use of macro data, Xiangyun et al. (2009) have prepared the Chinese household balance sheets for 2004–2007 based on the financial statistics provided in the stock of funds accounts and the estimates of physical assets. According to my superficial knowledge, this is probably the earliest study presenting the complete balance sheet of the household sector. The *China Financial Stability Report* (the People's Bank of China 2012) prepared by the People's Bank of China in recent years has listed and analyzed the financial assets and liabilities of the household sector and become the official publication of the relevant data.

On the whole, despite the high reference value of the above data, methods, theoretical framework used in the research findings, there are great differences and even apparent contradictions and controversies over the data quality, statistical scope and estimation methods (especially the estimation of housing values). To enrich and improve the discussion on this important topic of China's household assets and liabilities, this study will, from the macro perspective, tentatively compile the Chinese household sector balance sheets for the calendar years of 2004–2011 based on official data and our own estimates and carry out the corresponding analysis on this basis.

8.2 Compilation and Analysis of Chinese Household Balance Sheet

The following table lists Chinese household sector balance sheets for 2004–2011 based on our estimates.

Before starting the analysis, we will give some explanations on this balance sheet. In terms of household non-financial assets: first, due to the unavailability of data, this study has defined non-financial assets as household housing assets, rural productive fixed assets and cars based on the method proposed by Xiangyuan et al. (2009). But the household sector inventories defined by NBS (2007) do not include household food stocks, livestock, and inventories of self-employed industrial and commercial households. Second, the value of housing assets is calculated separately by urban and rural residents. Due to the special status of housing assets in the total assets of households, the specific estimation method will be introduced separately later. Third, with regard to "cars", due to unavailability of car sale data, the income from main business (or sales income) of the leading car products for the previous years released in *China Automotive Industry Yearbook* is used here, and the value of car asset stock held by residents was estimated based on the method proposed by Xiangyuan et al. Since the reference data are different, the value and the estimate of Xiangyun et al. are not directly comparable, but given the relatively small size of car assets, this difference has little impact on the total assets of household. Fourth, the "rural productive fixed assets" was calculated based on "the original value of productive fixed assets of rural household", "the average number of people per rural household" and "the rural population" released by the *Statistical Yearbook of China*.

In terms of household financial assets, the household financial assets for 2004–2010 listed in this table are directly cited from *China Financial Stability Report 2012*. However, as the People's Bank of China did not disclose the corresponding data in the subsequent report for 2013, the data for 2011 presented here were calculated based on the stock data for 2010 and the flow of funds accounts for 2011 (financial transactions). Only the item of "wealth management products" was estimated according to the relevant data of *China Financial Stability Report 2013*. It should be noted that based on the figures of 2004–2007, there are some differences between the data here and the research findings of Xiangyun et al. based on the stock of funds accounts, especially the differences in the values of the two items of "stocks" and "clients' margins of securities companies".

By definition, the household sector liabilities refer only to financial liabilities, while the latter in this study are limited only to loans. As loans are only roughly classified in *China Financial Stability Report*, the data for 2007–2011 here were cited from the data for December of various years in *Sources and Uses of Credit Funds of Financial Institutions in RMB* (*by Sectors*) prepared by the People's Bank of China. As this statistics began in 2007, and the data for the previous year were still based on *China Financial Stability Report 2012*.[2]

In addition, according to the compilation framework of NBS (2007), the external financial assets and liabilities of the household sector are blank items.

Based on the above table, we have tried to summarize the following six characteristics. First, during 2004–2011, the total assets of China's households expanded rapidly from 53.3 to 162.2 trillion yuan, slightly faster than the nominal GDP growth rate over the same period. Its ratio to GDP also rose accordingly from 3.3 times to 3.4 times. Meanwhile, the net assets of households (total assets minus total liabilities) increased from 50.3 to 148.6 trillion yuan, basically on a par with the nominal GDP growth rate. The rapid accumulation of household assets during this period was mainly attributed to sustained rapid economic growth, financial market development and rapid increased in asset prices.

Second, real estate is the most important asset item for households, and its share of total assets and non-financial assets in the study period maintained at 60 and 93%. From the absolute scale, the total value of real estate during 2004–2011 increased by nearly three times. The most important promoting factors include the increase in housing prices, expansion of per capita living space and increase in the relative size of urban population.

Third, based on the financial structure at the macro level, the expansion of financial assets is faster than that of real assets. As shown in Table 8.1, the ratio between the two items (i.e. financial correlation ratio) increased from 0.51 to 0.55 in 2004–2011. In fact, the ratio of household financial assets to GDP rose from 1.13 to

[2]It should be noted that, as far as the household sector is concerned, the data of *Sources and Uses of Credit Funds of Financial Institutions in RMB* and *Sources and Uses of Credit Funds of Financial Institutions in RMB and Foreign Currency* are extremely similar, so the difference is negligible. For example, in December 2011, the household loans in the two reports was 13.6 and 13.61 trillion yuan respectively.

Table 8.1 China's household sector balance sheets (unit: 100 million yuan)

Item/year	2004	2005	2006	2007	2008	2009	2010	2011
Non-financial assets	352,136	432,052	482,591	605,463	622,183	791,506	871,851	1,044,416
Real estate	327,442	402,986	449,503	567,003	578,168	739,113	809,023	962,875
Including: urban	279,680	343,745	384,977	496,085	502,205	655,928	719,433	807,348
Rural	47,762	59,241	64,526	70,918	75,963	83,185	89,590	155,527
Automobiles	13,642	15,960	19,274	23,576	28,118	35,123	44,637	54,458
Rural productive fixed assets	11,052	13,106	13,814	14,884	15,897	17,270	18,191	27,083
Financial assets	180,369	209,083	251,600	335,495	342,870	410,869	494,832	578,034
Currency	17,820	19,945	22,469	25,211	28,622	31,982	37,691	42,652
Deposits	129,575	150,551	171,737	181,840	228,478	268,650	315,642	363,332
Bonds	6293	6534	6944	6707	4981	2623	2692	1898
Stocks	8897	7865	17,001	51,604	20,157	47,374	56,477	59,755
Securities investment fund shares	1905	2449	5618	29,716	17,011	8383	7346	7952
Clients' margins of securities companies	1339	1566	3128	9904	4760	5695	4447	2607
Insurance reserves	14,113	18,315	22,680	27,097	37,831	46,226	52,667	59,084
Wealth management products of financial institutions	–	–	–	–	–	–	18,063	40,754
Settlement funds	−77	23	17	0	0	0	0	–
Other financial assets	504	1835	2005	3415	1030	−64	−193	–
Total assets	532,505	641,135	734,191	940,958	965,053	1,202,375	1,366,683	1,622,450
Financial liabilities (loans)	29,431	32,972	39,636	50,652	57,058	81,787	112,542	136,012
Consumer loans	–	–	–	32,729	37,210	55,334	75,064	88,717
Short-term	–	–	–	3104	4137	6378	9567	13,555
Mid- and long-term	–	–	–	29,625	33,073	48,956	65,497	75,162
Business loans	–	–	–	17,923	19,848	26,453	37,478	47,295

(continued)

Table 8.1 (continued)

Item/year	2004	2005	2006	2007	2008	2009	2010	2011
Short-term	–	–	–	12,792	14,555	19,550	24,781	30,198
Including: loans to farmer households	–	–	–	10,677	11,972	14,623	–	–
Mid- and long-term	–	–	–	5131	5293	6903	12,698	17,097
Net financial assets	150,938	176,111	211,964	284,843	285,812	329,082	382,290	442,022
Net assets	503,074	608,163	694,555	890,306	907,995	1,120,588	1,254,141	1,486,438

Sources: *Statistical Yearbook of China*, *China Automotive Industry Yearbook* and *China Financial Stability Report* for the years as well as *Sources and Uses of Credit Funds of Financial Institutions in RMB* and the flow of funds accounts (financial transactions) published by People's Bank of China

1.22 in the same period. This trend indicates that compared with the real economy, the development of the financial sector is faster. This is consistent with the assertion raised by the American economist Goldsmith that the financial correlation ratio shows an upward trend due to the expansion of the financial sector in economic development process.

Fourth, in all the items of financial assets, deposits remained the highest portion of financial assets held by households, but its share continued to decline from 71.8% in 2004 to 62.9% in 2011. In the meanwhile, the portion of cash (currency) and bonds also declined by 2.5 and 3.2% respectively. In sharp contrast, the portion of stocks, funds, insurance reserves and other "non-traditional" assets increased significantly (the portion of the three items together increased from 14 to 22%), while "wealth management products" appeared and developed rapidly. As shown in Table 8.1, the item increased by 226% only in the two years of 2010 and 2011, accounting for more than 7% of financial assets of (with a relative size close to that of currency) and had become an important form of asset allocation of households. But it is also noteworthy that a portion of assets fluctuated violently in the period. For example, the values of stocks and funds held by households soared during the stock market boom in 2007, reaching three times and five times of the values in 2006 respectively. In the following year, due to the impact of the international financial crisis, the values of stocks and funds held by households declined dramatically by 60 and 40%, respectively. Thus, the above data show not only the increasingly diversified trend of allocation of financial assets of the household sector in recent years but also the exposure of household assets to greater market risks with the development of financial intermediation (Fig. 8.1).

Fifth, during 2004–2011, the absolute size of household liabilities (loans) grew by 4.6 times, faster than the growth rate of total assets and financial assets. As shown in Fig. 8.2 below, the household debt-to-total assets ratio thus rose from

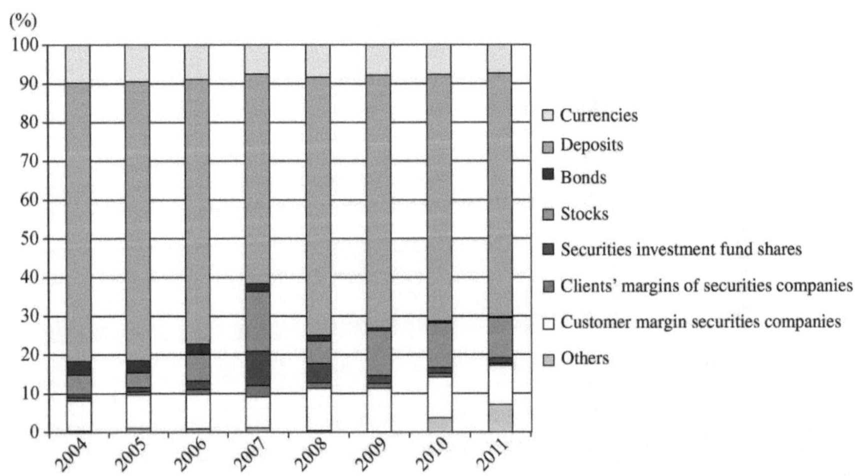

Fig. 8.1 Structure of household financial assets (totaling 100%). *Source* See the text

5.5 to 8.4%; the household debt to financial assets ratio rose from 16.3 to 23.5%. In particular, under the impact of the international financial crisis, the two debt to assets ratios of China's household sector rose continuously since 2007, so the financial risks of the sector and their contagion to the financial sector risk should arouse our attention. But there are three positive factors that should also be stressed. First, laterally compared with the developed countries, the overall debt burden of Chinese households remained at a low level. For example, as shown in Figs. 8.2 and 8.3, the debt-to-total assets ratio and debt-to-financial assets ratio of

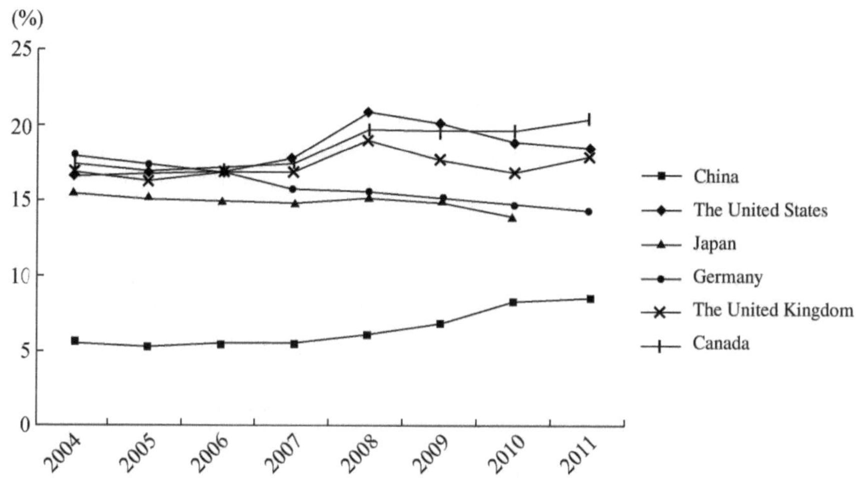

Fig. 8.2 International comparison of household debt to assets ratio (unit: %). *Source* See the text

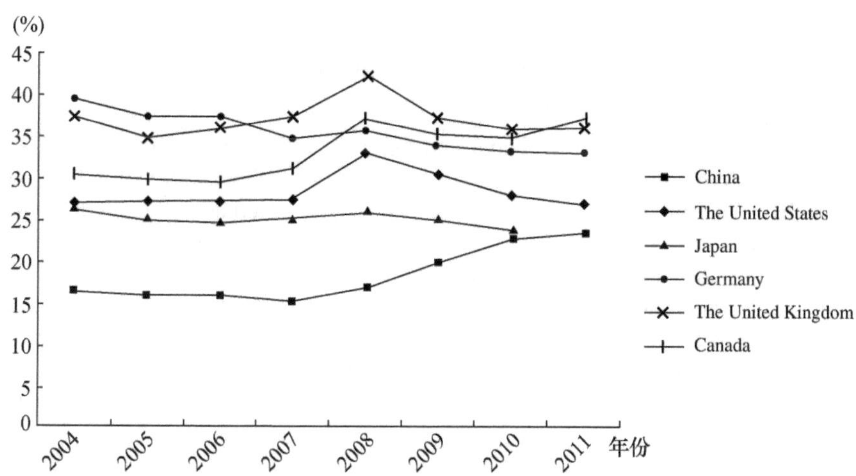

Fig. 8.3 International comparison of household financial debt to assets ratio (unit: %). *Source* See the text

the household sector in China were significantly lower than that of the United States, Japan, Germany, Britain and Canada in the same period. Second, from the perspective of loan defaults, according to the CBRC's data cited by *China Financial Stability Report 2013*, the ratio of non-performing personal consumer loans in China (including housing mortgage loans, auto loans and credit card loans) has continuously declined on the whole since 2006. Finally, in terms of maturity structure of debt, since 2007, the ratio of mid- and long-term consumer and business loans to financial liabilities remained at 68%, not showing an upward trend of short-term debt pressure. Based on the above analysis, we believe that the overall solvency and liquidity risk of the debts of China's household sector is low.

Sixth, there are some differences between our findings and those of related studies. For example, the study conduced by Xiangyuan et al. (2009) shows that, the household sector's total assets amounted to 61.7, 74.1, 85.3 and 110.2 trillion yuan in 2004–2007 respectively, higher than the estimates of this study in the same period. The main differences lie in the study by Xiangyun did not take into consideration the depreciation of housings and other issues, so they have to some extent overestimated the housing values. For another example, China Survey and Research Center of Southwestern University of Finance and Economics (2012) pointed out in its report that the assets per household in China in 2011 amounted to 1.2169 milion yuan, of which the assets per urban household amounted to 2.476 million yuan and those per rural household 377,000 yuan. If converted by the total number of households and other indicators, the data in Table 8.1 in this study show that per household assets in 2011 amounted only to 371,000 yuan. As the report is based on specific microscopic samples and its estimates of the values of business assets and housing assets held by households are different from those of this study, the data are not directly comparable.[3]

8.3 The Findings of the Study of Household Balance Sheet

Based on the data publicly available and our own estimates, in this chapter, we have tentatively compiled the balance sheet of the household sector in China for 2004–2011, and on this basis, analyzed and carried out international comparison of the structure and changing trend of household assets and liabilities. The study found that on the asset side, the household assets in China expanded rapidly in the study period and showed a significant structural change. That is, the traditional forms of asset holdings, such as deposits, cash and bonds, declined relatively in size, while housings, stocks, funds, insurance and other assets grew rapidly in size. This shows that with economic growth and development of financial markets,

[3]For the discussion on the survey data of Southwestern University of Finance and Economics, see the relevant reports of Jie (2012) as well as Ximing and Shi (2013).

wealth accumulation takes increasingly diverse forms. It should be emphasized that the value of a portion of assets, mainly housings and stocks, was significantly influenced by asset price fluctuations, and we remain highly vigilant on the uncertainty in this regard. On the liability side, the level of household debt burden kept relatively stable at the early stage, but since 2008 when the international financial crisis occurred, both the household debt to total assets ratio and debt to financial assets ratio showed an upward trend. Compared with the developed countries, they are still at a low level, but we should keep a close eye on their future trend. In addition, due to the conflicts between rigidity of debt and pro-cyclicality of asset prices, we should attach great important to the relationship between household liabilities and the fluctuation of the above asset prices.

Finally, it should be noted that, as the study is mainly based on macroeconomic data, we did not take into consideration the wealth distribution in the household sector and the impact of a number of microeconomic variables on assets and liabilities, such as age, occupation, education level and marital status. Therefore, in the future study, we may try to combine the macro data and micro survey to complement each other so as to have a more comprehensive understanding of the balance sheets of the household sector in China.

Chapter 9
Balance Sheets of Non-financial Corporations

9.1 Compilation of Balance Sheets of Non-financial Corporations

The compilation of balance sheets of non-financial corporations has profound significance in identifying the risks of the non-financial corporate sector and analyzing inter-sectoral risk contagion. Presently, China has not published the balance sheets of non-financial corporations, and the data related to the balance sheets of non-financial corporations that are available mainly include: (1) the data on assets and liabilities of nonfinancial corporations from the two economic census (2004 and 2008); (2) the data on assets and liabilities of state-owned enterprises throughout China; (3) the data on assets and liabilities of industrial enterprises above the designated size (with annual revenue of 20 million yuan or more from their main business operations) and enterprises in the industries of building, real estate, wholesale and retail trade; (4) the data on assets and liabilities of listed companies. Therefore, the balance sheets of non-financial corporations in China can only be compiled based on the estimates from the above four categories of data, and the above data are the benchmark data for compiling balance sheets of non-financial corporations in China.

Based on the above four categories of benchmark data, the balance sheets of non-financial corporations in China can be compiled roughly by two approaches. In the first approach, the time series data are projected year by year with the flow of funds accounts or the cross-sectional data based on the data on assets and liabilities of non-financial corporations in the base year (such as the data of year when the economic census was carried out). The flow of funds accounts in China mainly include the flow of funds accounts (physical transaction) prepared by NBS and the flow of funds accounts (financial transaction) prepared by the People's Bank of China. The changes in the total assets of the non-financial corporate sector is determined by the flow of funds accounts (physical transaction) and the flow of funds accounts (financial transaction) and can be calculated according to the total

Y. Li and X. Zhang, *China's National Balance Sheet*, China Insights,
DOI 10.1007/978-981-10-4385-7_9

assets (total assets that year = total assets in the previous year + total capital formation that year + other non-financial assets acquisitions less disposals + total application of funds that year) and total liabilities (total liabilities that year = total liabilities in the previous year − net financial investments + loans + corporate bonds + other foreign claims and obligations). Among these subjects, total capital formation and other non-financial asset acquisitions less disposals are the subjects of the flow of funds accounts (physical transaction), and total application of funds is the subject of the flow of funds accounts (financial transaction), net financial investment is the subject of the flow of funds accounts (physical transaction), and loans, corporate bonds and other external claims and obligations are the subject of the flow of funds accounts (financial transaction). The problems of the first approach mainly include: (1) there is the value incommensurability problem with direct addition and subtraction of the total assets and total liabilities in the previous period and the data of the flow of funds accounts in the current period, so adjustment must be carried out based on some assumptions; (2) the changes in the value of intangible assets in non-financial assets and business reputation etc. can not be reflected in this estimation approach; (3) the data of the flow of funds accounts (financial transaction) reflect the flow of funds produced in the income and expenditure and borrowing and lending activities of the non-financial corporate sector and other sectors (households, general government, financial institutions and the external sector), but does not reflect the borrowing and lending activities among the enterprises inside the non-financial corporate sector, which will result in underestimate of the assets and liabilities of the non-financial corporate sector. Duoduo (2013) has estimated the total assets and liabilities of non-financial corporations for 1992–2008 based on the data of the economic census using this approach and extrapolated the data for 2009–2011 based on some assumptions.

In the second approach, the time series data on assets and liabilities of some enterprises are extended to the time series data of all non-financial corporations through some assumptions. Presently, the time series data on assets and liabilities of some enterprises available include three categories: the data on assets and liabilities of industrial enterprises above the designated size and enterprises in the industries of building, real estate, wholesale and retail trade; the data on assets and liabilities of state-owned enterprises; and the data on assets and liabilities of listed companies. When the data of all non-financial corporations were estimated based on the data of part of the corporations, we need to consider: (1) the proportion of output of some enterprises to the output of all non-financial enterprises; (2) the proportional relationship between the same amount of output produced by some enterprises and other enterprises (all non-financial enterprises except some enterprises) and the assets needed. In general, the relationship between output and assets of an enterprise is related to the industry where the enterprise belongs to. In the above three categories of time-series data, no time-series data on the added value of state-owned enterprises have been directly released, so it is difficult calculate the proportion. In addition, the proportion of state-owned enterprises and listed companies in the industries will change over time, so the proportional relationship between the same amount of output produced by some enterprises and other enterprises and the assets needed is relatively instable, but this relationship is relatively stable when the data are broken down by industry. Therefore, based on the data by industry on assets and liabilities of industrial enterprises above the designated sized and enterprises in the industries of real estate, wholesale and retail trade and construction, as part of the data, we will be able to make more accurate estimation. Jun et al. (2012) carried out estimation using the second approach and used the data by industry on assets and liabilities of industrial enterprises above the designated size and enterprises in the industries of real estate, wholesale and retail trade, commercial and construction as the benchmark data. The main problem with the second approach is that the assumptions on which the estimation are made may be greatly different from the real economy and thus result in greater errors in the estimation data.

By making reference to the estimation method proposed by Duoduo (2013) and Jun et al. (2012), we will carry out estimation of the balance sheets of non-financial corporations for 2000–2012 using the second approach. The principle for estimation is that the fewer assumptions, the better, the more stable the assumptions, the better, and the closer the assumptions to the real economy, the better. Based on the above principle, we have further integrated the economic census on the basis of the estimation method proposed by Jun et al. (2012) so that some assumptions can be more closer to the real economy to achieve more accurate estimates.

The estimation method proposed by Jun et al. (2012) is briefed as follows. First, the estimation is made based on the experience of relevant statistical departments assuming that the size of assets of all industrial enterprises is 1.1 times of the industrial enterprises above the designated size; second, based on the data on total assets of industrial enterprises above the designated size in the industries of real estate, commercial and construction, the assets of all industrial enterprises are added up using the same method as mentioned above to get the size of total assets of the four industries; and finally, as the four industries account for more than 60% of non-financial and non-agricultural GDP, and the other industries are relatively asset-light, so the proportion of the other industries with respect to the four industries can be projected based on the ratio to GDP, and then the total assets of the other industries can be projected by assuming that the same output value contributed by the other industries only needs half of the assets of the four industries and added up to get the total assets of all non- financial enterprises (excluding agricultural enterprises). The total liabilities can be projected based on the debt to assets ratio as shown by the aggregate data of listed non-financial companies. The components of total assets and total liabilities can be projected according to all the ratios as shown by the financial data of non-financial listed companies.

The assumptions used by Jun et al. (2012) for estimation of total assets of non-financial enterprises mainly include: (1) the assets of all industrial enterprises is 1.1 times of the assets of industrial enterprises above the designated size, and the total assets of the industries of real estate, commercial and construction is also 1.1 times of the assets of industrial enterprises above the designated size; (2) the same output value contributed by the other industries only needs half of the assets of the four industries. The above two assumptions are mainly based on experience and intuitive judgment. In this book, the two assumptions are based on the data of the economic census (see Table 9.1), so they are more accurate, thereby improving the quality of estimates. First of all, according to the data of the 2004 and 2008 economic census, the assumption that the total assets of all industrial enterprises is 1.1 times of the assets of industrial enterprises above the designated size is more in line with the real economy, but this ratio is higher in the wholesale and retail trade industry, and this ratio in the four industries (real estate, wholesale and retail trade, manufacturing and construction) is around 1.2, so the estimation method proposed by Jun et al. (2012) has underestimated the assets. Therefore, in this book, this ratio is adjusted to 1.2. Second, Jun et al. (2012) assumes that the same output value contributed by the other industries only needs half of the assets of the four industries. Here, the other industries are further divided into transportation, warehousing, postal services, accommodation and catering and other tertiary industries. According to the data of the 2004 and 2008 economic census, we calculated the ratio of the assets needed by these industries to contribute the same output value in 2004 and 2008 to those of the four industries and got the average value, then we obtained that the ratio of the industries of transportation, warehousing and postal services is 0.95, that of the accommodation and catering industries is 0.41, and that of other tertiary industries is 1.07. Based on these ratios, the total assets of the four industries over the years and the proportion of the value-added of the four industries to the other industries, we have calculated and obtained the assets of transportation, warehousing, postal services, accommodation and catering and other tertiary industries and further aggregated the data to obtain the total assets of non-financial enterprises over the years.

Table 9.1 The data of the 2004 and 2008 economic census on assets and liabilities of enterprises by industry (unit: 100 million yuan)

Industries	2004		2008
	Total assets	Total liabilities	Total assets
Manufacturing	240,706.8	136,785	473,048.3
Construction	31,628.7	19,786.9	51,711.9
Transportation, warehousing and postal services	35,763.2	17,050.2	74,807.4
Real estate	69,774.7	50,653	208,750.1
Wholesale and retail	61,795.8	43,163.8	121,619.4
Accommodation and catering	6975.8	4222.2	11,079.1
Other tertiary industries (excluding the financial industry)	112,817.5	49,879.7	274,041.1
Financial industry	322,862.7	308,258.3	862,942.9
Total (including the financial industry)	882,325.2	629,799.1	2,078,000
Total (excluding the financial industry)	559,462.5	321,540.8	1,215,057

Sources *Communique on Major Data of the First National Economic Census of China* and *Communique on Major Data of the Second National* Economic Census *of China* published by NBS

The total liabilities can be projected based on the debt to assets ratio of non-financial listed companies. Here the total liabilities can be estimated in a similar way to the total assets, but as the debt to assets ratios contributing the same output value in different industries are not stable, the projections based on historical assets and liabilities are more accurate. Presently, we can obtain the time series data of non-financial listed companies and state-owned enterprises. As non-financial listed companies include state-owned enterprises and non-state-owned enterprises in various industries, the data of these companies reflect more comprehensive information, and their debt to assets ratio is close to the debt to assets ratio of non-financial enterprises, so here our projections are based on the data of non-financial listed companies.

The components of total assets and total liabilities of non-financial corporations are then projected in accordance with the ratios as shown by the financial data of non-financial listed companies. The assets of listed companies in the balance sheet are classified into current assets and non-current assets by liquidity, and the liabilities are classified into current liabilities and non-current liabilities by liquidity. In this book, by making reference to the methods of the Department of National Accounts of NBS (2007) and Jun et al. (2012), the total assets are classified into non-financial assets and financial assets. Non-financial assets include fixed assets, inventories and other non-financial assets, among which other non-financial assets include intangible assets, deferred assets, investment properties, productive biological assets, oil and gas assets, business reputation, development expenditures and so on.[1] Financial assets include monetary funds, inter-corporate credit (including notes receivable, accounts receivable, prepayments and other receivables), long-term equity investments and other financial assets. Total liabilities, i.e. financial liabilities, include short-term loans, long-term loans, inter-corporate liabilities (including notes payable, accounts payable, advances received, other payables and long-term payables) and other financial liabilities. Refer to Table 9.2 for the estimated data of the balance sheet of China's non-financial corporations for 2000–2012.

After being adjusted according to the data of the economic census, the estimated data in this book are closer to the data of the economic census. According to the 2008 Economic Census, the total assets of non-financial corporations amounted to 121,505.7 billion yuan, and the total assets of non-financial corporations estimated by Jun et al. (2012) were 98,478.2 billion yuan in 2008, which was underestimated to some extent. In this book, the estimated total assets were 117,503.6 billion yuan, which is closer to the real economy.

[1]The non-financial assets estimated by Jun et al. (2012) include fixed assets, inventories, intangible assets and business reputation. The scope non-financial assets estimated here is greater than the scope of estimate by Jun et al.

Table 9.2 Balance sheets of China's non-financial corporations for 2000–2012 (unit: 100 million yuan)

	2000	2001	2002	2003	2004	2005	2006	2007	2008	2009	2010	2011	2012
Total assets	305,597	337,278	377,044	434,909	579,604	653,428	770,083	933,596	1,175,036	1,361,800	1,656,649	1,968,060	2,296,500
Non-financial assets	168,003	202,834	235,972	276,116	380,298	446,071	534,237	621,686	818,446	905,483	1,067,983	1,255,309	1,408,252
Fixed assets	112,904	146,731	174,564	203,224	276,040	322,564	388,346	398,520	509,293	550,917	614,615	689,625	791,625
Inventories	42,777	44,757	47,928	58,447	83,048	99,670	117,449	138,784	178,448	211,319	286,998	366,971	437,733
Other non-financial assets	12,322	11,346	13,479	14,445	21,211	23,838	28,441	84,382	130,706	143,246	166,369	198,714	178,894
Incl.: intangible assets	9437	9102	9828	10,898	14,202	15,429	19,143	29,793	49,133	58,249	68,466	86,310	104,983
Financial assets	137,595	134,443	141,072	158,793	199,305	207,357	235,847	311,910	356,590	456,317	588,666	712,751	888,247
Monetary funds	46,187	48,435	51,150	57,003	72,332	72,802	87,822	118,855	144,516	191,830	246,891	285,166	312,411
Notes receivable	4308	5534	7608	11,151	13,767	14,236	17,468	21,578	20,882	27,075	41,011	56,925	59,534
Accounts receivable	32,162	25,853	26,458	28,949	37,321	40,984	44,439	51,852	58,962	77,851	101,530	133,159	166,383
Prepayments	10,475	9719	10,370	13,440	17,750	19,415	22,894	33,066	39,181	47,498	58,954	67,090	69,409
Other receivables	22,115	18,436	17,069	16,715	19,972	19,743	16,583	18,973	21,355	21,934	27,357	31,922	40,657
Inter-corporate credit	69,060	59,541	61,505	70,255	88,810	94,377	101,384	125,468	140,381	174,358	228,851	289,096	335,983
Long-term equity investments	18,628	20,206	21,998	24,978	32,051	34,105	39,097	37,503	45,531	48,318	61,848	70,977	88,217
Other financial assets	3719	6261	6419	6557	6113	6073	7544	30,085	26,163	41,812	51,077	67,511	151,637
Total liabilities	137,283	159,474	185,498	218,265	303,496	355,400	427,745	495,380	641,437	784,095	954,214	1,168,109	1,380,300
Short-term loans	43,443	47,732	51,519	61,723	82,919	89,688	99,464	101,485	138,278	131,690	171,056	194,875	232,260
Long-term loans	21,239	30,256	37,111	44,646	62,767	72,798	89,970	90,987	122,949	155,502	177,489	202,313	230,578
Notes payable	5826	9788	12,674	16,044	21,534	26,061	29,027	23,052	30,582	38,975	61,192	53,000	63,259
Accounts payable	19,037	19,703	25,700	31,741	44,753	56,484	68,127	93,891	113,174	149,846	209,560	235,198	278,227
Advances received	7372	7959	11,375	15,983	23,620	28,543	35,799	49,504	62,631	89,845	112,732	135,565	158,420
Other payables	13,294	13,886	14,337	16,925	22,927	24,989	31,764	39,688	47,442	52,560	63,788	77,227	89,222
Long-term payables	4049	4753	4832	3100	5248	4513	5551	7266	9483	9934	11,553	13,141	16,351
Inter-corporate liabilities	49,578	56,090	68,918	83,793	118,082	140,590	170,268	213,401	263,313	341,161	458,824	514,131	605,480
Other financial liabilities	23,022	25,396	27,949	28,104	39,728	52,323	68,043	89,507	116,897	155,742	146,844	256,790	311,982
Net assets	168,315	177,804	191,546	216,644	276,108	298,029	342,338	438,216	533,598	577,705	702,435	799,951	916,200
Net financial assets	312	−25,030	−44,426	−59,472	−104,190	−148,042	−191,898	−183,470	−284,847	−327,778	−365,547	−455,358	−492,052
Debt to assets ratio	0.449	0.473	0.492	0.502	0.524	0.544	0.555	0.531	0.546	0.576	0.576	0.594	0.601

Sources CCER's China financial database and the author's calculations

9.2 Analysis of Balance Sheets of Non-financial Corporations

9.2.1 Trend Analysis

(1) Total amount and structure analysis

As shown in Table 9.2, from 2000 to 2012, total assets, total liabilities and net assets have experienced rapid growth. Total assets rose from 30,559.7 billion yuan to 229,650 billion yuan, total liabilities from 13,728.3 billion yuan to 138,030 billion yuan, and net assets from 16,831.5 billion yuan to 91,620 billion yuan. As shown in Fig. 9.1, from 2000 to 2012, total assets and liabilities of non-financial corporations rose rapidly compared with GDP, while the ratio of net assets to GDP kept relatively stable. The faster expansion of corporate assets relative to GDP to some extent reflects a change in China's economic structure. With gradual promotion of industrialization and urbanization, the industries where more assets were needed to contribute the same output value such as capital-intensive industries developed faster, so the size of corporate assets relative to the total volume of the economy grew faster. The total liabilities to GDP ratio rose faster while the net assets to GDP ratio remained stable, reflecting that with the economic growth, the expansion of the non-financial corporate sector was largely reliant on financing through liabilities.[2]

In addition, China's non-financial enterprises have net financial debts, reflecting that enterprises have acquired non-financial assets with financial liabilities, and enterprises are net fund raisers in the debt market, and such is the case for most enterprise. Figure 9.1 shows that the net financial debt to GDP ratio of non-financial corporations has gradually increased since 2000 and remained stable since 2008, which to some extent reflects that the expanding trend of the size of non-financial assets acquired by the non-financial corporate sector with financial liabilities relative to GDP has slowed down since the occurrence of the financial crisis.

[2]In 2012, the liabilities to GDP ratio of non-financial corporations was 266%, higher than the ratio of outstanding balance of debt to GDP of 113% of non-financial corporations given in Sect. 6.2. This is mainly because "liabilities" and "debt" in the balance sheet are different concepts. According to the *Public Sector Debt Statistics-Guide for Compilers and Users* issued by IMF (2011), debt is liability presented in the form of debt instrument, so debt is only a portion of liability. The nonfinancial corporate debt given in Sect. 6.2 mainly includes loans from traditional sources, financial debt instruments (mainly including corporate bonds, short-term financing bonds, medium-term notes and corporate bonds etc.) and funds raised through credit intermediation activities outside the banking sector (mainly including trust loans, entrusted loans, banker's acceptance bills and other forms), while the inter-corporate liabilities in non-financial corporate liabilities and some other financial liabilities (such as dividend payable and accrued expense, etc.) are not included in the debt, and the inter-corporate liabilities accounted for 44% of total liabilities in 2012, so the ratio of non-financial corporate liabilities to GDP is far higher than the ratio of nonfinancial corporate debt to GDP.

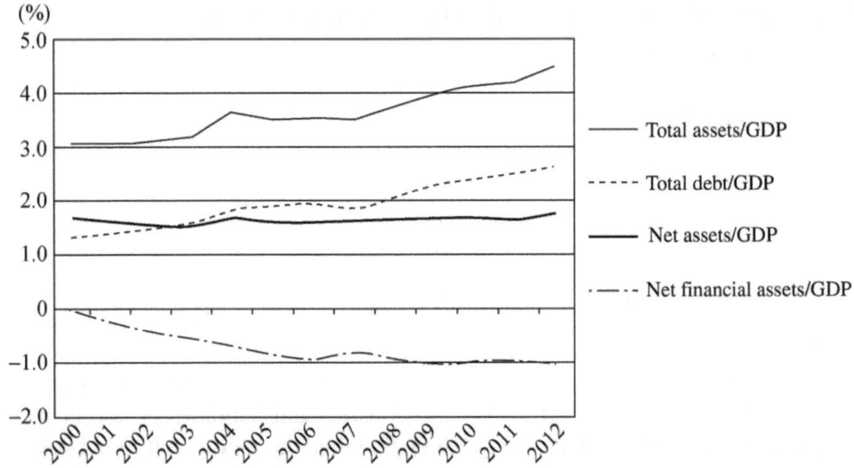

Fig. 9.1 The ratios of total assets, total liabilities and net assets to GDP of non-financial corporations

As shown in Fig. 9.2, in all components of total assets of non-financial corporations, fixed assets, inventories, monetary funds and inter-corporate credit (including notes receivable, accounts receivable, prepayments and other receivables) are the principal parts, among which fixed assets take a much higher proportion than other items. The proportion of fixed assets declined in 2012 compared with 2000, which to a certain extent may be related to the implementation of the new accounting rules in 2007. Under the new accounting rules, buildings and productive biological assets as investment properties included in the scope of fixed assets in the old accounting rules are no longer included in the accounting scope of fixed assets, so the accounting scope of fixed assets is smaller. In addition, under the new accounting rules, the scope of depreciation of fixed assets area is larger, which may result in decrease in the proportion of fixed assets.

Taking into account the impact of the new accounting rules on statistical scope, we have studied the changes in the proportion of fixed assets after 2007. As shown

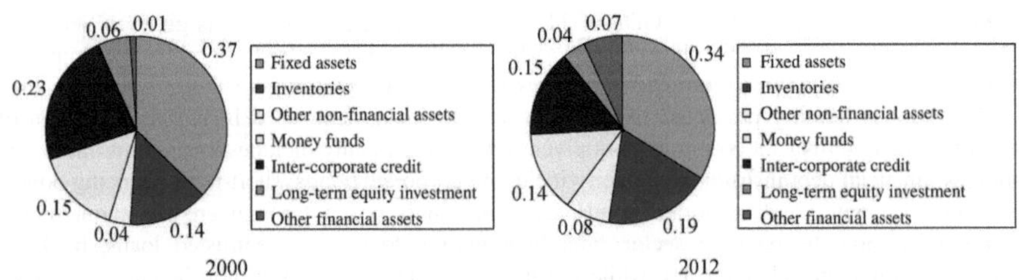

Fig. 9.2 Proportions of all components of total assets of non-financial corporations in 2000 and 2012

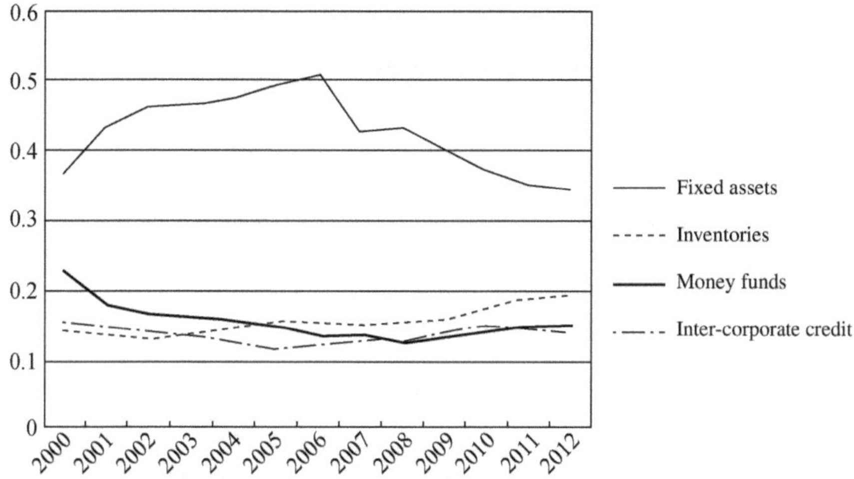

Fig. 9.3 The changing trend of proportion of main components of total assets of non-financial corporations

in Fig. 9.3, the proportion of fixed assets continued to decline from 43 to 34% during 2007–2012. This is mainly because the growth rate of inventories and inter-corporate credit was greater than that of fixed assets after the occurrence of the financial crisis in 2007, which to a certain extent is probably related to the fast increase of inventories resulting from the expectation of enterprises on the economic recovery and excess capacity and the fast increase of inter-corporate credit arising from the possible debt chain problem.

As shown in Fig. 9.4, in all components of liabilities of non-financial corporations, inter-corporate liabilities (including notes payable, accounts payable, advances received, other payables and long-term payables) accounted for the highest proportion and rose from 36% in 2000 to 44% in 2012, while the proportion of short-term loans declined significantly from 32% in 2000 to 17% in 2012. As the proportion of inter-corporate liabilities continued to rise and was much higher than the proportion of short-term loans, if a liquidity crisis occurs in the non-financial corporate sector, the risks may be first transmitted inside the sector.

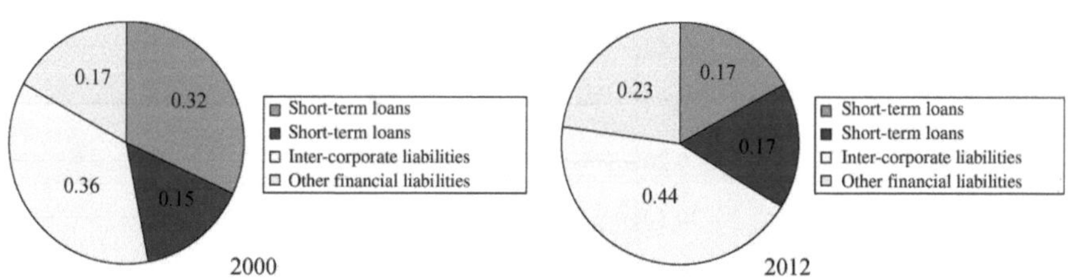

Fig. 9.4 Proportion of all components of liabilities of non-financial corporations in 2000 and 2012

(2) Ratio analysis

Figure 9.5 reflects the changing trends of the debt to assets ratio of non-financial corporations. As shown in the figure, the debt to assets ratio of non-financial corporations was showing a rising trend during 2000–2012 and rose from 44.9% in 2000 to 60.1% in 2012. It is generally believed that the optimal level of the debt to assets ratio is 40–60%. The debt to assets ratio of non-financial corporations in China has currently exceeded the upper limit. The rising trend of debt to assets ratio of non-financial corporations in China is to a certain extent related to the financing mode in China in which indirect financing takes the principal part and the strong investment-led capacity of local governments. Prior to 2007, the sustained growth or even overheating of China's economy and the promulgation of the stimulus policies after the occurrence of the financial crisis in 2007 have stimulated the investment demands of non-financial corporations, but as direct financing was always limited, non-financial corporations could only meet their investment demands by indirect financing, thus promoting the rise in the debt to assets ratio. In addition, local governments has a strong investment-led capacity, so an enormous sum of money has flown to LGFPs and some large state-owned enterprises, while these state-owned enterprises often have a soft budget constraint, which has also driven up the debt to assets ratio. For example, the debt to assets ratio of state-owned enterprises in China was 64% in 2011, higher than the average level of non-financial corporations. The gradual rise of China's debt to assets ratio and its trend to exceed the safety margin indicates that China currently has a certain degree of "capital structure mismatch", bringing the debt level of non-financial corporations to a situation that is likely to trigger a crisis.

Figure 9.6 reflects the changing trend of current ratio of non-financial corporations. The current ratio is the ratio of current assets to current liabilities. It is used to measure a company's ability to pay back its liabilities with its current assets before the maturity of its short-term liabilities. The current ratio reflects the liquidity of a company's assets, The higher the current ratio, the more capable the company is of paying its obligations. As shown in the figure, the current ratio of

Fig. 9.5 The changing trend of debt to assets ratio

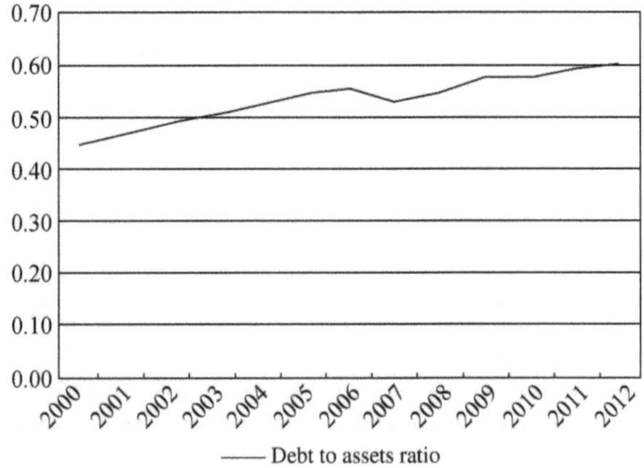

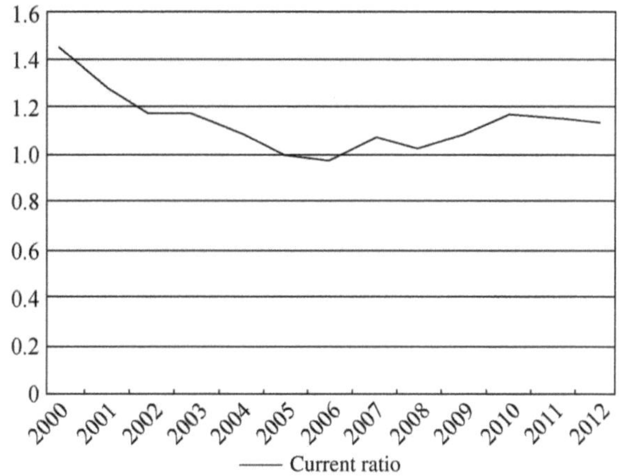

Fig. 9.6 The changing trend of current ratio

non-financial corporations appeared to have a decline trend after an initial ascent during 2000–2012 and declined from 1.45 in 2000 to 0.98 in 2006 and later experienced a gradual recovery and rose to 1.14 in 2012. It is generally believed that the current ratio should be greater than 2. A ratio above 2 suggests that even though half of current assets can not be cashed out in the short term, a company can still ensure that all current liabilities are repaid. China's non-financial corporations currently have a lower current ratio and are facing the "maturity mismatch" risk, and a short-term external shock is likely to trigger a liquidity problem. According to the analysis above, as the amount of inter-corporate liabilities is much larger than that of short-term loans, if a liquidity crisis occurs in the non-financial corporate sector, the risks may be first transmitted inside the sector.

As shown in the analysis above, there are "capital structure mismatch" and "maturity mismatch" problems in China's non-financial corporate sector.

Indirect financing is a major financing mode in China, and the vast majority of financial resources are allocated through bank intermediaries. This financial structure decides the high debt ratio of non-financial corporations in China. In a period of steady economic growth, bank loans with the advantages of low cost, low risk constitute the major source of corporate debt, but if the economy has entered a period of violent fluctuation and the economic growth rate is showing a decline trend, then a considerable part of corporate debt may form non-performing assets and thus impair the health of balance sheets of enterprises and banks. The analysis of leverage ratio in the general report shows that the corporate sector leverage ratio (proportion of corporate debt to GDP) reached 113% in 2012, higher than the threshold value of 90% of the OECD countries. Measuring by the total corporate liabilities in this chapter, its share of GDP has reached 266%, which requires keen vigilance. The interaction of "capital structure mismatch" and "maturity mismatch" of the non-financial corporate sector will possibly bring external shocks to the economy and lead to continuous contagion and amplification of risks and the formation of overall risks. Although China's government sector has huge sovereign assets, we still needs to consider the structural problems and should pay attention to the inter-sectoral risk contagion and amplification mechanism to avoid the formation of the overall risks that are difficult to control.

Chapter 10
Financial Sector Balance Sheets

10.1 Brief Introduction to the Statistical System for China's Current Financial Sector Balance Sheets

Theoretically, the financial sector balance sheet should include two levels: first, the balance sheets (summary) of various financial sub-sectors (including the central bank, banking, insurance, securities and trust etc.); second, the consolidated balance sheet of all financial institutions in the financial sector. Among them, the consolidated balance sheet of the financial sector is prepared by adding up the balance sheets (summary) of all financial sub-sectors and deducting the claims and obligations among the financial institutions. Thus, the preparation of complete balance sheets of the financial sub-sectors is the basis for the formation of the consolidated balance sheet of the financial sector. However, in reality, as there are many shortcomings in the preparation of the balance sheets (summary) of various financial sub-sectors, so far China has been unable to prepare the consolidated balance sheet of the financial sector covering all financial institutions. This is mainly because: (1) the balance sheets (summary) of various financial sub-sectors were prepared at different time points. The balance sheet of monetary authorities and other depository corporations began to be prepared in 1997, those of insurance companies and securities companies were prepared in 2007 and 2008 respectively, and those of the trust industry were prepared in 2010. (2) There existed a time lag in the preparation of the balance sheets (summary) of some financial sub-sectors. For example, the time for the preparation of the balance sheet (summary) of insurance companies and securities companies was one year later than the time for the preparation of the balance sheet (summary) of monetary authorities and other depository corporations. (3) The balance sheets (summary) of some financial sub-sectors are not fully structurally broken down and unable to fully reflect the relationship between claims and obligations among financial institutions and hinder the preparation of the consolidated balance sheet of the financial sector. For example, the balance sheet (summary) of insurance companies and securities

Y. Li and X. Zhang, *China's National Balance Sheet*, China Insights,
DOI 10.1007/978-981-10-4385-7_10

companies contain their claims and obligations respectively to other financial institutions, but the balance sheet of monetary authorities and other depository corporations does not include the broken-down claims and obligations to insurance companies and securities companies.

Therefore, China has currently formed two incomplete series of balance sheets of financial institutions. The first series is the *Depository Corporations Survey* (DCS) prepared by consolidating the balance sheets of monetary authorities and other depository corporations. As shown in Table 10.1, the DCS in 2011 is the brief balance sheet of depository corporations in the same year. Tables 10.2 and 10.3 represent the balance sheets of monetary authorities and other depository corporations in 2011 respectively. Specific preparation steps will not be listed due to limited space.

The second series is *Sources & Uses of Credit Funds of Financial Institutions in RMB*. The *Sources & Uses of Credit Funds of Financial Institutions in RMB* is essentially another form of balance sheet, in which the item of funds uses is similar to the assets item in balance sheet, and the item of sources of funds is similar to the item of liabilities and owners' equity in balance sheet. The greatest difference between *Sources & Uses of Credit Funds of Financial Institutions in RMB* and DCS is that the statistical scope of financial institutions also includes some other financial corporations, namely, trust and investment companies, financial leasing companies and car financial services companies, in addition to the central bank, commercial banks and policy banks. The *Sources & Uses of Credit Funds of Financial Institutions in RMB* is shown in Table 10.4.

Table 10.1 The DCS in 2011 (unit: 100 million yuan)

Net foreign assets	251644.5
Domestic credit	687971.6
Domestic credit: government debt	42363.92
Domestic credit: non-financial sector debt	600634.5
Domestic credit: other financial sector debt	44973.15
Liabilities: money and quasi money	851590.9
Money	289847.7
Money: cash in circulation	50748.5
Money: demand deposits	239099.2
Quasi-money	561743.2
Quasi-money: time deposits	166,616
Quasi-money: savings deposits	352797.5
Quasi-money: other deposits	42329.69
Deposits excluded from broad money	16809.07
Bonds	75409.69
Paid-in capital	28861.75
Other items (net)	−33055.3

Table 10.2 Balance sheet of other depository corporations in 2011 (unit: 100 million yuan)

Total assets	1,137,867
Foreign assets	24211.74
Reserve assets	176,422
Reserve assets: deposits with center bank	173004.1
Reserve assets: cash in vault	5101.574
Claims on government	49697.85
Central bank bonds	22323.96
Claims on other depository corporations	179,466
Claims on other financial corporations	34329.18
Claims on non-financial sectors	465395.2
Claims on other resident sectors	135214.4
Other assets	54224.67
Total Liabilities	1,137,867
(Nf) liabilities to non-financial institutions & households (Nf)	780043.9
Nf: deposits included in broad money	758512.7
Nf: deposits included in broad money: demand deposits	239099.2
Nf: deposits Included In Broad Money: Time Deposits	166,616
Nf: deposits included in broad money: savings deposits	352797.5
Nf: deposits excluded from broad money	16809.07
Nf: deposits excluded from broad money: transferable deposits	7118.482
Nf: deposits excluded from broad money: other deposits	9690.586
Nf: other liabilities	4722.111
Liabilities to central bank	6763.862
Liabilities to other depository corporations	85081.98
Liabilities to other financial corporations (Fc)	52210.89
Fc: deposits included in broad money	42329.69
External liabilities	7765.864
Bond issue	75409.69
Paid-in capital	28,642
Other liabilities	101948.9

10.2 Preparation of Balance Sheet of the Financial Sector

As many types of balance sheet (summary) of other financial corporations have still not been prepared, China is currently still not in a position to prepare the consolidated balance sheet of the financial sector covering all financial institutions. In this book, we will tentatively prepare the balance sheets of financial institutions, including the central bank, commercial banks and some of the other financial corporations (including insurance companies, securities companies, trust and investment companies, financial leasing companies and auto financing service

Table 10.3 Balance sheet of monetary authorities in 2011 (unit: 100 million yuan)

Total assets	280977.6
Foreign assets	237898.1
Foreign assets: foreign exchange	232388.7
Foreign assets: monetary gold	669.84
Foreign assets: other foreign assets	4839.492
Claims on government	15399.73
Claims on other depository corporations	10247.54
Claims on other financial corporations	10643.97
Claims on non-financial sectors	24.98933
Other assets	6763.309
Total liabilities	280977.6
Reserve money	224641.8
Reserve money: currency issue	55850.07
Reserve money: deposits of other depository corporations	168791.7
Deposits of financial corporations not included in reserve money	908.3654
Bond issue	23336.66
External liabilities	2699.438
Deposits of government	22733.66
Own capital	219.752
Other liabilities	6437.969

Source CEIC (According to the definition of "Financial Yearbook of China in 2009", the monetary authority refers to the People's Bank of China, and other depository corporations include: 1. policy banks; 2. commercial banks. (1) State-owned commercial banks. (2) Joint-stock commercial banks. (3) Urban banks. (4) Rural commercial banks. (5) Cooperative financial institutions: urban credit cooperatives, rural credit cooperatives and rural cooperative banks. (6) Foreign financial institutions. (7) Postal Savings Bank of China. (8) Financial corporations. Other financial corporations include: (1) insurance companies and pension funds (annuity). (2) Trust and investment companies. (3) Financial leasing companies. (4) Asset management companies. (5) Automotive financial services companies. (6) Financial guarantee companies. (7) Securities companies. (8) Investment funds. (9) Stock exchanges. (10) Other financial aid institutions.)

companies). The balance sheet of financial institutions is prepared by three steps: first, the *Sources & Uses of Credit Funds of Financial Institutions in RMB* is converted into the form of balance sheet of financial institutions. Second, the balance sheet of insurance companies and securities companies is simplified into the form that can be easily consolidated into the balance sheet of financial institutions. Third, the balance sheet of insurance companies and securities companies are consolidated into the balance sheet of financial institutions. Here we will prepare the balance of financial institutions in three steps.

Table 10.4 Sources and Uses of Credit Funds of Financial Institutions in RMB in 2011 (unit: 100 million yuan)

Sources and uses of funds	913226.33
Deposits	809368.33
Deposits of enterprises	410912.05
Personal deposits	353536.43
Fiscal deposits	26223.07
Financial bonds	10038.83
Cash in circulation	50748.46
Liabilities to international financial institutions	776.46
Other items (net)	42294.24
Loans	547946.69
Domestic loans	546398.25
Portfolio investment	96479.39
Shares and other investments	12824.72
Position for bullion & silver purchase	669.84
Position for forex purchase	253587.01
Assets with international financial institutions	1718.67

Source CEIC (According to information on the website of the People's Bank of China, the financial institutions in the balance sheet include the central bank, commercial banks, trust and investment companies, financial leasing companies and auto financing companies.)

10.2.1 Convert the Sources & Uses of Credit Funds of Financial Institutions in RMB *into the Form of Balance Sheet of Financial Institutions*

As shown in Table 10.5, to convert the *Sources & Uses of Credit Funds of Financial Institutions in RMB* into the form of Balance Sheet of Financial Institutions is to convert uses of funds and sources of funds in the former into assets and liabilities and paid-in capital in the latter respectively. Specifically, the difference between the Balance Sheet of Financial Institutions and *Sources & Uses of Credit Funds of Financial Institutions in RMB* in the form lies in: (1) in the balance Sheet of Financial Institutions, loans and deposits are no longer broken down; (2) portfolio investment, equity and other investments are combined into securities and investments; (3) The paid-in capital of other depository financial institutions is listed separately from the item "Other Items (Net)" of *Sources & Uses of Credit Funds of Financial Institutions in RMB*. The item of "Other Items (Net)" consists of paid-in capital of the central bank and other non-depository financial institutions, other capital of financial institutions, net assets of financial institutions with the real sector as well as errors and omissions and other items.[1]

[1]The net assets of financial institutions with the entity sector is a deduction item.

Table 10.5 The balance sheet of financial institutions converted from *Sources & Uses of Credit Funds of Financial Institutions in RMB* (unit: 100 million yuan)

	2000	2001	2002	2003	2004	2005	2006	2007	2008	2009	2010	2011
Assets	133,902	154,294	182,442	225,313	262,740	302,043	365,230	454,268	538,406	681,875	805,879	913,226
Total loans	99,371	112,315	131,294	158,996	178,198	194,690	225,347	261,691	303,395	399,685	479,196	547,947
Securities and investments	19,651	23,113	26,790	30,259	30,931	34,942	39,491	62,790	65,302	86,643	98,526	109,304
Position for bullion & silver purchase	12	256	337	337	337	337	337	337	337	670	670	670
Position for forex purchase	14,291	17,856	23,223	34,847	52,591	71,211	98,980	128,377	168,431	193,112	225,795	253,587
Assets with international financial institutions	576	754	798	873	683	862	1075	1073	941	1765	1693	1719
Liabilities and owners' equity	133,902	154,294	182,442	225,313	262,740	302,043	365,230	454,268	538,406	681,875	805,879	913,226
Total deposits	123,804	143,617	170,917	208,056	241,424	287,170	335,460	389,371	466,203	597,741	718,238	809,368
Financial bonds	30	51	90	2226	3955	5673	6483	11,505	20,852	16,203	13,527	10,039
Cash in circulation	14,653	15,689	17,278	19,746	21,468	24,032	27,073	30,334	34,219	38,246	44,628	50,748
Liabilities to international institutions	368	485	423	483	562	642	926	947	733	762	720	776
Owner's equity	−4954	−5548	−6266	−5197	−4670	−15473	−4712	22,110	16,398	28,923	28,766	42,294
Paid-in capital	7397	7660	8772	10,729	11,750	10,576	13,101	18,425	21,751	23,071	26,507	28,642
Other items (net)	−12,351	−13,208	−15,039	−15,926	−16,420	−26,049	−17,813	3685	−5353	5852	2259	13,652

Source CEIC

The following basic findings can be identified from the balance sheet of financial institutions as shown in Table 10.5.

First, the assets (liabilities) of financial institutions represented by commercial banks have expanded rapidly, and their ratios to GDP are showing an upward trend. As shown in Fig. 10.1, during 2000–2011, the assets-to-GDP ratio of financial institutions generally maintained an upward trend, but was different at different stages. The assets-to-GDP ratio rose from 135 to 166% during 2000–2003 and basically remained stable during 2003–2008, and this ratio was 171% in 2008. But it suddenly jumped to more than 200% in 2009. Such a sharp increase has partially reflected the changes in the Chinese monetary policy and economic growth. In 2000–2003, China was still in the shadow of the Asian financial crisis, and China implemented the easy monetary policy. From 2000 to August 2003, China's deposit reserve rate had remained at a low level of 6%, which had increased the monetary deriving capability of financial institutions and thus significantly increased the assets (liabilities) to GDP ratio of financial institutions. Since September 2003, with the stability and improvement of economic growth, the monetary policy began to tighten gradually and the deposit reserve rate was once increased to 17% in 2008. However, since the second half of 2008, in order to cope with the international financial crisis, China launched a RMB 4 trillion stimulus package, and the credit support from financial institutions became the core of the economic stimulus program. This has led to rapid expansion of the balance sheet of the financial sector and the sharp increase of their ratios to GDP in a short time.

Second, the changes in asset and liability structure. The proportion of loans to assets maintained a downward trend on the whole and declined gradually from 74.2% in 2000 to 60% in 2011. The main reason for the decline is that due to the sharp rise in foreign-currency-denominated assets of the financial sector, the position for forex purchase increased gradually from 10.7% in 2000 to 27% in 2011

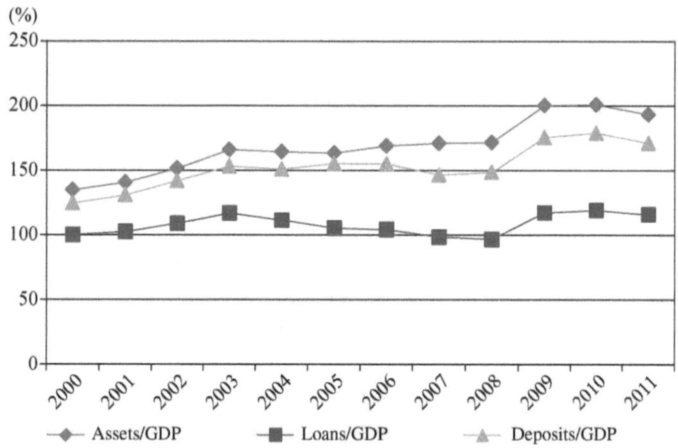

Fig. 10.1 Ratio of assets, deposits and loans to GDP of financial institutions

and had increased dramatically since 2003. This change was mainly attributed to the current account and capital account surplus caused by a sharp expansion of China's foreign trade since 2003. Due to China's special foreign exchange management system, foreign exchanges exist in the form of assets of banks, especially assets of the central bank. In the structure of liabilities and owners' equity, the proportion of total deposits declined gradually from 92.5% in 2000 to 88.6% in 2011, while bonds and other forms of liabilities had increased, which perhaps reflected that there were more diverse sources of funds in the financial sector than in the past, but deposits remains the dominant position.

10.2.2 Simplification of Balance Sheet of Insurance Companies and Securities Companies

To consolidate the Balance Sheet of Insurance Companies into the Balance Sheet of Financial Institutions, it is necessary to simplify the balance sheet of insurance companies. That is, the Balance Sheet of Insurance Companies shown in Table 10.6 is simplified into the form as shown in Table 10.7.

As shown in the simplified Balance Sheet of Insurance Companies in Table 10.7, the Balance Sheet of Insurance Companies has also rapidly expanded, but compared with GDP, no tendency change has taken place in the sample period, and its size has significantly been affected by the financial market. The ratio of assets to GDP fluctuated between 9.5–8.5% in 2007–2011 and was 9.4% in 2007 and 8.9% in 2011. Due to the characteristics of businesses of insurance companies, securities and investments are the major form of assets, followed by claims and obligations among financial institutions. Both valuations are significantly affected by financial market fluctuations, so in the bearish stock and bond markets, such as the 2008 financial crisis, their size to GDP had shrunk significantly.

The Balance Sheet of Securities Companies (summary) as shown in Table 10.8 is simplified using the similar method, and the results are shown in Table 10.9.

As shown in the Simplified Balance Sheet of Securities Companies in Table 10.9, the Balance Sheet of Securities Companies has also rapidly expanded. Likewise, due to its business properties, its assets to GDP ratio has been significantly affected by the capital market and was 1.1% in 2008, lower than the average level in the sample period. From the perspective of internal assets structure, the ratio of claims and obligations of securities companies to other financial institutions to total assets decreased significantly in the sample period, but the ratio of marketable securities & investments to total assets increased significantly. This is also largely due to the impact of the fluctuations of the capital market. The valuation of claims and obligations was less affected by the fluctuations of the capital market, while the ratio of marketable securities & investments to total assets was more seriously affected and increased from 57% in 2008 to 79.7% in 2011 with the rebound of the capital market after 2008.

Table 10.6 2011 balance sheet of insurance companies (unit: 100 million yuan)

Assets	60138.1
Monetary funds	2770.75
Held-for-trading financial assets	978.85
Redemptory monetary capital for sale	243.91
Premiums receivable	445.04
Policy holder pledge loans	656.32
Loans	810.01
Time deposits	14280.14
Available-for-sale financial assets	16051.57
Held-to-maturity investment	14738.4
Long-term equity investment	885.06
Fixed assets	745.62
Liabilities and owner's equity	60138.1
Financial assets sold under agreements to repurchase	2965.26
Insurance protection fund	18.651
Claims payable	541.45
Policyholder dividends payable	935.67
Unearned premium reserves	2369.77
Outstanding claim reserves	2185.48
Life insurance reserves	33183.48
Long-term health insurance policyholders reserves	1349.36
Policyholder savings and investment funds	6028.47
Paid-in capital	2965.59
Capital reserves	505.59
Surplus reserves	127.87
Retained profits	622.27

Source CEIC

Table 10.7 Simplified balance sheet of insurance companies (unit: 100 million yuan)

	2007	2008	2009	2010	2011
Assets	24936.4	26941.41	31762.94	38400.72	42134.82
Claims and obligations on other financial institutions	5853.94	6385.95	8823.35	11406.31	14329.54
Marketable securities and investments	19253.24	20727.59	25324.66	30792.34	32653.88
Loans	736.74	552.58	1710.03	2161.39	1466.33
Other assets	−907.52	−724.71	−4095.1	−5959.32	−6314.93
Liabilities and owner's equity	24936.4	26941.41	31762.94	38400.72	42134.82
Insurance reserves	20986.62	25398.745	26621.88	32103.11	39106.741
Paid-in capital	1007.76	1297.2	1878.53	2065.76	2965.59
Others	2942.02	245.465	3262.53	4231.85	62.489

Source CEIC

Table 10.8 Balance sheet of securities companies in 2011 (unit: 100 million yuan)

Assets		Liabilities and owner's equity	
Monetary funds	7960.81	Short-term loans	0
Incl.: customer deposits	6008.49	Incl.: pledged loans	0
Customer credit funds deposits	44.59	Placements from banks and other financial institutions	3.9
Own credit funds deposits	26.77	Held-for-trading financial liabilities	0.61
Deposit reservation for balance	875.15	Derivative financial liabilities	13.19
Incl.: customer excess reserves	707.85	Financial assets sold under agreements to repurchase	1866.2
Credit reserve payment	16.87	Receivings from vicariously traded securities	6820.79
Loans to banks and other financial institutions	7.9	Deposit of acting sale of securities for credit transaction	44.48
Financial capital	376.56	Receivings from vicariously sold securities	2.65
Financial securities	6.45	Wages payable	195.54
Held-for-trading financial assets	2638.54	Taxes and dues payable	77.2
Incl.: asset-backed securities	30	Interests payable	6.6
Derivative financial assets	16.35	Estimated liabilities	4.59
Redemptory monetary capital for sale	430.95	Long-term loans	105.85
Interests receivable	63.8	Bonds payable	59.01
Refundable deposits	182.45	Deferred income tax liabilities	6.45
Incl.: trading deposits	157.39	Other liabilities	217.22
Performance deposits	12.23	Incl.: accounts payable	123.62
Available-for-sale financial assets	1588.23	Other accounts payable	20.81
Held-to-maturity investment	92.58	Agency payment bonds	3.29
Long-term equity investment	852.37	Total liabilities	9424.29
Investment properties	20.56	Paid in capital (or share capital)	2135.9
Fixed assets	293.35	Capital reserves	1704.53
Incl.: construction in progress	3744	Less: treasury stock	0

(continued)

Table 10.8 (continued)

Assets		Liabilities and owner's equity	
Intangible assets	60.66	Surplus reserves	380.53
Incl.: membership fees	1015	General risk provisions	393.9
Goodwill	6.65	Trading risk provisions	370.5
Deferred income tax assets	83.6	Retained profits	1312.88
Other assets	165.58	Converted difference in foreign currency statements	0
Incl.: accounts receivable of margin trading	0.61	Owner's equity	6298.25
Accounts receivables	92.12		
Dividend payable	3.25		
Debt assets	1.94		
Vicariously cashed bonds	0.6		

Source DRCnet

Table 10.9 Simplified balance sheet of securities companies (unit: 100 million yuan)

	2008	2009	2010	2011
Assets	3584.9	4840.39	5675.04	6298.87
Claims and obligations of securities companies to other financial institutions	1713.37	1993.48	2131.29	1212.4
Marketable securities & investments	2053.92	3249.09	3960.57	5022.83
Other assets	−182.39	−402.18	−416.82	63.64
Liabilities and owner's equity	3584.9	4840.39	5675.04	6298.87
Paid-in capital	1640.85	1716.85	1891.95	2135.9
Others	1592.02	2709.67	3378.08	3769.85

Sources Infobank and DRCnet

10.2.3 Incorporating the Simplified Balance Sheet of Insurance Companies and the Simplified Balance Sheet of Securities Companies into the Balance Sheet of Financial Institutions

To incorporate the Simplified Balance Sheet of Insurance Companies into the Balance Sheet of Financial Institutions, we will continue to convert the Simplified Balance Sheet of Insurance Companies into the Survey of Insurance Companies as shown in Table 10.10, including: (1) the items of marketable securities & investments, loans, insurance reserves and paid-in capital of the Simplified Balance Sheet of Insurance Companies are incorporated into the corresponding items of the Survey of Insurance Companies; (2) the assets item of the Survey of Insurance Companies is obtained by adding marketable securities & investments and loans in the same table; (3) the item of "Other Items (Net)" of the Survey of Insurance Companies is obtained by subtracting "Assets & Obligations Among Financial Institutions" and "Other Assets" from the item of "Other Assets" in the Simplified Balance Sheet of Insurance Companies.

Table 10.10 Survey of insurance companies (unit: 100 million yuan)

	2007	2008	2009	2010	2011
Assets	19989.98	21280.17	27034.69	32953.73	34120.21
Marketable securities and investments	19253.24	20727.59	25324.66	30792.34	32653.88
Loans	736.74	552.58	1710.03	2161.39	1466.33
Liabilities and owner's equity	19989.98	21280.17	27034.69	32953.73	34120.21
Insurance reserves	20986.62	25398.745	26621.88	32103.11	39106.741
Paid-up capital	1007.76	1297.2	1878.53	2065.76	2965.59
Other items (net)	−2004.4	−5415.775	−1465.72	−1215.14	−7952.121

Source CEIC

Table 10.11 Survey of securities companies (unit: 100 million yuan)

	2008	2009	2010	2011
Assets	2053.92	3249.09	3960.57	5022.83
Marketable securities and investments	2053.92	3249.09	3960.57	5022.83
Liabilities and owner's equity	2053.92	3249.09	3960.57	5022.83
Paid-up capital	1640.85	1716.85	1891.95	2135.9
Other items (net)	413.07	1532.24	2068.62	2886.93

Source Infobank

Likewise, to incorporate the Simplified Balance Sheet of Securities Companies into the Balance Sheet of Financial Institutions, we will continue to convert the Simplified Balance Sheet of Securities Companies into the Survey of Securities Companies as in Table 10.11, and the method is summarized as follows: (1) the items of "Marketable Securities & Investment" and "Paid-in Capital" in the Simplified Balance Sheet of Securities Companies are incorporated into the corresponding items of the Survey of Securities Companies; (2) the "Assets" item of the Survey of Securities Companies is the item of Marketable Securities & Investments of the same table; (3) the item of "Other Items (Net)" of the Survey of Securities Companies is obtained by subtracting "Assets & Obligations among Financial Institutions" and "Other Assets" from the item of "Other Assets" in the Simplified Balance Sheet of Securities Companies.

The items of the Survey of Insurance Companies and the Survey of Securities Companies are incorporated into the Balance Sheet of Financial Institutions as shown in Table 10.5 to form the Balance Sheet of Financial Institutions Including Insurance Companies and Securities Companies as shown in Table 10.12. It should be noted that this table is not always comparable: (1) the balance sheets for 2000–2006 typically contained only the data of the central bank, commercial banks, trust and investment companies, leasing companies and auto finance companies, and the statistical scope of financial institutions was often adjusted; (2) the data of insurance companies were added for 2007 and onwards; (3) the data of securities companies were added for 2008 and onwards; (4) the paid-up capital data of trust and investment companies were listed separately for 2010 and onwards.

10.2.4 Shadow Banking and Financial Sector Balance Sheets

In recent years, the financing structure of the Chinese society has undergone some changes, which are mainly reflected in two aspects:

First, in the total social financing, the proportion of indirect financing (traditional bank loans) is decreasing, while the proportion of direct financing is increasing. Particularly, the proportion of bond financing is increasing significantly.

Table 10.12 Balance sheet of financial institutions including insurance companies and securities companies (unit: 100 million yuan)

	2000	2001	2002	2003	2004	2005	2006	2007	2008	2009	2010	2011
Assets	133,902	154,294	182,442	225,313	262,740	302,043	365,230	474,258	561,740	712,159	842,793	952,369
Total loans	99,371	112,315	131,294	158,996	178,198	194,690	225,347	262,428	303,947	401,395	481,357	549,413
Securities and other investments	19,651	23,113	26,790	30,259	30,931	34,942	39,491	82,043	88,083	115,217	133,279	146,981
Position for bullion & silver purchase	12	256	337	337	337	337	337	337	337	670	670	670
Position for forex purchase	14,291	17,856	23,223	34,847	52,591	71,211	98,980	128,377	168,431	193,112	225,795	253,587
Assets with international financial institutions	576	754	798	873	683	862	1075	1073	941	1765	1693	1719
Liabilities and owner's equity	133,902	154,294	182,442	225,313	262,740	302,043	365,230	474,258	561,740	712,159	842,793	952,369
Total deposits	123,804	143,617	170,917	208,056	241,424	287,170	335,460	389,371	466,203	597,741	718,238	809,368
Financial Bonds	30	51	90	2226	3955	5673	6483	11,505	20,852	16,203	13,527	10,039
Cash in circulation	14,653	15,689	17,278	19,746	21,468	24,032	27,073	30,334	34,219	38,246	44,628	50,748
Liabilities to international financial institutions	368	485	423	483	562	642	926	947	733	762	720	776
Insurance reserves	0	0	0	0	0	0	0	20,987	25,399	26,622	32,103	39,107
Paid-in capital	7397	7660	8772	10,729	11,750	10,576	13,101	18,425	21,751	23,071	27,245	29,513
Other items (net)	−12,351	−13,208	−15,039	−15,926	−16,420	−26,049	−17,813	2689	−7417	9513	6332	12,817

Data source CEIC, Infobank and DRCnet

The proportion of new loans in total social financing was 58.2% in 2011 and decreased 6.1 to 52.1% in 2012 and further decreased in the first quarter of 2013 to 44.7%, up 18.6% on a year on year basis. The proportion of corporate bond financing in total social financing was 10.6% in 2011, up 2.7% over 2010, and 14.3% in 2012, up 3.7% over 2011, and further increased in the first quarter of 2013 to 12.2%, up 2% on a year on year basis.

Second, the financial intermediation activities outside the traditional banking system have developed rapidly, and the off-balance-sheet financing of the real economy has increased significantly.

In 2011, the off-balance-sheet financing of the real economy through trust loans, entrusted loans and banker's acceptance bills accounted for 19.7% of total social financing, and its ratio to on-balance-sheet RMB loans in the same period was 33.8%. In 2012, the proportion of off-balance-sheet financing in total social financing rose to 23%, and its ratio to on-balance-sheet loans rose to 44.1%. In the first quarter of 2013, these two ratios further increased to 32.8 and 73.2% respectively.

What should be emphasized here is that the changes in the financing structure of the Chinese society, especially the rapid development of the shadow banking sector, make it complicated to prepare the financial sector balance sheet.

The FSB has defined shadow banking as "credit intermediation involving entities and activities (fully or partly) outside the regular banking system". According to this definition, the size of shadow banking is in fact the aggregate alternative monetary assets except bank money. The FSB also suggested that the government departments only strengthen supervision and risk control over those shadow banking activities where maturity/liquidity transformation and/or flawed credit risk transfer and/or leverage create important risks. This actually constitutes a narrow definition of shadow banking. Just as the *China Financial Supervision And Regulation Report 2013* issued by the Research Center for Financial Law and Regulation of the Chinese Academy of Social Sciences (2013) states, theorists or practitioners have different views on the definition of China's shadow banking system. In the narrowest scope, shadow banking includes only the two types of bank wealth management business and trust companies. In more large scope, it includes the narrowest scope, accounting companies, auto financial companies, financial leasing companies, consumer financial companies and other non-bank financial institutions. In the broad scope, it includes the narrow scope, interbank business, entrusted loans and other off-balance-sheet businesses, financing guarantee companies, micro lending companies, pawn shops and other non-bank financial institutions. In the broadest scope, it includes the broad scope and private lending. The report concluded that even in the narrowest scope, by the end of 2012 China had a huge shadow banking system, reaching 14.6 trillion yuan (based on the official data) or 20.5 trillion yuan (based on the market data). The former accounted for 29% of GDP and 11% of total banking assets, and the latter accounted for 40% of GDP and 16% of total banking assets. However, this estimation method has two major problems: first, there is no rigorous analysis of the relationship between financial institutions and businesses and credit expansion and liquidity creation, and there is considerable arbitrariness in calculation of shadow banking; second, there may exist overlapped calculation. In this book, the problem of overlapped calculation has been improved. In our view, China's shadow banking includes the two parts of wealth management products of financial institutions and informal financing. Among them, wealth management products of financial institutions (including the central bank, commercial banks, trust and investment companies, financial leasing companies and auto financing companies) consist of call deposits and margin deposits from enterprises, margin deposits and structured deposits of individuals, temporary deposits and other deposits, and its size reached nearly 9 trillion yuan at the end of 2011, which was close to the IMF's estimate (8–9 trillion yuan) (2012).[2] Obviously, these deposits and other deposits are mostly wealth management products created by financial institutions to circumvent interest rate control. Another estimate of informal financing was also quoted from the IMF (2012). IMF (2012) considered that as of the third quarter of 2012, China's informal financing accounted for 6–8% of GDP. We chose the highest value of 8% and multiplied it by the GDP of China in 2011 (about 47 trillion yuan) to get the informal financing of about 3.76 trillion yuan. On the whole, the size of shadow banking in China in 2011 was about 12.73 trillion yuan, accounting for 13.94% of total assets of financial institutions and about 1/4 of the GDP.

So far, there are many estimates on the size of shadow banking there are many, and the results are quite different. Here we could not expect to give a precise estimate, but what we should emphasize is that is very difficult to include the shadow banking sector into the financial sector balance sheet. This is because there are also assets and liabilities in shadow banks. For example, wealth management products reflect the liabilities of financial institutions, and trust loans and entrusted loans reflect the assets of financial institutions. Although it is theoretically feasible to break down the components of shadow banking into the items of "Assets" and "Liabilities" and include them into the financial sector balance sheets, but in practice, it would be very complicated and yet difficult to achieve. But even so, when we are talking about the financial sector balance sheets, we should not forget this important "dark matter" of shadow banking.

10.3 Appendix of This Chapter: Calculation Scope

If the transactions of financial institutions are divided into three categories, namely financial transactions of the financial sector and the real sector, real transactions of the financial sector and the real sector, and financial transactions within the financial sector, then there are three estimation methods for the preparation of balance sheet of financial institutions based on the scope of statistics: (1) the narrow scope method: this estimation method only carries out statistics of transactions of the

[2]The time for the estimate of the IMF (2012) is up to the end of third quarter of 2012.

financial sector and the real sector, while the real transactions of the financial sector and the financial transactions within the financial sector are excluded; (2) the medium scope method: this estimation method only excludes the financial transactions within the financial sector; and (3) the wide scope method: this estimation method covers all the three major categories of transactions of financial institutions. Obviously, the narrow scope method is used in this book for the preparation of balance sheet of financial institutions.

As the net value method is used to exclude the influence of related transactions, there is a close link between the three kinds of estimation methods for the balance sheet of financial institutions. Compared with the narrow scope method, the balance sheet of financial institutions prepared based on the medium scope method only lists other assets and other liabilities separately (including other capital items) but dose not calculate their net worth. In contrast, in the narrow scope method, other assets and other liabilities are included into other items (net). The balance sheet of financial institutions prepared based on the broad scope method further lists claims and obligations among financial institutions separately but does not calculate their net worth. In contrast, in the narrow scope method, the claims and obligations among financial institutions are included into other items (net) as net worth.

For different research purposes, different methods can be selected for the preparation of balance sheet of financial institutions. In view of the special nature of financial institutions as intermediaries, there is little influence on real transactions of the financial sector and the real sector, so there is little difference between the narrow scope method and the medium scope method. Therefore, in practical studies, the narrow and broad scope estimation methods are mostly used. The broad scope method was used by Cao and Ma (2012) in their study.[3] The narrow scope method is used in the DCS and *Sources of Credit Funds of Financial Institutions in RMB* prepared by the People's Bank of China and the Balance Sheet of Financial Institutions prepared in this book. As other net liabilities and other net assets are positive real numbers with a modest absolute value, the aggregate net value of claims and obligations among financial institutions is in theory close to zero, which results in a great difference between the results of the narrow and broad scope estimation methods. In 2011, for example, the total assets of the central bank and commercial banks estimated by the broad scope method is 141.88 trillion yuan, but it is merely 95 trillion yuan estimated by the narrow scope method, with a difference of up to 46.88 trillion yuan and the latter being nearly one-third less than the former.[4] From a purely technical perspective of preparation of national balance

[3]Cao and Ma: "Asking Advice for the National Balance Sheet", Finance, June 2012.

[4]The total assets of the central bank and commercial banks estimated using the broad scope method are obtained by adding up the total assets of Table 10.2. Balance Sheet of Depositary Corporations and Table 10.3 Balance Sheet of Monetary Authorities, and the total assets of the central bank and commercial banks estimated using the narrow scope method are obtained by adding up the foreign assets and domestic claims of Table 10.1. Depositary Corporations Survey plus the external liabilities of the central bank and commercial banks provided in Tables 10.2 and 10.3.

sheet, the balance sheet of financial institutions prepared using the broad scope method seems to be more reasonable. Strictly speaking, the DCS and *Sources of Credit Funds of Financial Institutions in RMB* prepared by the People's Bank of China and the Balance Sheet of Financial Institutions prepared in this book should belong to degraded balance sheets, in which some balance sheet information is not available. However, the Balance Sheet of Financial Institutions prepared using the narrow scope method not only highlights the nature of financial institutions as intermediaries, but also makes it convenient to focus on the analysis of financing services provided by the financial sector to the real sector. Therefore, we have selected the narrow scope estimation method in this book. In short, different estimation methods for preparing the financial sector balance sheet can corroborate each other and more fully reflect the mutual influence of the financial sector and the real sector.

Chapter 11
Central Bank Balance Sheet

As shown in Table 11.1, China central Bank Balance Sheet consists of two primary items: assets and liabilities, each of which has the following two secondary items. The assets and liabilities and their structural changes of the central bank in China over the years are analyzed as follows.

The item of "Liabilities" records the sources of funds of the central bank, the item of "Assets" records the uses and allocation of funds, and "Assets = Liabilities" shows the funds acquired by the central bank should be fully reflected in the uses of "Assets". If the liability side reflects that the central bank implements the monetary policies and influences the amount and flow of funds of commercial banks and other financial institutions and financial markets through taking on the debt, then the asset side reflects that the central bank implements the monetary policy intentions and adjusts the amount of money of commercial banks and other financial institutions and financial markets through the exercise of its rights as a creditor.[1]

11.1 Assets Item and Its Structural Changes

Table 11.2 shows that the size of assets in the central bank balance sheet increased rapidly during 1999–2012. The central bank's total assets increased from 3.92 trillion yuan in 1999 to 29.45 trillion yuan in 2012, an increase of 6.5 times in 13 years, with an average annual growth rate of up to 16.8%, higher than the growth rate of nominal GDP over the same period. This has led to gradual increase of the assets to GDP ratio of China's central bank (see Fig. 11.1). In 1985, the central bank's assets to GDP ratio was 30.27%, while the ratio reached 63.83% in 2010. The ratio maintained stable during 1985–2002 but increased rapidly after 2003 and decreased in 2011. The size of currency and assets of the central bank in

[1]Guogang (2010).

Y. Li and X. Zhang, *China's National Balance Sheet*, China Insights,
DOI 10.1007/978-981-10-4385-7_11

Table 11.1 China central bank balance sheet (subject setting)

Assets	Liabilities
Foreign assets	Reserve money (M1)
Foreign exchanges	Currency issue (M0)
Monetary gold	Deposits of financial corporations
Other foreign assets	Deposits of other depository corporations
Claims on government	Deposits of other financial corporations
Incl.: the central government	Deposits of financial corporations excluded from reserve money
Claims on other depository corporations	Bonds issue
Claims on other financial corporations	External liabilities
Claims on non-financial sectors	Government deposits
Other assets	Funds owned by bank
	Other liabilities
Total assets	Total liabilities

Source The Monetary Authorities and the *Balance Sheet* in 2008 prepared by the People's Bank of China

China have expanded rapidly, in respect of which the problems of so-called "money loss" and "excess liquidity" have aroused widespread concern.

Meanwhile, each sub-item of assets exhibits different variation characteristics. In the paragraphs below, we will analyze the size of each sub-item of assets and the characteristics of their structural changes and explore the causes behind.

11.1.1 Rapid Increase in Foreign Assets and Its Ratio to Total Assets

(1) In the central bank's asset structure, the ratio of foreign assets to total assets is highest and maintains a rapidly growing trend. This ratio increased from 36.91% in 1999 to 81.96% in 2012.
(2) Foreign exchange is a main form of allocation of foreign assets. The foreign exchange reserves held by the central bank amounted to 1.41 trillion yuan in 1999 and soared to 23.67 trillion yuan in 2012. Its ratio to total assets rose from 35.9% in 1999 to 80.35% in 2012. The economic background behind the substantial increase in forex reserves was the enormous surplus of "Goods", "Current Transfers", "Capital Account" and "Financial Account" in the balance of international payments and huge foreign currency inflows to China. As a country with a sovereign currency, foreign currencies are banned from circulation in China, so foreign exchange earnings of enterprises and individuals can

Table 11.2 The Assets of China central bank balance sheet during 1999–2012 (Unit: 100 million yuan)

Time	Foreign assets				Claims on government	Claims on other depository corporations	Claims on other financial corporations	Claims on non-financial sectors	Other assets	Total assets
	Total	Foreign exchange	Monetary gold	Other foreign assets						
1999	14,459	14,061	12	385	1583	15,374	3833	102		39,172
2000	15,583	14,815	12	756	1583	13,519	8600	110		43,930
2001	19,860	18,850	256	754	2821	11,312	8547			48,435
2002	23,243	22,107	337	798	2864	12,288	7240	207	5266	51,108
2003	31,142	29,842	337	963	2901	11,983	7256	206	8516	62,004
2004	46,960	45,940	337	683	2970	10,424	8865	136	9300	78,655
2005	63,339	62,140	337	862	2892	12,692	13,226	67	11,460	103,676
2006	85,773	84,361	337	1075	2856	6517	21,950	66	11,413	128,575
2007	124,825	115,169	337	9319	16,318	7863	12,972	64	7098	169,140
2008	162,544	149,624	337	12,582	16,196	8433	11,853	44	8027	207,096
2009	185,333	175,155	670	9509	15,662	7162	11,530	44	7804	227,535
2010.6	198,356	188,704	670	8983	15,621	8967	11,499	44	8446	242,932
2010.12	215,420	206,767	670	7983	15,421	9486	11,326	25	7598	259,275
2011.6	234,698	226,387	670	7641	15,405	9678	11,254	25	7019	278,079
2011.9	241,201	233,854	670	6677	15,400	9557	11,245	25	7485	284,912
2011.12	237,898	232,389	670	4839	15,400	10,248	10,644	25	6763	280,978
2012.3	240,695	235,800	670	4225	15,349	10,552	10,635	25	6767	284,022
2012.6	239,978	235,190	670	4119	15,349	13,304	10,625	25	6790	286,071
2012.9	240,191	235,297	670	4224	15,314	17,902	10,234	25	5993	289,658
2012.12	241,417	236,670	670	4077	15,314	16,701	10,039	25	11,042	294,537

Note The data in the table are acquired from the website of the People's Bank of China

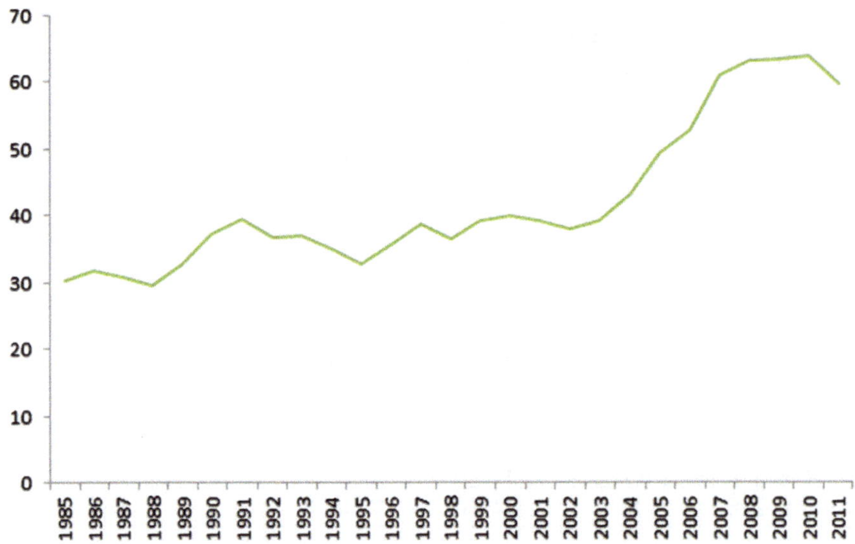

Fig. 11.1 Assets to GDP ratio of the central bank during 1985–2011

only be sold to the designated foreign exchange banks, the designated foreign exchange banks will then sell the portion beyond the position limit stipulated by the State Administration of Foreign Exchange in the interbank foreign exchange market, and the major buyer is the central bank. In this way, the state foreign exchange reserves are formed. In the past, in order to accumulate foreign exchange reserves, China had implemented a mandatory banking forex settlement and sale system. Presently, China has canceled the mandatory forex settlement and sale system, so enterprises and individuals can keep their foreign exchange earnings freely. As the double surpluses have brought huge foreign exchange assets, the central bank needs to use RMB to buy foreign currencies in the market, thus forming the inherent requirement for balance sheet expansion of the central bank. This mechanism is largely reflected in the central bank's position for forex purchase. The increase of foreign exchange on the asset side of balance sheet also corresponds at the same time to the money supply on the liability side.

(3) The item of "Monetary Gold" also increased significantly in the study period, but the absolute amount was low. According to the data published by the World Gold Council, as of 2012, China's official holdings of gold reserves totaled 1054 tons, making China the world's sixth largest holder of official gold reserve. Many researchers believe that this is not commensurate with the position of China as the second largest economy in the world and thus consider that there are some problems with the asset structure of China's central bank. In this regard, it should be noted that for many countries holding a large amount of gold reserves, such as the United States and Germany, their currencies are

international currencies, and their demands for foreign exchange reserves are relatively small. For example, the United States basically needs not hold other currency reserves, so it can hold a large amount of gold reserves.[2] But RMB is currently not an international currency, so it needs to keep more foreign exchange reserves to meet the transaction payment function and has correspondingly less demand for gold. Currently, the central bank's gold reserves mainly come from domestic gold mining acquisitions.

(4) Other foreign assets are mainly special drawing rights (SDR) of the IMF. China's SDRs have been very stable and increased by 5.997 billion yuan or about $9.296 billion only in 2008. In August 2007, to ease the pressure of excess liquidity due to foreign exchange payment, China's central bank requires commercial banks to pay the deposit reserves for RMB deposits with foreign exchanges. This portion of foreign exchange funds is accounted into the item of other foreign assets, resulting in the surge of the item in late 2007, and its ratio to total assets increased from 0.84% in 2006 to 5.51%. The ratio of other foreign assets to total assets declined after 2007 and reached 1.38% in 2012.

11.1.2 Claims on Government Expanded Substantially in 2007 and Basically Maintained Stable in the Remaining Time

Claims on government mainly include loans and overdrafts to government as well as government bonds. During 1999–2006, the balance of the item kept stable at 200 billion yuan, but increased sharply to more than 1.5 trillion in August 2007, and its ratio to total assets also increase from 2.2% in 2006 to 9.65% by the end of 2007. The main reason for the change is that the Ministry of Finance issued 1.55 trillion yuan worth of special government bonds in 2007, and the majority of funds raised were used to purchase foreign exchange from the central bank as the capital of China Investment Corporation. This reflected in the balance sheet of monetary authorities is the transfer of the corresponding amount of foreign exchange reserves to claims on government, resulting in a sharp increase of claims on government to total assets ratio to 9.65% that year. Claims on government had decreased since 2007 and reached 5.2% at the end of 2012.

Except for this portion of special government bonds, the central bank's claims on government mainly include two parts. First, financial overdraft. That is, the central bank and the Ministry of Finance negotiated on an overdraft amount and duration and directly credited it to the government's deposit account in the central bank and formed the government's liabilities to the central bank. This means the potential

[2]The gold reserves of the United States amounted to 8133.5 tons in January 2012.

increase in base money supply, but this method was ceased in China in 1994. Second, buying government bonds through open market operations. If the central bank purchases government bonds from the financial institutions, then the deposit accounts of the financial institutions in the central bank will increase equivalently, the total amount of base money will increase and money supply will expand. If the central bank purchases government bonds from the public, then the central bank will issue a check with an equivalent value to the trader and the trader can deposit the check into the depositary bank, the depositary bank will then hand over it to the central bank for payment, so the bank's deposit reserves and the base money supply will increase. If the operation is carried out in reverse direction, then money supply will be tightened.

11.1.3 Claims on Other Depository Corporations Remained Stable and Its Ratio to Total Assets Decreased

Claims on other depository corporations remained stable on the whole and amounted to 1.5 trillion yuan in 1999 and 1.67 trillion yuan in 2012 and was at a relatively low level in the middle of the study period. Its ratio to total assets was showing a downward trend and was 39.25% in 1999 and declined to 5.67% in 2012.

Claims on other depository corporations mainly reflect the central bank's re-lendings to commercial banks (based on different patterns of relending, re-lendings are divided into credit and rediscount relendings). Relending is a quantitative monetary policy instrument that is always planned ahead and characterized by administrativeness, passivity and low flexibility. Re-lending was once a main monetary policy tool of the central bank. After the People's Bank of China specially exercised the functions of the central bank in 1984, the credit fund management system characterized by "unified planning, division of funds, actual loans and deposits and mutual intermediation" was implemented. Under the former debit balance planning system, the People's Bank of China approved the borrowing bases for all specialized banks, thus laying the foundation that the central bank regulated the monetary base by relending. Over the next decade (1984–1993), re-lending became the most important channel for the central bank to adjust the monetary base and accounted for 70–90% of total monetary base supply. China's National Financial Work Conference in 1993 decided to reform the credit fund allocation system and reclaimed the right of all the branches of the People's Bank of China to adjust the size of re-lendings, and the main re-lending task of all branches was shifted to granting short-term funds to address the short-term position shortage of commercial banks. In 1998, the People's Bank of China canceled the mandatory plans for the size of loans of commercial banks, marking that re-lending started to become a real instrument for indirect regulation, and its position in the monetary policy regulation was decreasing.

Presently, the central bank's re-lending mainly plays the role of adjusting the position shortage of commercial banks and acts as the final lender by relending. After the 1998 Asian financial crisis and the 2007 financial crisis, its claims on other depository corporations have significantly increased, reflecting the role and status of the re-lending mechanism.

11.1.4 Claims on Other Financial Corporations Grew Rapidly for a Few Years, but Its Ratio to Total Assets Declined

Claims on other financial corporations increased in amount, especially in 1999–2006. However, its ratio to total assets decreased from 9.8% in 1999 to 3.41% in 2012.

Claims on other financial corporations mainly include the central bank's credit loans to other financial institutions such as asset management companies, trust and investment companies issued credit and bond repurchases. During 1999–2005, the central bank re-lent more than 1.2 trillion yuan to the four asset management companies of Cinda, Great Wall, Huarong and Orient Fund for acquisition of non-performing assets of state-owned commercial banks, leading to a substantial increase of claims on other financial corporations, and its ratio to total assets increased from 9.8% in 1999 from to 17.07% in 2006, but its size had shrunk continuously since 2007 and its ratio declined to 3.41% in 2012.

11.1.5 Claims on Non-financial Sectors are Relatively Small in Size and Its Ratio has been Declining

Claims on non-financial sectors declined from 10.15 billion yuan in 1999 to 2.5 billion yuan in 2012, and its ratio to total assets reached 0.26% in 1999 and up to 0.4% in 2002, but fell to 0.01% in 2012. Claims on non-financial sectors take a relatively small proportion in total assets.

11.1.6 Other Assets Remained Stable in Size, and Its Ratio to Total Assets Maintains a Downward Trend on the Whole

Other assets mainly include the collection trusted by the central bank and fixed assets, its size maintained at 500–1.2 trillion yuan, and its ratio to total assets of the central bank maintained a downward trend and was 3.75% in 2012.

Table 11.3 Assets structure of China Central Bank Balance Sheet in 1999–2012

Time	Foreign assets				Claims on government	Claims on other depository corporations (%)	Claims on other financial corporations (%)	Claims on other non-financial sectors (%)	Other assets (%)	Total assets (%)
	Total (%)	Forex (%)	Monetary gold (%)	Other foreign assets (%)						
1999	36.91	35.90	0.03	0.98	4.04	39.25	9.79	0.26		100
2000	35.47	33.72	0.03	1.72	3.60	30.77	19.58	0.25		100
2001	41.00	38.92	0.53	1.56	5.83	23.35	17.65			100
2002	45.48	43.26	0.66	1.56	5.60	24.04	14.17	0.40	10.30	100
2003	50.23	48.13	0.54	1.55	4.68	19.33	11.70	0.33	13.73	100
2004	59.70	58.41	0.43	0.87	3.78	13.25	11.27	0.17	11.82	100
2005	61.09	59.94	0.33	0.83	2.79	12.24	12.76	0.06	11.05	100
2006	66.71	65.61	0.26	0.84	2.22	5.07	17.07	0.05	8.88	100
2007	73.80	68.09	0.20	5.51	9.65	4.65	7.67	0.04	4.20	100
2008	78.49	72.25	0.16	6.08	7.82	4.07	5.72	0.02	3.88	100
2009	81.45	76.98	0.29	4.18	6.88	3.15	5.07	0.02	3.43	100
2010.6	81.65	77.68	0.28	3.70	6.43	3.69	4.73	0.02	3.48	100
2010.12	83.09	79.75	0.26	3.08	5.95	3.66	4.37	0.01	2.93	100
2011.6	84.40	81.41	0.24	2.75	5.54	3.48	4.05	0.01	2.52	100
2011.9	84.66	82.08	0.24	2.34	5.41	3.35	3.95	0.01	2.63	100
2011.12	84.67	82.71	0.24	1.72	5.48	3.65	3.79	0.01	2.41	100
2012.3	84.74	83.02	0.24	1.49	5.40	3.72	3.74	0.01	2.38	100
2012.6	83.89	82.21	0.23	1.44	5.37	4.65	3.71	0.01	2.37	100
2012.9	82.92	81.23	0.23	1.46	5.29	6.18	3.53	0.01	2.07	100
2012.12	81.96	80.35	0.23	1.38	5.20	5.67	3.41	0.01	3.75	100

Note The data in the table are from the website of by the People's Bank of China

As shown on the asset side of the central bank balance sheet, the central bank mainly controls the monetary base through the following channels. (1) Re-lending by the central bank to financial institutions. The central bank mainly controls the size and interest rate of credit loans and rediscounts. (2) Holding claims on government. This can be achieved by buying and selling bonds through open market operations. (3) Changing international reserves. The central bank can buy and sell foreign currencies in the foreign exchange market to affect the monetary base. (4) Changing net loans to other sectors. These transactions mainly include re-lending, rediscount, open market operations and foreign exchange market intervention. They are main ways for the central bank to implement macro-control, and any operation represents the change in the corresponding assets and at the same time means equivalence change in the monetary base (Table 11.3).

11.2 Liabilities Item and Its Structural Changes

The change in the amount and structure of liabilities of the central bank is mainly a reflection of the central bank's monetary policy direction and the results of regulation. For example, under the loose monetary policy conditions, the "Currency Issue" in the liabilities of the central bank will increase, but the "Deposits of Depositary Financial Institutions" will decrease. For example, under the tight monetary policy conditions, the "Currency Issue" in the liabilities of the central bank will decrease, but the "Deposits of Depositary Financial Institutions" will increase. Thus, the changes in the liabilities of the central bank reflect the trend of monetary policy and the central bank's regulation ability.

The liabilities structure of China Central Bank Balance Sheet during 1999–2012 is shown in Table 11.4. As the total assets and total liabilities of central bank balance sheet follow the accounting equation, i.e. total liabilities = total assets, the liabilities of the central bank had also grown rapidly since 1999 at a rate higher than the nominal growth rate of GDP in the same period.

In the following paragraphs, we will analyze the sub-items of liabilities of the balance sheet and their structural changes to explore the reasons behind: **the total liabilities of the central bank grew rapidly and reserve money took a dominant position**.

During 1999–2012, the central bank's total liabilities increased from 3.92 trillion yuan in 1999 increased to 29.5 trillion yuan in 2012. Among all items, reserve money took a dominant position, and the total amount of reserve money increased from 3.4 trillion yuan in 1999 to 25.2 trillion yuan in 2012. Reserve money accounted for 85.85% of total liabilities in 1999, and its proportion in total liabilities was at the lowest level of 60.04% in 2007 and was 85.68% in 2012.

Reserve money includes the two items of currency issue and deposits of financial corporations. In the early study period, both basically remained equal in size. In 1999, currency issue and deposits of financial corporations were 1.5 and 1.47 trillion yuan respectively. But later the deposits of financial corporations had a

Table 11.4 Liabilities structure of China Central Bank Balance Sheet during 1999–2012 (100 million yuan)

Time	Reserve money			Deposits of financial corporations excluded from reserve money	Bonds issue	External liabilities	Deposits of government	Own capital	Other liabilities	Total liabilities
	Total	Currency issue	Deposits of financial corporations							
1999	33,620	15,070	14,729	3822	119		1786	367	−541	39,172
2000	36,491	15,938	16,019	4534			3100	357	−553	43,930
2001	39,852	16,869	17,089	5894			2850	355	−517	48,435
2002	45,138	18,589	19,138	7411	1488	423	3085	220	754	51,108
2003	52,841	21,240	22,558	9043	3032	483	4955	220	474	62,004
2004	58,856	23,104	35,673	79	11,079	562	5832	220	2106	78,655
2005	64,343	25,854	38,391	98	20,296	642	7527	220	10,648	103,676
2006	77,758	29,139	48,459	160	29,741	926	10,211	220	9720	128,575
2007	101,545	32,972	68,416	158	34,469	947	17,121	220	14,837	169,140
2008	129,222	37,116	92,107	591	45,780	733	16,964	220	13,586	207,096
2009	143,985	41,556	102,429	625	42,064	762	21,226	220	18,653	227,535
2010.6	154,235	42,567	111,668	612	46,975	719	31,023	220	9148	242,932
2010.12	185,311	48,646	136,665	657	40,497	720	24,277	220	7592	259,275
2011.6	203,470	48,816	154,654	803	27,266	4866	34,542	220	6912	278,079
2011.9	212,204	52,203	160,001	861	22,451	4672	35,712	220	8793	284,912
2011.12	224,642	55,850	168,792	908	23,337	2699	22,734	220	6438	280,978
2012.3	226,684	54,379	172,306	1107	21,440	1847	23,085	220	9640	284,022
2012.6	228,051	54,294	173,757	1182	18,691	1097	27,550	220	9280	286,071
2012.9	236,033	59,178	176,855	1297	17,464	1242	28,149	220	5254	289,658
2012.12	252,345	60,646	191,699	1349	13,880	1464	20,753	220	4526	294,537

Note The data in the table are from the website of by the People's Bank of China

significantly higher growth rate and increased to 19.17 trillion yuan in 2012, while over the same period, the currency issue was only 6.06 trillion yuan. Therefore, the deposits of financial corporations rather than currency issue mainly accounted for the rapid growth in reserve money. In "Reserve Money", the increase or decrease of "Currency Issue" means the ease or tightness of monetary policy, while the increase or decrease of "Deposits of Financial Corporations" means the tightness and ease of monetary policy. Both have opposite monetary policy directions and effects. As far as this is concerned, the monetary policies after 2004 belonged to the tight monetary policies. Thus, it can be judged that over the past 13 years, the People's Bank of China primarily adjusted the debt capital and implemented the monetary policy intentions through "Currency Issue", but obtained capital through financial operation of "Deposits of Financial Corporations", so in this regard, the monetary policies were not easy in this period (Guogan 2012).

Reserve money is actually commonly called the monetary base in currency theory. Currency issue is cash issue, and deposits of financial corporations include required reserves and excess reserves of commercial banks. Deposits of other non-financial institutions in reserve money include deposits of government agencies and organizations, postal savings and so on. The monetary base will eventually form the cash in the hands of people, vault cash in commercial banks and reserve deposits of commercial banks at the central bank. In the central bank balance sheet, the supply of monetary base is reflected by increase of "Reserve Money" under the item of "Liabilities" (M1). Among them, "Currency Issue" shows the amount of cash supply (M0).

During 1999–2012, China's currency issue grew by 11.3% year on year, close to the GDP growth rate, and currency issue and economic development remained basically coordinated. Meanwhile, the central bank controlled the size of reserves of financial institutions at the central bank by adjusting deposit reserves. In 1999, to cope with the Asian financial crisis, China once lowered the reserve ratio to 6%, and later the deposit reserve ratio gradually increased from 6% to up to 21% in 2011 and 19.5% at the end of 2012. The adjustment of deposit reserve ratio has played an important role for the central bank to drain excess liquidity and also led to a sharp increase of financial corporations' deposits at the central bank. If 19.5% of the reserve ratio in 2012 was adjusted to 6%, then the amount of reserves at the end of 2012 would be reduced to 5.9 trillion, which is basically equal to the currency issue of 6.06 trillion.

11.2.1 The Size of Bond Issue and Its Ratio to Total Liabilities Increased and then Decreased

The size of bond issue and its ratio to total liabilities increased and then decreased, a total of 11.89 billion yuan worth of bonds were issued in 1999, this figure reached its highest level of 4.7 trillion yuan in June 2010 and later decreased continuously to 1.4 trillion yuan in 2012, and its ratio to total liabilities increased from 0.3% in 1999 to its highest level of 23.13% in 2006 and later decreased to 4.71% in 2012.

The particularity of central bank bond as special financial bond lies in short maturity period and strong controllability. It is a debt obligation issued to financial institutions to regulate the liquidity of financial institutions. When a central bank bond is used, the monetary base is drained, and when it is mature, the monetary base is supplied. In monetary policy regulation in many developing countries, the financial markets, particularly the bond markets, are underdeveloped, so central bank bonds tend to become the main instrument for open market operations, and this has become an important purpose for central bank bond issuance. The central bank bonds issued by the People's Bank of China are the so-called central bank bills. The role of central bank bond is to change the liability structure on condition that the central bank's total liabilities remains unchanged and change the asset structure of commercial banks on condition that their total assets remain unchanged. The direct policy effect is to change the amount of monetary base, which is similar to the reserve requirement ratio, but more flexible, because central bank bonds may be traded on the market.

Based on this role of central bank bond, it can be found that the amount of bonds issued and the reserve money are significantly negatively correlated in the short term. Based on calculation, we found that the correlation coefficient of ratio of bond issue to total liabilities and ratio of reserve money to total liabilities was 0.88 during 1985–2011. As shown in Table 11.5, when the ratio of bond issue to total liabilities increased from 0.3% in 1999 to 23.13% in 2006, the ratio of reserve money to total liabilities decreased from 85.83 to 60.48%. Therefore, the central bank can drain the monetary base in the hands of financial institutions through the issuance of bonds so as to tighten the monetary policy. Since 2008, the ratio of bonds issued by the central bank to total liabilities has gradually decreased to 4.71% in 2012, reflecting that the relatively loose monetary policy has been implemented since the occurrence of the financial crisis.

11.2.2 External Liabilities Continued the Upward Trend and Took a Relatively Small Proportion in Total Liabilities

During the study period, the central bank's external liabilities maintained an upward trend and increased from 42.3 billion yuan in 2002 to 269.9 billion yuan in 2011 and decreased slightly to 146.4 billion yuan in 2012. In the meanwhile, external liabilities took a relatively small proportion in total liabilities and accounted for 0.83% in 2002 and 0.5% in 2012. The central bank's external liabilities mainly include borrowings from foreign banks, liabilities to foreign central banks, loans

Table 11.5 Liabilities structure of China Central Bank Balance Sheet during 1997–2012

Time	Reserve currency			Deposits of financial corporations excluded from reserve money (%)	Bonds issue (%)	External liabilities (%)	Deposits of government (%)	Own capital (%)	Other liabilities (%)	Total liabilities (%)
	Total (%)	Currency issue (%)	Deposits of financial corporations (%)							
1999	85.83	38.47	37.60	9.76	0.30		4.56	0.94	−1.38	100
2000	83.07	36.28	36.47	10.32			7.06	0.81	−1.26	100
2001	82.28	34.83	35.28	12.17			5.89	0.73	−1.07	100
2002	88.32	36.37	37.45	14.50	2.91	0.83	6.04	0.43	1.47	100
2003	85.22	34.26	36.38	14.58	4.89	0.78	7.99	0.35	0.76	100
2004	74.83	29.37	45.35	0.10	14.09	0.71	7.41	0.28	2.68	100
2005	62.06	24.94	37.03	0.09	19.58	0.62	7.26	0.21	10.27	100
2006	60.48	22.66	37.69	0.12	23.13	0.72	7.94	0.17	7.56	100
2007	60.04	19.49	40.45	0.09	20.38	0.56	10.12	0.13	8.77	100
2008	62.40	17.92	44.48	0.29	22.11	0.35	8.19	0.11	6.56	100
2009	63.28	18.26	45.02	0.27	18.49	0.33	9.33	0.10	8.20	100
2010.6	63.49	17.52	45.97	0.25	19.34	0.30	12.77	0.09	3.77	100
2010.12	71.47	18.76	52.71	0.25	15.62	0.28	9.36	0.08	2.93	100
2011.6	73.17	17.55	55.62	0.29	9.81	1.75	12.42	0.08	2.49	100
2011.9	74.48	18.32	56.16	0.30	7.88	1.64	12.53	0.08	3.09	100
2011.12	79.95	19.88	60.07	0.32	8.31	0.96	8.09	0.08	2.29	100
2012.3	79.81	19.15	60.67	0.39	7.55	0.65	8.13	0.08	3.39	100
2012.6	79.72	18.98	60.74	0.41	6.53	0.38	9.63	0.08	3.24	100
2012.9	81.49	20.43	61.06	0.45	6.03	0.43	9.72	0.08	1.81	100
2012.12	85.68	20.59	65.08	0.46	4.71	0.50	7.05	0.07	1.54	100

Note The data in the table are from the website of by the People's Bank of China

from international financial institutions and central bank bills issued abroad. In theory, the purpose of external liabilities is mainly to balance international payments and maintain the stability of CNY exchange rate. In a special period, the central bank also needs to borrow from international markets to cope with a currency crisis or financial crisis.

11.2.3 The Size of Government Deposits Maintained the Upward Trend and Its Ration to Total Liabilities Maintained Relatively Stable

Government deposits increased from 178.55 billion yuan in 1999 to 2.08 trillion yuan in 2012, and its ratio to total liabilities increased from 4.56% in 1999 to 7.05% in 2012, maintaining relatively stable.

Government deposits are budgetary balance of payments of governments at all levels in the accounts of the central bank. Since 1999, with the rapid growth of China's economy, China's fiscal revenue has also grown rapidly, the financial positions of governments have been improved, and the surplus in the budget has increased. The ratio of the central government's deposits to its total liabilities also reached its highest level of up to 12.77% in 2010.

The increase in amount of government deposits at the central bank means a potential decrease of supply of monetary base. When financial funds are used, this is reflected as a decrease of "Deposits of Government" under the item of "Liabilities" of the central bank balance sheet and an increase of "Reserve Money" (mainly deposits of financial corporations), which means an increase in money supply, so government deposits and reserve money are negatively correlated in the short term. If financial overdraft is allowed, or the central bank grants loans to the government, then it will be direct reflected as an increase of "Claim on Government" under the item of "Assets" and an increase of "Reserve Money" (mainly deposits of financial corporations) under the item of "Liabilities".

However, the *Law of the PRC on the People's Bank of China* does not allow the central bank to release the monetary base in the form of financial overdraft. Article 29 of the Law provides that "The People's Bank of China shall not make an overdraft for the government, and shall not directly subscribe or underwrite State bonds or other government bonds." Article 30 of the Law provides that "The People's Bank of China may not provide loans to the local governments or government departments at various levels, to non-banking institutions, other units or individuals." Therefore, the central bank can buy bonds in the open market to regulate the money supply, but in theory should not directly finance government loans.

11.2.4 Other Liabilities Become a Positive Value from a Deduction Item and Took a Relatively Small Proportion in Total Liabilities

During the study period, "Other Liabilities" as a deduction item (i.e. negative value) of total liabilities of the central bank turned to a positive value and once took an important position in total liabilities and accounted for 8.77% in 2007. This means that, in addition to deposits of financial corporations and bond issue, the People's Bank of China was more reliant on sources of funds for other liabilities, which will affect the choice of monetary policy (Guogang 2010). But in recent years, the proportion of other liabilities has declined slightly and reached 1.54% in 2012.

11.3 Changes in China Central Bank Balance Sheet and Monetary Policy: Sterilization of Position for Forex Purchase

As shown in the central bank balance sheet, foreign exchange is the main existing form of assets of the central bank. This is mainly because since the 1990s, the competitiveness of many Chinese products gradually increased in the international markets due to their low prices, and foreign direct investment had also increased rapidly, leading to the long-term "double surplus" phenomenon of current account and capital account. In the table below, China's current account and capital account surpluses were growing, especially after 2003, leading to sharp increase of China's reserve assets and foreign exchange reserves, and the correlation coefficient of current account and capital account surpluses and forex reserve increment reached 0.99 (Table 11.6).

Under China's foreign exchange management system, the central bank needs to buy with RMB the foreign currencies that have flowed in as a result of current account and capital account surpluses, thus forming foreign exchange reserves and corresponding domestic RMB supply. This has also led to the rapid increase in the monetary base and inflationary pressure and asset bubble pressure through derivative deposits of commercial banks and money multiplier effect. This problem had particularly aroused widespread concern in 2007 when the stock market bubbles and rising inflation appeared. In such macro context, the independence and effectiveness of China's monetary policy has been challenged in recent years by capital inflows and rapid growth of position for forex purchase. Therefore, the central bank must drain excess liquidity due to the inflow of foreign currency by

Table 11.6 Balance of international payments and exchange rate (unit: $100 million)

Time	Current account	Capital and financial accounts	Sum of current account and capital account	Reserve asset increment	Forex reserve increment
1992	64.01	2.51	66.52	21.02	22.69
1993	119.03	234.74	353.77	17.67	17.56
1994	76.6	326.4	403	305.3	304.21
1995	16.2	386.8	403	224.8	219.77
1996	72.4	399.7	472.1	316.4	314.31
1997	369.6	210.1	579.7	357.2	348.62
1998	293.2	−63.2	230	64.3	50.69
1999	211.1	51.8	262.9	85.1	97.16
2000	205.2	19.2	224.4	105.5	108.93
2001	174.1	347.8	521.9	473.3	465.91
2002	354.22	322.91	677.13	755.07	742.42
2003	458.75	527.26	986.01	1170.23	1168.44
2004	686.59	1106.59	1793.18	2063.64	2066.81
2005	1341	1010	2351	2506	2526
2006	2327	526	2853	2848	2853
2007	3540	951	4491	4607	4609
2008	4124	463	4587	4795	4783
2009	2611	1808	4419	3984	3821
2010	3054	2260	5314	4717	4696

Source The State Administration of Foreign Exchange

massive monetary sterilization operations.[3] The role of monetary sterilization policy instrument has become a focus of concern and discussion among all circles in the world today and an urgent task decision makers are faced with.

Many economies have ever adopted the monetary sterilization policy, but it is mostly targeted for short-term international capital flows. For example, Germany and Japan are typical examples among the developed economies that have adopted the sterilization instrument to maintain the stability of exchange rate and prevent domestic inflation. Such is also the case for some emerging market countries. Since the 1990s, the major East Asian economies have been facing the continuous current account and capital account surpluses, so their sterilized intervention has become an important and conventional monetary policy strategy.

In theory, a commonly used monetary policy instrument can be used as the primary instrument of monetary sterilization policy, the general idea and principle of sterilization operation is: combined monetary policy instruments, maturity

[3]Zhu (2012) found that the position for forex purchase has significant short-term positive impact on the domestic price level, but the central bank's sterilized intervention policy can reduce the overall impact of the position for forex purchase on CPI.

structure and operating force are arranged reasonably to sterilize foreign exchange inflows and maintain moderate liquidity in the banking system and money supply and aggregate credit. In the context of rapid growth of foreign exchange, in order to control the domestic money supply and inflation, the People's Bank of China has sterilized the passive change in money supply arising from the double surplus of balance of international payments through open market operations, increasing the required reserve ratio, recovering re-lendings and issuing central bank bills so as to maintain price stability and promote economic growth.

However, the operating force and sustainability of sterilization operations are also affected by many factors. An important factor is the costs of sterilization operations. In general, the costs of the central bank's sterilization operations involve many aspects, including interest cost of central bank bills, interest cost of reserve deposits and even many hidden costs, such as financial market distortions, moral hazard and resource mismatch risk. Calvo (1990) pointed out that sterilization operations would lead to rising interest rates and induced huge financial costs, making sterilization operations unsustainable. The scale of monetary sterilization operations are also subject to some constraints, so it is often difficult to achieve complete sterilization (Christensen 2004). Yu (2003) pointed out that the gains and costs of monetary sterilization in China are asymmetric and will eventually need the government to bear the losses. Wu (2005) believes that the long-term sterilization policy will not only restrict the operation scope of monetary policy, but will lead to rising domestic interest rates, economic structural distortions, increase in "hot money" arbitrage motivation and thus systemic financial risks. Ping (2006) believes that the efficiency of central bank bills will gradually decrease and then are not sustainable. Yu (2010) has sorted out the documents about the un-sustainability of the two sterilization methods of central bank bills and deposit reserve ratio. Tan (2012) suggests that the scale of the central bank's monetary sterilization operations is significantly affected by the domestic market interest rates, and the higher the interest costs, the weaker the effectiveness of sterilization operations. Huangfu (2010) also believes that the effectiveness of the central bank's sterilization is significantly affected by the interest costs of sterilization operations, and in view of increasing foreign exchange reserves, to avoid excessive sterilization costs, the central bank is more inclined to use the means such as interest rates and open market operations to reduce the costs of sterilization.

Anyway, sterilization operations are very necessary for China today. Wu (2011) has calculated the amount and total sterilization ratio of sterilization measures on the monetary base during 1996–2010 according to China Central Bank Balance Sheet and related data (see Table 11.7).

As shown in Table 11.7, among the central bank's sterilization operations, the sterilization of reserves plays the biggest role. Guogang (2012) also believes that the main purpose for the central bank to continuously raise the deposit reserve ratio since 2001 is to obtain funds to hedge foreign exchange. The basic operation procedure is: the central bank raises the required deposit reserve ratio → financial

Table 11.7 Impact of position for forex purchase and sterilization measures on the monetary base (unit: 100 million yuan)

Time	Newly added amount of monetary base that year	Newly added amount of position for forex purchase	Amount of sterilization of the central bank that year	Amount of sterilization of reserves	Amount of sterilization of central bank bills	Amount of sterilization by repurchase	Amount of sterilization of re-lending	Total sterilization ratio (%)	Ratio of reserve funds to total amount of sterilization (%)
1996	6147.2	2764.6	1788.5	4784.7		11.7	−3007.8	64.7	
1997	3805.2	3072.2	1889.4	1777.0		0	112.4	61.5	
1998	247.6	440.4	−118.9	−1389.2		−701.9	1972.1	−27.0	
1999	3681.9	1013.2	−2406.0	135.3		−1919.7	−621.6	−237.5	
2000	2174.4	753.1	−2746.2	566.8		0	−3313.0	−364.6	
2001	4262.6	3812.8	2259.1	1899.3		810.3	−450.5	59.3	
2002	4743.6	4609.3	1875.4	1548.7		−103.5	430.2	40.7	
2003	7508.5	11458.9	4558.9	3923.5	1544.1	112.2	−1020.8	39.8	86.1
2004	6606.2	16,098.2	12385.9	4736.6	8047.5	50.0	−448.2	76.9	38.2
2005	5478.6	17441.4	7790.2	2727.7	9217.0	2880.0	−7024.4	44.7	34.9
2006	13414.7	22220.8	15807.8	11263.3	9444.6	−2330.0	−2570.0	71.1	71.3
2007	23736.3	25842.0	39136.8	21161.7	4728.6	4016.0	9230.5	151.4	54.1
2008	27850.7	34268.4	39263.3	27261.5	11310.7	205.7	485.5	114.6	69.4
2009	18213.7	25530.3	10904.3	11544.7	−3715.6	1488.3	1587.0	42.7	105.9
2010	41326.1	31612.1	29932.3	34235.9	−1567.0	−3300.0	563.4	94.7	114.4

institutions hand in the required reserves to the central bank → the central bank's "Deposits of Financial Corporations" increase → the central bank uses these funds to buy foreign assets from financial institutions (thus the "Foreign Exchange" of the central bank increases) → the RMB funds handed in by financial institutions to the central bank in accordance with the required deposit reserve ratio flow back to financial institutions.

In practical operation, there are mainly two measures used by the central bank to hedge foreign exchange to prevent the excessive growth of the monetary base: directly reduce the loans to financial institutions, non-financial institutions and government sector, and increase the issuance of bills to strengthen the sell repo operation. To make it convenient for analysis, the central bank balance sheet can be consolidated from the form as shown in Table 11.8 into Table 11.9 according to the relationship among all the items.

According to the principle of assets being equal liabilities, the following equation is true:

$$\begin{aligned} MB &= (A1 + A2 + A3 + A4 + A5 + A6) - (L2 + L3 + L4 + L5 + L6) \\ &= (A1 - L3) + (A2 + A3 + A4 + A5 + A6 - L4 - L5 - L6) - L2 \\ &= NFA + NDC - BI \end{aligned} \tag{11.1}$$

The expression of monetary base increment is:

$$\Delta MB = \Delta NFA + \Delta NDC - \Delta BI \tag{11.2}$$

Therefore, the supply structure of the monetary base consists of the three items of net foreign assets (NFA), net domestic claims (NDC) and bond issue (BI). The change in NFA and NDC will cause the change of the monetary base in the same direction, and BI will cause the change of the monetary base in the opposite direction. NFA is mainly affected by current account surplus or deficit and financial and capital account surplus or deficit, so it is an uncontrollable factor for the central bank's monetary policy. Ignoring the factors such as deposits of government, NDC and BI are uncontrollable factors for the central bank. Thus, to discuss the controllability of money supply is actually to investigate the power and position of uncontrollable factors affecting the monetary base (change in NFA and BI).

Based on the formula (11.2), we can obtain:

$$\Delta MB = \Delta NFA + \Delta DC \tag{11.3}$$

In the formula, $\Delta DC = \Delta NDC - \Delta BI$.

If the central bank's sterilization is complete, then there exists:

$$\Delta MB = \Delta NFA + \Delta DC = 0 \tag{11.4}$$

Table 11.8 China central bank balance sheet (subject setting)

Assets (A)	Liabilities (L)
Foreign assets (A1)	Reserve money (L1)
Foreign exchange	Currency issue (M0)
Monetary gold	Deposits of financial institutions
Other foreign assets	Deposits of non-financial corporations
Claims on government	Bond issue (L2)
Claims on other depository corporations (A3)	External liabilities (L3)
Claims on other financial corporations (A3)	Deposits of government (L4)
Claims on non-financial corporations (A5)	Own capital (L5)
Other assets (A6)	Other liabilities (L6)
Total assets	Total liabilities

Table 11.9 China central bank balance sheet (subject setting)

Assets (A)	Liabilities (L)
NFA: net foreign assets (A1-L3)	MB: monetary base (L1)
NDC: net domestic claims (A2 + A3 + A4 + A5 + A6 − L4 − L5 − L6)	BI: bond issue (L2)

Thus, according to Formula (11.4), in case of complete sterilization, the change in NDC ΔDC and the change in ΔNFA are inevitably equal in number but opposite in direction. Therefore, whether sterilized intervention is complete or not can be judged by estimating the central bank's reaction function. According to Sarno and Taylor (2001), the central bank's reaction function can be set as:

$$\Delta MB_t = v_1 \cdot \Delta NFA_t + v_2 \cdot cap\_gdp + v_2 \cdot \pi_t + \omega_t \tag{11.5}$$

In the formula, *cap_gdp* is the GDP growth rate gap, and π is the inflation rate. To estimate the formula (11.5), the data for the second quarter of 2002 and 2011 were selected. ΔMB and ΔNFA were calculated based on the central bank balance sheet, the inflation rate is the consumer price index, and the year-on-year data were converted into the quarter-on-quarter data. *cap_gdp* was obtained based on the GDP growth rate using the HP filter method. Thus, we obtain the following model by estimation:

$$\begin{array}{c} \Delta MB_t = 0.3819 \cdot \Delta NFA_t + 1.4324 \cdot cap\_gdp + 14.42\pi_t \\ (5.15) \qquad\qquad (4.48) \qquad\qquad (2.95) \end{array} \tag{11.6}$$

where $R^2 = 0.48$, $\bar{R}^2 = 0.45$, D.W = 1.8825, and those inside the parentheses are statistic data of T test.

According to Formula (11.6), on condition that other conditions remain unchanged, when NFA increases (or decreases) by one unit, the monetary base will

Table 11.10 Data of central bank balance sheet

Year	Net foreign assets	Net foreign assets increment (based on real value)	Reserve money of monetary authorities	Reserve money increment of monetary authorities (based on real value)	Reserve money increment caused by foreign assets (based on real value)
02Q1	18686.49		41221.1		
02Q2	19368.71	618.51	40554.5	−799.99	236.21
02Q3	20540.32	1071.98	39,864	−874.10	409.39
02Q4	22396.74	1803.95	45138.2	5156.27	688.93
03Q1	24355.23	1738.69	44113.3	−1378.95	664.01
03Q2	26270.89	1747.93	43206	−1110.58	667.53
03Q3	29044.35	2428.80	46730.4	2991.41	927.56
03Q4	30176.72	593.34	52841.4	5032.38	226.60
04Q1	32945.93	2084.96	50461.1	−3102.02	796.25
04Q2	35369.29	1676.29	51305.8	−62.98	640.18
04Q3	38402.1	2091.72	53,150	735.87	798.83
04Q4	45835.62	6375.47	58856.1	4733.32	2434.79
05Q1	50814.9	3969.27	57588.3	−1671.01	1515.86
05Q2	55341.4	3600.89	57360.2	−613.60	1375.18
05Q3	59479.9	3480.50	60771.2	2839.93	1329.20
05Q4	62697.7	2204.71	64343.1	2498.18	841.98
06Q1	67747.3	4054.46	62551.3	−1833.13	1548.40
06Q2	72728.4	3558.30	63096.2	−158.82	1358.91
06Q3	77485.8	3286.79	66187.1	1981.09	1255.23
06Q4	84846.3	5107.63	77757.8	8733.09	1950.60
07Q1	95015.5	6825.14	76990.1	−1920.38	2606.52
07Q2	103945.6	5699.14	82,664	3375.08	2176.50
07Q3	114765	6468.36	88048.7	2642.42	2470.27
07Q4	123877.9	4650.75	101545.4	8495.09	1776.12
08Q1	136488.2	7753.02	104224.2	655.99	2960.88
08Q2	148675.3	6879.06	115353.1	6582.55	2627.11
08Q3	157016.6	4838.60	117336.1	515.27	1847.86
08Q4	161810.9	2774.50	129222.3	8029.56	1059.58
09Q1	165300.8	7174.29	124276.7	−35.84	2739.86
09Q2	171131.4	3548.34	123929.7	−837.18	1355.11
09Q3	178973.4	3721.95	133406.6	5464.91	1421.41
09Q4	184571.3	2341.78	143,985	6356.45	894.33
10Q1	191372.3	2792.85	150032.8	2704.88	1066.59
10Q2	197637.2	1855.61	154234.5	960.87	708.66
10Q3	204094.9	2187.96	161320.3	3108.02	835.58

(continued)

Table 11.10 (continued)

Year	Net foreign assets	Net foreign assets increment (based on real value)	Reserve money of monetary authorities	Reserve money increment of monetary authorities (based on real value)	Reserve money increment caused by foreign assets (based on real value)
10Q4	214699.5	4109.04	185311.1	13702.25	1569.24
11Q1	221697.54	2262.48	192565.38	2752.72	864.04
11Q2	229831.43	2418.99	203469.88	4581.60	923.81

increase (or decrease) by 0.3819 unit correspondingly. Conversely, it means the sterilization coefficient of NFC is 0.6181. That is, 61.81% of the RMB increment corresponding to one unit increase of NFC has been sterilized by the central bank. According to Formula (11.6), we can calculate the increment of China's central bank reserve currency caused by foreign assets (see Table 11.10).

Chapter 12
Central Government Balance Sheet

12.1 Review of Documents on the Chinese Government's Balance Sheet

Since the outbreak of the international financial crisis, government balance sheets have aroused widespread attention. On the one hand, the size of government debt in the developed countries is increasingly expanding, government balance sheets are deteriorating, and the European debt crisis and the US federal government's debt ceiling have impaired the debt credit of the world's developed economic regions. This will endanger their own credit basis, and more seriously, US dollar and euro are two most important reserve currencies in the current international monetary system, the downgrade of credit rating for the US debt and European debt has also increased the systemic risk of the international monetary system. On the other hand, after the impact of the international financial crisis, China has launched the positive stimulus to restore its high economic growth, but has accumulated huge local government debt. The discussions on the financial situation and financial risks of the Chinese government will inevitably attract enormous attention.

Some earlier studies were more interested in government liabilities. For example, in analysis of non-performing assets of state-owned banks, Fan (1999) introduced the concept of "comprehensive national liabilities" as a measure of fiscal and financial risks in China. Zhang (2000) explored the sustainability of China's government debt. Liu and Zhao (2002) conducted comprehensive analysis of government liabilities and assets and classified government liabilities into four categories: (1) direct explicit liabilities: national bonds, wages in arrears, losses of grains on account and township debt; (2) direct implicit liabilities: pension funds, unemployment benefits and rural social security funds etc.; (3) explicit contingent liabilities: debt of other public sectors (policy financial bonds, railway sector bonds and external debt of state-owned enterprises and financial institutions), supporting funds of treasury bond investment projects and government guarantees etc.; (4) implicit contingent liabilities: non-performing assets of state-owned banks,

Y. Li and X. Zhang, *China's National Balance Sheet*, China Insights,
DOI 10.1007/978-981-10-4385-7_12

losses not made-up of state-owned enterprises and aids to the supply and marketing cooperative system and rural cooperative fund associations etc. They equate total government assets with total state-owned assets, i.e. the net worth of state-owned assets owned by the government, which mainly consists of two parts: operating state-owned assets and non-operating state-owned assets. Non-operating assets mainly include: stock assets of administrative institutions, agencies dispatched abroad and basic construction entities. The remaining are operating assets distributed in the industries and fields such as manufacturing, commerce, transportation, agriculture and financial services.

Undoubtedly, Liu et al. (2002, 2003, 2005) took the lead in making a detailed analysis of financial risks in China from the perspective of stock assets and liabilities, and their research findings are important in this field. However, due to the backward accounting system in China, unavailability of relevant statistical data and lack of previous studies, some studies are imperfect. The paper fails to finally form a complete balance sheet.

The preparation of national balance sheet (including government balance sheet) is a huge project, which will encounter difficulties in many aspects, such as acquisition and measurement of data on the asset side. Zhang (2006) clearly stated that as there were formidable obstacles in measurement of assets, the usefulness of government balance sheet was very limited. These obstacles include: first, the fair value of part of assets is not available and thus can only be measured based on historical costs, making the aggregate results meaningless; second, the fair value and historical costs of part of assets are not available, so it is impossible to list them (these assets include natural resources, cultural and natural heritages, management and technical innovation or software products, goodwill, human capital, social capital and so on); third, most of capital assets of government are for specific use, the market does not exist or is underdeveloped, so their net realizable value is usually much lower than their book value or appraised value.

Nevertheless, a central government balance sheet is relatively simple, and a number of countries in the world (including the US, Canada, UK and Australia etc.) have prepared their national balance sheets, among which the US has prepared the most detailed national balance sheet. A national balance sheet should essentially be a part of national account statistics system, and the flow indicators of national income statistics will eventually form the stock indicators of national balance sheet. There is a matching relationship between national income statistics and national balance sheet. The System of National Accounts, 2008 (2008SNA) is a statistical framework that provides a comparative, consistent and flexible set of macroeconomic accounts for policymaking, analysis and research purposes. It has been produced and released under the auspices of the UN, IMF, OECD, the European Commission and other international organizations. It represents an update of the System of National Accounts 1993 (1993SNA) and has made a number of changes in aspects such as statistical units and revisions in institutional sectoring, production boundary and output calculations, assets and capital formation, financial instruments & assets, government & public sector, and globalization-related issues. The US Federal Reserve and the US Bureau of Economic Analysis have jointly released the System of National Accounts prepared in accordance with the new standards of SNA2008, including the balance sheets of various sectors.

There are a huge number of state-owned enterprises in China (including financial and non-financial corporations), and it will still take some time for China to establish a unified national social security system. Such institutional difference poses a great challenge to preparing the balance sheet of the Chinese central government, and this is also the root cause for the current debate about the sustainability of China's debt burden. Due to unavailability of data, the studies of central government balance sheet have mainly adopted the direct enumeration method, which lists and estimates the items on the asset and liability sides and adds up the all items to get the difference between the sums as net worth (net assets). For example, according to the method adopted by Ma et al. (2012), on the asset side, there are non-operating assets, corporate equity held by the central government and investments of the four asset management companies and China Investment Corporation, while on the liability side, there are government bonds, liabilities of the Ministry of Railways and liabilities of four asset management companies and China Investment Corporation. In this method, the central government balance sheet is not formed by consolidating the basic data of balance sheets, so overlapped calculation or omission may exist, and the coverage and debt processing of central government balance sheet is not completely in line with with the international practice.

In this chapter, on the basis of existing data, we have used the basic concepts and methods of SNA2008 to tentatively prepare the balance sheet of the Chinese central government and carried out some simple analysis of the changes in the balance sheet of the Chinese central government for 2007–2011.

12.2 Preparation of Central Government Balance Sheet

The basic data on assets and liabilities of the central government balance sheet should come from the balance sheets of the economic entities involved in the central government's economic activities, so the central government balance sheet was formed by consolidating the balance sheets of various sectors. According to different standards, the central government balance sheets based on three scopes can be roughly prepared. (1) The narrow scope: based on the principle of separating the functions of the government from those of the enterprise, the central government balance sheet should only cover the budget entities, and state-owned corporations (including financial and non-financial corporations) should be included in the corporate sector, so their owner's equity should be included in the central government's equity investment. This is in line with international practice. (2) The medium scope: the coverage of the central government balance sheet is based on the scope of the economic activities the central government is involved in, and the state-owned corporations under the central government (including financial and non-financial corporations) are all included in the consolidated central government balance sheet. This is not in line with the international practice. According to the rules of SNA2008, the balance sheet based on this scope is equal to the public sector balance sheet rather than the general government balance sheet. (3) The broad scope: contingent assets and liabilities are added. This practice is useful for analyzing the potential level of debt, but does not comply with the accounting principles. Contingent assets and liabilities are assets and liabilities may occur in the future and thus should not be included in the current balance sheet.

Based on the definition of general government given by SNA2008, we have delineated the scope of the central government balance sheet and prepared the central government balance sheet based on the aforementioned narrow scope. The departments and units associated with the central government include: (1) the administrative departments under the central government, the public institutions administrated by the central government and the public institutions administrated by the central government as enterprises; (2) the financial and non-financial state-owned corporations under the control of the central authorities; (3) the social security accounts; (4) the central bank; (5) local governments; (6) the international departments.

The above six categories of institutional units are handled respectively in the following method: (1) apart from the administrative departments of the central government, as an entity of economic activities, the public institutions administrated by the central government as enterprises that belong to budgetary management units should also be included into the central government balance sheet. (2) The balance sheets of the financial and non-financial state-owned corporations under the control of the central authorities are consolidated into the corporate sector. The policy banks, the four asset management companies, China Investment Corporation, Huijin and other similar units are included in the (state-owned) corporate sector. But a portion of owner's equity of all these financial and non-financial state-owned corporations under the control of the central authorities belongs to the assets of the central government. (3) The relationship between the social security accounts and the central government balance sheet is relatively complicated. Presently, China's social security system is still in a fragmented state, the payers of each kind of insurance assume their own responsibilities, and the central government and local governments assume the responsibility of social insurance. Due to unavailability of the data on the central government's insurance accounts, here only the balance sheet of the National Council for Social Security Fund is included into the central government balance sheet. (4) Although the central bank in China is less independent than those in the developed countries, the central bank is generally included into the financial sector in the international practice. We have also adopted this international practice and did not include the assets and liabilities of the People's Bank of China into the central government balance sheet. We have only included the own capital on the liability side of the balance sheet of the monetary authorities into the item of financial assets of the central government and included the deposits of government into the item of deposits of the central government balance sheet. The claims of the People's Bank of China to the central government is included into the item of financial bonds of the central government.

(5) The relationship between the central government and local governments is mainly reflected through financial subsidies. This flow relationship is ultimately reflected in the balance sheet as an increase or decrease of treasury deposits, and the balance of treasury deposits has also included this relationship. (6) The economic contacts between the international departments and the units related to the central government have already been recorded in the balance sheets of these units. When consolidating them to form the central government balance sheet, the asset and liability relationship between the international departments and the central government will naturally form. As the data we have adopted do not cover such broken-down subjects, the central government balance sheet we have prepared does not provide a separate category of assets and liabilities of the international departments, but this category has been included in other subjects.

According to the above method, we have prepared the central government balance sheet by the following steps: (1) consolidate the balance sheets of the administrative units under the central government and the public institutions administrated by the central government as enerprises; (2) calculate the equity capital invested by the central government in state-owned enterprises according to the proportion of state-owned capital of the owner's equities of non-financial state-owned corporations (including those controlled and administrated by the central government) and financial state-owned corporations under the control of the central authorities; (3) consolidate the balance sheet of the he National Council for Social Security Fund; (4) add treasury deposits and own capital of the People's Bank of China into the asset side and add government bonds into the liability side. Finally, add up all the items to get total assets, total liabilities and net worth (Table 12.1).

12.3 Analysis of Central Government Balance Sheet

According to the above central government balance sheet, we can come to the following conclusions:

First, the central government's total assets and total liabilities grew rapidly, and its total assets grew faster. During 2007–2011, the central government's total assets increased from 14.1 to 25.8 trillion yuan, and its total liabilities grew from 5.6 to 7.7 trillion yuan, an average growth rate of 12.9 and 6.7% respectively based on the method of compound interest. Its net assets grew from 8.5 to 18 trillion yuan, an annual growth rate of 16.3%. In the 5 years, the growth rate of assets is 6.2% higher than that of liabilities (Fig. 12.1).

Second, the equity capital of state-owned enterprises took a large proportion in total assets of the central government. In the central government's total assets, equity capital invested in state-owned enterprises accounted for the highest proportion. In 2011, the equity capital invested by the central government in state-owned enterprises amounted to 17.2 trillion yuan, accounting for 66.8% of the central government's total assets, the equity capital invested in administrative

Table 12.1 Simplified Balance Sheet of the Chinese Central Government for 2007–2011 (unit: 100 million yuan)

	2007	2008	2009	2010	2011
Total assets	140905.9	164818.7	194291.9	230148.4	258055.2
Non-financial assets	16671.7	18933.8	22103.6	25876.7	29013.5
Inventory	291	256	287.1	375.3	440.4
Buildings	16270	18645.4	21722.9	25389.5	28507
Mechanical equipments	81.6	1.5	56.2	61.9	11.4
Intangible assets	29.1	30.9	37.4	50	54.8
Financial assets	124234.2	145884.9	172188.3	204271.7	229041.7
Cash and deposits	10973.1	11026.5	12361.8	13174.2	12100.3
Cash and payable deposits	10888.9	10937.8	12282.2	13087.9	12004.3
Time deposits	46.6	42.9	50.1	49.7	56.3
Unofficial currency	37.5	45.9	29.5	36.6	39.7
Bonds (assets)	0.7	0.7	0.6	0.6	0.6
Bonds held by asset management companies	0.7	0.7	0.6	0.6	0.6
Loans (assets)	0	0	0	0	0
Securities and investment fund shares	111592.3	133217.9	158123.4	188951.2	214528.7
Own capital of the People's Bank Of China's	219.75	219.75	219.75	219.75	219.75
Corporate equity & securities	86,561	105935.1	125,277	150,733	172283.9
Equity of administrative institutions	19488.5	22185.7	25715.3	29821.3	33660.2
Securities held by the social security fund	1584.4	1333.6	1880.5	2223.7	2432.7
Equity investments of public-private investment plan	3738.6	3543.7	5030.8	5953.4	5932.1
Advance payment	485.8	521.1	479.5	544.5	650.4
Other receivables	615.4	504.6	591	800.5	839.8
Accounts receivable	615.4	504.6	591	800.5	839.8
Others (miscellaneous assets)	567	614	631.9	800.7	921.9
Total liabilities and net worth	140905.9	164818.7	194291.9	230148.4	258055.2
Total liabilities	56059.6	57502.4	64680.3	72244.4	77531.9
Monetary liabilities	370.6	649.6	558.2	365.8	494
Cash and deposits (liabilities)	341.6	220.8	224.7	241.9	260.9
Trading liabilities	29	428.8	333.5	124	233.1
Bonds (liabilities)	52074.8	53271.6	60237.8	67548.1	72044.5
Financial bonds (including long-term bonds)	51467.5	52799.4	59737	66988	71410.8
External debt	607.3	472.2	500.7	560.1	633.7
Other loans	143.1	120.6	149.8	189.6	203.5

(continued)

Table 12.1 (continued)

	2007	2008	2009	2010	2011
Loans (mortgages) (liabilities)	1175.6	946.1	813.3	709.6	951.8
Other payables	1499.7	1635	1857.6	2075.9	2408.7
Others (miscellaneous liabilities)	795.9	879.6	1063.7	1355.3	1429.5
Net worth	84846.25	107316.3	129611.6	157904	180523.3

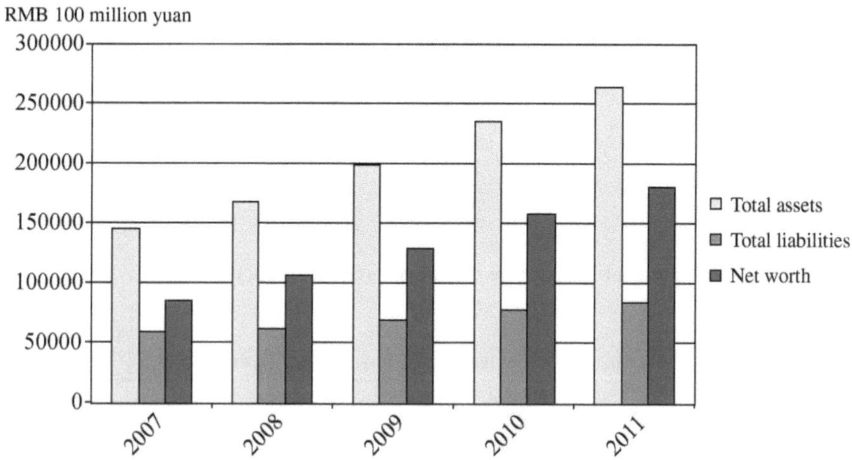

Fig. 12.1 Central government balance during 2007–2011

institutions accounted for 13.1%, assets of social security funds accounted for 3.2%, cash and deposits accounted for 4.7%, non-financial assets accounted for 11.3% and other assets accounted for 0.9% (Fig. 12.2).

Third, national bonds took a large proportion in the central government's total liabilities. In the central government's total liabilities, government bonds accounted for a large proportion. In 2011, the outstanding central government debt was 7.1 trillion yuan, accounting for 92% of the central government's total liabilities, short-term borrowings (including operating borrowings of social security funds) accounted for 0.6%, external debt accounted for 0.8% and other borrowings and accounts payables accounted for 1.5 and 5% respectively (Fig. 12.3).

Fourth, the equity of state-owned enterprises took a large proportion in the central government's net assets. As shown in the structures of total assets and total liabilities of the central government, the central government's net assets and total assets were mainly from its equity investment in state-owned enterprises. In 2011, the equipty capital invested by the central government in state-owned enterprises amounted to 17.2 trillion yuan, and the net assets of the central government amounted to 18.0 trillion yuan. If the equity capital invested by the central government in state-owned enterprises were excluded, the net assets of the central

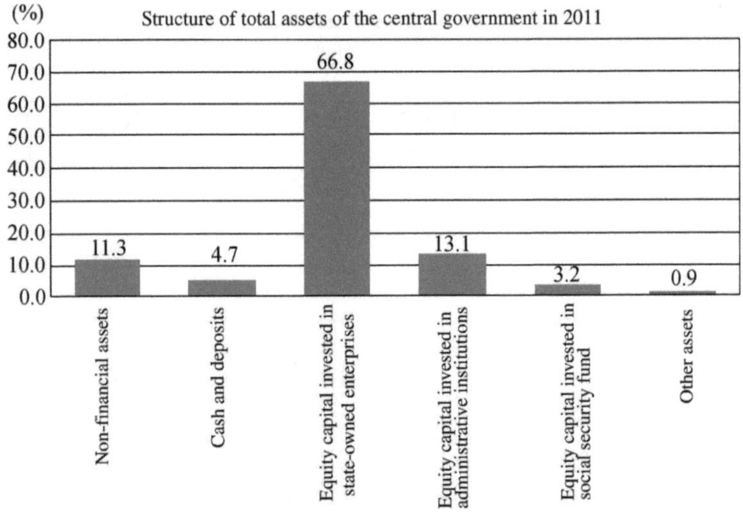

Fig. 12.2 Structure of total assets of the central government in 2011

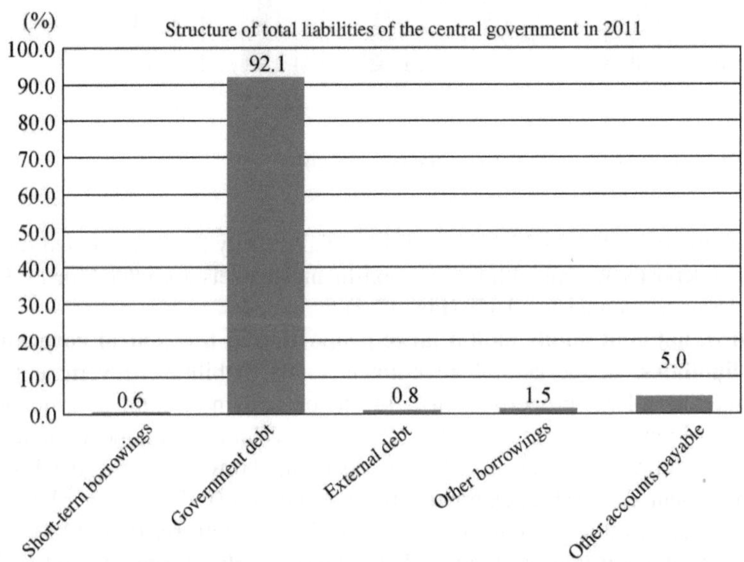

Fig. 12.3 Structure of total liabilities of the central government in 2011

government would be reduced to 0.8 trillion yuan. Therefore, the state-owned enterprises in China are crucial in maintaining a large proportion of net assets of the central government.

Fifth, the implicit debt in the field of social security may have a significant impact on the central government's assets and liabilities. The above analysis shows that the central government has huge net assets and seems to be at no debt risk. But as described above, the central government's assets and liabilities calculated here are based on the narrow scope, excluding contingent assets or contingent or implicit debt. If contingent or implicit assets and debt, especially the implicit debt arising from the debt of the social security system are added into the central government balance sheet, the results will be greatly different.

The implicit debt in the field of social security mainly comes from the old-age insurance. On the one hand, China's old-age insurance system starting from scratch has experienced the transition from the fully PAYG system to the partially funded system, thus forming the implicit pension debt. On the other hand, China's demographic structure will undergo fundamental change, birth rates are falling and the population is aging, which will lead to the sharp increase in pension spending, while the income growth will reduce. Such increase in spending and decrease in income growth will cause enormous pressure on the old-age insurance system. Base on the international experience, the pension funding gap is generally borne by the government.

According to the estimate of the research group, the transition cost stock of old-age insurance was 3.47 trillion yuan in 2011. Supposing 30% of the pension funding gap is borne by the central government, this means that only this item will bring the implicit debt burden of 1.04 trillion yuan to the central government. Coupled with the existing 2.2 trillion empty personal accounts, the implicit pension debt burden of the central government will rise to 1.7 trillion yuan.[1]

[1]This is the narrow-scope the implicit pension debt, and the incurrence of the debt is related to the transition of the old-age insurance system, without taking into consideration the pension payment gape arising from the population aging.

[illegible]

Chapter 13
Local Government Balance Sheet

Since the occurrence of the global financial crisis, due to the launch of the economic stimulus programs and the transfer of financial risk of the private sector, fiscal deficits and levels of government debt have significantly increased in some developed economies. The IMF has predicted that by 2014, except for Germany and Canada, the government debt to GDP ratio of the other countries of the Group of Seven (G7) will be over 100%. While the developed economies are plagued by the sovereign debt problems, there is also an increasing concern at home and abroad over China's sovereign debt, especially the hefty local government debt problem. Particularly, the rapid expansion of the debt of LGFPs in China's response to the financial crisis has brought some hidden risks. Therefore, it is particularly important to get a clear picture of the current status of assets and liabilities of local governments, identify the possible risk points and give recommendations to avoid the risks. Under such background, in this chapter, we will try to identify the types of assets and liabilities of local governments, assess local government debt risks, analyze the formation mechanism of local government debt and thus give the countermeasures to prevent risks.

13.1 Estimation of Local Government Assets

The assets of local government come in the following types:

13.1.1 Local Operating State-Owned Assets

Local operating state-owned assets are assets in respect of which local governments, as the contributors, invest resources into production and operation so as to obtain profits, including state-owned assets of non-financial and financial corporations.

Y. Li and X. Zhang, *China's National Balance Sheet*, China Insights,
DOI 10.1007/978-981-10-4385-7_13

State-owned assets of non-financial corporations are the main part of local state-owned operating assets. We have taken into account the debt of local state-owned non-financial corporations when estimating the local government debt, so the (total) state-owned assets of non-financial corporations was obtained by adding up the total assets and total liabilities of state-owned corporations. It should be noted that the total state-owned assets of state-owned corporations here is actually the concept of state-owned equity. Apart from the state-owned equity, the total owner's equity (i.e. total net assets) of state-owned corporations also include the equity of other owners (such as the equity of foreign, Hong Kong, Macao and Taiwan-funded enterprises, collective enterprises or individual owners in joint-venture, cooperative and joint-stock state-owned corporations). Only the state-owned equities in state-owned corporations from which the equity of other owners as mentioned above has been deducted are assets that can be truly disposed and used by the government. We have estimated the size of state-owned equity according to the data of the balance sheet of state-owned non-financial corporations. The basic method is as follows: calculate the proportion of state-owned capital according to the ratio of state-owned capital to paid-in capital in all sectors and then calculate the size of state-owned equity by multiplying the equity attributed to patent companies by state-owned capital.

The state-owned assets of local financial corporations mainly refer to all forms of investment of local governments in financial corporations and the equities formed by the investment as well as all other equities legally recognized to be owned by local governments. When estimating the local government debt in the next step, there is no directly corresponding debt of local state-owned financial corporations, so here we have only taken into consideration the size of state-owned equity rather than the total state-owned assets (i.e. state-owned equity plus liabilities). The estimation method is the same as that for the non-financial corporations, and the data are from statistics of financial indicators of state-shareholding financial corporations. It should be noted that, in state-owned assets of local financial corporations, the equity of other state-owned legal persons has been basically reflected in the balance sheets of non-financial state-owned corporations (based on the practical experience, a larger part of state-owned assets of local financial corporation belong to the legal persons of state-owned enterprises), but due to lack of further data, we are unable to estimate the share of non-financial state-owned corporations in the state-owned assets of local financial corporations, so it is impossible to exclude these assets.

13.1.2 Local Non-operating State-Owned Assets

Here local non-operating state-owned assets refer to the state-owned (public) properties occupied by administrative institutions and public institutions. As the support for the government to fulfill its functions in public administration and public affairs, this part of assets are the components of a country's sovereignty assets. As far as China is concerned, given the scale and characteristics of the government, this part of assets take an important position in the state's sovereign assets. According to the simplified balance sheets of local departments, we have added up the net assets of administrative institutions and public institutions.

13.1.3 Resource Assets Owned by Local Governments

Here we have mainly taken into account land resource assets owned by local governments (see related contents in Part 3 of this book for specific estimates). It should be noted that we tend to regard that land resource assets obtained by the method described above are all owned by local governments for the following reasons. On the one hand, urban land is nominally owned by the state, but under the existing land leasehold (transfer) system, based on the principle of separation of ownership and use right of land, local governments are empowered to be on behalf of the state to administer the land owned by the state and transfer the right to land use for many years and charge one-time land transfer fees. This has actually granted local governments greater rights to dispose land resources and share income. As an important manifestation of this right, land transfer fees need not be turned over to the central government and can be disposed and used by local governments. On the other hand, land in rural and suburban areas is nominally collectively owned, but can be turned into urban land through expropriation or requisition and become state-owned resource assets that can be leased by local governments. In summary, the valuation here can be recognised as the maximum value of local land resource assets.

13.1.4 Local Government Deposits at the Central Bank

These deposits mainly refer to the treasury deposits of local treasuries at all levels in the treasury single accounts at the People's Bank of China, namely the deposits of local budget funds in the treasuries (including general budget and fund budget). Treasury deposits and other public finance-cash in bank (various fiscal budget fund deposits at commercial banks not included in treasury deposits and part of special fund deposits designated by the Ministry of Finance to be deposited at commercial banks, as bank deposits reflected in the asset item of administrative institutions) together constitute public finance-cash in bank. It is a kind of fiscal assets managed and disposed by the financial departments at various levels on behalf of the governments at the corresponding levels. The data here are from the statistics of balances of local treasury funds.

13.2 Estimation of Local Government Debt

The Fiscal Risk Matrix is now widely used internationally for statistics on government debt. This method was first proposed by the senior economist Hanna (1998) of the World Bank in the World Bank Policy Research Working Paper published in 1998.

In this risk matrix, government liabilities can be divided into two types according to different criteria: from the viewpoint of legally mandated obligations, government liabilities can be divided into explicit and implicit liabilities. Explicit liabilities are specific obligations, created by law or contract, that governments must settle, while implicit liabilities represent moral obligations or burdens that, although not legally binding, are likely to be borne by governments because of public expectations or political pressures. From the viewpoint of liability incurrence conditions, they can be divided into direct liabilities and contingent liabilities. Direct liabilities are obligations that governments bear the responsibility to repay under any event, while contingent liabilities are obligations that may or may not come due, depending on whether particular events occur.

The two groups of liabilities can be combined to form four types of government liabilities, namely direct explicit liabilities (local government obligations in any event created by law or contract), direct implicit liabilities (moral obligations of government in any event but not created by law or contract), contingent explicit liabilities (legal or contracted obligations for governments to make payments only if particular events occur) and contingent implicit liabilities (liabilities or obligations, although not legally binding, are likely to be borne by governments if particular events occur).

Based on Hana's financial risk matrix, the Chinese local government debt can classified as follows:

13.2.1 Direct Explicit Liabilities

(1) Local government bonds

Article 28 of the *Budget Law* promulgated in 1994 clearly states: "The local budgets at various levels shall be compiled according to the principles of keeping expenditures within the limits of revenues and maintaining a balance between revenues and expenditures, and shall not contain deficit. The local governments may not issue local government bonds, except as otherwise prescribed by laws or the State Council." However, during the subsequent two financial crises, local government bonds appeared in some flexible and circuitous forms.

In 1998, to cope with the Asian financial crisis and expand domestic demands, China started to implement the proactive fiscal policy and issue long-term construction treasury bonds. In this process, in order to increase the funds for local economic and social development projects, the State Council decided to additionally issue a certain number of bonds, and the funds raised from issuing these bonds were re-lent by the Ministry of Finance to local governments. During 1998–2005, the central government issued a total of about 990 billion yuan of long-term construction treasury bonds, among which about a third were re-lent to local governments. The local government bonds under the bond re-lending mode were finally guaranteed by the credit of the central government, so they are in essence still "government bonds" issued by the central government and can not be regarded as local government bonds in a real sense.

Later in 2009, to cope with the international financial crisis and improve local governments' capacity to arrange funds and expand investment, according to the special provisions of the *Budget Law*, local governments were allowed to issue bonds officially. The governments of provinces and cities specifically designated in the state plan are issuers and repayers, and the Ministry of Finance should issue the bonds on behalf of local governments and pay principle and interest on the bonds and issuance fees on behalf of local governments. During 2009–2011, the size of local government bonds issued by the central authorities on behalf of local governments was 200 billion yuan each year. In the mode in which bonds are issued by the central government on behalf local governments, although local governments still have no independent right to issue bonds legally, at least nominal local government bonds had first appeared.

(2) Sovereign external debt of local governments

It mainly refers to loans from foreign governments and international financial organizations borrowed and managed in a unified manner by the central government on behalf of local governments (loans from the World Bank, the Asian Development Bank and IFAD), and it is in essence central debt transferred to loan fund.

This kind of external debt is managed by the central government on behalf of local governments, so in the *Brief Table of China's External Debt* for each year issued by the State Administration of Foreign Exchange, the local governments do not appear as debtors. Due to unavailability of data in this aspect, we have calculated the average ratio of local governments' sovereign external debt to China's total external debt (about 8%) according to the statistical data of the Ministry of Finance and assumed that the ratio remained largely stable. Then, we obtained the projected size of local governments' sovereign external debt by multiplying China's outstanding external debt of each year by the ratio and converted it to the size in RMB according to the average exchange rate at that time.

13.2.2 Implicit Direct Liabilities

Here we mainly take into consideration the social security's funding gap dominated by implicit pension debt. Based on the current distribution of administrative powers for the old-age insurance, the pension fund deficit is partially subsidized by the central government, while the majority should be borne by local governments. Calculated by 70%, the implicit pension liabilities of local governments in 2011 totaled about 2.43 trillion yuan.

13.2.3 Contingent Explicit Liabilities

(1) Debt for which local governments issued official guarantees

The debt guarantees provided by local governments do not necessarily form local government debt. If the guaranteed unit can timely fulfill its repayment obligation, then the local government can be exempted from the relevant responsibility, and such guarantee will not form local government debt. However, if the guaranteed unit fails to fulfill its repayment obligation, then the local government must assume the joint liability according to the guarantee contract or agreement and needs to use the budget to make the payment in advance. In such case, the debt guarantee provided by the government will form contingent liabilities.

Article 8 of the *Guarantee Law of the People's Republic of China* clearly states that "State organs cannot act as guarantors, except for sub-lending of loans from foreign governments or international economic organizations." But it is in fact a common practice that the local government provides guarantee or disguised guarantee (for example, the local government issues a repayment commitment, the local People's Congress agrees to include the repaid fund for a project in the budget, or the local government makes a repurchase commitment).

According to the *Results of National Audit of Local Government Debts* issued by the National Audit Office in June 2011, as of the end of 2010, the contingent liabilities arising from direct or indirect guarantees provided by local governments amounted to 2336.974 billion yuan. The audit results also revealed that the annual growth rate of outstanding local government debt during 2008–2010 was 23.48, 61.92 and 18.86% respectively. According to the *Audit Results of the Debts Held by 36 Local Governments* released by the National Audit Office in June 2013, the outstanding government debt grew by 12.94% during 2010–2012, with a projected annual growth rate of 6.27%. Assuming that the outstanding debt of local governments nationwide also grew at the same rate in 2011 and that the contingent liabilities arising from direct or indirect guarantees provided by local governments also grew at the same rate, then we can obtain this portion of debt stock in the corresponding year.

(2) Local public sector debt

The first is the debt of public institutions under local government departments. Particularly, the sectors such as transportation and education can carry out various investment and financing activities by extensively exercising the right to non-tax revenue on behalf of the government. Their funding sources are the public revenue collected, including funds and fees, and they can also borrow money from financial institutions by pledging the right to income. When this portion of debt is settled up, if the original debtor is unable to repay it, it will be translated into the direct debt of the local government.

According to the data of the National Audit Office, as of the end of 2010, the fund subsidies provided by local governments to public institutions and public service institutions totaled 1968.853 billion yuan. Excluding the debt for which local governments issued official guarantees (to avoid overlapped calculation with the secured debt above), the debt that will be repaid by government fiscal revenue and other related debt totaled 1783.192 billion yuan. Assuming that the annual growth rate of this portion of debt is the same as that of outstanding local government debt, we can obtain the portion of debt stock in the corresponding year.

Second, the debt of Local Government Financial Platforms (LGFPs).

It is currently a form of local government debt that has aroused widespread concern in various circles and most frequently discussed. The so-called "local government investment and financing platforms" refer to the economic entities with independent legal person status established by local governments and their departments and agencies by means of financial grants or injection of land, equities and other assets to raise funds for government investment projects. Since the 1990s, facing huge pressure on urban infrastructure construction, local governments have been establishing various special investment and financing companies or institutions to borrow money from banks or trust companies so as to bypass the *Budget Law* to realize extrabudgetary borrowing. In the wake of the Asian financial crisis, government investments were expanding, urban construction investment companies with the nature of local government investment and financing platform, which once acted as the borrowers, had repeatedly appeared in the "bank–government cooperation" with "bundled loan" agreements as the main contents. In 2002, Chongqing set up eight government construction investment groups, which was called by the World Bank as "Chongqing state-owned investment group model". Since then, LGFPs have been further promoted. In the process of tackling the international financial crisis, the People's Bank of China and CBRC jointly issued in March 2009 the *Guiding Opinions of the People's Bank of China and China Banking Regulatory Commission on Further Adjusting the Credit Structure to Promote the Rapid yet Steady Development of the National Economy*, which states that "we should support local governments to establish investment and financing platforms where conditions permit, issue corporate bonds, medium and long-term notes and other financing tools and broaden the financing channels of matching funds for the projects invested by the central government." Since then, the local government investment and financing platforms have emerged in large numbers.

According to the data of the National Audit Office, as of the end of 2010, local governments at provincial, municipal, and county levels had established 6576 financing platform companies, including: 165 at provincial level, 1648 at municipal level and 4763 at county level. Three provincial-level governments, 29 municipal-level governments and 44 county-level governments each had established over 10 financing platform companies. From the perspective of business scope of these companies, 3234 companies have the main function of financing government construction projects, 1173 companies have the function of financing and investing in government construction projects, and 2169 companies are also engaged in other businesses.

LGFPs mainly borrow money through three means:

First, bank loans. The relevant data are from the statistics of CBRC.

Second, urban construction investment corporation bonds (including corporate bonds, medium-term notes and short-term financing bonds etc.). This kind of bonds is nominally corporate bonds, but in essence are quasi government bonds, similar to municipal bonds abroad. The relevant data are from the statistics of bond market.

Third, infrastructure trust and other shadow banking channels. The total trust loans invested in infrastructure projects in the related years can be obtained according to the major business data of trust companies released by China Trustee Association (the data of 2009 are not available in the statistics, so the data at the end of the first quarter of 2010 are used).

It should be noted that, due to the relatively limited scale of financing of LGFPCs before 2009 and unavailability of relevant information, here we temporarily set the scale of financing in 2007 and 2008 to be 1 and 2 trillion yuan respectively.

13.2.4 Contingent Implicit Liabilities

(1) Non-performing assets of local financial institutions

Here we mainly take into consideration local banking institutions. Local banking institutions can be divided into two categories according to forms of ownership. One is local state-owned or state-controlled financial institutions, and the other is local non-state-owned financial institutions, including rural cooperative financial institutions. When non-performing assets and payment gap appear, from the perspective of nature of property right, the first category of local state-owned financial institutions will naturally be translated into direct debt of local government. For the second category of local non-state-owned financial institutions, to maintain financial and social stability, local governments will have to bear part of the final responsibility and pay the cost of direct rescue, which will also form local government debt.

CBRC has provided the total amounts of the five tiers of non-performing loans of banking institutions in different years (the data for 2007–2009 are total non-performing loans of commercial banks). According to the loan quality statistics of the central bank and local banks for 2010, we can obtain the proportion of non-performing loans of local banks (52.8%). Assuming that the ratio remained stable in recent years, then we can estimate the balance of non-performing loans of local banking institutions in the relevant years.

(2) Debt of local state-owned enterprises

Theoretically, local state-owned enterprises are corporate and market entities that enjoy full management authority and assume sole responsibility for their profits and losses, so they should take on their own debts. However, from the perspective of investors, there is an inseparable link between local governments and local state-owned enterprises. When enterprises are unable to repay their debts, local governments have to take the responsibility for repaying their debts. Furthermore, from the perspective of social stability, local governments will also provide a bailout to local state-owned enterprises and assume the role of the final payer. Therefore, the debt of local state-owned enterprises have indirectly formed contingent government debt of local governments.

The data here are from the balance sheets of state-owned non-financial corporations. It should be noted that local state-owned enterprises to a large extent include LGFPs as government-backed entities. To prevent overlapping, it is necessary to deduct the estimated size of the debt of LGFPs.

13.3 Preparation of Local Government Balance Sheet

Based on the above estimation method, we have tentatively prepared the simplified local government balance sheet (2007–2011) (see Table 13.1).

As shown in Table 13.1 above, during 2007–2011, the total assets of local governments increased from 49.87 to 89.98 trillion yuan, an increase of 0.8 times. In the structure of total assets, resource assets owned by local governments and local operating state-owned assets took a very large proportion and grew rapidly (see Fig. 13.1).

During 2007–2011, the total liabilities of local governments increased from 14.58 to 28.93 trillion yuan, an increase of 1.08 times. In the structure of total liabilities, the size of direct liabilities was relatively limited, contingent liabilities, especially contingent explicit liabilities, took a very large proportion and grew rapidly (see Fig. 13.2).

During 2007–2011, total assets and total liabilities of local governments were showing an expanding trend, while the growth rate of total assets was higher than that of total liabilities, so the net worth of local government has been growing and increased from 35.29 to 61.05 trillion yuan, an increase of 0.73 times (see Fig. 13.3). Therefore, from the perspective of net assets, local governments seems not to be exposed to extensive and overall debt risks.

Table 13.1 Simplified local government balance sheet: 2007–2011 (unit 100 million yuan)

	2007	2008	2009	2010	2011
Total assets	498,735.23	586,179.42	637,972.16	755,268.95	899,837.01
1. Local operating state-owned assets	132,688.47	156,721.1	183,431.44	233,896.12	292,156.98
2. Local non-operating state-owned assets	44,531.79	48,581.63	54,961.69	62,250.4	70,758.03
3. Resource assets owned by local governments	312,720.97	370,983.69	386,071.03	443,371.43	520,022
4. Deposits of local government at the central bank	8794	9893	13,508	15,751	16,900
Total liabilities	138,932.2	157,734.69	189,351.81	240,953.14	288,592.18
1. Direct explicit liabilities	2367.7	2167.76	4342.49	6972.84	9591.1
A. Local government bonds	–	–	2000	4000	6000
B. Local government sovereign debt	2367.7	2167.76	2342.49	2972.84	3591.1
2. Direct implicit liabilities	18,120.53	20,095.72	20,353.79	22,126.48	24,287.95
3. Contingent explicit liabilities	27,337.31	41,408.12	123,341.03	151,047.66	157,940
A. Debt for which local governments issued official guarantees	9833.79	12,142.77	19,661.57	23,369.74	24,835.02
B. Local public sector debt	17,503.52	29,265.35	103,679.46	127,677.92	133,104.98
(A) Debt of public service institutions under local government departments	7503.52	9265.35	15,002.46	17,831.92	18,949.98
(B) Debt of LGFPs	10,000	20,000	88,677	109,846	114,155
4. Contingent implicit liabilities	91,106.66	94,063.09	41,314.5	60,806.16	96,773.13
A. Non-performing assets of local financial institutions	6697.26	2958.15	2625.9	6566.74	5561.64
B. Debt of local state-owned enterprises	84,409.4	91,104.94	38,688.6	54,239.42	91,211.49
Net assets	359,803.03	428,444.73	448,620.35	514,315.81	611,244.83

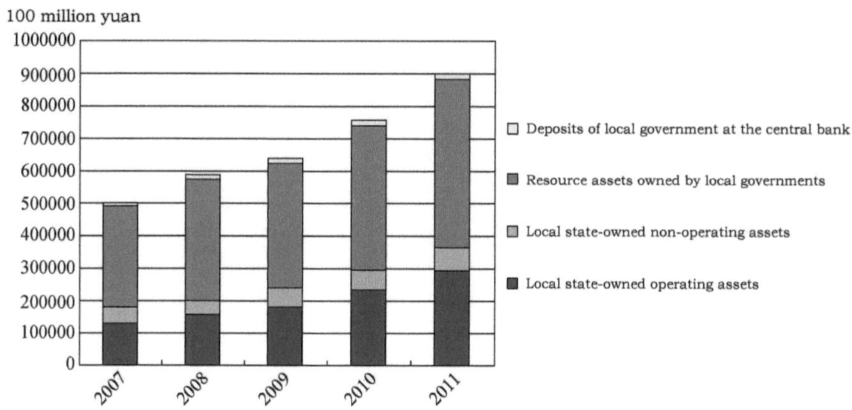

Fig. 13.1 Size and structure of total assets of local governments: 2007–2011 (unit: 100 million yuan)

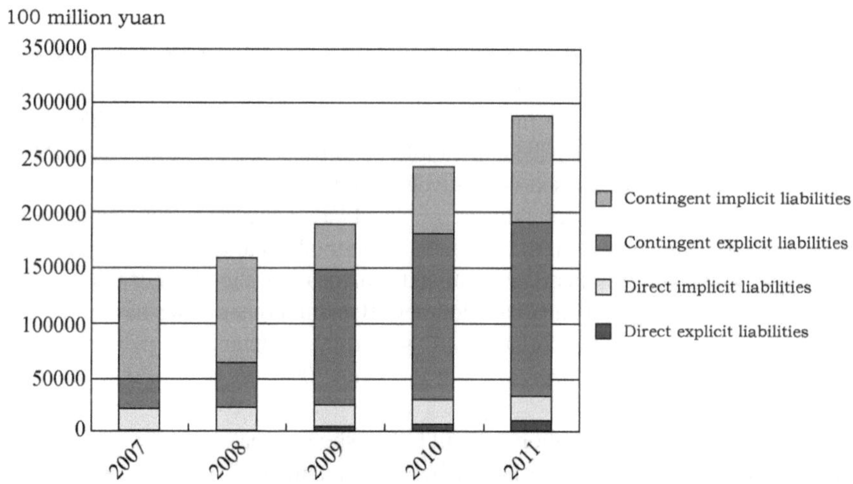

Fig. 13.2 Size and structure of total liabilities of local governments: 2007–2011 (unit: 100 million yuan)

13.4 Local Government Debt Risk Analysis

13.4.1 Hierarchical Distribution of Debt Risk

The debt risk of governments at the provincial level is lower, while the debt risk of governments at the prefecture and county-level is higher, especially the debt risk of governments at district- and county-level.

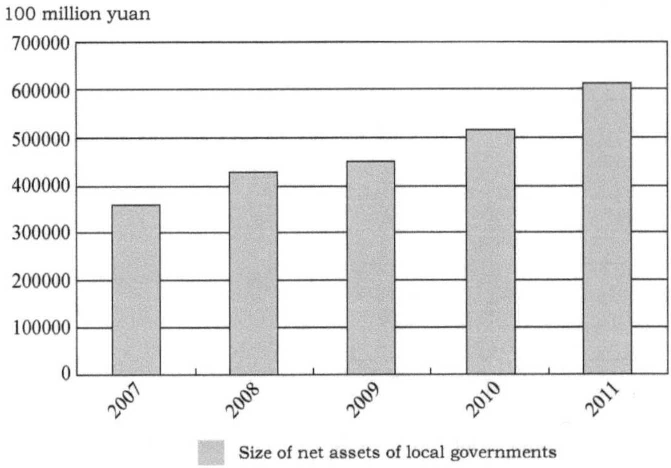

Fig. 13.3 Size of net assets of local governments in 2007–2011 (100 million yuan)

As far as governments at the provincial level are concerned, the size of debt is generally small (see Fig. 13.4), while their financial strength is generally powerful, and the asset quality of their financing platforms is relatively higher. The commercial banks have also provided favorable conditions for the loans of financing platforms, and the risk exposed is relatively small.

As far as governments at the county level are concerned, the county-level economy is less developed on the whole, and the total fiscal revenue is insufficient. Due to the low level of industrialization and urbanization, the effect of land finance is limited. Particularly, as China Development Bank and other banks have gradually expanded their loans to county-level government financing platforms (the county-level financing platforms account for about 70%), the debt risks at this level were further exposed.

The audit results of the National Audit Office showed that, as of the end of 2010, the ratio of debt that would be repaid by government fiscal revenue owed by 78

Fig. 13.4 Hierarchical distribution of outstanding debt of local governments at the end of 2010. *Source* The National Audit Office 2011

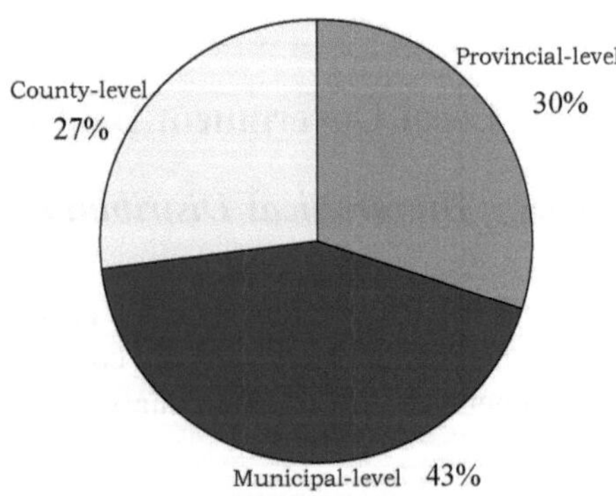

municipal-level governments and 99 county-level governments was higher than 100%, accounting for 19.9 and 3.56% respectively of the total debt of governments at the two levels. Due to inadequate solvency, some local governments can only take out new loans to repay old ones. As of the end of 2010, the proportion of new loans borrowed by 22 municipal-level governments and 20 county-level governments to repay old ones was over 20%. The debts of some regions were overdue, and the proportion of overdue debt of 4 municipal-level governments and 23 county-level governments was over 10%.

13.4.2 Regional Distribution of Debt Risk

Regionally, the overall judgment is that the debt risk in the central and western regions is greater than that in the eastern regions. Although the size of debt in the eastern regions was larger than that in the central and western regions (see Fig. 13.5), the eastern regions had a better economic foundation, ample government financial resources and higher land revenue, and the asset quality of their financing platforms was better, so they had stronger ability to resolve the debt risks. The central and western regions had a relatively weak economic foundation, inadequate financial capacity and limited land revenue, their asset quality was poorer than that of the eastern regions, so they were facing greater pressure in debt risk. Especially in the western regions, the debt risk was relatively concentrated, and in some places there was serious dislocation between their liabilities and debt repayment capability.

Particularly, it should be note that the proportion of urban fixed asset investment of the central and western regions continued to increase in recent years. In 2004, the urban fixed asset investment of 10 eastern provinces (municipalities) and the three northeastern provinces in accounted for 59.4% 6 central provinces accounted for 17.8% and 12 western provinces (autonomous regions and municipalities) accounted for 20.8%. As of 2011, the share of the eastern regions, including the three northeastern provinces, fell to 52.5% (among which the share of 10 eastern provinces fell to 42%), while the share of the central and western regions increased to 22.5 and 23.1% respectively. If the regional structure of urban fixed-asset

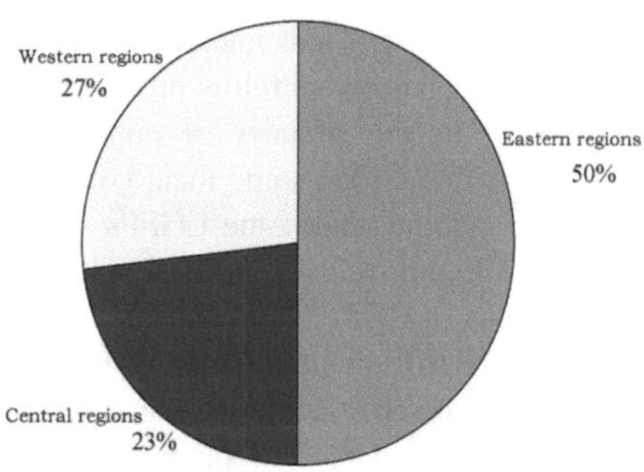

Fig. 13.5 Geographical distribution of outstanding debt of local governments by the end of 2010. *Source* The National Audit Office 2011

investment is approximated as regional distribution of debt, then the regional changes in the proportion of investment in fixed assets show that the debt risk in the central and western regions is gradually getting more serious.

13.4.3 Sectoral Distribution of Debt Risk

Sectorally, the highway sector, higher education institutions and hospitals in some regions are heavily in debt and bear enormous debt pressure.

According to the audit report of the National Audit Office, as of the end of 2010, the outstanding local government debt for highway construction was 1.116811 trillion yuan, of which the debt that would be repaid by government fiscal revenue was 75.402 billion yuan, the debt for which local governments issued official guarantees was 780.963 billion yuan, and other related debt was 260.446 billion yuan, accounting for 6.75, 69.93 and 23.32% respectively. In some regions, highways were in construction and initial operation period, the income was insufficient to pay the principal and interest on debt, so they had to take out new loans to repay old ones. In 2010, the proportion of new loans to repay old ones in the debt of the highway sector secured by local governments was 54.64%.

According to the audit report of the National Audit Office, as of the end of 2010, the government debt owed by 1164 local higher education institutions and 3120 public hospitals was 263.498 billion yuan and 97.774 billion yuan. Among them, the proportion of new loans borrowed to repay old ones in the debt for which local governments issued official guarantees and other related debt owed by 387 higher education institutions and 230 hospitals was over 50% in 2010, and the new loans to repay old amounted to 54.247 billion yuan and 9.529 billion yuan that year. 95 higher education institutions and 575 hospitals had overdue debt, which was 2.718 billion yuan and 3.042 billion yuan respectively.

13.4.4 Project-Based Distribution of Debt Risk

Projects can be roughly divided into two categories by debt risk: projects that can repay the principal and interest of debt by relying on their own stable operating income and projects with low profitability that need to be supported by government resources. In the process of coping with the financial crisis, with the rapid expansion of LGFPs, some local governments injected the assets that could hardly generate income, and some LGFPs at county level even had no operating income and were highly reliant on fiscal subsidies.

The data of CBRC show that as of the end of June 2010, LGFPs had borrowed a total of 7.66 trillion yuan, among which about 1.8 trillion yuan rely on the cash flow of projects to repay the principal and interest, accounting for 24%; 4 trillion yuan has inadequate source of repayment must rely on the second source of repayment to cover the principal and interest, accounting for 50%; and nearly 2 trillion yuan was invested to the projects in respect of which the borrowers and financial guarantees were not compliant or there were serious risks for repayment in the current period (for example, loans were misappropriated and loans were used as capital), accounting for about 26%. The audit results of the National Audit Office show that the governments in some places are highly reliant on the income from land transfer to repay their debt. As of the end of 2010, in the outstanding debt that would be repaid by local government fiscal revenue (6710.951 billion yuan), the debt for which local governments have committed to repaying with their land transfer income amounted to 2547.351 billion yuan, accounting for 38%, involving 12 provinces, 307 prefecture-level governments and 1131 county-level governments. These projects in absence of the first source of repayment have some hidden debt risks.

13.4.5 Term Distribution of Debt Risk

From the perspective of debt repayment terms, according to the audit report of the National Audit Office, as of the end of 2010, the outstanding local government debt due to mature in 2011 and 2012 accounted for 24.49 and 17.17%, that due to mature in 2013–2015 accounted for 11.37, 9.28 and 7.48% respectively, and that due to mature after 2016 accounted for 30.21%. This shows that the years of 2011–2013 is the peak time for maturity of local government debt. When debts are due to mature centrally, there is not enough cash flow for repayment and it is impossible to extend the maturity of the debts, the risk of default is likely to appear. What we should particularly note is that there often exists maturity mismatch in the balance sheets of LGFPs. On the one hand, their debts are mostly short-term bank loans with maturity of 3–5 years. On the other hand, the projects they have invested in are mostly mid and long-term urban infrastructure construction projects that take 5–10 years to generate cash flow and earnings. This has led to serious mismatch between debt maturity and cash flow distribution of projects, causing the liquidity payment problem. This kind of debt repayment "liquidity risk" should arouse wide concern.

13.5 Formation and Prevention of Local Government Debt Risk

There are deep-seated institutional causes for accumulation of local government debt risks. To prevent further accumulation of local government debt risks, a fundamental approach is to adjust the institutional factor to control the debt increase. This mainly involves the reform in four aspects: first, the reform of government functions; second, the reform of the investment and financing system; third, the reform of the taxation system; fourth, the reform of the financial system.

13.5.1 Reform of Government Functions

In recent years, with the emergence of the new development concept, some indicators measuring social development and sustainable development also began to be included into the assessment and evaluation system for local officials, but this positive change is still not enough to shake the core position of GDP in the entire evaluation system. Under the existing performance appraisal system and political incentive structure, economic growth and fiscal revenue growth has become an important signal display mechanism and the mechanism for the government at the higher level to identify the efforts of local governments, so economic development has become the core of all work of local governments.

Such strong preference for growth can be seen by comparing the GDP objectives of all provinces in their 11th Five-Year plans and 12th Five-Year plans. In the 11th Five-Year period, the target GDP growth rate is 7.5% at the state level and 10% at the local level, with the latter over 30% higher than the former. In the 12th Five-Year period, the target GDP growth rate is 7% at the state level and 10.5% at the local level, with the latter 50% higher than the former. The gap between the growth targets at the central and local levels is further broadened in the 12th Five-Year period. This expanding trend is particularly evident in the central and western regions: In the 6 central provinces, the average economic growth rate in their 11th Five-Year plans is more than 10%, while this figure is over 11% in their 12th Five-Year plans; in the 12 western provinces, the average economic growth rate in their 11th Five-Year plans is more than 10%, while this figure is over 12% in their 12th Five-Year plans. The pursuit of double growth in 5 years has almost become a universal goal.

Driven by such growth priority strategy, the governments at all levels devote most of their efforts to production and businesses and assume many economic development functions. In our view, local governments' overly penetration in the microscopic field and direct involvement in economic operation, especially their strong impulse in attracting investment and land management, have shown a distinct corporate behavioral characteristic. Professor Jean Oi at politics department of Stanford University had once used the concept of "local state corporatism"[1] for straightforward analysis of the corporate behavior of Chinese local governments. Judging from the present situation, the characteristics of such "local state corporatism" or local "construction (development)- oriented government" still universally exists.

[1]Oi (1992).

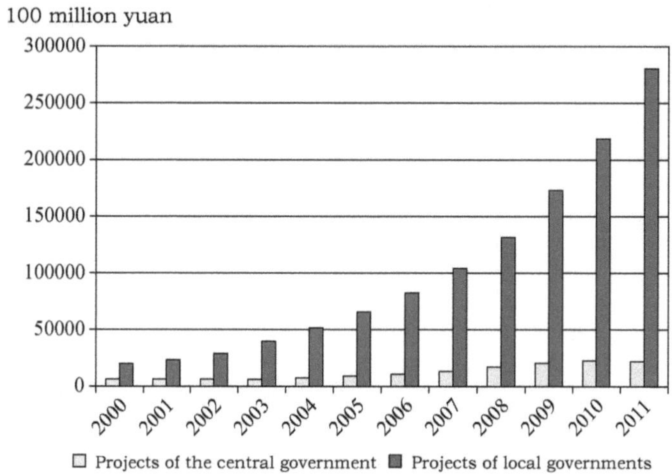

Fig. 13.6 Changes in urban fixed asset investment by relationship of administrative subordination. *Source* Statistical Yearbook of China 2012

To investigate the characteristics of such construction-oriented government, based on the information of *Government Finance Statistics Yearbook 2008* of the IMF, we have compared the structures of fiscal expenditure of the governments of relevant countries based on the functional classification. We have chosen the data for 2007 mainly in a bid to eliminate the distorted influence of governments' deep intervention in economic affairs in the abnormal event of the financial crisis on the structure of fiscal expenditure. As shown in Fig. 13.2, compared with the developed economies or the emerging and developing economies or the transitional economies and the traditional government-led East Asian economies, China's expenditure in economic affairs has taken a significantly higher proportion. In all countries for which data are available, China is the country that has highest spending in economic affairs except Bhutan, 13% higher than the country with the second highest spending in this aspect. Hierarchically, the characteristic of such construction-oriented government is largely reflected at the local level because the proportion of government's economic expenditure at the central level is not particularly high compared with the relevant countries (see Fig. 13.3).

The characteristics of the construction-oriented government at the local level can also be reflected in the subordinate relationship changes in urban fixed asset investment projects. As shown in Fig. 13.6, after entering the new century, the growth rate of local projects is much faster than that of projects under the central government. This has resulted in the increasing proportion of local projects, which has exceeded 80% since 2002 and reached more than 92.8% in 2011, showing that the dominant position of local investment has an increasing trend (Tables 13.2, 13.3).

In the institutional context of construction-oriented government, local governments' inner impulse to seek economic expansion has further given rise to the

Table 13.2 Comparison between the government fiscal expenditure structures of China and several other countries (2007, %)

	General public affairs	National defense	Public order and safety	Economic affairs	Environmental protection	Housing and community living facilities	Health	Culture and entertainment and religious affairs	Education	Social security
China	18.2	5.24	4.98	37.68	3.21	0.44	2.51	1.27	9.32	17.15
The United States	13.47	11.54	5.71	9.98	–	1.85	21.06	0.87	16.93	18.59
Germany	13.61	2.41	3.51	7.23	1.1	1.93	14.01	1.36	9.09	45.75
France	13.28	3.39	2.41	5.36	1.66	3.62	13.72	2.9	11.24	42.41
Italy	15.98	3.14	3.89	10.23	1.83	2.16	12.75	3.05	11.22	35.93
Japan	12.91	2.59	3.89	10.55	3.55	1.81	19.6	0.43	10.74	33.93
Singapore	12.37	27.99	6.24	9.81	–	12.19	6.04	0.48	20.82	4.07
Poland	12.58	3.89	4.72	10.15	1.4	1.7	10.62	2.64	12.72	39.57
Ukraine	7.66	3.04	5.25	13.54	0.66	2	9.05	1.9	14.01	42.89

Source: *Government Finance Statistics Yearbook* 2008 of the IMF

Table 13.3 Comparison between the expenditure structures of central governments of China and several other countries (2007, %)

	General public affairs	National defense	Public order and safety	Economic affairs	Environmental protection	Housing and community living facilities	Healthy	Culture and entertainment and religious affairs	Education	social security
China	60.49	11.37	1.82	19.67	0.03	0.27	0.16	0.32	1.22	4.65
The United States	13.4	19.96	1.53	5.91	–	1.95	25.18	0.15	2.39	29.54
Germany	14.56	3.68	0.5	5.37	0.06	0.71	20.35	0.15	0.59	54.03
Italy	19.98	3.52	4.08	6.39	0.4	0.5	13.54	0.83	10.9	39.87
South Korea	24.02	11.33	5.48	17.63	–	4.42	0.99	1.01	15.36	20.73
Singapore	12.37	27.99	6.24	9.81	–	12.19	6.04	0.48	20.82	4.07
Poland	13.88	4.63	5.29	6.8	0.21	0.42	11.58	0.9	11.48	44.82
Ukraine	23.52	3.65	6.24	11.58	0.58	0.59	3.1	0.84	5.81	44.08
Chile	7.71	6.51	7.02	14.3	0.32	1.49	15.94	0.71	17.24	28.76
Mexico	38.36	3.04	2.72	8.11	–	6.92	4.95	0.56	24.73	20.12

Source: *Government Finance Statistics Yearbook* 2008 of the IMF impulse of borrowing. To curb local governments' impulse of borrowing and control the corresponding debt risks, it is necessary to promote the transformation from a growth-oriented government to a public service-oriented one. This first requires to improve the performance appraisal system. In the design of the performance appraisal system and appraisal indicators, we should try to weaken the tendency of directly linking them with economic growth rate and gradually improve the quality and efficiency of economic growth and the degree of concern over social development, resource conservation and environmental protection so as to build a more scientific and more reasonable performance appraisal system. To better achieve this, we should improve the top-down appraisal mechanism and positively introduce the bottom-up appraisal mechanism with the public as participants. This is crucial to correct the behaviors of local governments.

13.5.2 Reform of the Investment and Financing System

By analyzing the investment areas of debt capital of local governments nationwide (the spending part) at the end of 2010 (see Fig. 13.7), we can find that the top three areas are municipal construction, transportation and land purchase, storage and consolidation, which together account for 72%. These three areas are directly related to urban infrastructure construction.

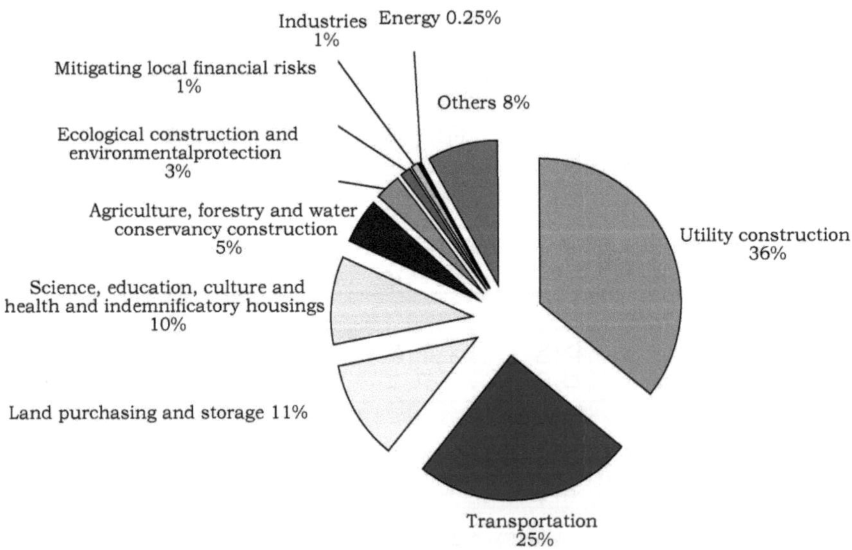

Fig. 13.7 Investment areas of debt capital of local governments nationwide at the end of 2010. *Source* The National Audit Office 2011

The infrastructure projects which local governments are currently involved in can be divided into four categories by the external progress and earning prospects. The projects in the first category are pure public welfare projects from which the services produced are provided free of charge. Even the daily operating costs and maintenance costs of these projects should be replenished from the outside, not to mention investment profits. Those in the second category are low-charge projects. The services generate earnings, but may not be able to compensate for daily operating costs and maintenance costs, and they are unable to recover the investment, let along make profits. Those in the third category are projects that charge fees. Their operating incomes are more than their operating expenses, but the investment can only be partially recovered, so it is difficult to rely on their own accumulation to complete the update of investment properties. Those in the fourth category are projects capable of fully recovering the investment and producing capital accumulation. In these four categories of projects, the first two categories can generate profits and thus are public welfare projects, the projects in the fourth category have earning prospects and thus are commercial in nature, while whether those in the third category can generate proficts depend on individual situations.

According to the above classification, the government is generally responsible for investing in the non-profit and public welfare projects that have no or low economic benefits and non-public capital is unwilling to enter, while commercial projects that can generate profits and non-public capital are willing to invest usually achieve a good equilibrium through market competition, so there is no need for government intervention. But for a long time, due to the obstacles in the investment and financing system, there are restrictions for private capital to enter the field of infrastructure. The analysis of fixed asset investment structure in the infrastructure sector in 2011 in Table 13.4 shows that only a small amount of private capital has entered this sector. Due to government's over commitment, some quasi-public welfare projects in the field of infrastructure that can generate stable operating income through operation and management and thus can be partially marketized as well as the non-public welfare projects that can assume sole responsibility for their own profits and losses and operate fully according to the market principles are unable to attract sufficient private capital, thus increasing local government debt risks.

To alleviate the financial pressure, the situation of local government-led infrastructure investment should be changed, and the Public–Private Partnership (PPP) should be used to prompte the transition of local governments from the first investors to the last investors. That is, their investment scope should be limited mainly to the non-profit and public welfare area where private capital is unwilling to enter and should in principle no longer invest in profitable commercial areas. For quasi-public welfare projects that can generate stable operating income and non-public welfare projects that have good market prospects, we should relax restrictions on market access for private capital and strive to achieve commercial operation as soon as possible. By transferring the ownership or operation rights to social forces, we can realize the transfer of government risks to market risks.

Table 13.4 Fixed assets investment structure infrastructure sectors, 2011 (unit 100 million yuan)

	Total investment	Item		
		State holding	Group holding	Private holding
Electricity, heat generation and supply	11,603.5	8636.6 (74.4%)	459.2 (4%)	1999.9 (17.2%)
Gas production and supply	1244.4	610.1 (49%)	41.7 (3.4%)	503.2 (40.4%)
Water production and supply	1811.3	1271.1 (70.2%)	165.8 (9.2%)	286.4 (15.8%)
Railway transportation	5915	5760.0 (97.4%)	26.4 (0.4%)	110.9 (1.9%)
Urban public transportation	2225.3	2122.9 (95.4%)	29.1 (1.3%)	50.2 (2.3%)
Air transportation	835.8	748.7 (89.6%)	59.9 (7.2%)	20.7 (2.5%)
Telecommunications and other information transmission services	1680.3	1262 (75.1%)	27.5 (1.6%)	75.5 (4.5%)

Source China Statistical Yearbook 2012

13.5.3 Reform of the Taxation System

As far as local finance is concerned, to realize the reciprocity between income and expenditure, there are roughly two different matching methods, namely direct and indirect matching. The former means that in fiscal decentralization system design, the expenditure of governments at various levels and the fiscal income at the corresponding levels are basically equivalent. The latter means that in fiscal decentralization system design, the matching between income and expenditure of local governments at the corresponding levels will not be taken into consideration in division of income, but instead after the income is centrally collected by the central government, the matching between income and expenditure of local governments at various levels is achieved through transfer payment. This in fact also involves two different forms of fiscal delegation, namely the form of fiscal delegation in which expenditure responsibility and income power are delegated simultaneously and the form of fiscal delegation in which only the expenditure responsibility is delegated while the income power is not delegated. In the latest domestic and foreign papers on political economics, these two different forms of financial delegation are distinguished and it is found that: there is great difference between the two forms of fiscal delegation in management performance: the form of fiscal delegation in which only the expenditure responsibility is delegated, but the income power is not delegated and thus local governments need plenty of transfer payments from a higher level, and the form of fiscal delegation in which expenditure responsibility and income power are delegated simultaneously. The former is likely to generate a series of costs arising from distortion of local incentives. Some domestic and international studies show that in some developing countries, such as the Latin American countries, the financing through transfer payment from a higher level under delegation of expenditure responsibility has resulted in increased moral hazards, spending and debt of local governments.[2]

Further analysis shows that transfer payments may give rise to moral hazards of local governments. This is because transfer payments may result in the imperfectness of the accountability system for officials and thus cause soft budget constraints, which will reduce the use efficiency of financial allocations. The relevant studies show that in a long term, compared with the relief of tax to be paid to the central government, the central government's total grants (especially unconditional non-matching subsidies) have much greater effect in stimulating the spending of the governments receiving subsidies. Meanwhile, a government grant to a recipient municipality increases the level of local public spending more than an increase in local citizen income of an equivalent size. That is, the budgetary spending stimulated by the central government's grants may have weaker hard constraints on local governments than the budgetary spending stimulated by local tax income increase. This phenomenon is called "flypaper effect". That is, money sticks where it hits, like a fly to flypaper.[3] An important reason for forming such a situation is that: if a local government's spending exceeds its budget and results in a deficit, it may not be responsible for the gap, while the gap will be filled by the subsidy provided by the government at a higher level afterwards, then the local government is in a simple status as an income recipient. Since the subsidy is not its own income, but a cheap money, which may makes the local government to have a "fiscal illusion" and stimulate its excessive spending, and this may result in an unreasonable spending direction and inefficient use of funds. Undoubtedly, the presence of soft budget constraint has, to a certain extent, induced an increase in the fiscal deficit of local governments and leaves local finance trapped in a vicious circle.

The analysis of China's relevant institutional tax decentralization arrangement using the above theory shows that: it largely shows the indirect matching between income and expenditure of local governments and the characteristics of asymmetric decentralization of expenditure responsibility and income power. As shown in Fig. 13.8, since the tax decentralization reform was launched, the self-sufficiency rate of central finance is showing an overall upward trend, while the self-sufficiency rate of local finance is showing an overall downward trend. Thus, local finance was more reliant on the central finance's transfer payments, and both the proportion of the central finance's subsidies in local disposable financial resources and the proportion of transfer payments in local fiscal expenditure were at a relatively high level (in 2009, the central government's subsidies accounted for 46.8% of local disposable financial resources nationwide, and 39.1% of local fiscal expenditure was from the central government's transfer payments). When most part of a government's spending does not come from its own sources of revenue, its budget

---

[2]Fei et al. (2008).

[3]For the typical analysis of flypaper effect, refer to Gramlich (1969, 1977), Henderson (1968), Inman (1988).

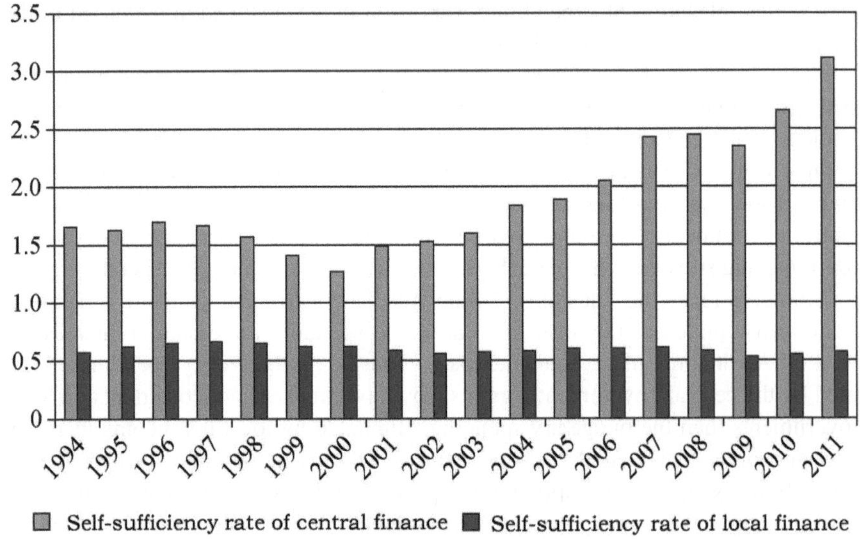

Fig. 13.8 Changes in self-sufficiency rate of the central and local governments since the tax decentralization system was adopted. *Note* Financial self-sufficiency rate = income at the corresponding level of governments at various levels/expenditure at the corresponding level. It was calculated based on *Statistical Yearbook of China* for various years

constraints will be softened and its behavioral accountability will also be reduced accordingly.

Moreover, although under the current budget system, local governments are not allowed to issue public bonds, the fact is that local governments have borrowed a large amount of debt through various informal channels in disguised forms. Under the background that local bond issuance is non-public and non-transparent, and due to the lack of an effective supervision and constraint mechanism, soft budget constraints and moral hazards have been formed, which has ultimately led to disorderly growth of local government debt.

For this reason, we should try to change the situation of asymmetric decentralization between expenditure responsibility and income power and local finance's highly reliance on transfer payments, alleviate the derived local government financing pressure derived therefrom and change the distorted behavioral pattern. In the division of administrative powers, while continuing to give full play to the role of local governments, while the central government's expenditure responsibility should be appropriately strengthened. The expenditure responsibility in the fields of pension, compulsory education of floating population's children, jurisdiction, food and drug supervision, cross-basin river governance and cross-regional pollution control can be appropriately handed over to the center government. In the division of financial power, we should take increasing local autonomous fiscal revenue as the core goal, improve the main types of local tax, reasonably divide the shared taxes and reform the tax system in which tax rights are overly concentrated.

In the meanwhile, the Ministry of Finance started to issue bonds on behalf of local governments in 2009 and the central government started a trial program in 2011 to allow Shanghai, Zhejiang and Guangdong and Shenzhen to issue bonds directly. We should take these as an opportunity and give local governments the creditor right and allow them to issue bonds publicly in the capital markets. Through the implementation of local government sunshine financing system, we can gradually improve the transparency of local government debt risk, and form effective supervision over local governments' borrowing through market-oriented approach so as to enhance constraints on local financial budget and debt, inhibit financial opportunistic behaviors and curb the borrowing impulse.

13.5.4 Reform of the Financial System

Observing the funding sources of local government debt, we have found that: bank loans account for an absolutely large proportion (see Fig. 13.9). This means that in the process of debt expansion, the impact on the existing banking system and credit behaviors should not be ignored. In fact, it is both the lending impulse of the banking sector and the borrowing impulse of local government that has amplified the size of local government debt.

(1) The lending impulse resulting from concentrated ownership structure of state-owned commercial banks

Presently, although the state-owned commercial banks have undergone the joint-stock reform and listed in the capital market, the basic ownership pattern has not changed very much. By the end of 2010, in the ownership structure of entire banking sector in China, state-owned shares accounted for 53.85%, state-owned legal person shares accounted for 6.81%, and non-state-owned shares accounted for 39.34%. Among them, in the ownership structure of the five major banks of ICBC, ABC, BOC, CCB and BCM, state-owned shares accounted for 68.19%,

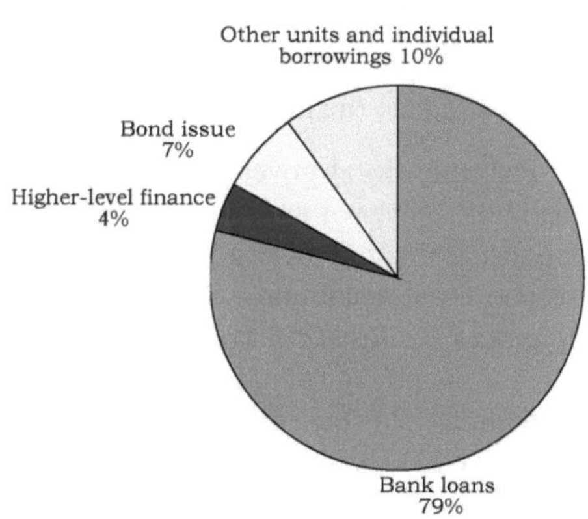

Fig. 13.9 Funding sources of local government debt by the end of 2010. *Source* The National Audit Office 2011

state-owned legal person shares accounted for 1.36% and non-state-owned shares accounted for 30.45%. In the ownership structure of the 12 joint-stock banks nationwide, state-owned shares accounted for 3.60%, state-owned legal person shares accounted for 25.93% and non-state-owned shares accounted for 70.47%.

Under such ownership structure, the government as the main investor provides a kind of implicit risk guarantees with the state credit and the status as the final rescuer, soft budget constraints and moral hazards arising thereof are likely to stimulate the lending impulse of state-owned Banks. Especially there is some natural link between local governments and state-owned banks, so the state-owned banks prefer lending money to local governments. This is because, in the financial structure in which indirect financing still occupies the absolute dominant position, dye ti a higher degree of risk aversion of the state-owned commercial banks with a powerful position, coupled with the asymmetric distribution of constraints on loans and incentive mechanisms arising from incomplete commercial reform and interest rate market-oriented reform, local governments with various tacit supports are particularly favored. While the state-owned banks play the "quasi-fiscal" role and provide credit support to priority projects of local governments, their risk awareness will weaken, and the size of loans will expand in an uncontrolled manner. Since the occurrence of the international financial crisis, the tendency of credit financial-orientation has exacerbated, there is increasingly obvious trend that loans are centrally provided to the national key projects. This to a certain extent has reinforced the "local government complex" of bank loans.

(2) The lending impulse resulting from the "too big to fail" pattern of banks

After entering the new century, the market share of assets of banking institutions has changed to some extent (see Fig. 13.10), but the basic pattern dominated by large commercial banks has not substantially changed. The share of large commercial banks in the assets of banking institutions has remained above 50%, and although it declined to a level below 50% in 2011 but still reached 47.3%. This relatively concentrated distribution pattern of assets has highlighted the systematic importance of large commercial banks, the government thus tends to provide some kind of implicit guarantees to avoid going bankrupt, which has in turn led to moral hazards of their lending behavior.

(3) The lending impulse resulting from quasi-fiscal tendency of local financial institutions (mainly including urban commercial banks)

Presently, local governments, relying on the resources at their disposal, especially the power of appointment, still have great control over local financial institutions, and some local governments even take urban commercial banks as their second fiscal institutions. Some places dominate the integration of local financial resources by fostering financial holding groups and strengthen local controlling interest, including strengthening the holding position in rural cooperative financial institutions. In the indirect-financing-based financial structure with with the executive-led characteristics, local governments still have significant influence and

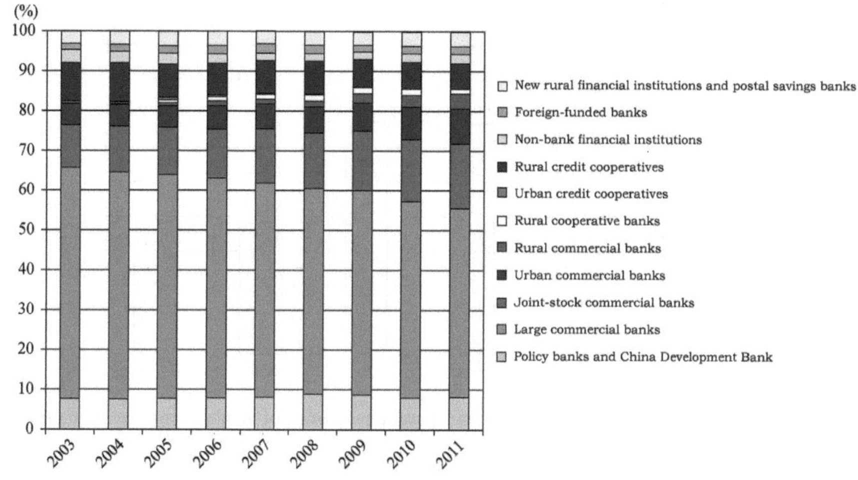

Fig. 13.10 Changes in distribution of total assets of banking institutions. *Source* The 2010 Annual Report of CBRC

discourse power over how to allocate funds to local investment projects. Moreover, in the process of guiding local financial institutions' allocation of funds, local governments can provide various forms of guarantees or disguised guarantees for loans, or use land as collateral to apply to banks for mortgage loans and access to cheap financial resources. To some extent, once a local governments has taken hold of land, this means that it has grasped the right to allocate financial resources in the region. Under the background of government-led resource allocation, "bank-government cooperation" is still a typical mode that local governments dispose financial resources. It should also be noted that, in the existing centralized financial system (vertical financial supervision), less financial risk control responsibilities are delegated to local governments, thereby forming the non-reciprocity between investment and financing incentives and risk control. This has also induced local government to use huge bank loans to support their investment expansion preference. Thus, the investment impulse of local government has gradually evolved into the credit expansion impulse of local banking institutions.

(4) The lending impulse resulting from the traditional extensive business model of banks under the interest rate control

Presently, the income of most commercial banks are mainly from the difference of interest rate, so they are highly reliant on expanding the size of loans. According to the investigation by the IMF (2011) on 17 major commercial banks in China, the proportion of interest income in operating income has maintained at higher than 80% (see Fig. 13.11) in recent years. In such case, even the reform measures such as introduction of strategic investors and listing are adopted, the inter-bank credit market competition pattern and under the pressure of market competition, banks

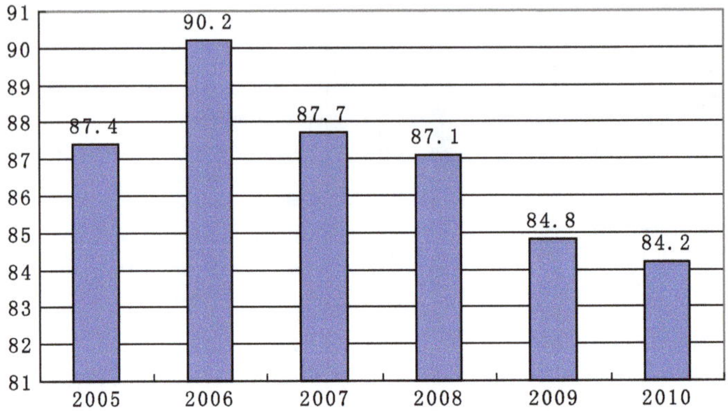

Fig. 13.11 Proportion of interest income in operating income of major commercial banks in recent years (%). *Source* The IMF 2011

still tend to seek cooperation with local governments and strive to increase the size of loans.

To effectively curb the lending impulse in the banking sector, we should fundamentally change the financial system dominated by state-owned banks and encourage the development of non-state-owned banks, promote competition the banking sector and further strengthen risk control from the ownership relations. We should continue to deepen the reform of state-owned and state-holding commercial banks to really change their operating mechanism and operation mode. Meanwhile, we should further promote the market-oriented interest rate reform, positively develop direct financing and establish a multi-level capital market system. We should pay particular attention to regulate governments' land mortgage loans and investment guarantees for enterprises and promote the transformation from executive-led to market-oriented allocation of financial resources.

Chapter 14
External Sector Balance Sheet

International Investment Position (IIP) is a country's external sector balance sheet reflecting a country or region's financial assets, financial liabilities and their component stocks to other countries or regions in the world at a particular point of time, in which external financial assets consist of outward FDI, outward portfolio investment (equity securities and debt securities), other outward investments (trade credits, loans, currencies and deposits, and other assets) and reserve assets (monetary gold, special drawing rights, reserve position in the IMF and foreign exchanges), and external financial liabilities consist of inward FDI, inward portfolio investment (equity securities and debt securities) and other inward investments (trade credits, loans, currencies and deposits, and other assets). The changes in the items of IIP may be caused by either transactions or price changes or exchange rate changes. IIP and BoP Statement together constitute a complete international account system of a country or region.

Presently, the IMF has published the IIPs of most countries, and China started officially publishing the IIP data for 2004 and the following years in 2006. IIP may to some extent reflect a country's ability to respond to potential risks in the face of external shocks. For example, a large amount of international reserves tend to show that a country has a strong ability to respond to external shocks. The analysis of aggregate indicators including total assets, total liabilities, net assets and structural indicators can help identify a country's main problems and conflicts in external economic activities and better forecast potential economic risks so as to take early policy response.

The analysis below will be mainly based on the ideas such as what characteristics IIP reflects, what risks it can reveal and which factors will influence it. First, we will introduce the main characteristics of China's IIP and its formation causes and carry out international comparison, then analyze how the external sector balance sheet methodology reveals the risks and finally analyze the affecting factors of IIP (mainly including total external assets, total external liabilities and net external assets) through international comparison and panel data method and roughly judge the future trend of China's IIP.

Y. Li and X. Zhang, *China's National Balance Sheet*, China Insights,
DOI 10.1007/978-981-10-4385-7_14

14.1 Main Characteristics of China's IIP and International Comparison

14.1.1 Main Characteristics of China's IIP

Table 14.1 gives the data on China's IIP from 2007 to 2012. Its main characteristics is that the external assets are mainly foreign exchange reserves concentrated in the monetary authorities; the external liabilities are mainly inward FDI in the private sector; external assets and external liabilities increased year by year and external assets grew faster than external liabilities, so external net assets are positive and increased year by year.

Figures 14.1 and 14.2 show the proportions of all components of China's total assets and foreign reserve assets in 2012. As shown in the figures, China's total assets mainly consisted of foreign exchange reserves, and due to relatively strong liquidity and controllability of foreign exchange reserves, this is conducive to safeguarding the financial safety. As shown in Fig. 13.3, foreign exchange reserves have been growing in recent years, which was mainly accountable for China's sustained and rapid growth of foreign assets. But the proportion of foreign exchange reserves to total external assets began to gradually decline in 2009, and the contribution of reserve assets to the increment of total external assets in 2012 fell to 30%, far lower than the average annual contribution rate of 65% in 2004.

Figure 13.4 shows that the total external liabilities mainly consisted of inward FDI, and the increase in inward FDI was mainly accountable for the increase in total liabilities. Since 2008, inward FDI and other investment in China has accelerated, leading to rapid increase in total external liabilities. As inward FDIs are mostly highly stable long-term investment behaviors, the likelihood of short-term impact is small for them. This structure is conducive to a certain extent to guard against financial risks. The ratio of inward FDIs to total external liabilities started to declined in 2009 mainly because of divestment and liquidation of inward FDIs and outflow of loans of foreign shareholders and after the financial crisis (Figs. 14.3, 14.4).

As shown in Fig. 14.5, China's total external assets and total external liabilities are showing an upward trend, reflecting the gradual expansion of China's opening up and the increasingly closer contact with the world economy. As the total external assets grew faster than the total external liabilities, the net external assets are positive and increasing year by year, but the growth rate of net external assets has slowed down significantly since 2008, which is related to the decrease of net exports and divestment and liquidation of inward FDIs after this financial crisis. China's enormous net external assets indicate that it has strong international solvency and external financial influence and has become an important force in the international capital supply. But holding enormous net external assets does not mean a strong financial strength. For example, the United States owes enormous external net liabilities but its financial strength is strongest, so a country's financial strength depends largely on the degree of development of its financial market, the

Table 14.1 China's international investment position during 2007–2012 (Unit: $100 million yuan)

Item	2004	2005	2006	2007	2008	2009	2010	2011	2012
Net assets	2764	4077	6402	11,881	14,938	14,905	16,880	16,884	17,364
A. Assets	9291	12,233	16,905	24,162	29,567	34,369	41,189	47,345	51,749
1. Outward FDI	527	645	906	1160	1857	2458	3172	4248	5028
2. Portfolio investment	920	1167	2652	2846	2525	2428	2571	2044	2406
2.1 Equity securities	0	0	15	196	214	546	630	864	1298
2.2 Debt securities	920	1167	2637	2650	2311	1882	1941	1180	1108
3. Other investments	1658	2164	2539	4683	5523	4952	6304	8495	10,437
3.1 Trade credits	432	661	922	1160	1102	1444	2060	2769	3387
3.2 Loans	590	719	670	888	1071	974	1174	2232	2778
3.3 Currencies and deposits	553	675	736	1380	1529	1310	2051	2942	3816
3.4 Other assets	83	109	210	1255	1821	1224	1018	552	457
4. Reserve assets	6186	8257	10,808	15,473	19,662	24,532	29,142	32,558	33,879
4.1 Monetary gold	41	42	123	170	169	371	481	530	567
4.2 SDR	12	12	11	12	12	125	123	119	114
4.3 Reserve position in the IMF	33	14	11	8	20	44	64	98	82
4.4 Foreign exchanges	6099	8189	10,663	15,282	19,460	23,992	28,473	31,811	33,116
B. Liabilities	6527	8156	10,503	12,281	14,629	19,464	24,308	30,461	34,385
1. Inward FDI	3690	4715	6144	7037	9155	13,148	15,696	19,069	21,596
2. Portfolio investment	566	766	1207	1466	1677	1900	2239	2485	3364
2.1 Equity securities	433	636	1065	1290	1505	1748	2061	2114	2622
2.2 Debt securities	133	130	142	176	172	152	178	371	742
3. Other investments	2271	2675	3152	3778	3796	4416	6373	8907	9426

(continued)

Table 14.1 (continued)

Item	2004	2005	2006	2007	2008	2009	2010	2011	2012
3.1 Trade credits	809	1063	1196	1487	1296	1617	2112	2492	2915
3.2 Loan	880	870	985	1033	1030	1636	2389	3724	3680
3.3 Currencies and deposits	381	484	595	791	918	937	1650	2477	2446
3.4 Other liabilities	200	257	377	467	552	227	222	214	384

Source The website of the state administration of foreign exchange

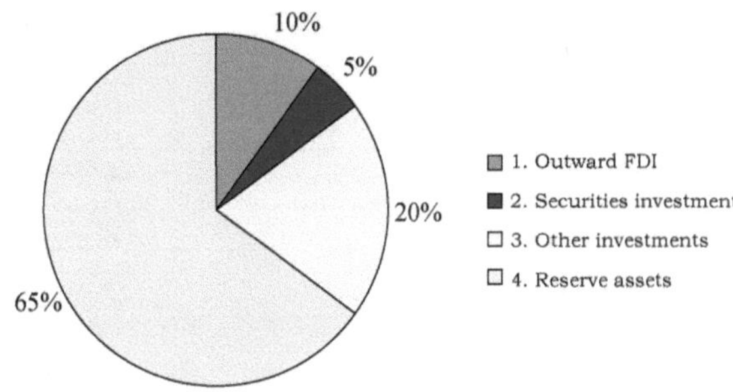

Fig. 14.1 Components of China's total external assets in 2012

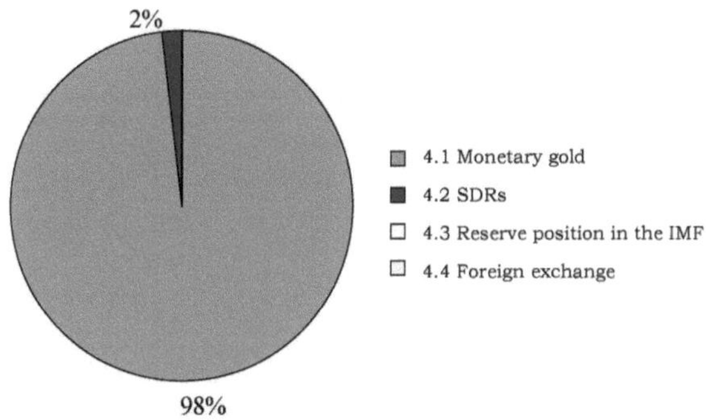

Fig. 14.2 Components of China's reserve assets in 2012

international competitiveness of its financial sector, the internationalization degree of its sovereign currency and other factors.

When ignoring the net errors and omissions, there exists an equation for the BoP: current account balance + capital and financial account balance + change in reserve assets = 0, and it can be transformed to obtain: change in reserve assets = current account balance + capital and financial account balance, in which the negative change in reserve assets means net outflow of reserve assets, i.e. the accumulation of reserve assets, from which we can observe that the increase of reserve assets was mainly from the "double surplus" of current account and capital account. The above equation can also be converted to: current account balance = change in reserve assets—capital and financial account balance, i.e. the international economic equation: current account balance = net capital outflow (including the private sector and the government sector), from which we observe that China's high net external assets was mainly the result of accumulation of current account surpluses year after year.

China's industrialization and export-oriented policies have led to a huge trade surplus, and continuous trade surplus had led to accumulation of net external assets, while in the previous forex settlement and sale system and the subsequent intervention in the foreign exchange market, the continuous accumulation of net external assets was mainly reflected as the rapid increase in foreign exchange reserves. The accumulation of China's huge external assets mainly consisting of foreign exchange reserves has constituted a distinctive characteristic accumulation

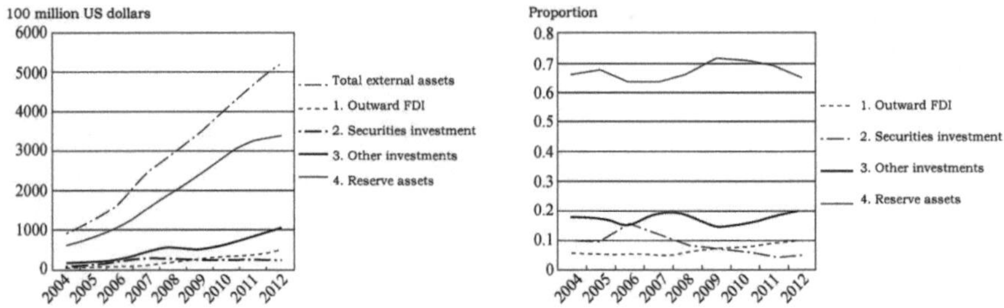

Fig. 14.3 Components of China's total external assets ($100 million) (*left*) and the changing trend of their proportions to total assets (*right*)

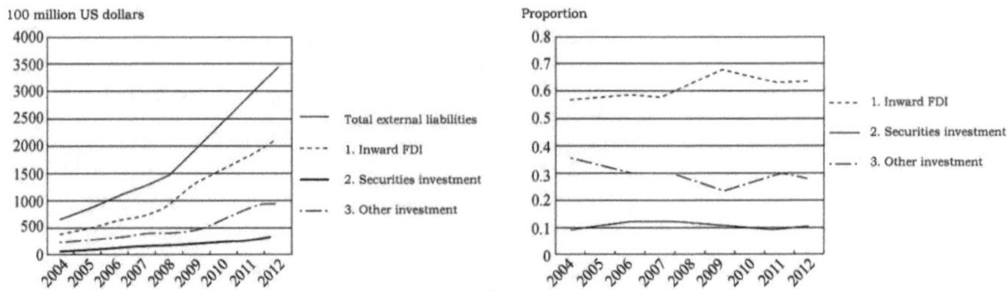

Fig. 14.4 Components of China's total external liabilities ($100 million) (*left*) and the changing trend of their proportions to total liabilities (*right*)

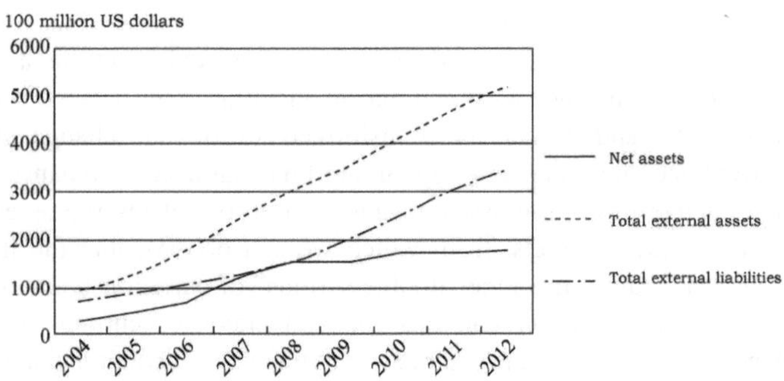

Fig. 14.5 The changing trend of China's total external assets, total liabilities and net assets ($100 million)

of assets in China, which is to some extent the result of the Chinese government's active choice to maintain a certain target exchange rate. As foreign exchange reserves are an important means for the government of a country to intervene in the foreign exchange market and stabilize the exchange rate of its own currency. Holding adequate foreign exchange reserves helps improve a country's international solvency and credit, enhance its ability to resist risks and safeguard the national economic and financial security. In the 1998 Asian financial crisis, it was because the government of the HKSAR held plenty of foreign exchange reserves that it won a victory in the battle of maintaining the stability of Hong Kong dollars. In addition, China's external liability structure mainly consisting of inward FDIs is also related to the preferential policies for investment in the specific stages of development, inward FDIs help introduce advanced technologies and optimize the enterprise management system, playing a positive role in China's economic growth and financial stability.

But on the other hand, the problems with the current structure of external assets have begun to gradually appear. As the external assets are mainly concentrated in the government sector, while the external liabilities are concentrated in the private sector, there is subject mismatch in China's external financial assets and liabilities. Although China's IIP data are denominated in US dollars, in fact China's external assets are mainly denominated in foreign currencies, while its liabilities are primarily denominated in the local currency, the appreciation of RMB against the major currencies will inevitably bring a net loss of assets and liabilities. Moreover, the rate of return of external liabilities is much higher than that of external assets, which have led to the loss of China's welfare. Excessive foreign exchange reserves will force the central bank to put excessive local currency into circulation, resulting in inflationary pressures.

The external balance sheet is a reflection of long-term accumulation of external economic activities, and the total amount and structural characteristics of external assets and liabilities are decided by the development stages and characteristics of an economy. The characteristics of China's current external assets and liabilities are decided by the development stages and characteristics of China's economy as well as the specific considerations of the Chinese government over the past period or the choice the Chinese government had to make under certain constraints, which to a certain extent is the result of the government's weighing and choice among maximum gains, risk resistance and economic growth. With economic development, the corresponding structure of foreign assets and liabilities will be gradually adjusted, and in recent years, the proportion of reserve assets and inward FDIs was showing a downward trend. China should also positively reform the external sector based on the law of different stages of economic development, further optimize the structure of foreign assets and liabilities and gradually reduce the negative impact that external assets and liabilities may bring on the economy.

14.1.2 International Comparison

In the following paragraphs, we will mainly carry out comparative analysis of total amount and structure of external assets and liabilities of the United States, Japan, Germany and China. As shown in Fig. 14.6, the ratios of total external assets, total external liabilities and net external assets to GDPs of the United States, China, Japan, Germany and China were all showing an upward trend during 2005–2012, among which Germany saw the greatest growth rate while China saw the lowest one. Except the United States, other countries had net external assets, while the United States had net external liabilities and its net external liabilities to GDP ratio was rising which was mainly related to many years of trade deficit in the United States and the continuous trade surplus in the other three countries.

As shown in Fig. 14.7, the proportions of all components of external assets of the United States, China, Japan and Germany roughly maintained stable. The size of reserve assets of the United States and Germany were smallest, accounting for about 2% of their total assets, Japan's reserve assets accounted for nearly 20% of its total assets, while China's reserve assets accounted for nearly 70%. Japan had the highest proportion of outward portfolio investment to total assets, followed by the United States and Germany, which was about 30%, and China's outward portfolio investment had declined year by year and accounted for less than 5% in 2012. The United States had the highest proportion of outward FDIs to total assets, which was nearly 30%, followed by Germany and Japan, and China's outward FDI accounted for nearly 10% of its total assets in 2012. On the whole, in the components of total external assets, China's reserve assets accounted for the majority of its total external assets, Japan's portfolio investment took the highest proportion, while the United States and Germany had a very low proportion of reserve assets, and the other items of external assets of the United States and Germany were relatively balanced, accounting for a similar proportion.

As shown in Fig. 14.8, the proportions of all components of external liabilities of the United States, China, Japan and Germany also roughly maintained stable.

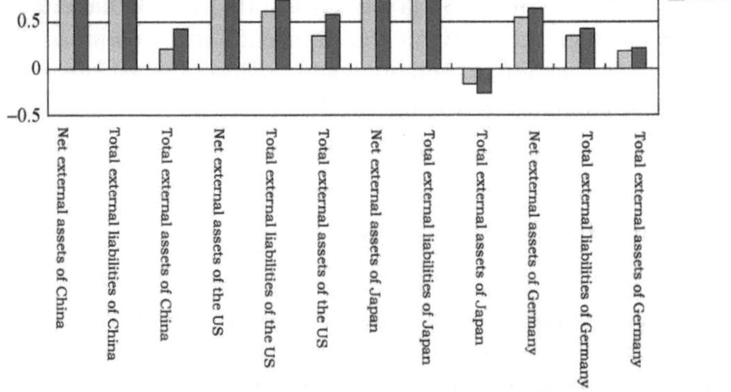

Fig. 14.6 Ratios of total external assets, total external liabilities and net external assets to GDPs of the United States, China, Japan, Germany and China *Source* IMF's International Financial Statistics database

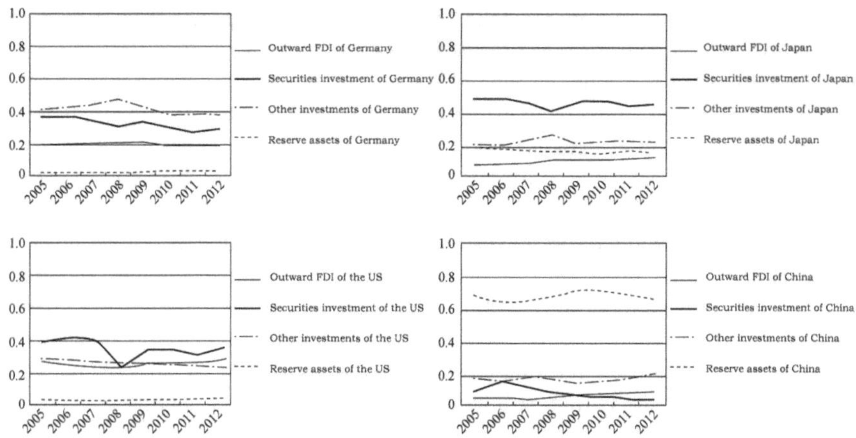

Fig. 14.7 Proportions of all components of total external assets of the United States, China, Japan, Germany. *Sources* IMF's International Financial Statistics database and the author's calculations

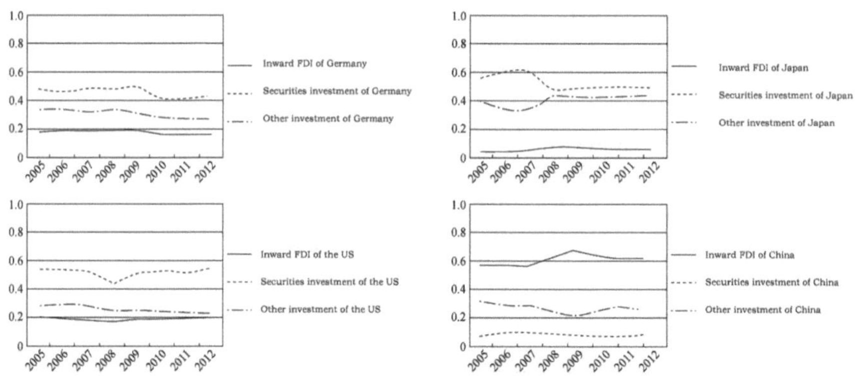

Fig. 14.8 Proportions of all components of total external liabilities of the United States, China, Japan, Germany. *Sources* IMF, International Financial Statistics database and author's calculations

China's inward FDI accounted for more than 60% of its total external liabilities, the highest among the four countries, followed by the United States and Germany, accounting for about 15%, and Japan inward FDIs accounted for 5%. The proportion of portfolio investment of the United States, Japan and Germany was higher than that of inward FDI and other investment, which was about 50%, while China had a smaller proportion of portfolio investment than inward FDI and other investments, which as less than 10%. On the whole, in the components of total external liabilities, the United States, Japan and Germany had the highest proportion of portfolio investment, followed by other investment and inward FDI, while China had the highest proportion of FDI, followed by other investments and portfolio investment, and its portfolio investment accounted for a relatively lower proportion, which was attributed to the immaturity and low degree of openness of the capital market in China.

The international comparison also reveal the structure of China's external assets and liabilities, which is characterized by reserve assets accounting for a large proportion of external assets and FDIs accounting for a large proportion of external liabilities. The total amount and structure of a country's external assets and liabilities are decided by its status in the international division of labor, level of development of its financial system as well as its foreign economic and trade policies and other factors. The structure of external assets and liabilities will change gradually with the change of the above factors. As mentioned earlier, China should also positively initiate the relevant reform to gradually reduce the possible negative impact brought by the current structure of external assets and liabilities.

14.2 Risk Revelation by the External Balance Sheet

In the following paragraphs, we will discuss the default risks of external liabilities and balance sheet mismatch risk revealed by the external balance sheet.

14.2.1 Default Risks of External Liabilities

The outbreak of a external debt crisis in a country is attributed to the level of its external debt crisis, debt threshold and unexpected shocks. A country's external balance sheet may reflect the level of its external debt and its debt threshold to some extent, thus playing the role of giving the early warning signs of an external debt crisis.

When other conditions remain unchanged, the higher the level of external debt, the higher the likelihood of an external debt crisis. But in some countries, a debt crisis may break out at a lower level of external debt, while some other countries may be able to maintain a high level of external debt for many years, so the debt threshold is critical for the probability of outbreak of an external debt crisis. Debt thresholds are related to many factors such as a country's economic growth and volatility, the history of debt default, institutional factors, the level of foreign exchange reserves, the countries with a high level of debt intolerance have a lower debt threshold. Reinhart and Rogoff (2010) pointed out that the debt intolerance can be systematically identified by a relatively few variables (including a country's history of default and high inflation). If a country has a higher the level of foreign exchange reserves, its corresponding debt threshold will be higher and it will have a higher bearing capacity for external debt.

In addition, some unexpected factors have also played an important role in the outbreak of an external debt crisis. Reinhart and Rogoff (2010) pointed out that a country's default is generally the result of complex cost—benefit analysis after considering the political and social factors rather than just an economic and financial event. The social, political and economic issues behind the default are very complex. A country's default is usually mainly decided by its willingness to repay rather than its solvency, a defaulting country generally has to make the strategic decision on whether repayment (full repayment) is necessary. Furthermore, in some circumstance in which a default is the result of a liquidity crisis rather than the solvency problem, the impact on confidence may play a critical role in the outbreak of a debt crisis. As long as the creditors are confident, the borrowers will be able to easily roll over their loans, but if the creditors lose confidence for some reasons (probably external reasons), the loans will collapse and the liquidity crisis will occur. Therefore, from the technical point of view, a country may sometimes be faced with multiple equilibria, which means the difference between default and non-default of a country is sometimes very small. For a given debt structure and assuming that all participants pursue their own interests, judgments based on expectations and confidence may produce different equilibrium results. Before the burst of confidence bubbles, even a relatively weak economy can run smoothly for a long time and often many debt problems are hidden.

An external balance sheet can reflect the size and structure of a country's external debt and the size of its foreign exchange reserves, thus providing some basis for judging the probability of the outbreak of an external debt crisis. In addition to the stock indicators presented by an external balance sheet, many flow indicators and domestic economic indicators, such as the level of capital flows and the level of import and export etc., can better alert a country to a crisis. The study by Reinhart and Rogoff (2008) shows that the conditional probability of the four crises, namely external sovereign debt default (or restructuring), currency crash, inflation crisis and banking crisis, is significantly higher than the unconditional probability in the event of large capital inflows. That is, in the event of capital inflows, the probability of financial crisis is higher. In addition, when the financial crisis occurs in a country, it will increase the probability of outbreak of a crisis in another country through contagion.

Due to the impact of unexpected factors and the complexity of debt threshold etc., it is difficult to provide the level of external debt and some other threshold values as the definite warning signs for the outbreak of a crisis and accurately predict the point of time for the outbreak of a crisis, but through the combination of stock and flow indicators, it is still possible to make more accurate and early judgments on the probability of the outbreak of an external debt crisis through some ambiguous signals so as to timely take response measures to avoid the outbreak of a large-scale crisis. Based on China's current situation, China's external debt is still at a low level, especially compared with its huge foreign exchange reserves with relatively high liquidity. In addition, China has imposed extensive control over capital accounts, so the likelihood of the outbreak of an external debt crisis is very small.

14.2.2 Balance Sheet Mismatch Risks

Balance sheet mismatch risks include maturity mismatch, currency mismatch and capital structure mismatch. Maturity mismatch mainly refers to the mismatch in the maturity of sources of funding of shareholders and their use, so liquidity problems may lead to default or debt restructuring and other risks. Currency mismatch means that the net worth or net income (or both) of a shareholder's equity is very sensitive to exchange rate changes (due to its net debt or net assets denominated in foreign currencies), so the changes in exchange rate may bring losses to the shareholder. Capital structure mismatch risk will occur when a shareholder is overly reliant on debt financing, while the proportion of the capital or owner's equity in financing is too low.

A sectoral balance sheet (including the government, non-financial corporations, financial corporations and the household sector) may reflect the maturity mismatch, currency mismatch and capital structure mismatch at the sectoral level, while an external balance sheet may reflect the overall maturity mismatch, currency mismatch and capital structure mismatch a country is facing. As an external balance sheet can be seen as a summary of financial assets and liabilities of the balance sheets of various sectors, the balance sheet mismatch risk a country is facing on the whole tend to show one or some sectors are facing the balance sheet mismatch risk.

According to Allen et al. (2002), the overall maturity mismatch of a country is mainly reflected by the contrast between the short-term external debt and the liquidable hard currency reserves held by the government and the private sector. A country's overall currency mismatch is reflected by the net external assets (or net liabilities) denominated in hard currency, while a country's overall capital structure mismatch is reflected the contrast between its net external debt stock and net FDI stock.

For maturity mismatch, it is difficult to acquire the data on China's liquidable hard currency reserves, but the ratio of outstanding short-term external debt to foreign exchange reserves was 16.3% in 2011, and the average ratio was about 13.5% during 2007–2011, which shows a small maturity mismatch risk on the whole. For currency mismatch, in recent years, China has held enormous net external assets (mainly foreign exchange reserves) denominated in foreign currencies (primarily the US dollars), so China is facing serious currency mismatch on credit, which is greatly different from the currency mismatch on debt the countries most seriously affected by the Asian financial crisis and this crisis were facing, so China's external assets will face huge book losses when the exchange rate appreciates. For capital structure mismatch, China's net FDI stock (the difference between inward FDI and outward FDI) was $1656.8 billion in 2012, its outstanding external debt amounted to $ 736.99 billion, the difference between its net external debt stock was further smaller than its outstanding external debt, so its net external debt stock was far less than its net FDI stock. China's external financing is largely effected through equities rather than debts, so it is essentially facing no capital structure mismatch risk. At the national level, China is mainly facing currency mismatch risk, while such currency mismatch risk is mainly reflected in the government sector holding enormous foreign exchange reserves.

An external balance sheet reveals the mismatch risks a country is facing as a whole and further illustrates the mismatch risks probably existing in one or several sectors of the country. Based on the external balance sheet and the balance sheets of all sectors, we can better judge the mismatch risks various sectors are facing and the overall mismatch risks China is facing. When there exists the balance sheet structure mismatch, a country and its relevant sectors are more vulnerable to the impact of uncertainty shocks, and the balance sheet mismatches will affect investors' confidence and willingness to invest, thus further amplifying the impact of uncertainty shocks. After being impacted, the mismatch risks will be transmitted among the sectors, and the interaction of different mismatch risks will further be amplified and may eventually form overall risks. Therefore, like the external debt default risks, the mismatch risks may not erupt in a longer period of time, but it is necessary alert the mismatch risks reflected by the balance sheet and take necessary measures to cope with them as soon as possible.

14.3 Analysis of the Affecting Factors of IIP

14.3.1 International Comparison

In the following paragraphs, we will carry out international comparison of the historical data to get an intuitive understanding of the impact of the stages of economic development and global imbalances and other factors on IIP. There is a great difference between the starting and ending time for the IIP data of various countries published by IMF (for example the starting time for the IIP data of China is 2004), so when the IIP data of various countries published by IMF are added up, the time for publishing the last country's IIP data shall be used as the starting point of time, thus limiting the use and analysis of the data. Therefore, the IIP data for the previous years estimated by Lane and Milesi-Ferretti (2007) are used here for international comparison of the IIP historical data.

As shown in Fig. 14.9, regardless of developed countries and emerging market countries, the total external assets and total external liabilities are approximately equal and show the same upward trend. As the total external assets and total liabilities of developed and emerging market countries reach an equilibrium on the whole, the developed and emerging market countries as a whole did not had huge net external assets or net external liabilities. In addition, it can be observed that although the size of total external assets and total external liabilities of the developed countries is much greater than the size of total external assets and total external liabilities of the emerging market countries, the external total assets of the emerging market countries grew faster than those of the developed countries. The size of external total assets of the developed countries in 2010 is 26 times as much as that in 1982, while the size of total external assets of the emerging market countries in 2010 is 56 times as much as that in 1982. This is mainly because the economic scale of the emerging market countries grew faster than that of the developed countries.

As shown in Fig. 14.10, the proportion of the total external assets and liabilities of the developed countries in the world's total assets and total liabilities (here the world means the sum of the developed countries and emerging market countries) is far greater than the proportion of the total external assets and liabilities of the emerging market countries in the world's total assets and total liabilities, and these two proportions basically maintain stable. The size of total external assets and liabilities of the developed countries is about nine times as much as that of the emerging market countries. As shown in Figs. 14.9 and 14.10, the stage of development is an important factor affecting the size of total external assets and liabilities, but it has no definite influence on the size of net external assets.

As shown in Fig. 14.11, although the proportion of the total external assets and liabilities of the developed countries in the world's total assets and total liabilities tended to be stable, the growth rate of total external assets and liabilities was greater than the GDP growth rate, and the proportion of total external assets and liabilities

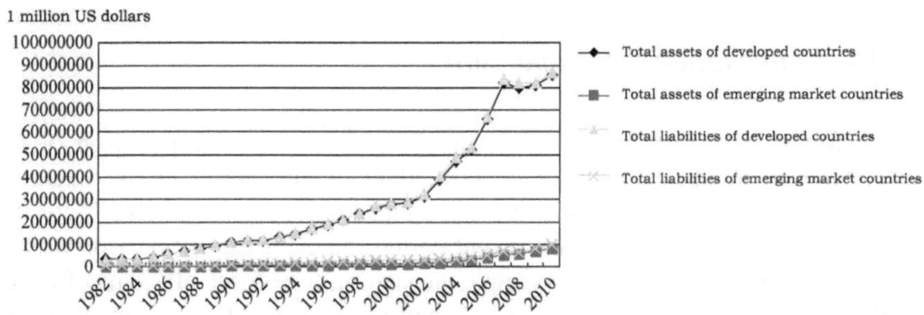

Fig. 14.9 Total external assets and total external liabilities of developed and emerging market countries

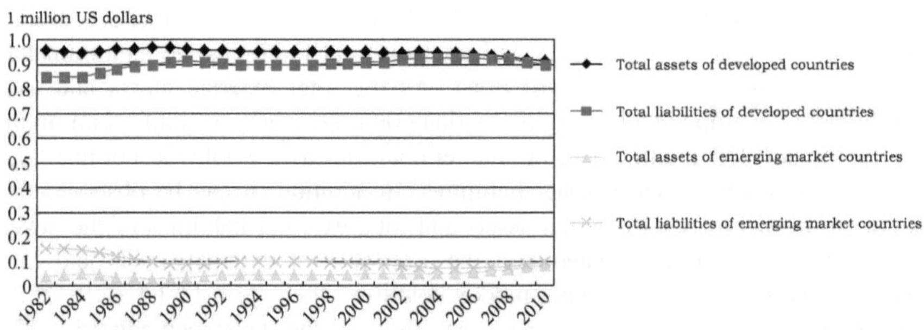

Fig. 14.10 Proportion of total external assets and liabilities of developed countries and emerging market countries in the world's total assets and total liabilities

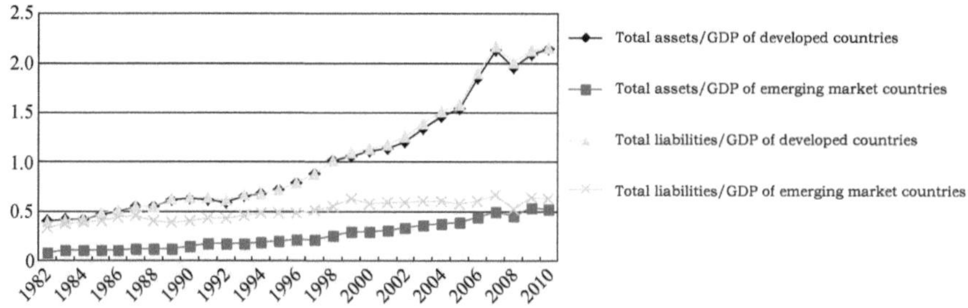

Fig. 14.11 Proportion of total external assets and liabilities of developed countries and emerging market countries to their GDPs

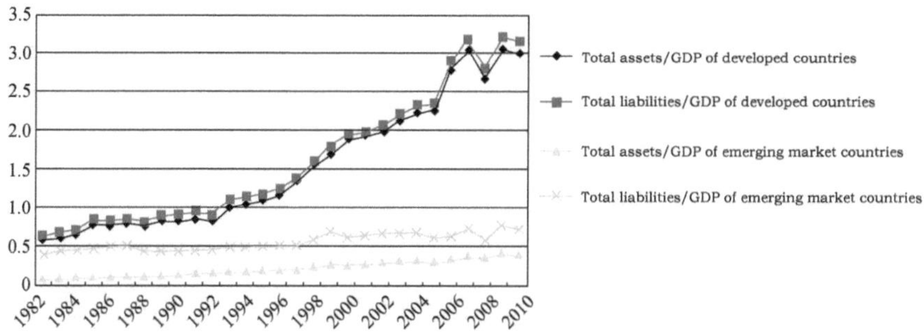

Fig. 14.12 Proportion of total external assets and liabilities of developed countries and emerging market countries to their GDPs (excluding the four countries of the US, Japan, Germany and China)

of the developed countries to their GDPs was showing a rapid upward trend since the 1980s. In this process, the imbalances in the global economy are further aggravated, so it is important to examine the causal link between the two. If the major countries causing the global imbalances are excluded, the rising trend of the proportion of total external assets and liabilities of the countries to their GDPs would slow down, this could to a certain extent reflect that there is a link between the rapidly risking trend of the proportion and the global imbalances. But the changing trend of the proportion of total external assets and liabilities of both developed and emerging market countries to their GDPs as shown in Fig. 14.12 after the four countries causing the global imbalances, i.e. the United States, China, Japan and Germany, are excluded, show that the proportion of total external assets and liabilities of the developed countries to their GDPs was further increased. This shows that the global economic imbalances are no the main factor for the rapid rising of the proportion of total external assets and liabilities of the developed countries to their GDPs, and the rapid rising of this proportion may be attributed to the factors such as low degree of capital control, continuously improved trade openness and rapid development of financial derivatives in the developed countries since the 1990s.

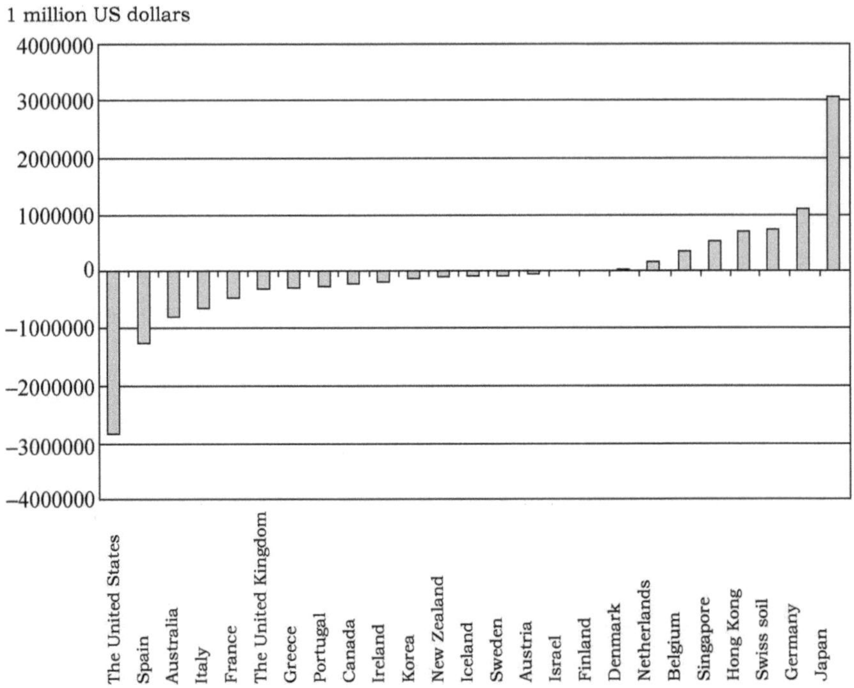

Fig. 14.13 Net external assets of the 25 developed countries in 2010

As shown in Figs. 14.13 and 14.14, among the 25 developed countries, 10 had net external assets (Israel, Finland, Denmark, the Netherlands, Belgium, Singapore, Hong Kong, Switzerland, Germany and Japan). Among the 21 emerging market countries, 3 had net external assets (Malaysia, Argentina and China). Most emerging market countries had net external liabilities. It can be observed that there is not a very close relationship between a country's net external assets and its stage of development, and the status of a country in the international division of labor is the important factor affecting its net external assets. In the 46 sample countries, the United States had the largest net liabilities, the top three countries by net assets were China, Germany and Japan, and the US, China, Japan and Germany were mainly accountable for the imbalances in the world economy, which was consistent with their status in the international division of labor. Figure 14.15 reflects the proportion of the current account balance of the US, China, Japan and Germany to their GDPs. It can be observed that since the 1980s, the proportion of the current account balance of the four countries to their GDP had continued to increase.

The main conclusions from the international comparisons include: (1) there is a significant relationship between total external assets and liabilities and stages of economic development, and the developed countries are highly open economically and financially, so they have a higher level of total external assets and liabilities, and due to the factors such as low degree of capital control, continuously improved

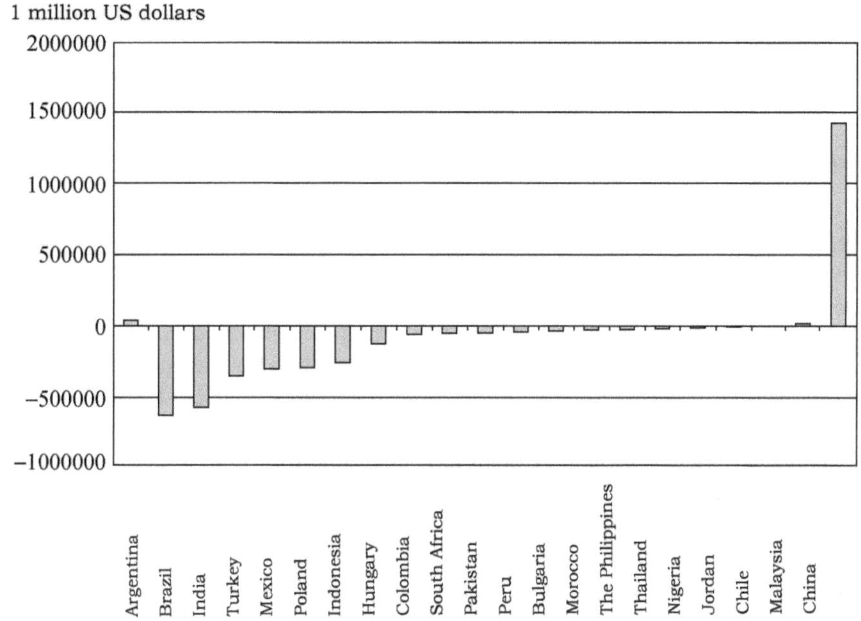

Fig. 14.14 Net external assets of the 21 emerging market countries in 2010

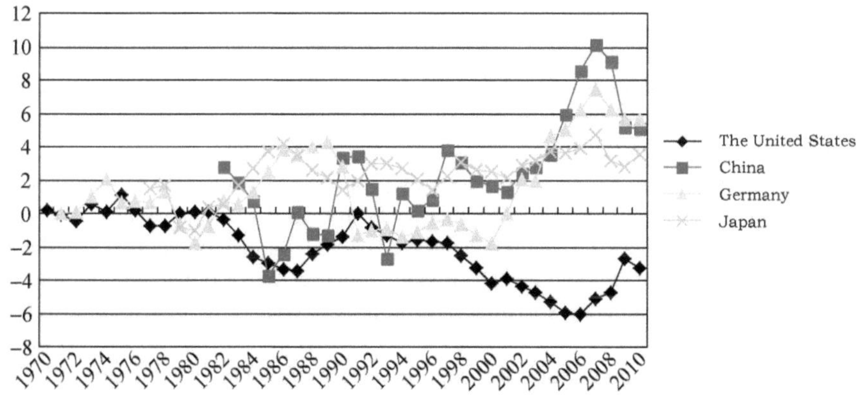

Fig. 14.15 Proportion of current account balance of the four countries of the US, China, Japan and Germany to their GDPs

trade openness and rapid development of financial derivatives in the developed countries since the 1990s, the proportion of total external assets and liabilities of the developed countries to their GDPs was showing a rapidly rising trend since the 1980s; (2) there is not very close relationship between net external assets and stages of economic development, and the net external assets of a country is related to its status in the international division of labor. The global economic imbalances have mainly affected the net external assets of the relevant countries, but have little influence on their total external assets and liabilities.

14.3.2 Panel Analysis of the Factors Affecting IIP

In the following paragraphs, we will use the panel data method to further analyze the factors affecting total external assets, total external liabilities and net external assets. As the problem of the different starting points of time for publishing the IIP data of different counties can be addressed by establishing the unbalanced panel data model in panel analysis, we will use the IIP data published by IMF in panel analysis, and these data are more accurate than the estimated data of Lane and Milesi-Ferretti (2007). Here the panel data of the 28 developed countries and 27 emerging market countries are used, and the maximum time period is from 1988 to 2010.

The size of a country's external assets and liabilities is limited by the size of its economy, so the country's GDP is used here as the proxy variable of its economic size and its total external assets/GDP, total external liabilities/GDP and net external assets/GDP ratios as explanatory variables respectively.

Lane and Milesi-Ferretti (2008) have empirically studied the factors driving the financial globalization, among which the total external assets (total liabilities)/GDP can reflect a country's level of financial globalization. They have proposed the variables affecting the total external assets (total liabilities)/GDP ratio, including trade openness, per capita GDP, population size, degree of capital control, level of domestic financial development, and distinguished the two dummy variables of the EU countries and the international financial center. The results of panel regression show that the impact of degree of capital control is not significant, the impact of the other variables is significant and consistent with the expected direction.

By referring to the explanatory variables proposed by Lane and Milesi-Ferretti (2008), the explanatory variables in this study for total external assets/GDP and total external liabilities/GDP include degree of capital control, trade openness, level of economic development and level of financial market development, and the proxy variables of all explanatory variables and impact expectations of explained variables are as follows.

The degree of capital control: the data on degree of capital control are from the estimates of Chinn and Ito (2008). The greater the value, the lower the degree of capital control. As the probability of short-term changes in the degree of capital control in a country is small, the data for 2009 are directly used as the data on degree of capital control for 2010. The lower the degree of capital control, the greater the size of a country's total external assets and total liabilities.

Trade openness: it is expressed by the ratio of total exports and imports to GDP. The higher the trade openness, the greater the size of a country's total external assets and total liabilities.

Level of financial market development: it is expressed by the ratio of total capitalization of the stock market and a country's sum of credits provided by the banks to GDP. The higher the level of financial market development, the greater the size of a country's total external assets and total liabilities.

Level of economic development: per capita GDP is used as a proxy variable. The higher the level of economic development, the greater the size of a country's total external assets and total liabilities.

According Hausman inspection, coupled with the nature of the data of degree of capital control as an explanatory variable, each model uses a variable intercept form with random effects. As the developed countries and emerging market countries may have different economic environments and structures, here a regression is carried out for all the countries, the developed countries and the emerging market countries. The regression results of total external assets and total external liabilities are shown in Tables 14.2 and 14.3.

The regression results in Tables 14.2 and 14.3 show that in the three categories of samples of all the countries, the developed countries and the emerging market countries, trade openness, per capita GDP and level of financial market development have significant influence on the total external assets and liabilities of the three categories of samples and the symbol is consistent with the expectation. This result is similar to the result of Lane and Milesi-Ferretti (2008). But unlike the result of

Table 14.2 Regression result for total external assets

	All the countries	Developed countries	Emerging market countries
Number of samples	881	515	366
Degree of capital control	-0.0668^{**}	-0.0824^{*}	0.0037
Trade openness	0.0120^{***}	0.0154^{***}	0.0037^{***}
Per capita GDP	0.0001^{***}	0.0001^{***}	0.00005^{***}
Level of financial market development	0.0032^{***}	0.0033^{***}	0.0015^{***}
R^2	0.5495	0. 5811	0.3138

*, **, ***Represent the significance levels of 10, 5 and 1% respectively

Sources IFS database, WDI database, Chinn and Ito (2008) database

Table 14.3 Regression result for total external liabilities

	All the countries	Developed countries	Emerging market countries
Number of samples	881	515	366
Degree of capital control	-0.0900^{***}	-0.2104^{***}	0.0452^{***}
Trade openness	0.0116^{***}	0.0138^{***}	0.0051^{***}
Per capita GDP	0.0001^{***}	0.0002^{***}	0.00006^{***}
Level of financial market development	0.0031^{***}	0.0026^{***}	0.0020^{***}
R^2	0.4331	0.4635	0.4290

*, **, ***Represent the significance levels of 10, 5 and 1% respectively

Sources IFS database, WDI database, Chinn and Ito (2008) database

Lane and Milesi-Ferretti, the influence of degree of capital control on the total external assets of the emerging market countries is not significant, and although its influence on the total external liabilities of the emerging market countries is significant, but the symbol is contrary to the expectation; its influence on the total external assets and liabilities of the developed countries and all the countries is significant and the symbol is consistent with the expectation. This result to some extent shows that for the countries with a relatively lower overall degree of capital control, the degree of capital control has some explanatory power for the size of total external assets and liabilities, and the countries with a lower degree of capital control will form a large size of total external assets and liabilities and thus have a high level of financial globalization. But for the emerging market countries with more stringent capital control, the degree of capital control has limited explanatory power for their total external assets. Often due to more stringent capital control, these countries can form enormous total external assets through the government's holding of foreign exchange reserves, but the higher the degree of capital control, the higher the total external liabilities of the emerging market countries, which is probably because a higher degree of capital control to some extent reflects a lower level of economic development while these countries tend to form a larger size of total external liabilities.

The regression results in Tables 14.2 and 14.3 show that the higher the level of development of a country, the higher the level of trade openness, the higher the level of financial market development and the greater the size of total external assets and liabilities. This regression result further explains the continuously rising trend of total external assets and liabilities in recent years with China's rapid economic development and the continuously rising of level of trade openness and financial market development and warns that with further development of China's economy in the future, its total external assets and liabilities will continue to rise.

A country may have a high level of external assets and liabilities, but its net external assets may be positive, basically balanced or negative. The factors affecting a country's net external assets are different from those affecting their total external assets and total liabilities. Lane and Milesi-Ferretti (2008) proposed that the factors affecting a country's net external position mainly include the level of economic development, demographic factors, the level of government debt, and the situation of the financial sector, but did not carry out further regression analysis. In this study, we will further analyze the factors affecting a country' net external assets based on the panel data.

By referring to the results of Lane and Milesi-Ferretti (2008), in this study, the explanatory variable for net external assets/GDP takes into consideration the labor population, per capita GDP and government debt. In addition, Xu and Yao (2008) proposed that the comparative advantage of the financial sector versus the manufacturing sector may be an important factor affecting net external assets and global imbalances, so we have introduced the comparative advantage of the financial sector versus the manufacturing sector as an explanatory variable, and the proxy variable of the explanatory variables and the expected influences of the explained variables are as follows.

The comparative advantage of the financial sector versus the manufacturing sector: it is obtained by r1:r2, here r1 is the ratio of the total capitalization of the stock market and a country's sum of credits provided by the banks to GDP, and r2 is the ratio of the value added of the manufacturing sector to GDP. The higher the ratio, the greater the comparative advantage of the financial sector relative to the manufacturing sector and the lower the level of net external assets.

The proportion of the working population: it is expressed by the proportion of the population aged 15–64 to the total population. The greater the proportion of the working population to the total population, the higher the savings rate, the greater the current account balance and thus the greater the size of net external assets because net external assets are the accumulation result of current account balance.

Government debt: it is expressed by the ratio of the central government debt to GDP. The greater the government debt burden, the lower the national savings and thus the smaller the net external assets.

The regression result for net external assets is shown in Table 14.4. As shown in Table 14.4, government debt has significant influence on the net external assets of three categories of samples, and the symbol is consistent with the expectation. The greater the government debt, the lower the national savings and the smaller the net external assets.

The proportion of the working population has significant influence on the net external assets, but its influence is negative in the developed countries and positive in the emerging market countries. This result may to some extent explain the strong positive relationship between the proportion of the working population and the savings rate in the emerging market countries. But in the developed countries, the proportion of the working population has little influence on the savings rate, and the savings rate is also affected by a variety of other factors. For example, Japan, as a country with a large aging population, has a lower proportion of the working population than the US, but its savings rate is higher than that in the United States.

Per capita GDP has significantly negative influence on the net external assets of the emerging market countries, and its influence in all the sampled countries and the

Table 14.4 Regression results for net external assets

	All the countries	Developed countries	Emerging market countries
Number of samples	429	269	160
Proportion of the working population	−0.0244*	−0.0742***	0.0185**
Per capita GDP	0.0000	−0.00001	−0.00007***
Government debt	−0.0082***	−0.0121***	−0.0030***
Comparative advantage of the financial industry versus the manufacturing sector	0.0027***	0.0033***	−0.0126**
R^2	0.1426	0.1975	0.2020

*, **, ***Represent the significance levels of 10, 5 and 1% respectively

Sources IFS database and WDI database

sampled developed countries is not significant. Its less significant influence in all the sampled countries is consistent with the conclusion of international comparison. Its significant influence range in the emerging market countries may to some extent show that the countries with a lower level of economic development may expect to hold more net external assets to cope with economic risks. In the range of developed countries, the level of economic development has no consistent impact on net external assets. For example, Germany, Japan and the United States have a greater per capita GDP, but have different sizes of net external assets.

Although the comparative advantage of the financial sector versus the manufacturing sector has significant influence in the emerging markets and developed countries but in the opposite directions. The regression results are not consistent with the expectation. This may be due to the important impact of international division of labor on net external assets, but the comparative advantage of the financial sector versus the manufacturing sector measured by the ratio of the value added of the financial sector to that of the manufacturing sector does not fully reflect this pattern of international division of labor. For example, the ratio of the value added of the financial sector to that of the manufacturing sector in Germany and Japan was higher than that in the other countries, but Germany and Japan had greater comparative advantages over these countries and held more net external assets. Some empirical studies show that the level of financial development indeed have a significant negative effect on net external assets and is in line with the expectation, such as the results of the study by Xu and Yao (2008), Lisheng and Bo (2011).

The above measurement and analysis results can explain to some extent the fact that with China's rapid economic development in recent years, greater trade openness is increasingly and rising level of financial market development, its total external assets and liabilities have shown a continuously rising trend and due to China's status in the international division of labor, its net external assets have continuously accumulated. Based on the results of international comparison and econometric analysis, we can make a rough estimate of the future trend: with further development of China's economy and greater trade openness, the proportion of total external assets and liabilities to GDP will continue to rise, but with the global economic rebalancing, decline of the working proportion and further development of financial market, China's net external assets to GDP may gradually decline.

Appendix

Trend Analysis Including the Country (Based on Lane and Milesi-Ferretti Database 2007)

Developed countries (25): Australia, Austria, Belgium, Canada, Denmark, Finland, France, Germany, Greece, Hong Kong, Iceland, Ireland, Israel, Italy, Japan, Korea,

Netherlands, New Zealand, Portugal, Singapore, Spain, Sweden, Switzerland, the United Kingdom and the United States.

Emerging market countries (21): Argentina, Brazil, Bulgaria, Chile, China, Colombia, Hungary, India, Indonesia, Jordan, Malaysia, Mexico, Morocco, Nigeria, Pakistan, Peru, Philippines, Poland, South Africa, Thailand and Turkey.

Countries Included in Panel Analysis (Based on IMF's IIP Database)

Developed countries (28): Australia, Austria, Belgium, Canada, Czech Republic, Denmark, Estonia, Finland, France, Germany, Greece, Hong Kong, Iceland, Ireland, Italy, Japan, Korea, Netherlands, New Zealand, Portugal, Singapore, Slovakia, Slovenia, Spain, Sweden, Switzerland, the United Kingdom and the United States.

Emerging market countries (27): Argentina, Brazil, Bulgaria, Chile, China, Colombia, Hungary, India, Indonesia, Jordan, Kazakhstan, Latvia, Lithuania, Malaysia, Mexico, Morocco, Nigeria, Pakistan, Peru, Philippines, Poland, Romania, Russia, South Africa, Thailand, Turkey and Ukraine.

Part III
Related Topics

Chapter 15
Pension Gap and Implicit Debt Forecast

15.1 Introduction

Promoted by the previous government, China has gradually established and improved the social pension system in recent years. In 2005, the *Decision of the State Council on Improving the Basic Old-age Insurance System for Enterprise Employees* established and improved the mixed old-age insurance system framework that features social pooling plus personal accounts. The *Guiding Opinions of the State Council on Trials of A New Type of Old-Age Insurance for Rural Residents* in 2009 and the *Guiding Opinions of the State Council on Trials of the Social Old-age Insurance for Urban Residents* in 2011 have respectively established the basic old-age insurance framework for rural and urban residents. These policies and measures have improved the basic old-age insurance system in China, and China's social security and social welfare thus achieved leap-forward development in a short time and there is a substantial increase in the coverage of the old-age insurance.

However, in order to honor the government's commitments to workers and residents in old-age insurance, China needs to pay huge pensions to safeguard the life of the elderly population. In particular, the current personal account accumulation system of the old-age insurance for workers in China is far from perfect, and pensions are mainly paid through the accumulation of cash-basis social pooling, while the basic pensions in the old-age insurance system for residents are mainly from the subsidies of the government. Under such institutional arrangement, the government bears the responsibility to repay, so the commitments to workers and residents in old-age insurance have become implicit government debt. In the future, population aging is accelerating in China, so the spending in this area will increase substantially, which will pose a serious pressure on the government's finance and impair the healthiness of the government balance sheet. This potential problem was particularly serious in the wake of the European debt crisis erupted in 2010. Since the European government debt crisis erupting in 2010, the governments throughout

Y. Li and X. Zhang, *China's National Balance Sheet*, China Insights,
DOI 10.1007/978-981-10-4385-7_15

the world have paid great attention to the debt issues, and a series of studies by IMF (2009, 2010), the European Union and other international organizations also show that the long-term funding gap of their social security system is an important factor behind the soaring government debts of these countries.

Then is China's current old-age insurance system stable and sustainable? Will it lead to serious government debt problems? How much is the pension pressure on government finances? How to deal with the funding shortage that may occur? These are the issues we must consider. The central government should take precautions and rationally design the pension reform plan. We should establish and improve the old-age insurance system covering all citizens and avoid the high debt burden caused by the policies that give overly high benefits, which may also endanger the national balance sheet health and weaken the international competitiveness of China.

In this chapter, we will use a model of population growth and migration to predict the population structure of China during 2010–2050, and on this basis, we will create an actuarial model for assessment of the old-age insurance system, analyze and predict China's pension income, expenditure and payment gap in the future, calculate the amount of government subsidies required to maintain the current old-age insurance system and warn over the debt risks that may caused by the old-age insurance's funding gap. This chapter is structured as follows: in Sect. 15.2, we will further discuss the institutional framework and the basic conditions of China's current old-age insurance system, summarize and analyze the documents available and introduce the basic framework and calculation methods of this study. In Sect. 15.3, based on the data of the 2010 population census, coupled with data of the sampled population surveys in the previous years, we have predicted the population structure and size of China during 2010–2050 from the three dimensions of urban-rural structure, age structure and gender structure. In Sect. 15.4, on the basis of the overall population prediction data, we will identify the population size and structure of the old-age insurance for residents and workers through reasonable assumptions and analysis and calculate the corresponding old-age insurance's funding gap and implicit debt. In Sect. 15.5, we will further carry out scenario analysis and policy simulation to observe the changing trend of pension gap and implicit liabilities when there are changes in some policy variables such as (return on investment) ROI of pension funds, retirement age (pensionable age) and pension replacement rate, thus providing the scientific basis for the adjustment of China's pension policy. Section 15.6 is the summary and conclusions of this study.

15.2 The Basic Framework and Funding Gap Calculation Method of China's Old-Age Insurance System

Due to the factors in development stage and institutional aspects, China's social old-age insurance system, which started from scratch, is in a gradual process of establishment and reform. Like other areas of the Chinese society where the "dual track system" universally exist, the old-age insurance is a multi-track system. Presently, China's old-age insurance is divided into the two parts of the old-age insurance for workers and residents, in which the old-age insurance for workers also includes the two types of the old-age insurance for enterprise employees and for staff of government organs and institutions, while the old-age insurance for residents is divided into the two types of the old-age insurance urban and rural residents.

15.2.1 The Framework of the Current Basic Old-Age Insurance System

(1) The Old-Age Insurance for Workers

The old-age insurance for employees of enterprises. At present, the policies for the old-age insurance for employees of enterprises mainly include the *Circular of the State Council on Deepening the Reform of the Old-Age Insurance System for Employees of Enterprises* (Guofa No. [1995] 6), the *Decision of the State Council on Establishing A Unified Basic Old-Age Insurance for Employees of Enterprises* (Guofa No. [1997] 26) and the *Decision of the State Council on Improving the Basic Old-Age Insurance for Employees of Enterprises* (Guofa No. [2005] 38). On the contribution side, according to the policies, the contribution rate towards the basic old-age insurance to be paid by enterprises should, in general, not exceed 20% of their total payroll, and the contribution rate towards the basic old-age insurance to be paid by individuals should be 8% of their salaries, so the total contribution rate shall be less than or equal 28%. The contributions paid by individuals will go entirely into their personal accounts, and the contributions paid by enterprises will go into the pooling accounts. On the expenditure side, as the old-age insurance system has undergone several reforms since its establishment, and in different reform trials, different measures were taken for different groups of people. Enterprise retirees are divided into three categories by the retirement time and the time starting to work: the retirees who had retired before the end of 2005 (the old men), the retirees who started to work before 1997 and retired after 2005 (the middle age men) and the retirees who started to work after 1997 (the new men). The pension payment methods for the three categories of people are slightly different. For the new men, the pensions include two parts: basic pension from social pooling account and pension from personal accounts; for the middle men, as the pension system had initially established, the contributions in personal accounts started to be paid in 1997 (or 1995), the time for paying contributions is too short and there is insufficient fund accumulation, so apart from the basic pension and the pension in individual accounts, the transitional pensions are paid to guarantee a reasonable pension for them; for "the old men", the basic pensions are still paid according to the original provisions, and their pension level should be substantially equal to the basic pension of the new men who have paid contributions in full plus the pension in individual accounts.

The old-age insurance for staff of government organs and institutions. In the past planned economy system, government organs, public institutions and enterprises were controlled by the government, and the income and pension systems for them were basically the same. In the 1990s, the market-oriented reforms exposed enterprises to market, and the basic old-age insurance system for employees of enterprises was established. But the reforms did not cover the old-age insurance for staff of government organs and institutions, and their pensions were not included in the social security system and continued to be borne by the government. Government organs and institutions and individuals did not need to pay premiums, the premiums were uniformly paid by the state finance, and the pensions were also uniformly borne by the finance. In 2008, the State Council issued the *Pilot Program for the Reform of the Old-age Insurance System for Staff of Public Institutions*, and gradually integrated the old-age insurance system for staff of public institutions and the old-age insurance system for employees of enterprises and determined to carry out trials in the five provinces and municipalities of Shanxi, Shanghai, Zhejiang, Guangdong and Chongqing. However, as the current pension replacement rate for the staff of public institutions is significantly higher than that for the employees of enterprises, the reform under the present circumstances would lead to a sharp reduction of pensions of the staff of public institutions, so it has encountered considerable resistance. According to the relevant surveys and news coverage, the current reform of the old-age insurance system for staff of public institutions is proceeding very slowly.

(2) The Old-Age Insurance for Residents

The old-age insurance for urban residents. The *Guiding Opinions of the State Council on Trials of the Social Old-age Insurance for Urban Residents* (Guofa No. [2011] 18) established the basic institutional framework of the old-age insurance system for urban residents, which combines social pooling with individual accounts. Residents aged 60 and above who do not enjoy the basic old-age insurance for workers and other pension benefits specified by the state can receive a monthly base pension. Pension benefits consist of two parts: base pension and pension from personal accounts. The base pension is provided by the central government and local governments, and the basic social pension set by the Central Government is 55 yuan per person per month. Local governments may increase the pensions according to the actual situations, and the increased pensions should be paid by local governments. For the pension from personal accounts, the monthly calculation and distribution amount of pension is the total amount of personal account divided by 139. Individual contributions and the subsidies paid by local governments for insured persons should be credited to individual accounts, and the pensions in personal accounts should be paid from the accumulated funds in personal accounts. The trials of the old-age insurance for urban residents has started July 2011 and should achieve full coverage in 2012.

The old-age insurance for rural residents. The *Guiding Opinions of the State Council on Trials of A New Type of Old-Age Insurance for Rural Residents* issued in 2009 established the basic institutional framework of the old-age insurance for rural residents, which also combines social pooling with personal accounts. Rural residents aged 60 and above who do not enjoy the basis old-age insurance for workers and other pension benefits specified by the state can receive a monthly base pension. From the policy perspective, except for the significant differences between the standards of contributions to personal accounts, other institutional arrangements in the old-age insurances for rural and urban residents are basically the same. According to the Opinions, the trials of the new rural pension scheme should be implemented in 10% of the country's counties (cities, districts and banners) in 2009 and should cover all rural pensionable-age residents by 2020.

15.2.2 Definition and Nature of Pension Gap and Debt Risk

The pension gap and implicit debt discussed in this chapter mean that under the current institutional arrangements, in order to honor the government's commitment in old-age insurance to staff on active duty, retirees and residents, the government should provide subsidies and funds to support the old-age insurance through financial expenditure. In the funded system, unless under extreme circumstances, otherwise the government is liable for paying the pensions.[1] But as China is currently adopting the PAYG (social pooling) pension scheme, which is actually a scheme of earmarked payroll taxes, the government levies taxes on the contemporary labor force, and the taxes are used for the pensions of the contemporary retirees, while the base pension in the old-age insurance for residents is entirely paid from government subsidies, so the government has the ultimate responsibility for repaying these two parts of pension.[2]

The financial debt arising from the pension gap is a kind of implicit liabilities. It is not directly reflected in the current assets and liabilities and financial balance sheet of the government, but over time, due to a substantial increase in pension expenditure, the debt may become explicit in a short time, resulting in enormous pressure on the government's assets and liabilities and financial income and expenditure. Meanwhile, it is also a contingent liability, whether there will be a

[1]For example, due to the risk of investment return, if the failure in pension fund investment causes dramatic shrinkage of pension, then the government might subsidize pensions for humanitarian consideration.

[2]The funded system is essentially to realize the smoothing of the income of individuals in the life cycle through this system and safeguard their old-age income and living through compulsory savings. The PAYG system is essentially tax collection and transfer payment of the incomes of people of different generations so as to achieve the purpose of income smoothing.

pension gap, how large its size will be and how much pressure it will cause on the government finance depend on the specific circumstances in the future and there is great uncertainty.

An important contingent factor for the pension gap is the uncertainty of the pension-related policies. China's current old-age insurance system is still in the process of transition and gradual improvement, and there is still a long way before establishing a sound old-age insurance system. In the future, there is great uncertainty in what course China's old-age insurance will follow and how the policies will change, which also leads to great uncertainty in the debt risk from the pension gap.

Now we will like to give the basic definitions of the estimated funding gap and implicit liability. There are a variety of ways to measure the pension gap and implicit liabilities. First, the current pension gap, which is equal to the difference between the pension expenditure and pension income of the year. If income is greater than spending, there is a surplus, while if spending is greater than income, there is a deficit. Second, implicit pension liability (cumulative gap) is the sum of total present value of annual pension payment gaps in a number of years in the future from a starting point. The current gap is a flow concept, while implicit liability (cumulative gap) is a stock concept. The liability here is the net liability from which the contribution income of pension is deducted. Third, the transition costs, which mean the pension gap and implicit liabilities arising from insufficient funds accumulated in the personal accounts of "the old men" and "the middle men" due to the transition from the fully PAYG system to the partially funded one which was piloted in 1995 and widely promoted in 1997. The transition costs are theoretically part of the implicit pension liabilities.

In addition, as the implicit debt defined in this study refers to the pension commitment to staff on active duty and retirees in the old-age insurance for workers, so if workers on active duty started to work in 2010 and are now 20 years old or older, then they will have at least retired before 2050 if the retirement age is 60. Therefore, the abovementioned "a number of years from a starting point" in this study refer to the years of 2010–2050.

15.3 Prediction of Size and Structure of the Population in China During 2010–2050

To accurately predict the future size and structure of the population is the basis for study and analysis of pension gap and debt risk issues. Based on the current situation, the rapidly aging of the population structure in China is an inevitable trend, which will radically reduce the relative proportion of the population who pay the contributions and the population who receive the benefits, increase the amount of government subsidies and thus may lead to the payment crisis. As China has already established an wide-covering basic old-age insurance system for urban workers and initially established the old-age insurance system for urban and rural residents, and the central government has specified the corresponding pension payment standard, so in this study we will try to estimate the full-scope pension spending and income deficit and implicit liabilities covering the old-age insurance systems for workers and residents. This task requires us to have a clear picture of the future urban and rural population structures. In this section, we will reasonably determine the parameters of birth, death and migration of population and predict the population structure during 2010–2050 on the basis of the 2010 census and other basic data.

15.3.1 Setting of Parameters of Birth, Death and Migration of Population and Establishment of Population Prediction Model

(1) Underestimation of Birth Rate and Adjustment

According to the data of the National 1% Population Sample Survey in 2005, the total fertility rate of Chinese women of childbearing age (15–49 years old) was 1.33, while according to the data of the 2010 census, the total fertility rate of Chinese women of childbearing age has fallen to 1.188, making China a country with almost the world's lowest fertility rate. However, the existing research findings show that China's official statistics has significantly underestimated the fertility rate. On the one hand, the underestimation of fertility rate is due to the miss reporting, and this is mainly due to incomplete statistics, and part of the newborns were not included into the official statistics. On the other hand, the newborns were underreported due to the birth control policy.

The phenomenon of official fertility rate underestimation can be confirmed from many aspects. For example, according to the age data in the historical demographic data, the population of i-year-old children, after deducting the deaths, will become $i + 1$ years old in the next year, and the population should be equal. However, the actual data show that the younger population will be include into the statistics through various ways as they are growing up, which has led to an increase in population. Based on the annual demographic statistics data during 1989–2009, Ma (2012) found that the population of the newborn group (0–4 years old) was significantly lower than the population (5–9 years old) in 5 years later, with the gap reaching 5.9–13.2%. In another example, the primary school enrollments can also confirm the underestimation of fertility rate, and the primary school enrollments over the years significantly exceed the population in the official statistics of corresponding ages (assuming a 7-year-old admission age).

In this study, we have calibrated the fertility rate using the primary school enrollments. At present, the enrollment rate of China's primary school-age children is more than 99%, so there should be no problem in using the primary school enrollments as the real statistic value of young population. Then, we have compared the primary school enrollments in *Education Statistical Yearbook of China* of the previous years and the official population statistics and calculated the corresponding underestimated degree of fertility rate. Finally, we have identified that the current underestimated degree of fertility rate in Chinese is 18%. That is to say, only 82% of newborns are included into the official statistics. Then we have amplified the birth probability of women of childbearing age in urban and rural areas based on this result, and after adjustment by this method, China's total fertility rate is 1.4486, which is 1.082, 1.4161 and 1.7615 respectively for cities, towns and villages.

Theoretically, the two-child policy is promulgated, the fertility rate will increase, but according to the international experience, with further improvement of the level of economic development and national income, the fertility rate will be further reduced, the combined action results of the both can hardly be known. Meanwhile, we can hardly judge when China will implement the two-child policy. Therefore, it is quite difficult to judge how China's future fertility rate will change, and for simplicity, we assume that China's fertility rate will remain unchanged at the adjusted level during 2010–2050.

(2) Birth Sex Ratio Overestimate the Problems and Adjustment

As mentioned above, a very important reason for the underestimation of fertility rate is the underreporting due to the birth control policy. Undoubtedly, to hedge the birth control policy, as compared with boys, girls are more likely to be underreported, which will lead to the overestimation of the gender ratio at birth in official statistics. This problem can also be confirmed by some data. For example, even taking into account the deaths, the gender ratio of the younger population in China will also gradually reduce with the increase of age, and the male to female ratio in the primary school enrollments is significantly lower than the corresponding male to female ratio in the official demographic statistics.

To correct this problem, we have compared the male to female ratio in the primary school enrollments in *Education Statistical Yearbook of China* and the corresponding ratio in *Population Statistics Yearbook of China* to obtain the degree of overestimation of the gender ratio at birth. According to the *2010 Education Statistical Yearbook of China*, the male to female ratio of the school-age population aged 6–11 in the primary school enrollments is 1.159 on average, and the male to female ratio of the population who started to go to school at 6 years old is 1.16, while the average male to female ratio of the school-age population aged 6–11 in *Population Statistics Yearbook of China* in the same period is 1.217, and the male to female ratio of the population aged 6 is 1.247, which is 1.074 times and 1.05 times of the former respectively. Meanwhile, we found that the degree of overestimation of the gender ratio in the population statistics gradually reduces with the increase of age, and the male to female ratio is only overestimated by 1.01 times at the age of 11.

Therefore, we assume that the male to female ratio is overestimated by 1.07 times. The male to female ratio calculated according to the data of the 2010 population census is 114: 100, and after adjustment, it becomes 107: 100, assuming that this gender ration remains unchanged for the population born during 2010–2050. It should be noted that as there is no separate data on the primary school enrollments in urban and rural areas, we are unable to estimate the separate gender rates at birth for urban and rural areas, and the gender rate at birth for cities, towns and rural areas was adjusted by 1.07.

(3) Mortality and Life Expectancy Adjustment

Based on the deaths of all ages/the average population of all ages in the 6th population census, we have obtained the mortality data of all age groups. Based on the age-specific mortality data, we can calculate the population life expectancy of the population aged zero that year. The life expectancy is calculated as follows:

$$\text{Life expectancy 预期寿命} = \sum_{i=0}^{N} (i + 0.5) \times \text{prob}(i) \tag{15.1}$$

where prob (i) is the death probability of a person who lives to the age of i, equal to:

$$\text{prob}(i) = \text{death}\ (i) \times \prod_{n=0}^{i-1} (1 - \text{death}(n)) \tag{15.2}$$

where death (i) is the mortality rate calculated based on the census data in all age groups.

The following table is the life expectancy of the population calculated by this method and based on the 2000, 2005 and 2010 population censuses or the data of the sampled surveys (Table 15.1).

Obviously, with economic development and further improvement of the level of medical security in China, the life expectancy of residents will continue to increase. Therefore, we need further give the changing ways of mortality and life expectancy in future. After comparing a variety of ways to improve life expectancy, we selected the following schemes: the average life expectancy of the population in the three time periods in the above table shows that the life expectancy in 2005 is 2.71 years higher

Table 15.1 Life expectancy of the population during 2000–2010

	Cities		Towns		Rural areas		Average
	Male	Female	Male	Female	Male	Female	
2000	74.39	78.65	72.60	77.08	68.71	72.04	73.91
2005	76.88	81.39	74.44	79.77	71.21	76.02	76.62
2010	79.43	83.43	76.92	81.43	72.94	78.24	78.73

It should be noted that perhaps because of the different mortality rates in the basic data and other reasons, the life expectancy calculated here is not consistent with the life expectancy released by the Chinese official statistics authority, and the official result is significantly lower. For example, China's average life expectancy in 2000 in the official statistics was 71.4 years old than that in 2000, the average life expectancy in 2005 is 2.12 years higher than that in 2010, and the growth rate of life expectancy during 2005–2010 is 78.12% as much as that during 2000–2005. By assuming that the growth rate of life expectancy of residents in cities, towns and villages decreased by 78.12% in every five years in future, we can calculate the growing trend of life expectancy in the future. That is, assuming that the increase of life expectancy obeys the following formula:

$$\Delta E_t = E_t - E_{t-5} = (\Delta E_{t-5}) \times 0.7812 = (E_{t-5} - E_{t-10}) \times 0.7812 \qquad (15.3)$$

Through this growth mode, the life expectancy is increasing but its growth rate is decreasing. As shown in Fig. 15.1, according to this growth mode, the average life expectancy will reach 85.2 years by 2050, which is basically consistent with the forecasting given in the *Overview Of China's Sustainable Development* of the Chinese Academy of Sciences that the life expectancy for the Chinese people will reach 85 years by 2050. After getting the life expectancy, we then calculated through reverse-reasoning the mortality rate corresponding to the life expectancy by urban and rural areas, gender and age and predict the future size and structure of population based on this mortality rate.[3] Assuming that the mortality rate will change once every 5 years, then the extrapolated mortality rate in 2010 can be used for 2010–2014 and the extrapolated mortality rate in 2015 can be used for 2015–2019, and the rest may be deduced by analogy.

(4) Migration Probability Estimation and Urbanization for Cities, Towns and Villages

Another issue that must be considered is the impact of urbanization on the population structure. China's old-age insurance system is still an urban-rural dualistic system, the basic old-age insurance for workers is concentrated in urban areas, while there is slightly difference in the old-age insurance for urban and rural resident. This requires us to distinguish between the urban and rural populations and take into consideration the impact of rural-urban migration on the demographic structure and the old-age insurance. The existing research findings provide no estimation on the rural-urban migration probability in China by age and gender, and to compensate for this shortcoming, we have estimated the probability of the current population migration using the data on population changes over the years by urban and rural areas, gender and age.

Simply speaking, based on the 1% National Population Sample Survey in 2005, the 0.1% sample population survey in 2006–2009 and the data of the 2010 population census, we can project the population over the years by urban and rural areas, gender and age.[4] Excluding the population of deaths, if the population aged i in rural areas in the year t is lower than the population aged year $i - 1$ in the year

[3]That is, assuming that the mortality rate of all ages reduces by x times in the same proportion, and then find the value of x that makes the calculated life expectancy equal to the predicted life expectancy, and finally adjust the mortality rate.

[4]It should be noted that the actual population sampling ratio is not exactly equal to 1 or 0.1%.

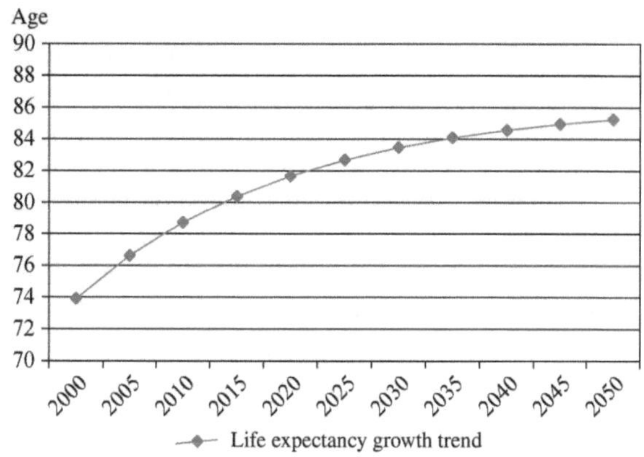

Fig. 15.1 Growing trend of average life expectancy

$t - 1$, it can be assumed that this part of the population have migrated to the cities and towns. On the contrary, excluding the net deaths, if the population aged i in urban areas in the year t is higher than the population aged year $i - 1$ in the year $t - 1$, then it can be assumed that the increased population are migrated from rural areas. In this way, we can get the following formula:

$$\mathrm{P} = \mathrm{Inc}/\mathrm{Pop} \tag{15.4}$$

- P is the probability of migration of rural population to towns of age $i - 1$
- Inc is town population increase of age i in year t minus death people
- Pop is rural population of age $i - 1$ in year $t - 1$

Likewise, we can get the probability of migration of rural population to towns by sex and age. As serious errors are like to occur in the calculation results for a particular year, the results for the 5 years of 2005–2010 were averaged to reduce calculation errors.

Meanwhile, due to the absence of further data on migration between towns and cities, for simplicity, we assume that there is no migration between towns and cities, and based the current situation, this assumption has no effect on the results. This is because in the calculation, we found that after excluding the deaths, only the rural population of all ages has reduced on the whole, which is reflected as in net outward migration, while the population of towns and cities after excluding the deaths is reflected in net inward migration. Then, whether the population of cities is from rural areas or towns has no effect on the population structure. Here is a simple example. Supposing there are 100 people in rural areas, 100 people in cities and 100 people in towns, now 10 people have moved from villages to cities, 10 people have moved to towns, and 5 people have moved from towns to cities, then the population structure becomes 80: 115: 105. But if we do not know how many people have move from cities into towns, then now assuming 15 people have moved from villages into cities and 5 people have moved from villages into towns, we will get the same results in the changes in population structure. Therefore, due to the absence of further data on migration between cities and towns, and cities and towns present net inward migration, we assume that there is no migration between cities and towns. In addition, when calculating the pensions, the pensions of cities and towns will be consolidated, so it will not interfere the pension calculation.

In addition, we assume that migration between cities, towns and villages only occurs for people aged 1–50, and there is no migration of the population for those aged over 50. First, we found after calculation that the age of 50 is an important threshold for rural-urban migration, and once rural residents are more than 50 years old, the probability of their migration to cities and towns is basically close to zero (see Fig. 15.2). Second, the calculation of births, the childbearing age of women is 15–49 years old, therefore the population aged over 50 will have no impact on the fertility status of cities and towns. Finally, if a rural resident does not move to get a job in a city and acquire the pension eligibility when he/she is young, then it can be expected that he/she is unlikely to acquire the eligibility for the old-age insurance for urban workers if he/she moves to a city later (e.g. over 50 years old).[5] From this perspective, we also assume that people aged more than 50 will no longer move into cities and towns. After all, the ultimate goal for us to predict the population structure is to investigate pension issues. Moreover, we assume here that there is also migration in children and teenagers (aged 1–15), which is different from the assumption of Ma (2012). We found after calculations that there is also a higher probability of migration in children and teenagers. Although minors do not have the independent ability for economic behaviors, they may move into cities and towns with their parents. The gradually declining trend of probability of migration for them is very close to the changing trend of the population aged above 20. This result supports the above point.

In summary, according to the calculation results of probability of migration among cities, towns and villages, during 2005–2010, the expected probability of a rural resident remaining in a village from birth to the age of 50 is 10.3% for male and 14.6% for female. We have predicted the population migration by using the calculated probability of migration of rural population to cities and towns by age and gender as the probability of migration of rural population to cities and towns during 2010–2050.

[5]According to the document Guo Fa No. [2005] 38, an individual who has achieved the legal retirement age, but contributed less then 15 years, would not be entitled the basic pension, the accumulate savings of pension in his personal account can be defrayed one-off and the relationship of insurance will be terminated.

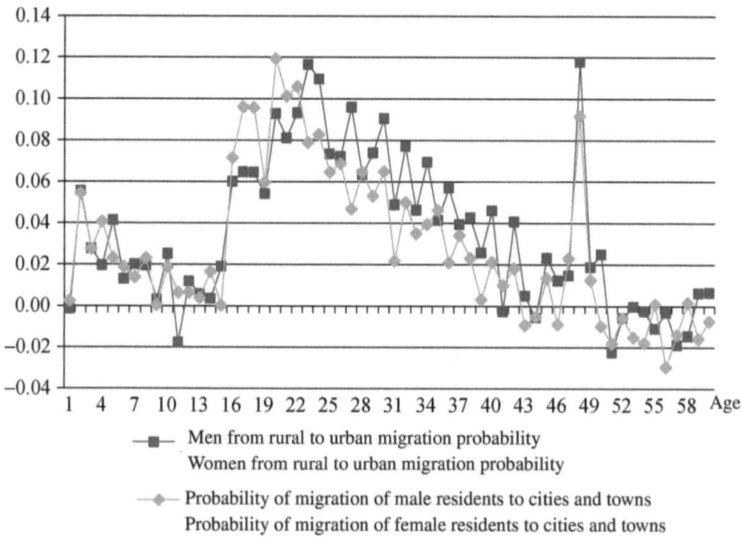

Fig. 15.2 Probability of migration of rural residents to towns by gender and age. *Source* The author's estimates

15.3.2 Prediction of the Population Structure During 2010–2050

On the basis of the above parameter setting, we have predicted the future population structure of China according to the population data for cities, towns and villages of the 2010 population census by gender and age.[6] Meanwhile, we combined the population predication data for cities and towns into the population predication data for urban areas. Some important characteristics data in the prediction results are as follows:

(1) Population Size and Urbanization Rate

As shown in Fig. 15.3, the prediction results show that China's total population will peak at 1.415 billion in 2027 and later will start to gradually decline to reach 1.313 billion by 2050. The urbanization rate (population in cities and towns/total population) will maintain a steady upward trend. During 2010–2030, the average urbanization rate will increase by 1% per year from 0.5 to 0.71, which is consistent with the target urbanization rate in China's future urbanization plans recently revealed by the National Development and Reform Commission. After 2030, due to the reduction and serious aging of the rural population, the pace of urbanization for

[6]Meanwhile, we have combined the predicted population data for cities and towns into the predicted urban population data.

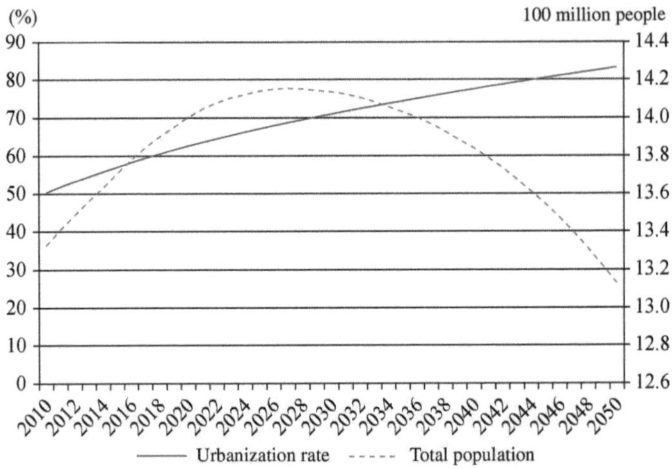

Fig. 15.3 Total population and urbanization rate in future

rural residents will slow down significantly, and the urbanization rate will eventually reach 83% by 2050. The urban population in this period will remain the growing trend and grow gradually from 670 million to 1.092 billion by 2050, and at that time the urban population will stop growing. But the rural population in this period will maintain the downward trend.

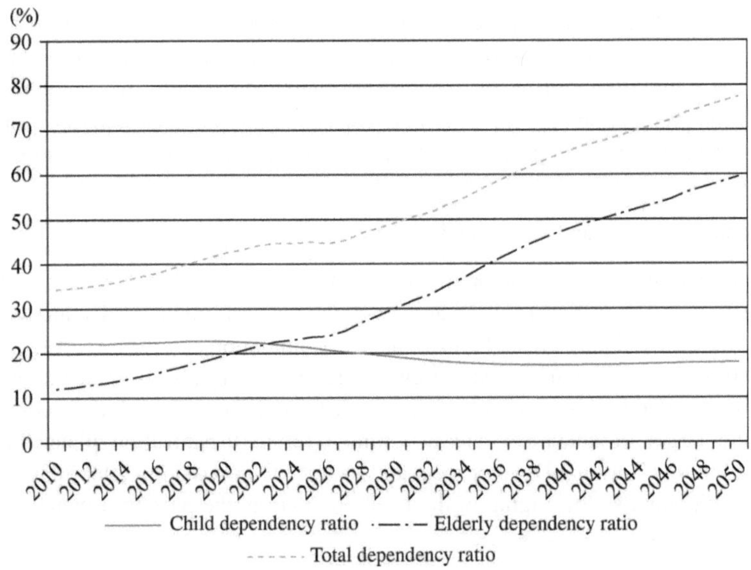

Fig. 15.4 Changing trend of the dependency ratio of the population

(2) Changing Trend of the Population Age Structure

Figure 15.4 shows the prediction diagram of the elderly dependency ratio, the children dependency ratio and the total dependence ratio in China during 2010–2050. Here the elderly is defined as the population aged 65 and above, children is defined as the population aged 0–14 and the working population is the population aged 15–64. The results show that the children dependency ratio in China will maintain a steady and slightly downward trend, and the children dependency ratio is about 20% and will reduce to 17.95% by 2050. The elderly dependency ratio will maintain a steady upward trend, but will rise sharply especially after 2027 largely because the massive baby boomers born after 1962 will gradually get old, and the elderly dependency ratio will reach 59.46% by 2050. The overall changing trend of the overall dependency ratio is substantially consistent with the elderly dependency ratio, and the overall dependency ratio will rise to 77.4% by 2050.

The urban population structure is relatively more younger. As shown in Fig. 15.5, the dependency ratio of children in cities and towns will experience an increase and then decrease process and will increase gradually from 18% in 2010 to 20.45% in 2023 and later will start to gradually decline to reach 17% by 2050. The elderly dependency ratio will remain a steady upward trend and will rise gradually from 10% in 2010 to 46.5% in 2050. The total dependency ratio will increase gradually from 28% in 2010 to 63.6% in 2050. The cause for the lower dependency ratio of the urban population is the presence of rural-urban migration, and more

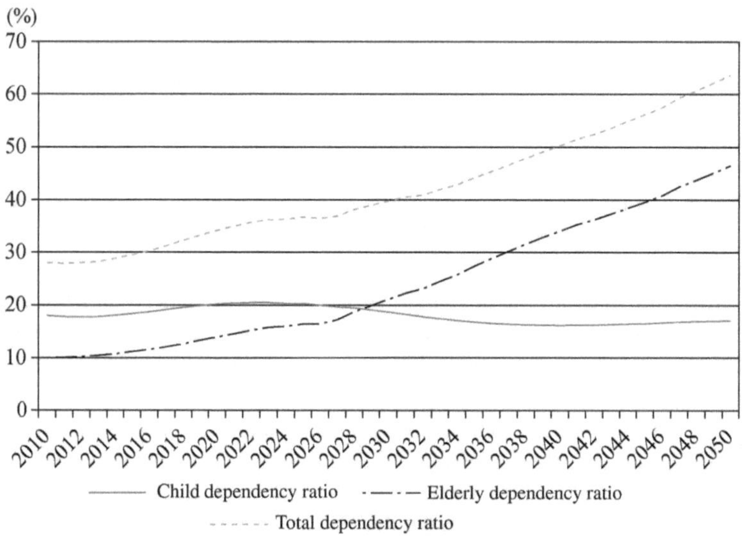

Fig. 15.5 Changing trend of the dependency ratio of the urban population

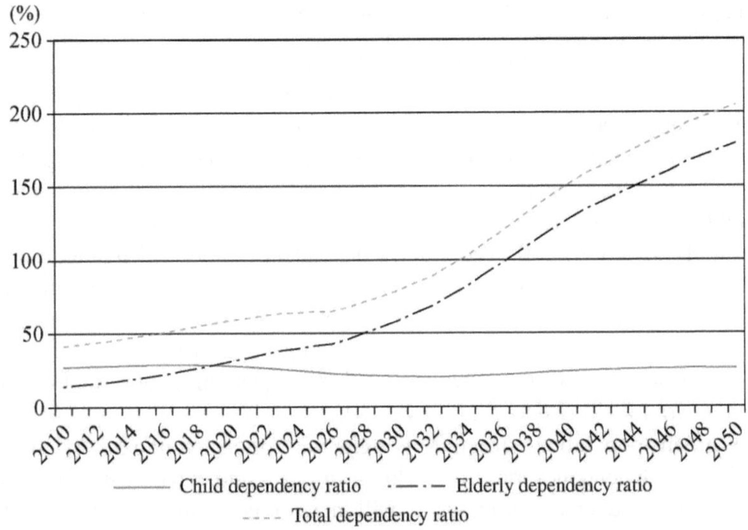

Fig. 15.6 Changing trend of the dependency ratio of the rural population

rural young people in rural areas will migrate to urban areas, thus the working-age population in urban areas will keep booming for a long time.

The dependency ratio of the rural population is worrying. As shown in Fig. 15.6, the children dependency ratio in rural areas has increased slightly from 27.1% in 2010 and then will gradually decrease in 2017 and reach 20.1% in 2031 and then start to gradually increase to reach 25.9% in 2050. The elderly dependency ratio will remain a rapid upward trend. The elderly dependency ratio was only 14.21% in 2010 but will increase to 178.8% in 2050, expanding by more than 10 times. The total dependency ratio will keep pace with the elderly dependency ratio and increase from 41.29% in 2010 to 204.7% in 2050. That is to say, a worker should raise more than two elderly people or children on average. It is the result that we have use the scope of age of 15–64 in the statistics for labor force. If we adopt the scope of age of 20–60, this ratio will be higher.

Undoubtedly, when studying the rural dependency ratio issue, it is also necessary to take into account the actual situation. That is, the elderly in rural areas are not necessarily raised by the rural laborers. Due to rapid urbanization, young people may have migrated to urban areas, but their parents are left behind in rural areas, then the responsibility of supporting their parents in rural areas is actually borne by part of the urban population. Therefore, from the perspective of practical supporting responsibility, the elderly dependency ratio in cities and towns may be underestimated, while the elderly dependency ratio in rural areas has been overestimated.

In any case, it is undoubted that the dependency ratio of the population in China, especially in the elderly dependency ratio, will increase sharply in the future. This will pose a huge challenge to the pension issues of the elderly in the future.

15.4 Population Estimation of Workers and Residents with Old-Age Insurances

15.4.1 The Population Prediction of Urban Workers with Old Age Insurances

As mentioned above, China's old-age insurance is a multi-track system and currently is divided into the two parts of the old-age insurance for workers and the old-age insurance for residents, in which the old-age insurance for workers includes the old-age insurance for employees of enterprises and the old-age insurance for staff of government organs and institutions. In the old-age insurance for workers, retirees are divided into three categories by the retirement time and the time starting to work: the retirees who had retired before the end of 2005 (the old men), the retirees who started to work before 1997 and retired after 2005 (the middle men) and the retirees who started to work after 1997 (the new men). Slightly different pension policies are implemented for various categories of retirees. We will make use of relevant data to predict the size and structure of the beneficiary population of the old-age insurances for workers and residents.

(1) Prediction of Retirees Who Had Retire Before the End of 2005 (The Old Men)

According to the document Guofa No. [2005] 38, for retirees who had retired prior to the end of 2005, the base pensions should still be paid according to the original provisions, while the base pension adjustment measures should be implemented simultaneously. Although the time of their contribution payment may be very short, to safeguard their livelihood, their pension level should be substantially equal to the base pension of the new men who have paid contributions in full. The data of *Statistical Yearbook of China* show that the total number of enterprise retirees totaled 40.052 million in 2005, but their gender and age structures were not distinguished. Here, with regard to the gender structure, the male to female ratio of urban retirees from the data of 1% national population sample survey in 2005 are used as the proxy variable of the male to female ratio of enterprise retirees, and the result is the female/male ratio = 105.77/100, and there are more women than men. The reasons lie in that (1) the statutory retirement ages for women are younger; (2) the middle-aged and old women have a lower mortality rate than men, which has led to more working men than working women but more female retirees than male retirees. With regard to the age structure, we assume that the age structure of those who have been retired is consistent with the overall age structure by gender of the urban population in the same period, and male workers retire at the age of 60 and female workers retire at the age of 53, then we get the number of workers who have retired before 2005 by gender and age.

Assuming that the mortality rate of "the old man" and its changes is the same as the mortality rate of the urban population by gender and age of the above overall population predictions, we predicted the changes in size and structure of "the old man" in the future on this basis. As shown in Fig. 15.7, with the gradual death of the elderly, the elderly population is also declining, and by 2050, the elderly population will only be 853,000, and the elderly men have been more than 100 years old, the elderly women has reached 98 years old. This part of population are gradually disappearing.

(2) Prediction of the Number of Retirees Who Started to Work Before 1997 and Retired After 2005 (The Middle Men)

According to the document Guofa No. [2005] 38, people who started to work before 1997 and retired after 2005 are referred to as "the middle men". As the time of their contribution payment is short, there is little accumulated money in their personal accounts. To safeguard their livelihood, apart from base pension and pension from personal account, the transitional old-age pension is paid to them. According to the data of *Statistical Yearbook of China*, there were a total of 58.116 million urban pensioners who had retired from enterprises in China in 2010, and deducting the predicted number of retirees who had retired before the end of 2005, 22.421 million new retirees were added after 2005. Assuming that the retirement age is 60 for male workers and 53 for female workers, then the age structure of the newly added retirees during 2005–2010 is 60–64 for men and 53–57 for women in 2010. The gender ratio of this portion of population is assumed to be equal to the male to female ratio of urban retirees in the corresponding age groups in the data of the 2010 census, which is 100/132, and based on the population structure data of the corresponding age groups in the Sixth population census, we have projected the age structure of retirees who retired 2006–2010.

The number of "the middle men" who retired after 2010 was predicted based on the total size and structure of the population. After dividing the above data on the

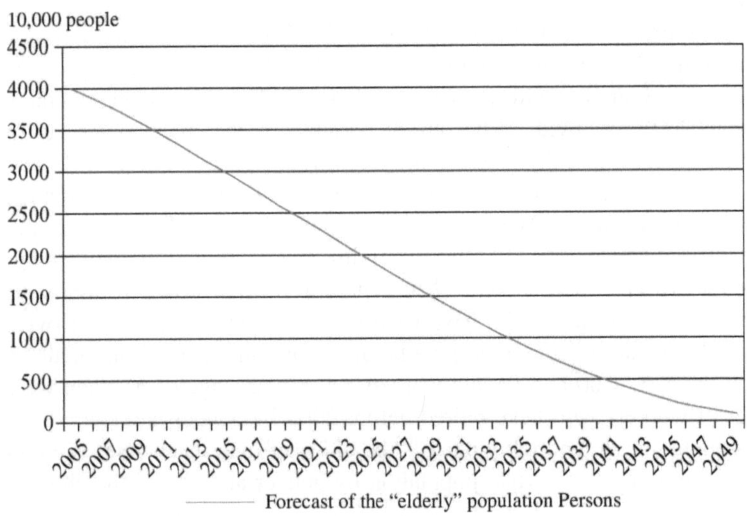

Fig. 15.7 Prediction of the number of the retired "old men"

retired population during 2005–2010 by the total size of the urban population at the corresponding age group, we have obtained the proportion of the pensioners who had retired from enterprises during 2005–2010 to the total urban population at the corresponding age group, which is 0.7373 for men and 0.6313 for women. This means that presently 73.73% of men in urban areas will become beneficiaries of the old-age insurance for workers after reaching the retirement age and 63.13% of women in urban areas will become beneficiaries of the old-age insurance for workers after reaching the retirement age. With the continuous expansion of the coverage of the old-age insurance for urban workers and further regulation of the labor market, it is expected this proportion will continue to increase in the future. In this study, we assume the proportion of pensioners who have retired from enterprises in urban areas will increase by 1% each year after 2010 and will no longer increase when reaching 80.73% for men and 70.13% for women. We did not set a higher proportion because there is still the population covered by the old-age insurance system for those who are not employees of enterprises, the non-working population as well as the population not covered by the old-age insurance system due to other factors.[7]

Like "the old men", the mortality rate of "the middle men" and its changes are assumed to be the same as the mortality rate of the urban population by gender and age of the above overall population predictions. In the above parameter setting, the prediction results of the change in the number of "the middle men" is shown in Fig. 15.8 below.

The number of the retired middle men will grow rapidly at the beginning, but the growth rate will decline slightly by 2030 because there will then be no newly added female retirees as "the middle men", and the number of the retired middle men will peak and reach 198 million by 2036. There will be no newly added male retirees as "the middle men" after 2036, so the middle men will grow old continuously, and the number of the middle men will decline to 141 million in 2050.

(3) Prediction of Retirees Who Started to Work After 1997 (The New Men)

The employees of enterprises who started to work after 1997 (the new men) are required to pay contributions and can draw the base pension and the pension from personal account after retirement. This portion of population are actually successors of "the middle men". Therefore, the basic parameter setting is the same as that of "the middle men", and the prediction results are shown in Fig. 15.9. In the current retirement age setting, "the new men" will not appear until 2030. However, due to the factors such as a specific population structure and a higher life expectancy, the number of the retired new men will grow rapidly and reach 215 million by 2050, and they will become major enterprise pension beneficiaries.

[7]According to the international experience, even if the developed countries where there is a sound old-age insurance system, the coverage of old-age insurance is only about 90% (Holzmann 2009). In the past, the proportion of China's urban employment maintained at a level close to 90%, so even the old-age insurance coverage reaches 90%, the proportion of the population covered by the old-age insurance to the total population is less than 81%.

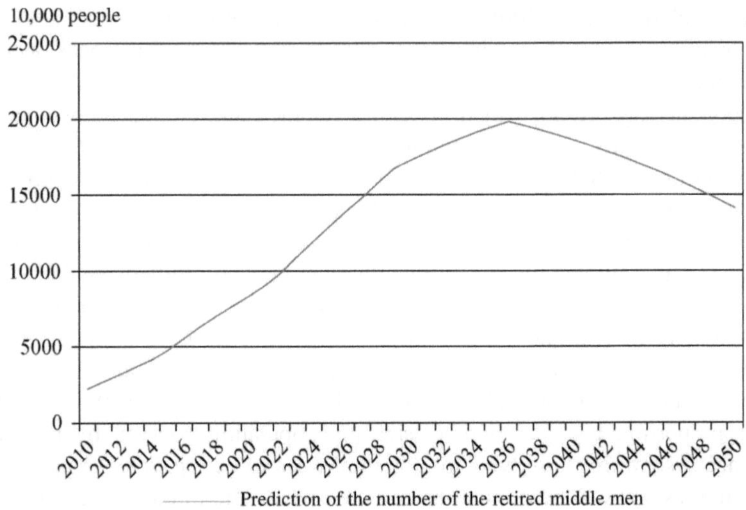

Fig. 15.8 Prediction of the number of the retired middle men

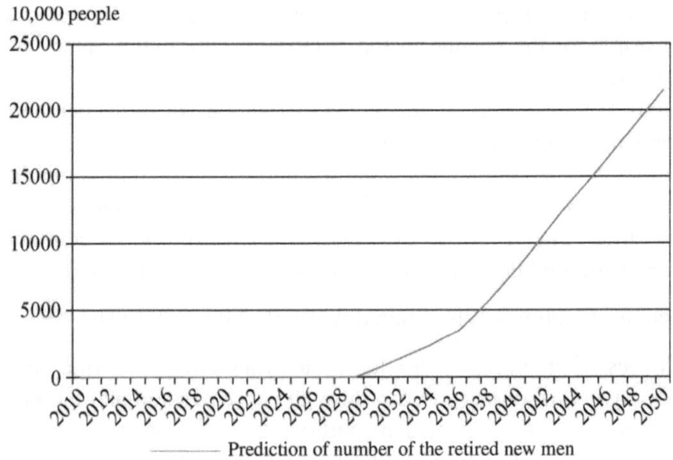

Fig. 15.9 Prediction of number of the retired new men

(4) Prediction of the Number of Pensioners Who have Retired from Government Organs and Public Institutions

According to the *Statistical Yearbook of China*, the total number of old-age pensioners of government organs and public institutions reached 4.933 million in 2010. The gender ratio of this portion of population was replaced by the gender ratio of retirees in urban areas at the corresponding age group (men aged 60 and women aged above 55) in the 2010 population census, and the result is the

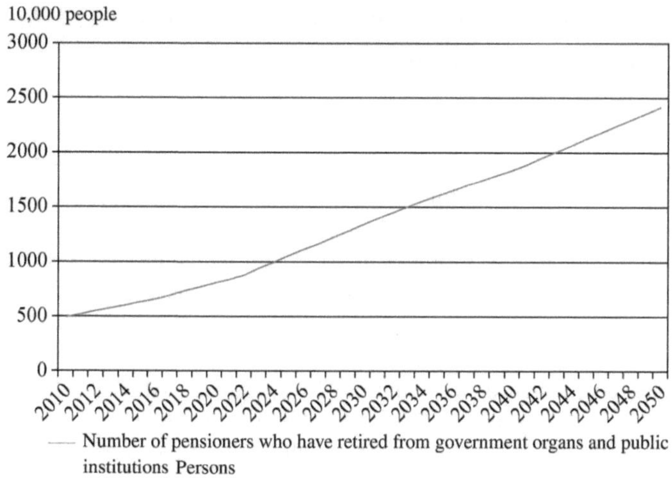

Fig. 15.10 Number of pensioners who have retired from government organs and public institutions

female/male ratio = 114.7/100. Based on this, we projected that the retired female population is 2.6354 million, and the retired male population is 2.2976 million. Meanwhile, assuming that their age structure is the same as the age structure of the overall urban population at the corresponding age group. After dividing this portion of the retired population of government organs and public institutions by the size of the overall urban population at the corresponding age group, we have obtained the ratio of the pensioners who have retired from government organs and public institutions to the total urban population in the corresponding age group, which is 6.02% for male pensioners and 4.48% for female pensioners. There is great uncertainty in the current reform of the old-age insurance for staff of government organs and public institutions, so it is difficult to judge how this ratio will change in future. For simplicity, we assume that the ratio of the pensioners of government organs and public institutions to the total urban population remain unchanged at 6.02 and 4.48%.

The mortality setting is consistent with that of enterprises. On the basis of the above parameter setting, we can predict the number of pensioners of government organs and public institutions, and the results are shown in Fig. 15.10.

Based on the current retirement age setting, the number of pensioners of government organs and public institutions will gradually increase and reach 24.17 million by 2050. But compared with the pensioners of enterprises, this size is still small.

15.4.2 Prediction of the Number of Urban Workers Who Pay the Old-Age Insurance

Like the old-age pensioners, the premium payers of the old-age insurance for urban workers are also divided into employees of urban enterprises and staff of government organs and public institutions. According to *Statistical Yearbook of China*, the number of in-service workers of urban enterprises who have participated in the old-age insurance was 178.2 million in 2010, and the gender ratio of the working population in the 2010 population census was used as the gender ratio of the in-service workers who have participated in the old-age insurance (123:100) to get the number of in-service male and female workers who have participated in the old-age insurance, which is 9830 and 7992 respectively. After dividing the size of this portion of population was divided by the size of the urban population at the corresponding age group, we have obtained the ratio of the current in-service male and female workers who have participated in the old-age insurance to the total urban population at the corresponding age group, which is 0.4345 and 0.4194 respectively. In the future, with further improvement of the old-age insurance system, it is expected this ratio will further improve. Thus this ratio is same as the ratio of persons who enter enterprise retired population and persons who enter the pension population. It is assumed that this ratio will increase by 0.01 point each year to reach 0.5045 and 0.4894 respectively.

Meanwhile, the number of in-service staff of government organs and public institutions who have participated in the old-age insurance was 15.796 million in 2010, and based on the gender ratios of the urban working population by industry and age in the 2010 population census, we have projected the gender ratio of in-service staff of government organs and public institutions, and the result is the male/female ratio = 1.117.[8] In this way, we calculated the number of in-service male and female staff of government organs and public institutions who have participated in the old-age insurance, which is 8.334 and 7.462 million respectively. Assuming that the age structure of this portion of population is the same as that of the overall urban population at the corresponding age group, we can obtain its age structure. Then, dividing the number of in-service staff by the total urban population at the corresponding age group, we can obtain the ratio of in-service male and female workers of government organs and public institutions who have participated in the old-age insurance to the total urban population at the corresponding age group, which is 4.09 and 4.21% respectively. Likewise, as there is great uncertainty in the future reform of the old-age insurance for staff of government organs and public institutions, for simplicity, we assume that that the ratio of the in-service staff

[8]The industries used include 7 industries where state organs and public institutions are concentrated in, namely state organs, Party organs, the CPPCCs, the democratic parties, education, health, research and experimental development. In the meanwhile, the retirement age for female cadres in state organs and public institutions is 55, the age range for men and women in the calculations here is 20–59 and 20–54 respectively.

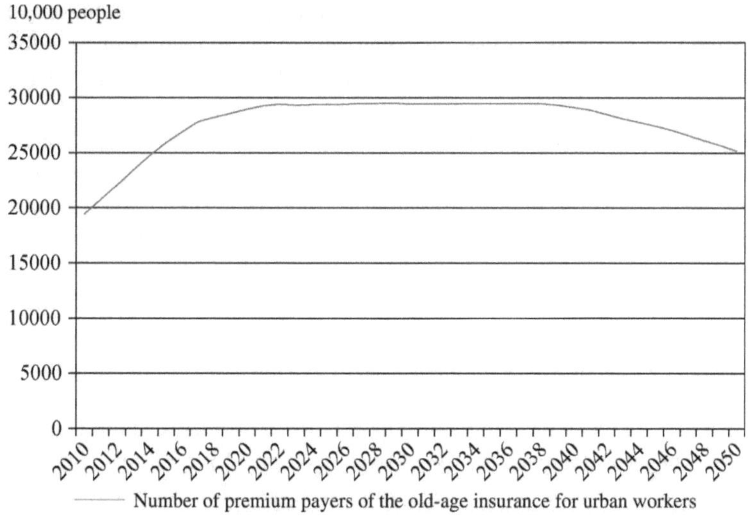

Fig. 15.11 Prediction of the number of premium payers of the old-age insurance for urban workers

of government organs and public institutions who have participated in the old-age insurance to the total urban population will remain unchanged in the future.

In this way, based on the above parameters and the predicted structure of the urban population in the future, we can predict the number of the premium payers of the old-age insurance for urban workers. As shown in Fig. 15.11, the premium payers of the old-age insurance for urban workers can grow rapidly in the future, but the growth rate will decrease gradually. During 2021–2038, the average size of this portion of population will remain at a stable level of 295 million, and later due to the impact of population aging and slowdown of urbanization, the urban working population will decline, and the number of premium payers will also decline and reach 252 million by 2050.

15.4.3 Prediction of the Beneficiary Population of the Old-Age Insurance for Urban and Rural Residents

Assuming that the urban residents who have not been covered by the old-age insurance for employees of enterprises and staff of government organs and public institutions are all the basic beneficiaries of the old-age insurance for urban residents. Thus, with the predicted data of the size of the total urban population at the corresponding age group—the old men—the middle men—the new men—the beneficiaries of the old-age insurance for government organs and public institutions are the predicted data of the basic beneficiaries of the old-age insurance for urban residents. The rural population at the corresponding age group are all the basic beneficiaries of the old-age insurance for rural residents (for the sake of simplicity, we assume that rural residents do not participate in the basic old-age insurance for urban workers). After multiplying the predicted beneficiaries of the old-age insurance by the ratio of the number of actual pensioners to the number of basic beneficiaries, we have obtained the predicted data of the actual beneficiary population of the old-age insurances for urban and rural residents.

Apart from the old-age insurance systems for urban workers, China's the old-age insurance system for urban and rural residents has also been gradually established. According to the document Guofa No. [2011] 18, the trials on the insurance system would start in July 2011, while the Chinese government explicitly stated in 2012 that the basic old-age insurance system for urban residents should achieve full coverage. The expected pace for the old-age insurance for rural residents is slightly slower. According to the document Guofa No. [2009] 32, China initiated the trials on the new old-age insurance for rural residents in 2009, and the trials of the new rural pension scheme should be implemented in 10% of the country's counties (cities, districts and banners) in 2009 and will expand gradually to cover all rural pensionable-age residents by 2020

Although it is now still in the pilot stage legally, in fact the old-age insurance for residents has been advanced very rapidly. Based on the relevant statistical data, the old-age insurance will actually be expanded at the pace more faster than the predetermined pace of full coverage by 2020. The *Statistical Bulletin on the 2012 Human Resource and Social Security Development in China* shows that all the county-level administrative regions in China have fully carried out the social old-age insurance for urban and rural residents by the end of 2012 and have basically achieved the full coverage. According to the official statistics, the number of people aged above 60 covered by the old-age insurance for urban and rural residents reached 91.57 million by the end of 2011, which is 67% of our predicted basic beneficiaries of the old-age insurance for urban and rural residents, while the number of people aged above 60 covered by the old-age insurance for urban and rural residents reached 130 million in 2012, accounting for 92% of the beneficiaries of the old-age insurance for residents. Therefore, the old-age insurance for residents has been advanced very rapidly in China. Just as what are stated in the bulletin of the Ministry of Human Resources and Social Security, the old-age insurance for urban and rural residents have at least basically achieved full coverage institutionally.

In the future, with further improvement and promotion of the system, we assume that the proportion of residents actually over the age of 60 to the people covered by the old-age insurance for residents will continue to increase and reach 95% in 2013 and then continue to increase by 1% and maintain at 98% from 2016 to 2050. On the basis of setting the above parameters and predicted data of the overall population, we can estimate the number of pensioners of the old-age insurance for urban and rural residents during 2010–2050, and the results are shown in Fig. 15.12.

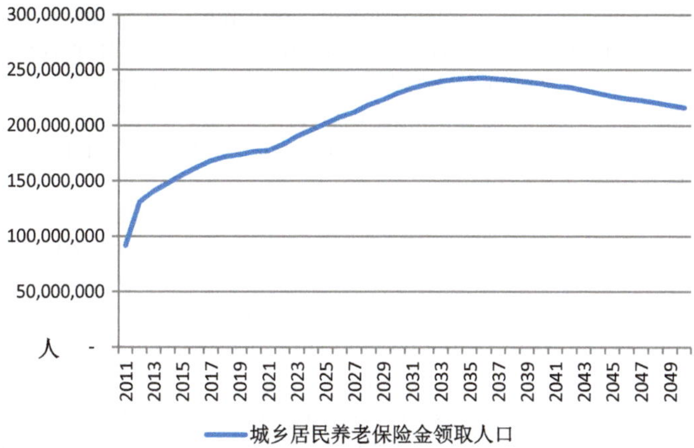

Fig. 15.12 Number of pensioners of the old-age insurance for urban and rural residents

15.5 Prediction of Pension Gap and Implicit Debt

Based on the prediction of the overall size and structure of population and a series of parameter settings, we have discussed and estimated the size and structure of various portions of the pension-covered population during 2010–2050. In this section, we will project the pension gap and implicit debt during 2010–2050.

15.5.1 Setting of Benchmark Parameters

The estimates involve a series of parameters, including GDP growth rate, the price index, the average wage level, state fiscal revenues and expenditures, pension contribution rate, pension replacement rate and pension investment return rate etc. Here the benchmark parameter settings for pension revenues and expenditures are given here as follows:

(1) Price index: Assuming the annual price growth rate is 2.3% in the future and the GDP deflator and the consumer price index follow this growth rate.
(2) GDP growth rate: China's GDP growth rate was 7.7% in 2012. Given the weak economy in the first half of 2013, we assume that the growth rate of the whole year is 7.625%, and the real economic growth rate in the coming years will fall by 0.125% each year and reach 3% by 2050. The reasons for selecting such a change in economic growth include: one is for simplicity and the other is that based on this rate, combined with the projections of the total population in the future in this study, by 2050, China's per capita GDP will reach 269,000 yuan (the price in 2010). Calculated based on the exchange rate of US dollar against RMB of 6.2, the per capita GDP will reach $43,400. According to the studies

by a number of international research institutions, such as PricewaterhouseCoopers (2013) and Goldman Sachs (2012), it is believed that by 2050, the per capita GDP of the US will reach about \$85,000–\$90,000, while the per capita GDP of China will reach about 50% of the level of the US.[9] Therefore, the prediction that China's per capita GDP is \$43,400 in 2050 is also consistent with these studies.

(3) Wage growth rate: Assuming that the growth rate of average wage of the whole society is equal to the GDP growth rate × the price growth rate, i.e. equal to the nominal GDP growth rate.
(4) State fiscal revenues and expenditures: The ratio of China's state revenues and expenditures to GDP was 0.2259 and 0.2427 respectively in 2012, assuming that this proportion remains unchanged in the future.
(5) Financial subsidies at various levels to the pension funds: Presently, the income of the basic old-age insurance for urban residents and workers mainly come from two parts: the income from contributions and the income from financial subsidies at various levels. In addition, there is a small amount of interest income. In 2012, governments at various levels granted 264.8 billion yuan in subsidies to the pension fund system, accounting for 2.1% of state fiscal expenditures, and this proportion was basically stable in the past three years. Assuming that this proportion remains unchanged in the future.
(6) Investment return rate and debt interest rate: China have imposed strong constraints on investment of pension fund. Presently, the income of pension funds is equal to the interest income of one-year fixed deposits. It is assumed that this approach is still adopted in the future, and the yield rate is the annual interest rate of 3%. If the pension deficit occurs, the relevant departments need to borrow to pay for pensions, so it is assumed that the interest rate of liabilities is 5%.
(7) Pension contribution rate: presently, under the relevant law of the China, the pension contribution rate is 28%, of which 20% should be paid by enterprises and go into the pooling account and 8% should be paid by individuals and go into their personal accounts. But the income from contributions/the pension payers/the average wage of the whole society, the average actual contribution rate was only 15.49% during 2010–2012. There is significant difference between the actual contribution rate and the statutory contribution rate, and this is attributed to many aspects. For example, the contribution rate towards the basic old-age insurance to be paid by enterprises should, in general, not exceed 20% of their total payroll, so 28% is the upper limit of the contribution rate, and the contribution rate towards the basic old-age insurance to be paid by

[9]Affected by the economic crisis, the estimates made by the latest studies more were more conservative, the estimate of per capita GDP of the US in 2050 US is lower. Citigroup (2011) and ADB (2011) estimated that the per capita GDP of the US in 2050 would reach approximate to \$100,000, while PricewaterhouseCoopers (2013) and Goldman Sachs (2012) estimated that it would be \$85,000–90,000, but many studies considered that China's per capita GDP would reach about 50% of that of the United States.

individual industrial and commercial households and flexible employees is lower. But the main reason may be that there are differences in the level of the average wage of the whole society and the average level of wages for premium payment of workers. The statistical scope for the former is wider than the latter. According to the data of the Statistical Bulletin of the Ministry of Human Resources and Social Security, we projected that the ratio of the average level of wages for premium payment to the average wage of the whole society was about 55% in 2011 (Wang and Ren 2013). In this study, it is assumed that the actual payment rate will remain unchanged at the 2012 level of 15.32%.

(8) Pension replacement rate: The pension replacement rate benchmark level of various groups of people, we used the settings of Ma (2012). That is, the replacement rate for the old men is 42.6%, that for the middle men will gradually reduce from 42.3 to 32% and remain unchanged, and that for the new men will remain unchanged at 32%. The replacement rate for staff of government organs and public institutions will remain unchanged at 63.5%.

(9) Pension standards for residents: According to the document Guofa No. [2009] 32 and the document Guofa No. [2011] 18, the minimum standard of pension benefits for rural and non-working urban residents is 55 yuan per person per month, and local governments may increase the standard of pension benefits according to the actual situations, and the increased pension benefits should be paid by local governments. Due to the lack of data on the pension standards increased by local governments, the minimum standard of 660 yuan per year was used as the standard in the base period, and it is assumed that the increase rate of pension standard in the future is equal to the nominal GDP growth rate.

15.5.2 Estimates of Pension Gap and Implicit Debt in Reference Scenario

Based on the above the benchmark parameter setting, we have set the relevant equation for the income and expenditure of the old-age insurance system to obtain the estimation results. We will first make an estimate of the income and expenditure and implicit liabilities of the old-age insurance for urban workers and then make an estimate of the subsidies to be provided by the governments for the old-age insurance for urban and rural residents, and then add up the subsidies to be provided by the governments for the old-age insurance for workers and residents to get the total implicit debt burden of the old-age insurance of the whole society.

(1) Estimation of the Income and Expenditure of the Old-Age Insurance for Urban Workers

Based on the estimation result of the income and expenditure of the old-age insurance for urban enterprise employees as shown in Fig. 15.13, during 2010–2021, the income from contributions is sufficient to cover the pension expenditure with a slight surplus. But starting in 2022, the old-age insurance for

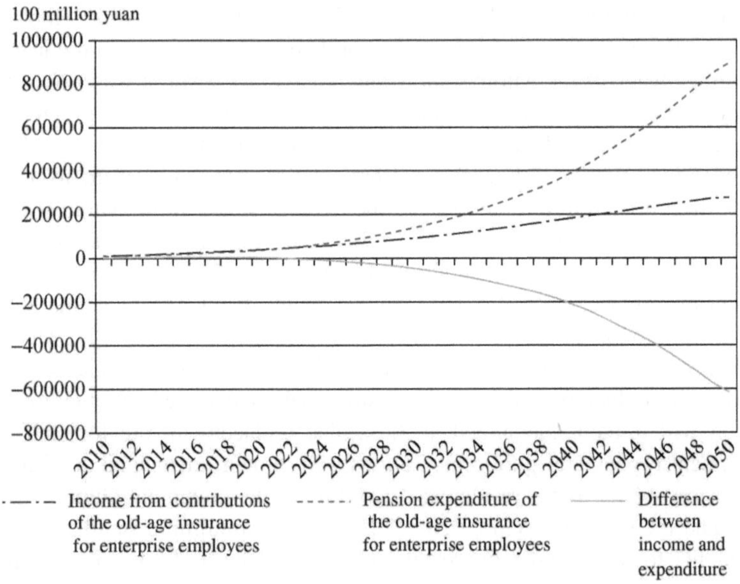

Fig. 15.13 Estimation of the income and expenditure of the old-age insurance for urban enterprise employees

enterprise employees will be unable to strike a balance between income and expenditure. In 2050, the funding gap of the old-age insurance for urban enterprise employees will reach 61.6 trillion yuan (the price in 2050).

The income and expenditure of the old-age insurance for staff of government organs and public institutions is slightly different. As shown in Fig. 15.14, as the current pension replacement rate for the staff of government organs and public institutions is overly high, there was a deficit of income over expenditure of the old-age insurance for staff of government organs and public institutions from the very beginning. In 2050, the funding gap of old-age insurance for staff of government organs and public institutions will reach 9.64 trillion yuan. As the number of staff in government organs and public institutions is relatively small, its funding gap is much smaller than that the old-age insurance for enterprise employees.

Adding up the income and expenditure of the old-age insurances for enterprises and government organs and public institutions, coupled with the income from subsidies of government at various levels, we have obtained the estimated total income and expenditure of the old-age insurance for urban workers. As shown in Fig. 15.15, there is a surplus of income over expenditure of the old-age insurance for urban workers 2010–2022, and starting from 2023, there will be a deficit of income over expenditure, and it is necessary to use the accumulated surplus to make up the funding gap. By 2029, the cumulative surplus will be used up, and if the

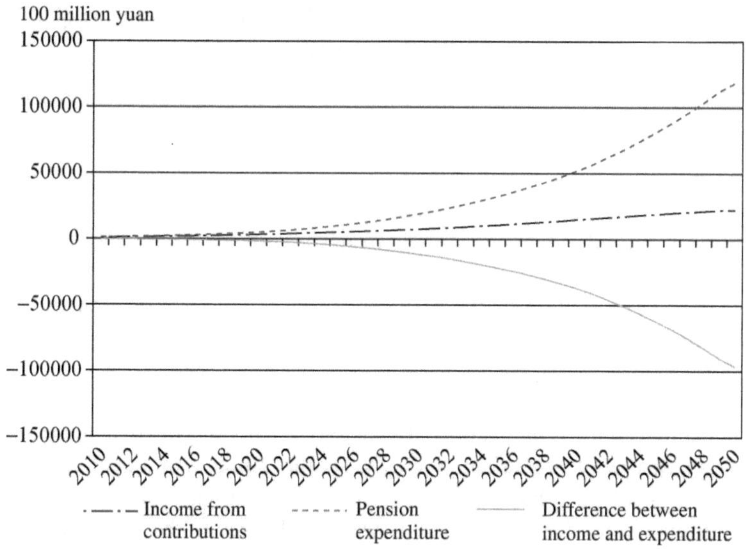

Fig. 15.14 Estimation of income and expenditure of the old-age insurance for staff of government organs and public institutions

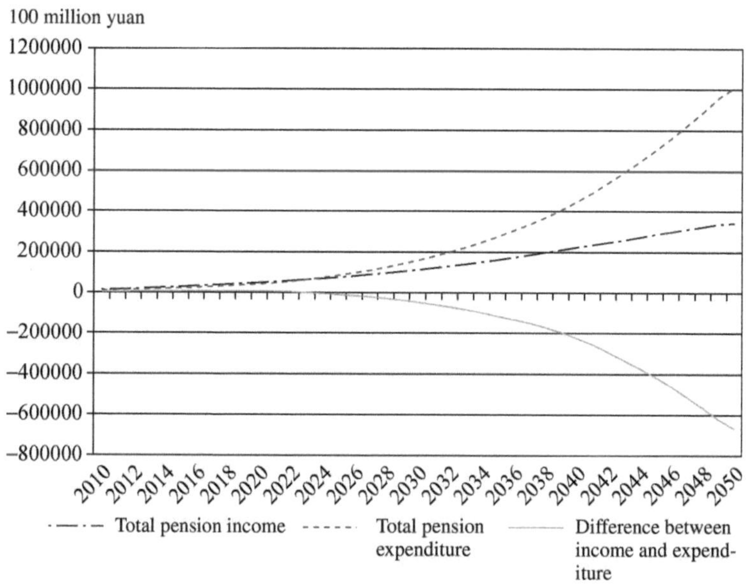

Fig. 15.15 Estimation of income and expenditure of the old-age insurances for urban and rural residents

government does not take any action, then by 2050, the cumulative gap will reach 802 trillion yuan, accounting for 91% of the GDP in 2050.

(2) Estimation of Income and Expenditure of the Old-Age Insurances for Urban and Rural Residents

In theory, there is no social unified raising of the old-age insurances for urban and rural residents, the base pension is fully paid from the government budget, and the pension from individual accounts is from the money accumulated in residents' individual accounts. Based on the previous parameter setting, we have made an estimate of the expenditure on the base pension of the old-age insurances for urban and rural residents (subsidies from the government) and the results are shown in Fig. 15.16.

As shown in Fig. 15.16, although the expenditure on the base pension of the old-age insurances for urban and rural residents is growing rapidly, there still exist the old-age insurance for urban workers, so the number of beneficiaries of the old-age insurances for urban and rural residents is relatively small, and this part of expenditure is mainly for rural resident. Meanwhile, due to the low guarantee level of the base pension of the old-age insurance for residents, this part of expenditure is actually very small compared with the pension expenditure for urban workers. But as this part of expenditure is entirely borne by the governments, it is also quite a large expenditure burden for the governments.

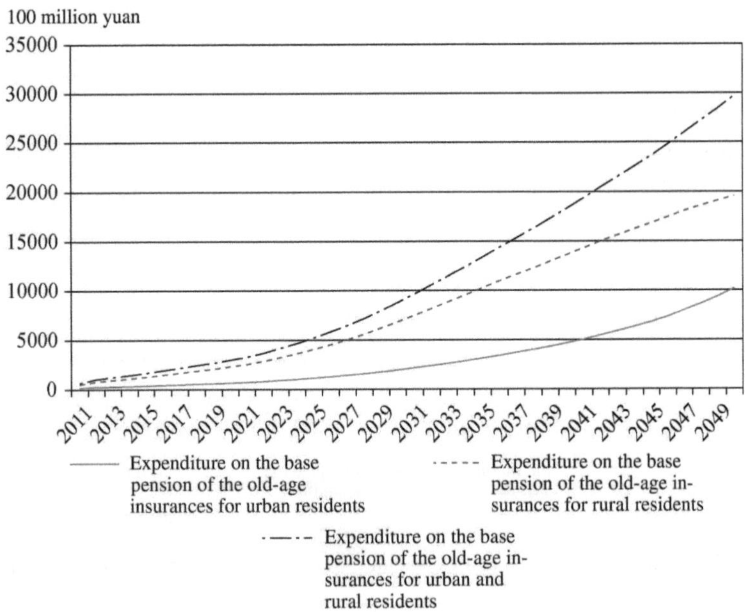

Fig. 15.16 Estimation of the expenditure on the base pension of the old-age insurances for urban and rural residents (government expenditure)

(3) Estimation of the Fiscal Pressure for Maintaining the Old-Age Insurance System and the Overall Implicit Pension Debt

The previous calculations show that, if the funding gap of the old-age insurance for urban workers appears and the accumulated surplus is insufficient to cover the gap, and if the government does not take any action, then by 2050 the cumulative gap will reach 802 trillion yuan, accounting for 91% of the GDP in 2050. But in the study carried out by Ma Jun, the calculation result of this variable is 83%.[10] But it is unrealistic to assume that the government does not take any action and lets the gap expand arbitrarily. Now let's simulate such a policy scenario. That is, when the funding gap of the old-age insurance for urban workers appears and the accumulated surplus is insufficient to cover the gap, the government will take measures rather than abdicate its responsibilities. A concrete measure is that the governments grant subsidies to make up for the pension fund to be spent each year so that the annual accumulated surplus of the pension fund is zero. This means that the governments will assume responsibility for the pension benefits, but only limited to fill the pension gap. In the meanwhile, we combine the income and expenditure items of the old-age insurances for urban workers and for urban and rural residents so as to estimate the overall fund pressure for maintaining the old-age insurance system on the society and the government finance.

The financial subsidies needed to be granted by the governments to bring the accumulated surplus of pension fund down to 0, coupled with the original income from the subsidies granted by the governments at various levels for the old-age insurance for workers and the subsidies for the base pension of the old-age insurance for rural and urban residents, constitute the total amount of government subsidies to maintain the old-age insurance system. Dividing this amount by that year's GDP and the government expenditure, we have obtained the ratios of the total amount of government subsidies to maintain the old-age insurance system to GDP and the government expenditure. The results are shown in Figs. 15.17 and 15.18.

As shown in the figures, the ratio of total pension expenditure to GDP has increased gradually over time from 2.73% in 2011 and to 11.85% in 2050. Before 2029, the ratios of total fund needed to maintain the old-age insurance system to the government expenditure and GDP ratio are not high. This is because the funding gap of the old-age insurance for urban workers will not yet appear, and the cumulative balance will remain positive. Starting from 2030, as the accumulated surplus of the old-age insurance for urban workers will be insufficient to cover the funding gap, the government will need to increase subsidies, so these two ratios will start to grow rapidly. By 2050, the ratios of the total amount of government subsidies to maintain the old-age insurance system to GDP and the government expenditure will reach 8.46 and 34.85% respectively. That is, about one-third of the

[10]The result was converted to 2011, but as the discount factor is the nominal GDP growth rate, this ratio should be the same in theory in 2011 and 2050.

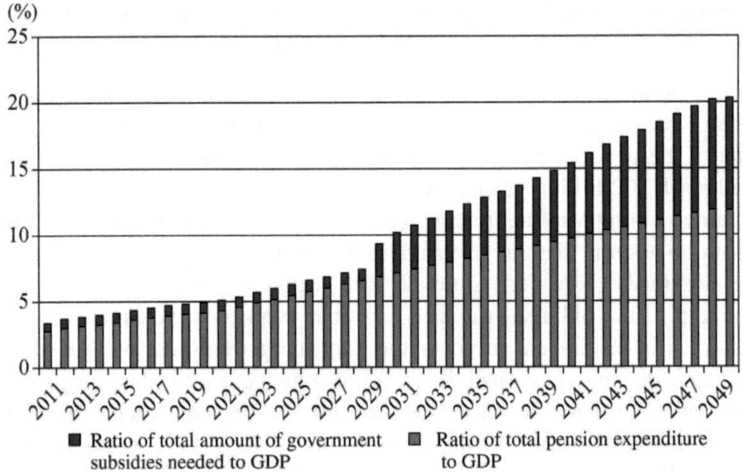

Fig. 15.17 Ratio of the total amount of government subsidies to maintain the old-age insurance system to GDP. *Note* The ratio of total pension expenditure to GDP is the ratio of the total pension payment to GDP, which consists of two parts: the total amount of government subsidies to maintain the old-age insurance system + the expenditure of endowment insurance payment

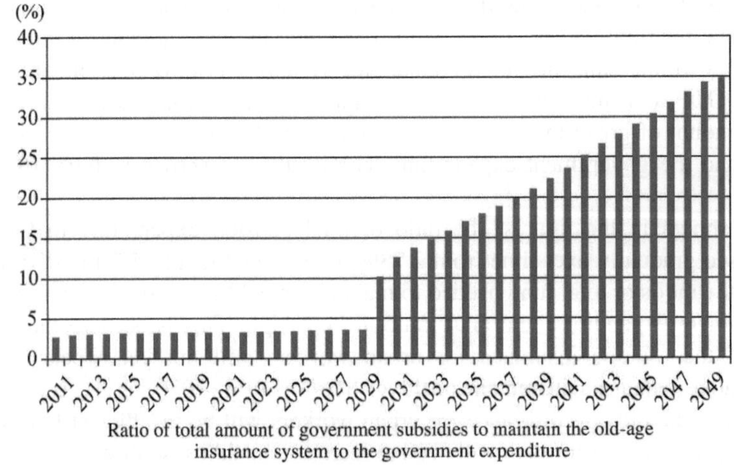

Fig. 15.18 Ratio of the total amount of government subsidies to maintain the old-age insurance system to the government expenditure

government expenditure will be used to cover the funding gap of the old-age insurance system.[11]

The government subsidies needed each year during 2010–2050 were discounted to 2011,[12] and the government subsidies over the years were added up to get the implicit debt of the entire old-age insurance system, which totaled 62.5 trillion yuan, accounting for 132% of the GDP in 2011, in which the implicit debt of the old-age insurance for urban workers amounts to 46.5 trillion yuan, accounting for 98% of the GDP, plus the original subsidies from the governments at various levels, the implicit debt reaches 56.4 trillion yuan, accounting for 119% of the GDP; the implicit debt of the old-age insurance for rural and urban residents amounted to 6.08 trillion yuan, accounting for 13% of the GDP.[13]

With regard to the ratio of accumulative implicit pension debt to GDP, if the debt ratio is more than 100%, the debt seems very serious. But as the debt is repaid on average in many years, the fiscal pressure it poses on the economy and the government seems much smaller. According to the estimate, the total pension expenditure to GDP ratio will reach 11.85% by 2050 under the reference scenario, and this result is basically close to the current level of some European welfare states (see the relevant contents in Part 1 of this book).

15.5.3 Estimation of Transition Costs of the Old-Age Insurance System

The above estimated implicit pension debts are wide-scope data. There are also narrow-scope implicit pension debts, the so-called transition costs. The *Circular of the State Council on Deepening the Reform of the Old-Age Insurance System for Employees of Enterprises* (Guofa No. [1995] 6) introduces the model combining social pooling with personal accounts for the basic old-age insurance and emphasizes to establish a multi-level social security system. The document Guofa No. [1997] 26 further confirms this model and requires to transit from the fully PAYG system to a partially funded one. However, this has resulted in a problem: the retirees had contributed no money or little money to their personal accounts when they were in-service, but it was necessary to safeguard their livelihood after retirement, while in the new model that features social pooling plus personal

[11]One t factor that must be taken into account is China's fiscal revenue to GDP ratio is significantly lower than those in the developed countries. The revenue and expenditure to GDP ratios in the developed countries are mostly about 40%.

[12]The current year nominal GDP growth rate is used as the discount factor. It is convenient to use the nominal GDP as a deflator because although the absolute amount changes after discounting, the ratio of a certain amount to GDP will remain unchanged, thus avoiding a significant impact of the setting of a discount factored on the analysis results.

[13]Please note that the implicit debt here is net debt because it has excluded the expenses the old-age insurance can cover.

accounts, the contributions paid by in-service workers should theoretically go into their personal accounts, then there was a funding gap between the contributions left in the pooling account and the pensions to be paid for "the old men" and "the new men". This is the so-called "transition costs" of the old-age insurance system.

For a long time, who should bear the costs incurred in the transition has not been completely solved. When designing the reform scheme for the old-age insurance, China failed to adopt a special method to handle the transition costs, but expected to gradually eliminate the costs through increasing the contribution rate of enterprises, expanding the pension coverage and combining social pooling with personal accounts (Song et al. 2000; Jia et al. 2007).[14] In such case, enterprises and in-service employees needed not ois perhaps morenly to pay premiums to their personal accounts (the obligation under the partially funded system), but also to provide pensions to retired workers (the obligation under the PAYG system—the transition costs). Transition costs and "empty personal accounts" were closely linked, and as no measure was taken to address the funding gap, the old-age insurance administration departments had to divert funds from personal accounts to ensure the payment of pensions for retired workers, which led to the emptiness of the personal accounts of in-service employees under the new payment system and the degeneration of the nominal system of social pooling plus personal accounts into a de facto PAYG system.

Many domestic and foreign institutions have estimated the amount of China's implicit pension debt, but some estimates focused on the size of the implicit pension debt arising from the transition costs. However, scholars have not formed consistent views on the definitions of transition costs, and there are differences in calculation methods, parameter selection and other aspects. According to the definition given by Sun (2001), transition costs consist of two parts: the base pension paid to "the old man" and the transitional pension paid to "the middle men". This definition was also adopted by Jia et al. (2007) who projected the transition costs and implicit debt by calculating the expenditure of the two parts. Wang et al. (2001) believed that the transition of the old-age insurance system resulted in the empty personal accounts, so they defined in their calculations the transition cost as the financial expenditure on the transition of personal pension accounts from nominal empty accounts into fully funded accounts. That is, assuming that the old PAYG system is still used for in-service workers and retirees who participated in the old-age insurance before 2001, and a new fully funded personal account system is established for workers who participated in the old-age insurance after 2001, then the government subsidies needed to safeguard the pension benefits of people participated in the old system are the transition costs.

[14]Some scholars were opposed to this. For example, Sun (2001) believes that the transition costs should be borne the government rather than individuals and enterprise. On the one hand, it is unfair for individuals and enterprises to bear the transition costs. On the other hand, this would diminish the enthusiasm of individuals and enterprise to participate in the old-age insurance and thus lead to decline in contribution rate.

He (2001) criticized the studies of some scholars and believes that some scholars researchers believe that there are two mistaken ideas in estimation of implicit debt and transition cost. First, the government's pension commitments in the old system are fully classified as debt. Based on this idea, it is erroneous to fully classify the base pension paid to "the old man" as transition costs because 20% of pooling accounts still remain in the new system and this part of pooling accounts should originally be used to pay the base pension to retirees, and the middle men have also paid contributions. Second, the transition costs are estimated by assuming that the old system is terminated and the new system is put in place in one step. In fact, assuming that the pension commitments for the ole men and the middle men remain unchanged, the PAYG income and expenditure method continues and the contribution rate of enterprises does not temporarily reduce, then the transition costs to be raised by the government will greatly reduce.

In our view, the definition given by Zhao (2006) is perhaps more accurately. He proposed that now that the transition costs are incurred due to the establishment of the new system on the basis of the old system, then the transition costs can be acquired by comparing the difference between the pension input for establishing a new system on the basis of the old system and the income and expenditure of the new pension system on the assumption that there is no burden of the old system. He estimated that the transition costs that may be incurred each year during 1996–2076, but the basic data he was reliant on, especially the estimated data of the population are somewhat rough, and the population changing trend of the old men and the middle men is somewhat strange. Ma (2012) has also used the definition given by Zhao Junkang to calculate the transition costs. Specifically, the pension replacement rate on the assumption that there is no burden of the old system and the actual scenario are as follows (Table 15.2).

Then calculate the pension expenditure difference under two scenarios to get the transition costs arising from pension gap.

Here, we have also used the definition given by Zhao Junkang and Ma to estimate the size of the transition costs and implicit debt of the old-age insurance and its changes. The estimate results of the transition costs of each year during 2000–2050 are shown in Fig. 15.19. The annual transition costs of the old-age insurance for employees of enterprises are 100–4000 million yuan (at current prices). In 2000, the transition costs accounted for nearly 50% of the pension expenditure of enterprises.[15] During 2000–2011, the cumulative transition costs of the old-age insurance for employees of enterprises reached 1.84 trillion yuan. As mentioned above, the funding gap caused by the transition costs were mainly filled through diverting the funds from personal accounts. According to *China Pension Report 2012*, by the end of 2011, the empty amount of the personal accounts in the basic old-age insurance system for urban residents and workers reached 2.2 trillion

[15]This was partially because at that time there were only the old men, the old men did not have any accumulated money in their personal accounts, so a considerable part of the pension fund exists in the form of transition costs and paid through misappropriation of the funds in personal accounts.

Table 15.2 Setting of the replacement rate for estimation of the transition costs

	Replacement rate of the new system on the assumption that there is no burden (%)	Replacement rate of the real new system (%)
The old men	32	Remaining unchanged at 44
The middle age men	32	Reducing gradually from 44 to 32
The new men	32	32

Source Ma (2012)

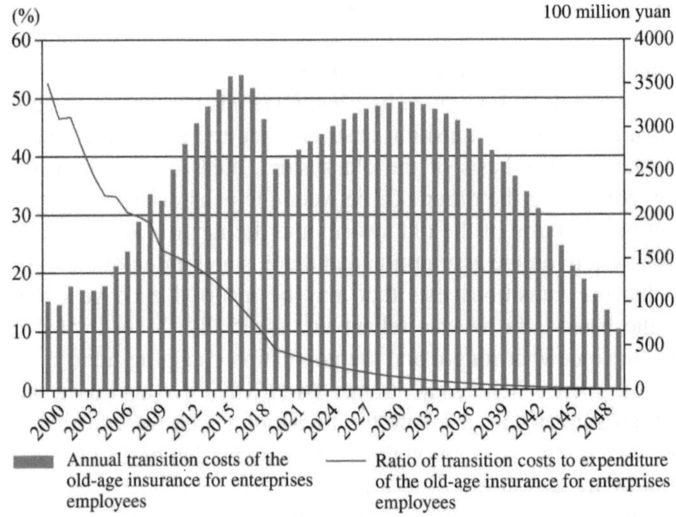

Fig. 15.19 Transition costs accounted for enterprise retirees pension expenditure ratio

yuan, much greater than the cumulative transition costs we calculated. This is partially because there were also the transition costs incurred during 1996–1999. Assuming that the transition costs in the 4 year are equal to the level in 2000, then they exactly amount to 2.24 trillion yuan.

Figure 15.20 shows the estimated retained transition costs[16] (at current prices) in these years and their ratios to GDP. Due to the impact of price and demographic factors, the retained transition costs have increased from 1.53 trillion in 2000 to 3.6 trillion yuan in 2014 and later maintained the gradual downward trend. The ratio of transition costs to GDP has maintained a downward trend. In 2011, the retained transition costs amounted to 3.47 trillion yuan, accounting for 7.33% of the GDP.

[16]The stock of transition costs, i.e. the discounted transition costs that still need to be paid in the future. The transition costs that have been incurred have already been reflected in the empty accounts of the personal accounts of old-age insurance.

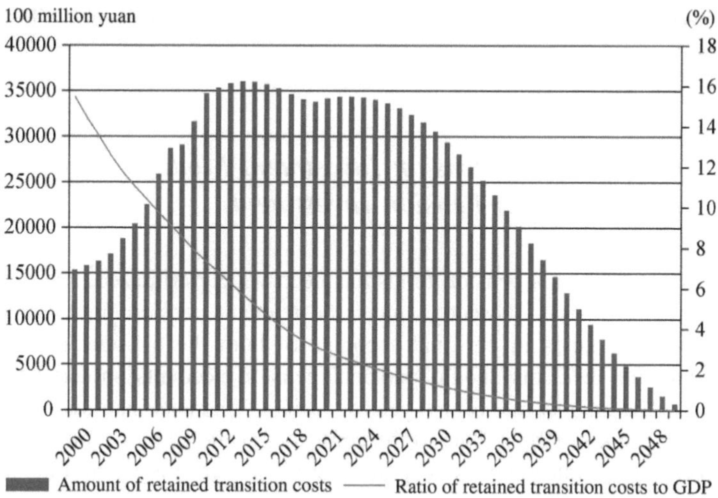

Fig. 15.20 Amount of retained transition costs

As mentioned in the previous paragraph, the implicit debt we calculated reached 56.4 trillion yuan in 2011, accounting for 119% of the GDP. As the transition costs are part of the implicit debt, so we can break down the implicit debt to get the ratio of the implicit debt caused by the transition to total implicit debt of the old-age insurance for workers, which is 7.5%, while the ratio of the implicit debt caused by the population aging to total implicit debt of the old-age insurance for workers was 92.5%. Thus, it can be found that the transition costs are very important in the short term and have formed serious emptiness of personal accounts. But in the long term, the implicit pension debt caused by the population aging will be more serious.

However, from the perspective of the government responsibilities, the transition costs are direct implicit debt, so the government should take direct responsibility for repayment, while the implicit pension debt caused by the population aging is largely a kind of contingent implicit debt, and the government repayment responsibility is relatively small.

15.6 Further Analysis and Simulation of Pension Income and Expenditure Scenario

In this section, we will carry out further scenario analysis and policy simulation of pension income and expenditure to examine pension income and expenditure and debt burden under different parameter settings. The actual work is to set parameters and carry out sensitivity analysis in particular of relevant policy variables to examine the effects of the policies. In the paragraphs below, we will change the variables such as pension investment return rate, retirement age, pensionable age and pension replacement rate to examine the impact of these possible policy measures on the pension gap.

15.6.1 Changing the Pension Investment Mode to Improve the Returns of Pension Investment

The low ROI of China's pension funds has been widely criticized, and the risk of devaluation even exists. Presently, under the relevant pension fund management law, the pension funds in personal accounts of both the old-age insurances for workers and for residents should personal pension accounts should be accrued according to the interest rate of one-year deposits of financial institutions issued by the People's Bank of China. Due to the control over the Chinese financial system, the deposit interest rates always keep at a very low level for a long time and may even be lower than the inflation rate during periods of high inflation, so the pension funds are at risk of devaluation. Low ROIs have also limited the enthusiasm of enterprises and residents to participate in the old-age insurance.

Of course, from another perspective, due to the serious problem of current empty pension accounts, when personal accounts are not fully funded, there are great risks to hastily change the investment mode to improve the pension investment returns. On the one hand, there is no money in the empty personal accounts, so personal accounts are not fully funded, to improve the returns of investment is out of the question in actual operation at least for the part of personal accounts. On the other hand, if we promise a higher ROI to the public, but personal accounts are not fully funded, investment returns are not accumulated, it is tantamount to draw a blank check to the public, and there will be more serious problems in the future when pension commitments for personal accounts should be honored. Finally, there will also be investment risks.

Nevertheless, the investment returns of pension funds in China is indeed too low. According to the data provided by Dai, Chairman of the National Council for Social Security Fund, more than 90% of China's pension funds are deposited in bank accounts and are not used in investment tools with higher returns, and in the coming 10 years, the average annual investment return rate will be less than 2% (Dai 2011). If we can effectively increase the ROI of pension funds, this will to some extent promote the financial sustainability of pension funds. In particular, if a low nominal ROI is still used on the pension payment side (for example, the deposit rate is still used), while on the management side, pension funds can have a higher ROI, this will be able to greatly improve the funding strength and self-sustainability of pension funds to better respond to the future potential funding gap when an aging population appears.[17] In this regard, the National Social Security Fund is a

[17]But the old-age insurance management agency guarantees the minimum rate of return, and even in the event of the investment risk, it must guarantee the payment at the minimum rate of return.

successful model. Due to its multiple and flexible investment channels, the National Social Security Fund has realized a total investment return of 277.1 billion yuan in the 10 years since its establishment, with an average annual ROI of 9.17%, 7.03 higher than the average annual inflation rate over the same period of time.

In short, professionals, the public or scholars have been calling to open stock markets to pension funds. Here, we assume that the investment mode for pension funds in China is changed and pension funds are allowed to be invested in high-risk high-return bond and equity markets to increase their ROI and observe the impact of this policy on pension income and expenditure. We raised the ROI from 3 to 9% in the benchmark parameter setting, but the pension expenditure level remains unchanged and then carry out re-estimation (see Fig. 15.21).[18]

As shown in Fig. 15.21, the ROI is set at 3%, the accumulated surplus of pension funds of the old-age insurance for workers will peak in 2023 and reach 10.66 trillion yuan and will be used up by 2030. If the ROI is increased to 9%, the accumulated surplus of pension funds of the old-age insurance for workers will peak in 2026 and reach 18.3 trillion yuan, and with the increase of the pension gap, the accumulated surplus will be used up by 2032. By 2050, the accumulated pension gap of the old-age insurance for workers will reach 760 trillion yuan, which is 5.2% lower than the reference scenario of 802 trillion yuan, accounting for 87% of the GDP that year.

Therefore, the increase in ROI will be somewhat helpful to enhance the sustainability of the old-age insurance for workers, but the effect seems not strong enough, and the cumulative pension gap will be postponed by more than two years. By 2050, the cumulative pension gap will be reduced by only 5.2%, and the policy effect will be relatively disappointing.

15.6.2 Raising the Retirement Age and the Pensionable Age of Residents

Presently, China's retirement age is significantly younger compared with other countries. According to *Circular on Issues Concerning Stopping and Correcting the Handling the Early Retirement for Employees of Enterprises in Violation of the Rules and Regulations of the State*, for enterprises, the retirement age is 60 for male employees, 50 for female employees and 55 for female cadres. In the benchmark parameter settings in this study, the retirement age is 60 and 53 for male and female employees of enterprises respectively, and the retirement age is 60 and 55 for male and female staff of government organs and public institutions respectively. Compared with the US, Japan, Europe and other OECD countries, China's retirement age is significantly younger.

[18]Like the previous studies, the pension payments calculated here included the original subsidized by government at all levels.

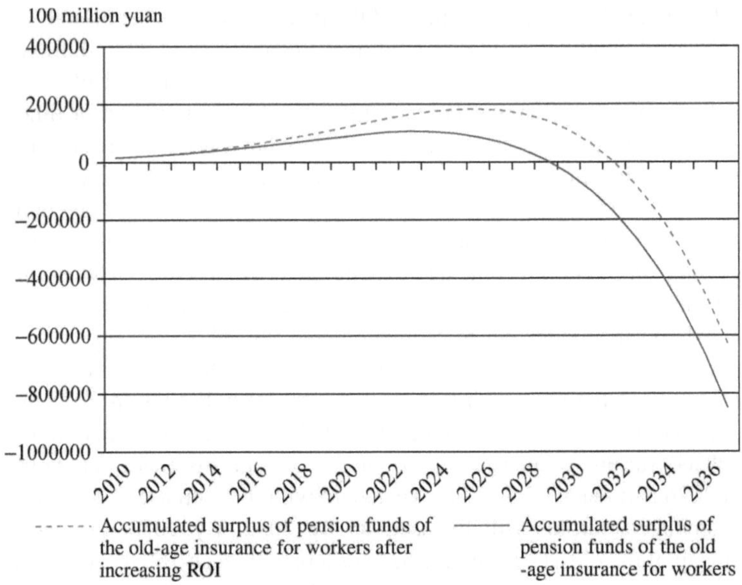

Fig. 15.21 Impact of increasing ROI on the pension surplus of the old-age insurance for workers

An extension of the retirement age is consistent with the extension in life expectancy. In the past, due to the shorter life expectancy, the retirement age was young. With the improvement of nutritional status and medical care level, life expectancy and people's health levels are improving rapidly, so people are physically capable of working for a longer time. Meanwhile, in one sense, an appropriate extension of the retirement age is also in the interests of the people. On the one hand, after all, working wages are higher than pension income, and on the other hand, under the funded system, the increase in the retirement age can help accumulate more personal account pensions for workers.

However, people may be less willing to retire at a later age in the arrangements of the PAYG system than in the funded system. This is because the overall level of pension benefits in the PAYG depends on the level of wages of workers before retirement but is not necessarily related to the years of working, particularly the years of pension contribution. Thus, the increase in years of working is not in their interests. In addition, the higher the pension replacement rate, the stronger workers' motive for early retirement. Perhaps the above factors are mainly accountable for the resistance of the general public to the current discussions in raising the retirement age.

An extension of the retirement age can on the one hand help reduce the number of pensioners and thus reduce the pension spending and on the other hand increase the base population for pension contribution, thereby increasing the pension income. Here, we will change the retirement age for workers of enterprises and government organs and public institutions in the benchmark mode. and extend the age for receiving the base pension for the old-age insurance for residents to study the effect of increasing the retirement age in the aspect of pension gap and financial subsidy pressure.

Specifically, we assume that the reform of the retirement age will start in 2015 and there are two reform options: high-speed and low-speed reform schemes to gradually raise the retirement age. The reform timetable is shown in the following Table 15.3. The high-speed reform scheme will start reforming in 2015, the retirement age and the pensionable for various groups of people will increase by 1 year every 2 years to gradually increase the retirement age for male and female workers to 65 and 60 respectively, the pensionable age is the same as the retirement age for male workers, and later the retirement age will no longer be adjusted. The low-speed reform scheme will start reform in 2015, but the adjustment pace is to increase by 1 year every four years at a slower pace. Below we give the policy simulation results of the high-speed and low-speed reform schemes.

(1) Estimation results of the high-speed reform scheme

As shown in Fig. 15.22, the high-speed reform scheme has a very significant role in reducing the pension gap and easing the financial pressure brought by the pension expenditure. In the reference scenario, the accumulated surplus will be used up by 2030 and the cumulative pension gap will reach 802 trillion yuan by 2050, accounting for 91% of GDP. While in the high-speed reform scheme, the cumulative surplus of the old-age insurance for urban workers will not be used up until 2043, and a large cumulative gap will appear after 2043. By 2050, the cumulative gap will 197.5 trillion yuan, accounting for 23% of GDP. Therefore, the high-speed reform scheme plays a very significant role in reducing the pension gap.

Extending the age for receiving the base pension for the old-age insurance for residents can also help reduce the base pension spending for residents. As shown in Fig. 15.23, the reform of extension of the retirement age can reduce the number of pensioners, so the base pension spending for the old-age insurance for residents is also significant lower than that in the reference scenario and will only account for 84% of the reference scenario in 2050.

Consolidating the income and expenditure of the old-age insurances for workers and for residents, we can get the ratio of the government subsidies needed to maintain the current old-age insurance system to GDP, and the results are shown in Fig. 15.24. In the reference scenario, to maintain the old-age insurance system, government subsidies should start to be significantly increased in 2030, and the ratio of government subsidies to GDP will rise to 8.46% in 2050. But in the high-speed reform scheme, government subsidies will not be significantly increased until 2044 because the accumulated pension surplus of the old-age insurance for workers are used up, and the ratio of government subsidies to GDP will rise to 4.97 in 2050, which is much better than the circumstances in the reference scenario.

Table 15.3 Setting of the reform schemes for retirement age and pensionable ages of residents

	High-speed scheme				Low-speed scheme			
	Male workers	Female employees of enterprises	Female staff of government organs and public institutions	Pensionable age	Male workers	Female employees of enterprises	Female staff of government organs and public institutions	Pensionable age
2015	61	54	56	61	61	54	56	61
2017	62	55	57	62	61	54	56	61
2019	63	56	58	63	62	55	57	62
2021	64	57	59	64	62	55	57	62
2023	65	58	60	65	63	56	58	63
2025		59			63	56	58	63
2027		60			64	57	59	64
2029					64	57	59	64
2031					65	58	60	65
2033						58		
2035						59		
2037						59		
2039						60		

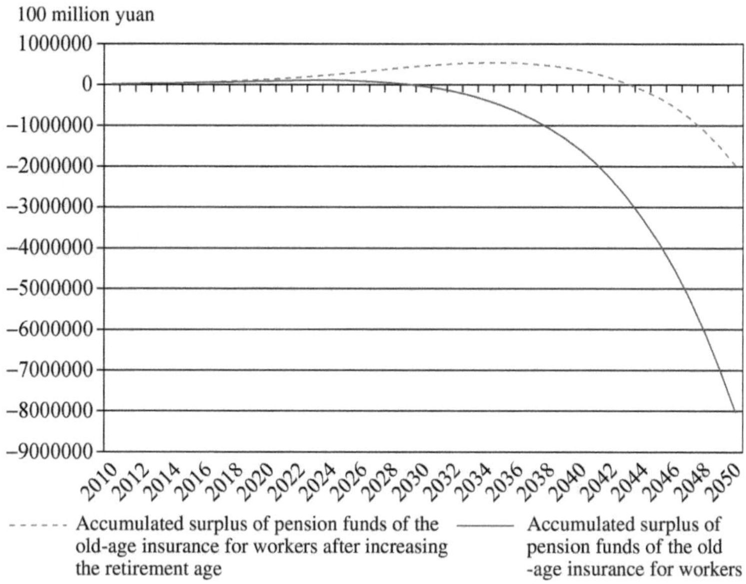

Fig. 15.22 The cumulative pension surplus of the old-age insurance for urban workers in the high-speed reform scheme

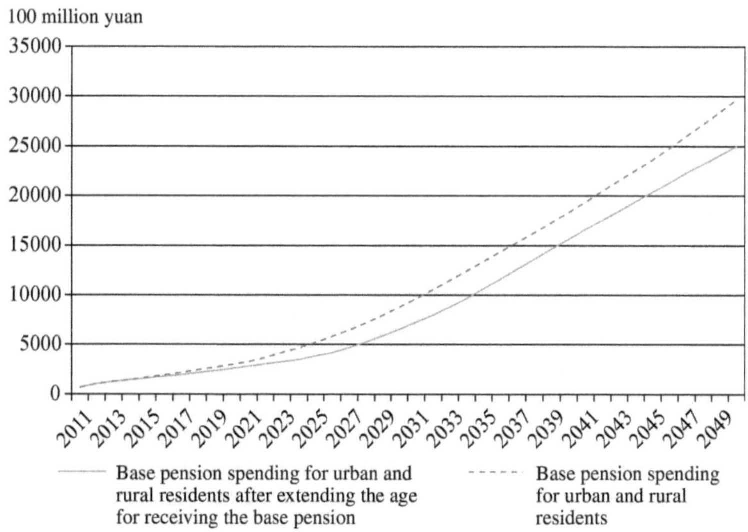

Fig. 15.23 The base pension spending for urban and rural residents in the high-speed reform scheme

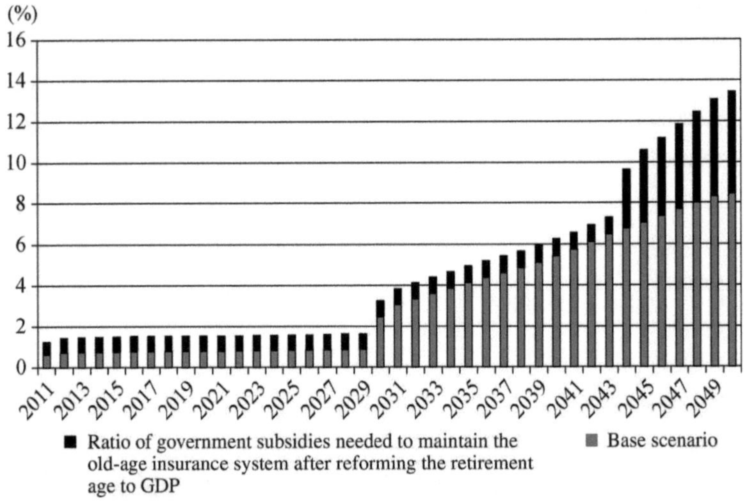

Fig. 15.24 Ratio of the government subsidies needed to maintain the old-age insurance system to GDP in the high-speed reform scheme

(2) Estimation results of the low-speed reform scheme

The effect of the low-speed reform scheme is shown in Fig. 15.25. Based on the calculation results, even if the pace of extending the retirement age and the pensionable age of residents is adjusted from 1 year every 2 years to 1 year every 4 years, this policy measure still has a very strong effect. In the low-speed scheme, the accumulated surplus of the old-age insurance for workers will not be used up and become negative until 2041, which is 2 years earlier than the high-speed scheme. By 2050, the cumulative pension gap of the old-age insurance for workers will reach 248.4 trillion yuan, accounting for 28% of the GDP that year, an increase of 5% compared with 23% in the high-speed scheme. As shown in Fig. 15.26, even in the low-speed scheme in which the age for receiving the base pension for residents is extended, the base pension expenditure for urban and rural residents is still significantly lower than the baseline situation.

To sum up, extending the retirement age and the pensionable age for residents is a very potent measure to reduce the pension gap and ease the financial pressure of government in the old-age insurance. In addition, even if the pace of extending the retirement age and the pensionable age of residents is adjusted from 1 year every 2 years to 1 year every 4 years in the low-speed scheme, the policy effect will not be greatly reduced.

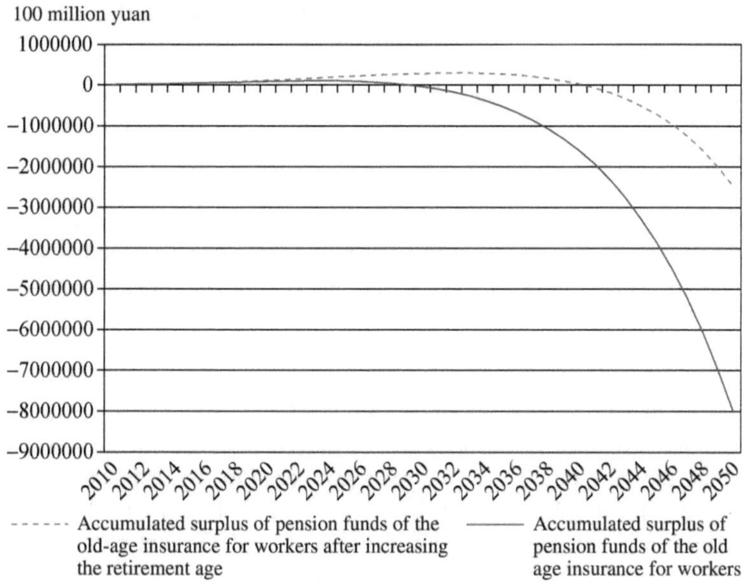

Fig. 15.25 The accumulated pension surplus of the old-age insurance for workers in the low-speed scheme

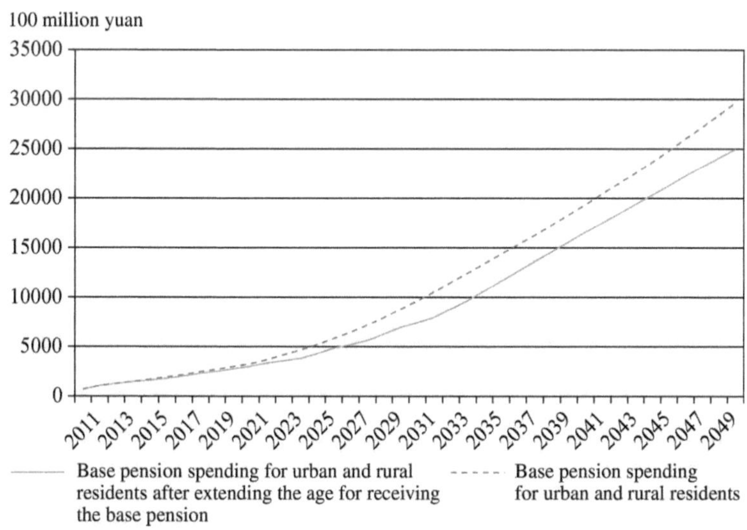

Fig. 15.26 The base pension expenditure for urban and rural residents in the low-speed scheme

15.6.3 Maintaining a High Pension Replacement Rate

In the parameter setting in the reference scenario, we assume that the pension replacement rate of the old-age insurance for employees of enterprises will fall to 32% in the future, and in fact the overall pension replacement rate for workers was about 44.69% in 2012 (calculated based on the social average wage). Here we assume that the average pension replacement rate for employees of enterprises and staff of government organs and public institution remains unchanged at 44.69% in the future and carry out re-estimation, and the re-estimation results are shown in Figs. 15.27 and 15.28.

It can be anticipated that, to maintain the current relatively high pension replacement rate, the future pension gap and financial pressure in China will be much greater than the reference scenario. By 2025, the accumulated pension surplus of the old-age insurance for workers will be used up and become negative, 4 years earlier than the year of 2029 in the reference scenario. By 2050, the cumulative pension gap will reach 1332 trillion yuan, much higher than 802 trillion yuan in the reference scenario, accounting for up to 152% of the GDP that year.

The government subsidies needed to maintain the old-age insurance system will also increase significantly. Starting from 2025, the amount of subsidies should significantly increase, and by 2050, the ratio of the government subsidies to GDP to maintain the current level of pension replacement rate will rise to 11.95%, while the total pension expenditure to GDP ratio will rise to 15.34%, significantly higher than 11.85% in the reference scenario.

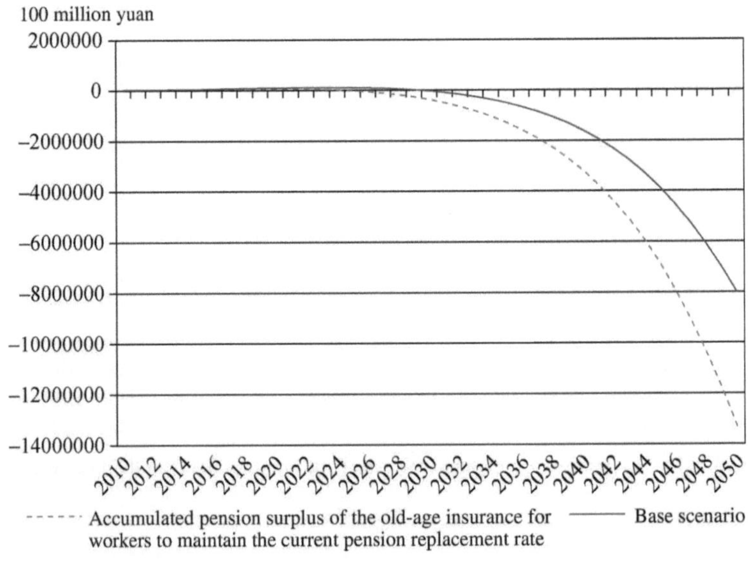

Fig. 15.27 The accumulated pension surplus of the old-age insurance for workers to maintain the current pension replacement rate

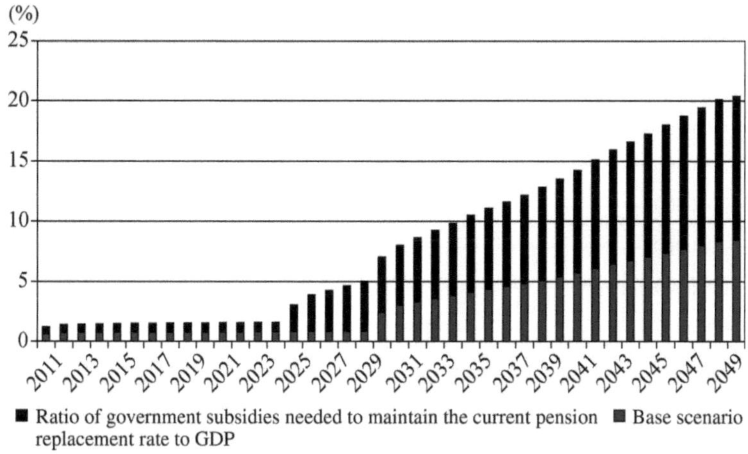

Fig. 15.28 Ratio of the government subsidies needed to maintain the current old-age insurance system to GDP

15.6.4 Combined Effect of Increasing the ROI and the Retirement Age and Maintaining a High Replacement Rate

We certainly expect that the pension benefits of workers and residents in China can be effectively safeguarded in the future. But in order to reduce the pension gap and avoid the occurrence of a debt crisis and the reduction of the international competitiveness of China, we must make a choice in policies. If we must make trade-offs between the alternatives of raising the retirement age (the age to receive the base pension) and maintaining a relatively high replacement rate, we believe that it is more preferable to raise the retirement age and maintain a relatively high replacement rate than to maintain a low retirement age while reducing the pension replacement rate. The second scheme will not only reduce the level of pension benefits for the retired workers, but also result in the shortage of labor supply and reduce China's international competitiveness. Instead, the first scheme can also give a higher level of security for the retired workers while ensuring labor supply.

Below we try to implement a comprehensive reform program, which combine the three scenarios of ROI, retirement age and pensionable age discussed in this section and tentatively increase the ROI, retirement age and pensionable age without reducing the replacement rate (the high-speed reform scheme).

The estimation results are shown in Figs. 15.29 and 15.30. In the comprehensive reform scheme, even if the replacement rate is maintained at a high level, but as the other two policy measures play a strong role, the pension payments of the old-age insurance will still be greatly improved. Compared with the reference scenario in which the accumulated pension surplus will be used up by 2029 and the scenario in which only a high replacement rate is maintained and the accumulated pension

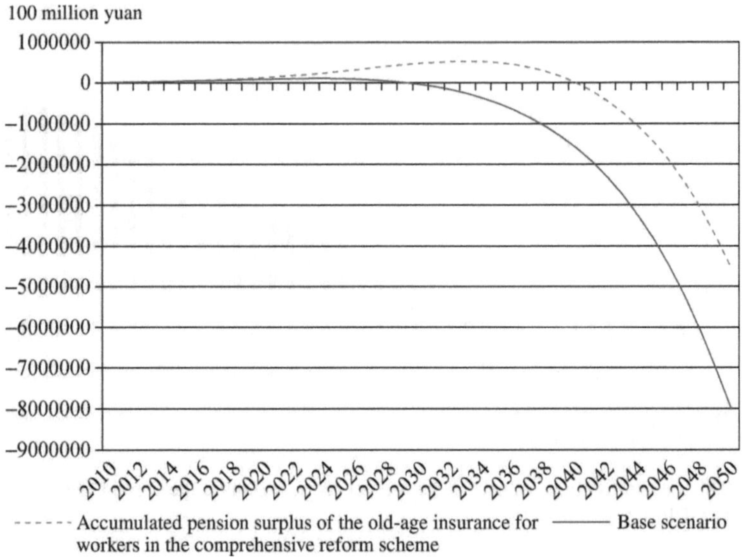

Fig. 15.29 The accumulated pension surplus of the old-age insurance for workers in the comprehensive reform scheme

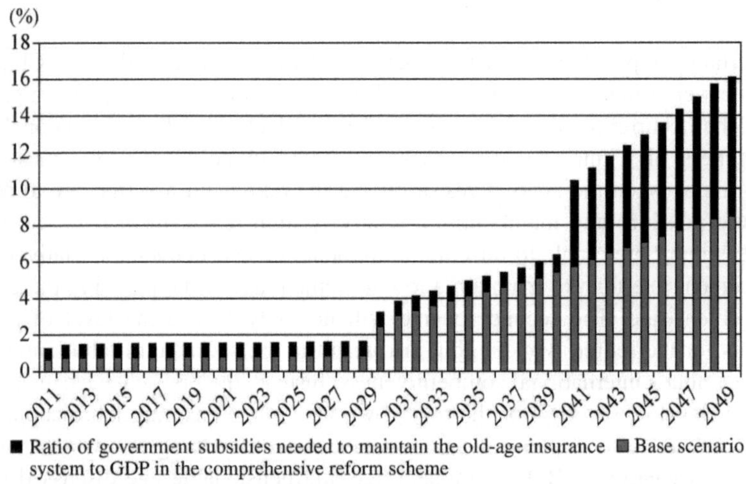

Fig. 15.30 Ratio of the government subsidies needed to maintain the old-age insurance system to GDP in the comprehensive reform scheme

surplus will be used up by 2025, the comprehensive reform scheme postpones this point of time to 2040. By 2050, the cumulative pension gap of the old-age insurance for workers will reach 455.4 trillion yuan, accounting for 52% of the GDP that, which is also greatly lower than 91% in the reference scenario and 152% in the scenario with a high replacement rate.

In the comprehensive reform scheme, the size of the government subsidies needed to maintain the old-age insurance system is also significantly reduced, and the point of time is greatly postponed. In the reference scenario, the government subsidies should be significantly increased from 2030 n to maintain the old-age insurance system, but in the comprehensive reform scheme, it is not until 2041 that the government subsidies should be significantly increased, only to be a substantial increase in government subsidies to pension insurance, and the point of time is postponed by 11 years. By 2050, government subsidies to GDP ratio will reach a level of about 7.64%.

15.7 Summary

In this study, we have used a model of population growth and migration to predict the population structure of China during 2010–2050, and on this basis, we have created an actuarial model for assessment of the old-age insurance system, analyzed and predicted China's pension payments in the future through reasonable assumptions and careful calculation and calculated the amount of government subsidies required to maintain the current old-age insurance system. The estimation results show that if under the current old-age insurance system persists, a huge pension gap will appear in the future as the population aging gathers pace. If the government does not take any action and lets the gap expand arbitrarily, the accumulated pension surplus will be used up by 2029, and the pension gap of the old-age insurance for workers will reach 802 trillion yuan by 2050, accounting for 91% of the GDP that year. Coupled with the expenditures of the old-age insurance for residents, the pension payment pressure will be greater. Assuming that the government will raise funds for the old-age insurance system through financial subsidies to ensure that the accumulated pension surplus is greater than or equal to 0, then the implicit debt arising from government subsidies during 2010–2050 discounted to 2011 will reach 62.5 trillion yuan, accounting for 132% of the GDP in 2011, in which the implicit debt of the old-age insurance for urban workers amounts to 46.5 trillion yuan, accounting for 98% of the GDP, plus the original subsidies from the governments at various levels, the implicit debt reaches 56.4 trillion yuan, accounting for 119% of the GDP; the implicit debt of the old-age insurance for rural and urban residents amounted to 6.08 trillion yuan, accounting for 13% of the GDP. By the end of 2050, the ratio of China's total pension expenditure of the whole society (including the old-age insurance for workers and residents) to GDP will reach 11.85%, which is close to the current level of some European states with high welfare.

In addition, we have also estimated the transition costs of the old-age insurance for enterprise employees. The total transition cost in 2011 was 3.47 trillion yuan, accounting for 7.33% of the GDP in 2011. The transition costs are part of the implicit pension liabilities and the main cause for the empty personal accounts of the current old-age insurance system, but based on the calculation results, the implicit debt arising from the transition costs only makes up a small part of the total pension liabilities. The implicit debt arising from the transition accounts for 7.5% of the total implicit debt of the old-age insurance for workers, while the implicit debt arising from the aging of the population accounts for 92.5% of the total implicit debt of the old-age insurance for workers. Therefore, the implicit debt arising from the aging of the population in the future is more worrying.

In this study, we have also analyzed the impact of some policy measures and system designs on the financial sustainability of the old-age insurance system under various scenarios. It is found that an extension of the retirement age and the age to receive the base pension for residents can play a good role and significantly reduce the pension gap. In addition, increasing the ROI of the pension funds will also be somewhat helpful, but the effect is relatively small. But maintaining a high pension replacement rate will significantly increase the level of potential pension debt. We prefer the comprehensive reform scheme in which the retirement age and the age to receive the base pension as well as the ROI are increased while a high pension replacement rate is maintained.

Based on the international experience, to solve or alleviate the pension funding gap problem, there are usually several alternatives for the government to choose. First, the internal reform of the old-age insurance system, which focuses on lowering the level of pension benefits, raising the retirement age and other methods to reduce the pension spending and the implicit pension debt; second, privatization of state-owned enterprises and state-owned assets obtain the cash flow and achieve the swap between state-owned assets and pension liabilities; third, raising funds to support the old-age insurance system through raising the taxes, issuing bonds and providing financial subsidies. Here, we will mainly discuss the policy effects of the first alternative, but the second and third alternatives are also important measures, in which dividends of state-owned assets or sale of state assets have been discussed by many scholars, while the third alternative is often neglected. The economic development over the past 30 years in China is characterized by a government-led catch-up model. government expenditure under this model places too much emphasis on construction but little emphasis on people's livelihood. With further development of China's economy and further improvement of infrastructure construction in the future, the fiscal expenditure and debt burden in construction may be reduced so that more funds can be used to strengthen social security, and the government will be also be able and should bear more responsibility for social security.

Chapter 16
Study of Value of Housing Assets of Residents

In recent years, people have been paying great attention to the real estate market. But based on the author's knowledge, relevant discussions mostly lack of rigorous data support. In this study, we will try to, from a macro perspective, estimate the value of the residential housings in the previous years (from 1998 to present) since the market-oriented reform of the Chinese housing market and carry out expand relevant analysis on this basis.

16.1 Estimation of the Value of Residential Housings

16.1.1 Value of Urban Residential Housings

Clearly, in the existing urban–rural dual social structure in China, urban residential housings constitute the main part of the total price of residential housings. In general sense, the discussions on the real estate market also mainly focus on the urban real estate market. Therefore, the discussions here also focus on this.

The specific estimation steps are as follows. First, we have calculated the floor space of urban residential housing stock over the years based on the per capita housing floorage of permanent urban residents and the urban population provided in the household survey of NBS. Second, about the depreciation issue. Here, we have adopted the annual depreciation rate of 3% based on the provision of the tax law that the minimum depreciation period of housings should be 20 years and taking into account the actual situation that the life expectancy of housings is generally about 40–50 years. In addition, strictly speaking, the price of real estate property consists of two parts: the price of housing property and the price of land property, while the latter is generally not depreciated. According to the data for 1998–2011 released by NBS, we have calculated that the price of land transfer (land acquisition costs) roughly accounts for one fifth of the total housing sales. Accordingly, we

Y. Li and X. Zhang, *China's National Balance Sheet*, China Insights,
DOI 10.1007/978-981-10-4385-7_16

carried out depreciation based on 80% of the price of housings (this is equivalent to the depreciation rate of 2.4%). Third, the depreciated housing area calculated in this way is multiplied by the average selling price of new residential housings in urban areas in the corresponding year to get the total price of urban housings.

The calculation formula is as follows:

$$住房总价值_t = \boldsymbol{\alpha}\boldsymbol{\beta}' p_t;$$
$$\boldsymbol{\alpha} = (A_t, A_{t-1}, \ldots A_{1979});$$
$$\boldsymbol{\beta} = (1, 0.976, \ldots (1\text{-}0.03 \times 0.8\text{n}))'; \qquad n = t - 1979$$

住房总价值 The total value of houses

In the formula, the vector $\boldsymbol{\alpha}$ represents the floor space of housings newly built over the years (A_t), the vector $\boldsymbol{\beta}$ represents the linear depreciation coefficient, and p_t represents the average housing price in the year t.

It should be noted that, due to the unavailability of data, the above calculation has ignored the impact of the floor space of stock housings in 1978 and before on the floor space of housings in the investigation period. But as this initial stock value is small and there exists depreciation, this ignorance has little impact on the estimation of housing value. In fact, the floor space of stock housings was only 1.155 billion square meters in 1978. Even if all the stock housings were considered as being newly built in 1978, according to the above depreciation method, the stock housings have depreciated to 50% of their original value in the starting year of the study period 1998. Based on the total value at that time of 1.1 trillion yuan, it only accounts for 11% of the housing value of 10.1 trillion yuan that year as estimated in this study. In addition, it should be noted that, due to depreciation, 1998 is actually a year that was most seriously affected by this issue, and its subsequent impact has gradually weakened.

In addition, as the reference, we have also estimated the value of housings that have not been depreciated. That is, the unadjusted floor space of stock housings that year is directly multiplied by the total value acquired based on the average sales price of newly built housings.[1] According to this method, the value of urban residential housings was 112.8 trillion in 2011.

As shown in Fig. 16.1, since the market-oriented housing reform, the total value of urban housings has increased rapidly by nearly 8 times from 10.1 trillion yuan in 1998 to 80.7 trillion yuan in 2011. In the meantime, except for 2006, 2008, 2010 and 2011, the housing value generally grew faster than the nominal GDP over the same period, resulting in an increase of the ratio between the two from 1.7 to 1.2 times. This is attributed to the increase in the unit price of housings and per capita living space, the expansion of the urban population and other factors. In fact, during 1998–2011, the above three indicators increased by 269, 175 and 166% respectively.

In addition, it can also be seen from Fig. 16.1 that the per capita housing price also grew faster the disposable income of residents in most years (2008 is still a

[1]Xiangyun et al. (2009) have ever adopted the same estimation method.

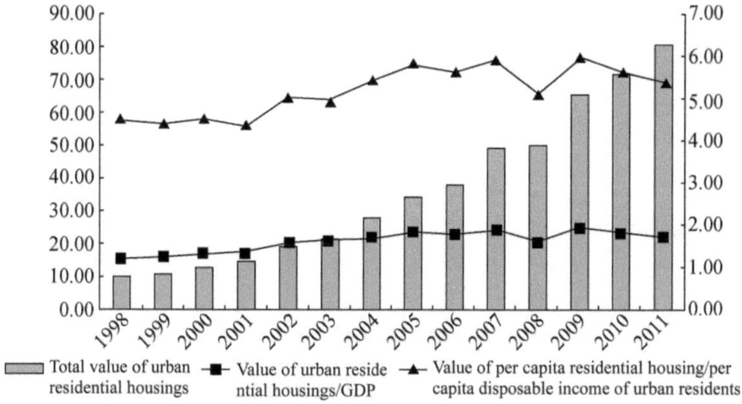

Fig. 16. 1 Ratio of the value of urban residential housings to the income of urban residents (after depreciation) (*Note* 1. Refer to the text for the depreciation method for the price of real estate property. 2. The value of urban housings is expressed by the *left axis*, and the unit is one trillion yuan; the remaining two ratios are expressed by the *right axis*.)

notable exception), resulting in an increase of the ratio between the two from 4.5 to 5.4 times. In particular, this indicator better reflects residents' actual affordability for housing expenses. The data here can be interpreted as the average price and the average space of housings a typical urban resident can afford with the total income in about 4–6 years.

It should be noted that the above results are also different from the estimates of some scholars. For example, according to the estimate of Wang Tao, the total value of urban housings in China in 2010 was about 30 trillion yuan, accounting for 75% of GDP.[2] Although the annual depreciation rate of 3% was also used, his calculation of housing area is based on the total floor space of residential housings in 1985 plus the accumulated area of housings completed subsequently. Based on the actual situation in China, as the considerable size of self-built housings and housings of small property right are not included in this statistic data, this statistic scope is too narrow. Relatively speaking, the household survey data adopted by us may better reflect the people's actual housing conditions. In another example, based on the survey data of Aldo Center, Yunwen et al. (2010) has obtained the average per household housing value of 239,800 and 157,900 yuan in 2005 and 2007. If converted based on the total number households in cities and towns in China, the total value of urban housings was 45.5 and 32.9 trillion yuan. The magnitude of decline is clearly inconsistent with the general intuition, and the author did not provide further explanation.

[2]Refer to caixin.com: http://economy.caixin.com/2011-02-23/100228236.html.

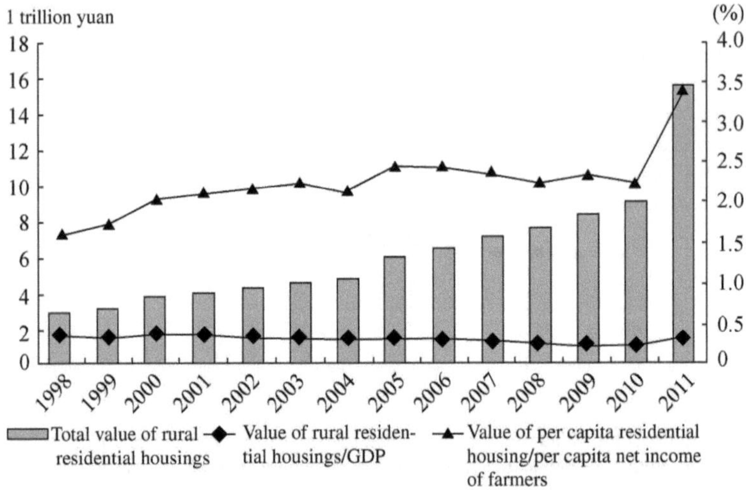

Fig. 16.2 Ratio of rural housings to income (*Note* The value of rural housing is expressed by the *left axis*, and the unit is 1 trillion yuan; the remaining two ratios are expressed by the *right axis*.)

16.1.2 The Value of Rural Housings

With regard to the value of rural residential housings, we still used the data of the household survey conducted by BNS. The calculation method is as follows:

$$\text{The value of rural residential housings} = \text{living space per capita} \times \text{the rural population} \times \text{the price of rural housings at the end of the year}$$

It should be emphasized that the housing price provided here is the average year-end price provided by NBS rather than the average price of housings newly built this year, so it can be understood as having taken the depreciation into account.[3] Figure 16.2 shows the corresponding estimation results: during the study period, the value of rural housings increased from 2.9 to 15.6 trillion yuan, an increase of only 5.4 times, significantly slower than the increase in the value of urban housings and also slower than the increase of the nominal GDP over the same period. The per capita value of housings in rural areas to the net income rose from 1.62 to 3.4 times, faster than the increase rate in cities and towns, but this ratio is far lower than the similar indicator of cities and towns.

[3]It should be noted that, according to China Statistical Yearbook 2012, the unit price of rural housings at the end of 2011 was 654 yuan, an increase of 67% over the previous year, which resulted in the sharp increase in the value of rural housings in 2011.

16.2 Ratio of Housing Value to Income–International Comparison

The above analysis shows that, since the market-oriented housing reform, the value of residential housings relative to GDP or income of residents in China have increased, but does this mean that the risk of real estate market has also increased substantially? In the following paragraphs, we will try to discuss this issue from the perspective of international comparison.

Firstly, from the perspective of housing value/GDP ratio, we have compared the data of China with those of the United States, Japan, Europe and other major developed countries. In particular, here we have selected the data of 2006 and 2008 with a view to reflect the different presentations of the housing market before and after the international financial crisis. As shown in Fig. 16.3, either the urban housings alone or the urban and rural housings together, the ratio of housing value to GDP in China is still at a low level compared with the developed countries. On the one hand, this is because China's urbanization process is far from over, the value of part of real estates (especially in rural real estates) have not yet been fully reflected. On the other hand, from the perspective of macroeconomic operation, although under the premise that the economy maintains a rapid growth momentum, the risk of Chinese real estate market is controllable on the whole, but when a structural or trending deceleration appears, the corresponding market risk in the economy will also be more serious.

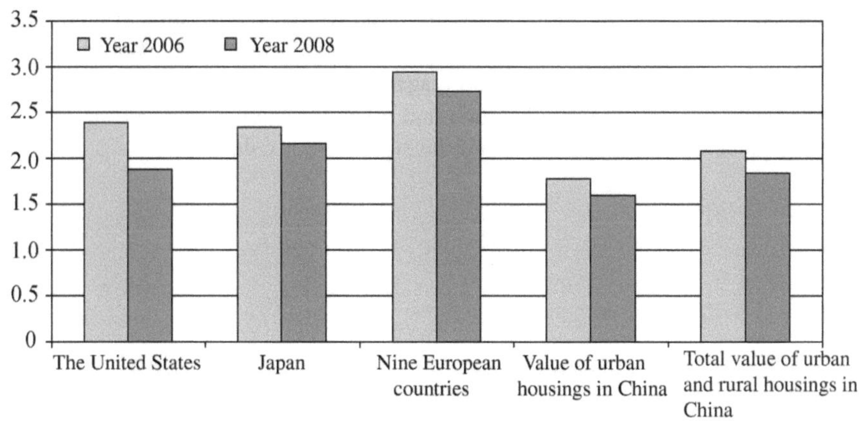

Fig. 16.3 The different presentations of the housing market before and after the international financial crisis (*Note* 1. The estimates of the housing values of the US, Japan and 9 European countries are from MGI (2009), and the GDP data are from the IMF. 2. The 9 European countries refer to Belgium, Denmark, France, Germany, Italy, the Netherlands, Norway, Spain and the United Kingdom.)

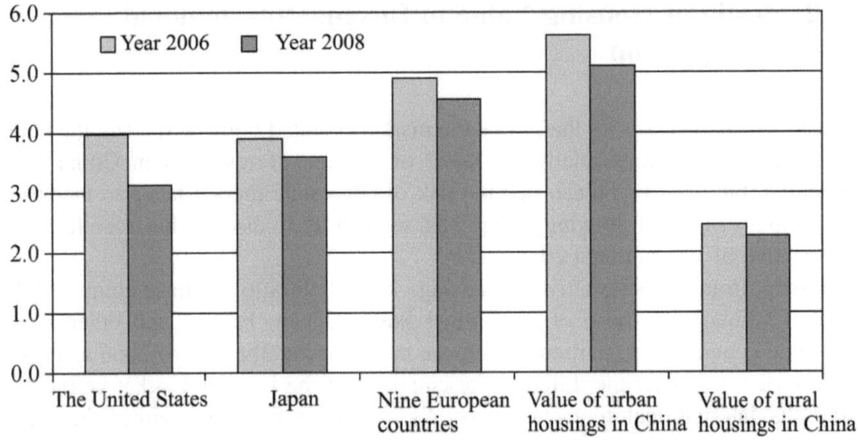

Fig. 16.4 International comparison of housing value to income ratio [*Note* Here, the GDPs of the United States, Japan and the 9 European countries is multiplied by 0.6 to get the income of residents. The empirical value, i.e. the ratio of workers' remuneration to GDP, is consistent with the results of many empirical researches based on the developed economies (see Arpaia et al. 2009)]

Secondly, we have compared the ratio of housing value to income of China with those of other countries. As shown in Fig. 16.4, the ratio of housing value to disposable income of urban residents is higher than those in the developed countries examined. This is partially because the residents' income to GDP in China ratio is low (which is less than 40% in recent years, but this ratio is generally 60% in the developed countries). In addition, in the context of accelerating urbanization, income growth largely lags behind the growth of housing prices, and the corresponding financial risks (such as mortgage defaults) are constantly being accumulated. Of course, if the data for rural and urban areas are combined, the ratio of housing value to income in China will be significantly reduced.

Appendix: Related Data on the Valuation of Real Estates

Year	Value of urban housings	Value of rural housings	Total value of urban and rural housings	Ratio of value of urban housings to GDP	Ratio of value of rural housings to GDP	Ratio of total value of urban and rural housings to GDP	Ratio of per capita value of urban housings to disposable income	比 Ratio of per capita value of rural housings to disposable income
1998	10.12	2.91	13.03	1.20	0.35	1.55	4.48	1.62
1999	11.20	3.13	14.33	1.25	0.35	1.60	4.37	1.73
2000	12.96	3.76	16.72	1.31	0.38	1.69	4.50	2.06
2001	14.44	4.01	18.45	1.32	0.37	1.69	4.38	2.13
2002	19.36	4.20	23.56	1.61	0.35	1.96	5.00	2.17
2003	21.83	4.54	26.37	1.61	0.33	1.94	4.92	2.25
2004	27.97	4.78	32.75	1.75	0.30	2.05	5.47	2.15
2005	34.37	5.92	40.29	1.86	0.32	2.18	5.83	2.44
2006	38.50	6.45	44.95	1.78	0.30	2.08	5.62	2.46
2007	49.61	7.09	56.70	1.87	0.27	2.14	5.93	2.40
2008	50.22	7.60	57.82	1.60	0.24	1.84	5.10	2.27
2009	65.59	8.32	73.91	1.92	0.24	2.16	5.92	2.34
2010	71.94	8.96	80.90	1.79	0.22	2.01	5.62	2.26
2011	80.73	15.55	96.29	1.71	0.33	2.04	5.36	3.40

Note 1. The unit of housing value is one trillion yuan

2. The value of urban housings has been depreciated (see the text for the specific method)

3. GDP, per capita disposable income of urban residents, per capita net income of rural residents and other data are from *Statistical Yearbook of China*

Chapter 17
Comparison of National Wealth of China and the US and Estimation of the Value of Land Resources in China

17.1 Interdependence of Wealth and Income

People often come to measure the wealth of a country with a gross domestic product (GDP), but in fact this indicator simply reflects the income flow in a period of time (e.g. one year). Obviously, whether a country is rich or poor is not only related to the income in the current period or in the future, but also closely related to the long-term capital accumulation its "generations". The latter is the national wealth we are to discuss here.

By definition, national wealth refers to the stock of welfare of all citizens in a country. It can be understood as the sum of a country's "financial resources", "material resources" and "human resources". Unlike the income flow (e.g. GDP), national wealth has a bearing on the long-term welfare of future generations and is an important reference for measuring development sustainability. In this sense, national wealth can be seen as the core of researches on macroeconomics. It is worth noting that, as the father of modern economics, Adam Smith firmly focused his researches on the wealth of nations and stated out that "to maintain and augment the stock which may be reserved for immediate consumption is the sole end and purpose both of the fixed and circulating capitals" (Smith 1996, p. 259).

However, despite the importance of the concept of national wealth, either policy makers or scholars did not attach due importance to it and often "tolerate" the one-sidedness of GDP and other flow indicators. This problem seems to be particularly serious in China. There are roughly three causes for this. First, in the initial stage of reform, there was an incredibly huge gap between the total GDP and GDP per capita of China and those of the developed countries, even including many developing countries, such as India. It is such remarkable "income divide" that the Chinese people generally have the feeling that "our GDP has caught up with and even surpassed other countries". Second, in the above context, China has emphasized over the years that the size and growth rate of GDP should be the standard for assessment of local officials. Although this governance model produced a positive

Y. Li and X. Zhang, *China's National Balance Sheet*, China Insights,
DOI 10.1007/978-981-10-4385-7_17

impact in a certain period and a certain range, it also further enhanced the profit-oriented style of GDP worship, thus ignoring the sustainability of long-term wealth accumulation and development. Third, as wealth and other stock indicators are in theory not yet mature, and there are also many operational difficulties in statistical practice, reliable stock indicators are not only difficult to obtain, but also not easy to undergo longitudinal comparison in time sequence and lateral inter-country comparison.

Of course, it should also be noted that stressing "wealth" do not means to exclude or belittle "income". Obviously, without accumulation of wealth, income is not sustainable, and without continuous income flow, accumulation of wealth is out of the question. There exists a dialectical unity in the relationship between the two, and the key is to find the right point of balance.

17.2 Comparison of the National Wealth of China and the United States

It is gratifying that, in recent years, people have become increasingly concerned about the issue of sustainable development (particularly from the perspectives of resource and environmental constraints and human capital accumulation), direct discussions worldwide on national wealth is gradually increasing. Here are three examples as follows.

First, the World Bank published two reports on the wealth of nations in the world in 2006 and 2011 (World Bank 2006, 2011). The World Bank first calculated all the comprehensive wealth, namely the sum of discounted value of consumption flows (discount rate of 4%) in the future periods (25 years, about one generation). Then, the national wealth is divided into four parts: produced, natural, human and institutional capital (such as the laws, government efficiency and social trust etc.). The specific estimation method is: produced capital: the historical data of investment is estimated by the "perpetual inventory method"; natural capital: reserves of underground minerals, arable land, pasture and forest resources, and estimating their currency value based on the world market prices and regional production costs; intangible human capital and institutional capital: the difference between comprehensive wealth and produced and natural capital.

Based on this method, the World Bank (2011) has estimated the national wealth of nearly 120 countries in the three years of 1995, 2000 and 2005. The study found that the proportion of produced capital in the comprehensive wealth was about 18% and remained stable in the countries with different income levels, but was larger in the lower middle income countries, which was 24; the proportion of natural capital was 5%, but there was great differences among the countries and it was obviously reversely associated with the income level. That is, the proportion of natural capital was relatively smaller in the rich countries but larger in the poor countries.

Table 17.1 Estimation of the wealth of China and the United States in 2005 (2005, US dollars) (World Bank 2011)

Country	Total national wealth (trillion yuan)	Natural capital	Produced capital and urban land (trillion yuan)	Intangible capital (trillion yuan)	Net IIP (trillion yuan)	Per capita national wealth	Per capita intangible capital
China	25.09	5.23 trillion yuan (incl. underground mines: 1.05 trillion yuan)	7.85	11.64	0.37	19,234	8921
The United States	217.62	4.1 trillion yuan (incl. underground mines: 1.03 trillion US dollars)	29.66	185.92	−2.06	734,195	627,246

World Bank (2011)

Finally, the proportion of intangible capital as residual (including human and institutional capital) was 77% and was positively correlated with the income level.

Particularly, the World Bank has estimated the different types of capital in China and the United States, and the results are shown in Table 17.1. As shown in the table, there are great differences between the wealth of the two countries. On the one hand, structurally, China's intangible capital accounts for a significantly lower proportion, while its natural and produced capital accounts for a larger proportion. This shows that the later-development countries have attached more importance to the accumulation of factories, mines, land and other "tangible" wealth in economic development, but to a large extent neglected the augment in human, institutional and other "intangible" wealth. On the other hand, in terms of the size of wealth, the per capita national wealth and intangible assets of the United States were 38 times and 70 times of China's, while its per capita nominal GDP was "only" 25 times that of China's over the same period. Thus, in the process of rapid rise, the Chinese people should be soberly aware that the rise of wealth is much more difficult, while the only way to achieve this goal is sustainable and healthy development. In addition, as shown in Table 17.2, the changes in the accumulation of wealth in the two countries have some common characteristics. That is, either per capita wealth or comprehensive wealth of China calculated at comparable prices achieved positive growth in 1995, 2000 and 2005, showing the path of sustainable economic development.

Following the World Bank, Kenneth Arrow, the Nobel Laureate in Economics, and his collaborators (Arrow et al. 2007, 2010) studied the national wealth China and other countries and its sustainability of growth. Based on the data of 1995–2000, Arrow et al. directly calculated natural, human and reproducible capital, petroleum capital gains as well as loss of carbon emissions and added them up to estimate the comprehensive wealth (see Tables 17.3 and 17.4). Among them, natural capital includes oil, natural gas, bauxite, copper, iron, gold, lead, nickel, phosphorus, forests and land; human capital was calculated by the years of schooling, wages and remaining working years; the data of reproducible capital was from Klenow and Rodríguez-Clare (2005), and the net external wealth (IIP) was taken into account; petroleum capital gains refers to the price appreciation arising from the reduction of oil reserves; loss of carbon emissions refers to the impact of carbon dioxide emissions caused by the "greenhouse effect" on the economy.

Recently, the *Inclusive Wealth Report 2012* (UNU-IHDP and UNEP 2012) prepared by the relevant agencies and the task team of the United Nations further

Table 17.2 Changes in the wealth of China and the United States (2005, US dollars) (World Bank, 2011)

Country	Total national wealth (trillion yuan)			Per capita intangible capital		
	1995	2000	2005	1995	2000	2005
China	11.86	18.07	25.09	9845	14,310	19,234
The United States	155.87	188.42	217.62	585,347	667,626	734,195

World Bank (2011)

Table 17.3 Estimation of the national wealth of China (prices in 2000; Unit: one trillion US dollars) (Arrow et al. 2010)

Year	Total wealth	Natural capital	Human capital	Reproducible capital	Oil capital gains (changing amount)	Carbon emission loss (changing amount)
1995	16.05	3.85	8.49	3.71	–	–
2000	19.40	3.85	9.39	6.47	−0.31	−0.00

Arrow et al. (2010)

Table 17.4 Estimation of the national wealth of the United States (prices in 2000; Unit: one trillion US dollars) (Arrow et al. 2010)

Year	Total wealth	Natural capital	Human capital	Reproducible capital	Oil capital gains (changing amount)	Carbon emission loss (changing amount)
1995	79.21	5.69	60.09	13.43	–	–
2000	84.89	5.70	64.80	15.92	−1.37	−0.17

Arrow et al. (2010)

expanded the study of Arrow et al. separately calculated the four types of capital, i.e. non- reproducible oil and mine, land, physical and human capital and weighted and added them up with the shadow prices as weights to obtain the inclusive wealth of 20 countries worldwide during 1990–2008. Its main difference from the report of the World Bank is that the sustainable wealth accumulation path was not pre-assumed and the comprehensive wealth was not calculated based on the present discounted value of future consumption stream. In a sense, the study conducted by the United Nations can better measure the sustainability of economic growth.

Tables 17.5 and 17.6 list the estimates of this study related to China and the United States.

As there are many differences in the studies conducted by the World Bank, Arrow and the United Nations in the estimation methods, statistical scope, parameter assumptions and other aspects, the estimates of wealth are different and not completely comparable. Nevertheless, the three studies show consistency in some important aspects. First, there was a large gap between the comprehensive wealth and per capita wealth of China and the United States, which was greater than the difference between the GDPs of the two countries. This has particularly highlighted the differences between the stock and flow perspectives. Second, structurally, the national wealth of China consists mostly of physical capital-including produced and natural capital-based, while the national wealth of the United States mainly consist of human capital. This to a certain extent reflects the poor economic growth quality and sustainability in China. Of course, the broader comparative studies conducted by the World Bank and the United Nations show that the respective structural characteristics of the national wealth of China and the United States are universal in the developing and developed countries. Finally, at the dynamic level, the three studies show the growing trend of the national wealth of

Table 17.5 Inclusive wealth of China and the United States in 2008 (US dollars in 2000) (UNU-IHDP and UNEP 2012)

Country	Total inclusive wealth (trillion yuan)	Reproducible capital (trillion yuan)	Human capital (trillion yuan)	Natural capital (trillion yuan)
China	19.96	6.16	8.73	5.07
The United States	117.83	22.34	88.87	6.62

UNU-IHDP and UNEP (2012)

Table 17.6 Changes in inclusive wealth of China and the United States in 2008 (US dollars in 2000) (UNU-IHDP and UNEP 2012)

Country	Total inclusive wealth			Per capita inclusive wealth		
	1990 (trillion yuan)	2000 (trillion yuan)	2008 (trillion yuan)	1990	2000	2008
China	11.90	15.23	19.96	10,394	12,003	15,027
The United States	86.44	102.54	117.83	341,211	362,979	386,351

UNU-IHDP and UNEP (2012)

the two countries in the study period, and the increase in human and reproducible capital was especially obvious, while there was little change in the absolute size of natural capital and its size decreased significantly. This indicates that the economic growth paths of the two countries in the study period meet the criteria for sustainable development.

17.3 Estimation of Natural Capital of China: Land Resources

The above studies of the Chinese experience provide valuable reference and have enlightening significance, but due to the short study period and many omissions in statistical scope and indicators, it is difficult to accurately and comprehensively reflect the national wealth of China accumulated in its rapid economic growth period. The domestic scholars have made considerable classified estimates of the national wealth of China, and particularly in the framework of growth accounting, the related estimates of physical capital stock[1] (such as Zhang et al. 2004, The Research Group 2010) and human capital stock (such as Qian et al. 2009; Fan 2000) are relatively mature. In this study, we will tentatively estimate and analyze the size and changing trend of Chinese land and resources that have been less discussed (part of the natural capital).

[1]Similar to produced capital as mentioned in the studies of the World Bank.

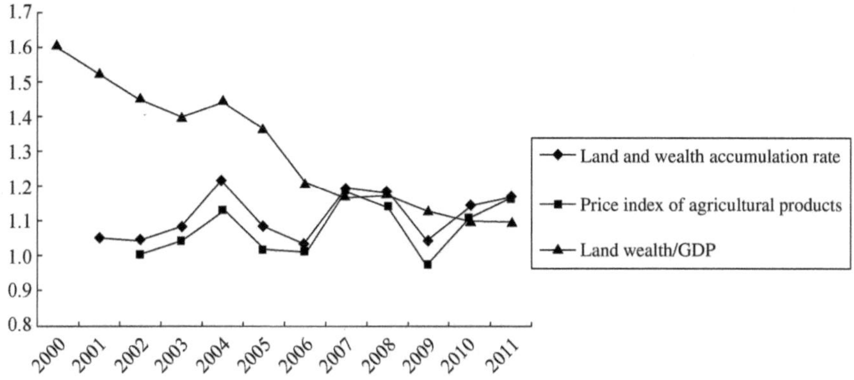

Fig. 17.1 Changing trend of China's land resources. *Source* Estimates of the research group

Based on the basic research idea of the World Bank (2006, 2011), the total present value is understood as the sum of the present value of net output (i.e. total receipts less cost, or resource rent) acquired from resources in a certain future period. This is the general understanding or definition of economic value of a kind of resource in economic theories. Due to limitation in data, we have not calculated separately the gains of different types of resources such as arable land, grassland and forests but used the "total output of agriculture, forestry, animal husbandry and fishery" instead and adopted the uniform rent rate of 40%.[2] In addition, like the World Bank, we used the 25-year discount period and the discount rate of 4%.

On this basis, the author has estimate the value of land resources in China over the years since 2000, and its related trend is shown in Fig. 17.1. On the one hand, although the value of land resources rose from 16 trillion yuan in 2000 to 52 trillion yuan in 2011 (current prices), its ratio to GDP decreased by 1.6–1.1 times in this period. This indirectly shows a downward trend of the status and role of land resources as an important component of natural capital in national wealth and economic growth. This phenomenon has also further confirmed the research findings described above. On the other hand, as the wealth of each year was calculated in accordance with the current prices of that year, we compared the speed of land resource wealth accumulation as shown in Fig. 17.1 (the nominal growth rate) and the price index of agricultural products. As shown in the figure, the growth rate of China's land resource wealth was generally faster than the price index of agricultural products over the same period, indicating that it was in a sustainable growth path.

[2]The standard of 40% of rental rate was acquired based on the estimate of the World Bank (2006). In fact, the World Bank has listed the following data: arable land rental rate (total of nine crops): corn 30%, rice 51, wheat 34%, bananas 42%, grapes 31%, apples 36%, oranges 36%, soybean 27% coffee 8% and pastures 45%.

Table 17.7 Comparison of estimates of value of land resources (Unit: one trillion US dollars)

Studies/year	1995	2000	2005	2008
This study	–	1.93	3.08	5.34
The world bank (2006)	–	2.16	–	–
The world bank (2011)	–	–	4.19	–
Arrow et al. (2010)	2.92	–	–	–
The United Nations (2012)	3.30	3.36	3.44	3.41

Note 1. The estimates in this study are converted into the current prices in US dollars based on the annual average exchange rate
2. The estimates of the World Bank (2006) are based on US dollars in 2000, including forests, non-timber forests, protected areas, arable land and pasture; the estimates of the World Bank (2011) are based on US dollars in 2005
3. The estimates of Arrow et al. are based on US dollars in 2000, including wood and forest benefits and land
4. The estimates of the United Nations are based on US dollars in 2000, including arable land, pasture, forests and fishery resources

As the references, we compared this estimate with the above-mentioned three studies. As shown in Table 17.7, due to the differences in estimation methods, diameter, assumptions and other aspects, there are some differences in the findings of the studies. It is worth emphasizing that the above studies have not excluded the technological advance factors from the accumulated value of land resources (or generally assume various types of capital subject to the same rate of technological progress), but obviously, technological advances can make the same unit of land to create more income. Due to this shortcoming, land resources in different periods are entirely incomparable even after deducting the price factor. Therefore, further studies are needed for a comprehensive, sophisticated estimate of land resources.

Chapter 18
A International Comparative Study of Balance Sheet

18.1 Introduction

As an analytical framework from the stock perspective, the national balance sheet has a very important theoretical and practical significance for the study of economic growth, financial structure, distribution of wealth, development mode and sustainability (Carlson 1991). In this chapter, we will first make a brief introduction to the size and structural change of the national balance sheets of the United States, Japan, Germany, Britain, Canada and other countries based on the publicly available data. Then on this basis, combined with the development characteristics of the developed economies, summarize and interpret the common characteristics of the national balance of each country. However, this should be noted that in the existing domestic and foreign documents, the studies of national balance sheet seems never to been a "famous school". Particularly, the national balance sheets of different countries come in different forms and have different contents, and the data are disclosed continuously, which brings more difficulties for the comparative study of China's national balance sheet with the national balance sheets of other countries and greatly limits the completeness and accuracy of the analysis here.

18.2 The Experience of the United States

18.2.1 Early Studies of Goldsmith et al.

As the world's largest economic power, the United States started early to prepare its national balance sheet and carried out related accounting. Goldsmith et al. started the pioneering task of formulating sectoral and aggregate national balance sheets of the United States for a number of years from the early twentieth century to 1980 and

Y. Li and X. Zhang, *China's National Balance Sheet*, China Insights,
DOI 10.1007/978-981-10-4385-7_18

carried out detailed analysis of the structure and changing trend of each constituent item (see Goldsmith and Lipsey 1963; Goldsmith 1966, 1982).

In the following paragraphs, we will briefly review the early findings of Goldsmith et al.

Goldsmith et al. found that during 1900–1980, the nominal value of the US balance sheet expanded at an annual pace of about 6.5–6.7%,[1] faster than the nominal growth rate of GNP over the same period. This increased the wide-scope capital/output ratio from 9.7 in 1900 to 12.4 in 1980.[2] In other words, the United States experienced a more significant balance sheet expansion in this period.

The studies above also revealed the structural changes in the balance sheet of the United States. First, in terms of asset categories, the proportion of land, minerals and other natural resource assets in the total national assets of the United States dropped significantly during 1900–1953. By wide scope, the proportion declined from 17% in 1900 to 7.1% in 1953 and rebounded later, but only reached 10.7% in 1980; the proportion of reproducible physical capital also declined but at a slower pace of from 34.2% in 1900 to 29.3% in 1980. In the same study period, financial assets first expanded and then shrank, which resulted in an "inverse U" shape change of the financial correlation ratio (i.e. ratio of financial assets to physical assets). That is, it increased from 0.95 in 1900 to 1.62 in 1953 and later declined to 1.49 in 1980 (wide scope).[3]

Second, in terms of components of assets, the proportion of assets of households and non-profit organizations of the US in the total assets remained basically unchanged at a level of 40% during 1900–1979; the proportion of assets of non-financial corporations and other business units shrink significantly from 47% in 1900 to 25.8% in 1979; in the meanwhile, the relative size of the assets of the general government (including federal and local governments) and financial institutions significantly increased from 4.6 and 10.3% to 13.5 and 21.2% respectively.

Finally, in terms of other aspects of asset and liability structure, the debt/total assets ratio and debt/physical asset ratio significantly increased in the above study period. By wide scope, the former rose from 0.23 in 1900 to 0.47 in 1980, while the latter rose from 0.44 to 1.16 in the same period. This better suggested the worsening trend of the debt burden and risk accumulation of the US economy at the macro level. In addition, the liquidity of assets (current assets/total assets) improved during 1900–1953, but began to decline ever since then. In the meanwhile, the proportion of external assets to total assets of the US also experienced great volatility: rapidly increased from −2% in 1900 to 1% in 1929, and later continued to decline to close to zero.

---

[1]If the price changes are excluded, the growth rate of the real value was about 3–3.4%.

[2]Calculated based on the narrow scope, the growth rate will be slightly smaller, i.e. from 7.4 times to 8.0 times.

[3]Carlson (1991) found according to the analytical framework of Goldsmith and the relevant data of the Fed that the relevant interrelation ratio of the United States was lower than 1.3 in 1948, dropped to about 1.15 after several fluctuations in the mid 1970s. But later it rose continuously to nearly 1.5 in 1990.

In general, the study by Goldsmith et al. shows that since the beginning of the last century, especially since World War II, the United States experienced a significant, prolonged process of financial deepening, and the position and role of the financial sector and financial assets was increasingly important in the economic system. However, the increasing dependence of the US economy on the financial sector exposed it to higher financial risks. Obviously, this posed new challenges to preventing and resolving the financial crises.

18.2.2 Characteristics and Trend of the US Balance Sheet in Recent Years

Following Goldsmith et al., the Fed had compiled the national balance sheet excluding financial assets and liabilities for the years after World War II in the early 1990s, i.e. the sheet of net national wealth or net assets (see the Federal Reserve System 1991; Carlson 1991),[4] but for various reasons, this task was suspended later. In recent years, the Fed's Flow of Funds Accounts (see Kennedy 2012) only listed the balance sheets of residents and non-profit organizations (or the household sector) and the non-financial private sector (incorporated or unincorporated) and the financial assets and liabilities of other sectors, but did not include the non-financial assets of the government sector, the financial sector and the external sector. Therefore, many analyses based on the US national balance sheets are inevitably incomplete (see Rutledge 2009).

In the following paragraphs, we will give a brief introduction to the characteristics and trends of assets and liabilities of various economic sectors of the US in recent years based on the Fed's flow of funds accounts and other relevant information. Particular, Table 18.1 lists some information of the US national balance sheet in 2011.

Firstly, the household sector. On the asset side, this sector's total assets was \$73.52 trillion in 2011 or about 4.9 times of the US GDP, of which 32% were non-financial assets, worth \$23.29 trillion (including nearly 78% of real estate properties); 68% were non-financial assets, worth \$50.23 trillion (mainly composed of deposits, equity and pension accounts). On the liability side, the liabilities of this sector was \$13.48 trillion in 2011, mainly composed of real estate mortgages (73%) and consumer credit (19%). As the difference between total assets and liabilities, the net assets of residents and non-profit organizations amounted to \$60.04 trillion or about four times of the US GDP. It is noteworthy that, in recent years, especially before and after the 2007 subprime lending crisis, both the absolute and relative size of the assets and liabilities of residents and non-profit organizations in the US experienced some significant changes. First, as shown in Fig. 18.1, the sector's total assets and two sub-assets rapidly expanded during 1980–2006 (both faster than the

[4]In the data of the Fed, this item is numbered C.9 release.

Table 18.1 The national balance sheet of the United States in 2011 (part) (unit: 1 billion US dollars)

Sector	Non-financial assets	Financial assets	Total assets	Financial liabilities	Total net assets
Residents and non-profit organizations	23,288.9 Incl.: real estate: 18,182.8	50,229.4 Incl.: deposits: 8651.1; Equities: 17723.9; Pensions: 13147.1	73,518.3	13,481.0 Incl.: housing mortgage: 9818.7; Consumer credit: 2508.2	60,037.3
Nonfinancial incorporated business	14,971.0 Incl.: real estate: 8768.1	15,073.8	30,044.8	13,739.3 Incl.: credit market instruments (bonds and commercial paper etc.): 8031.6	16,305.5
Nonfinancial unincorporated business	9524.6 Incl.: real estate: 8557.6	3470.5	12,995.1	5561.5 Incl.: credit market instruments: 3773.3	7433.6
Financial sector	NA	65,969.0 Incl.: credit market instruments: 38,216.3; Corporate equities: 11,053.2	NA	62,339.9 Incl.: credit market instruments: 13793.8; Pensions: 13,147.1	NA
Federal government	NA	1349.1	NA	12,262.2	NA
State and local governments	NA	2524.8	NA	3715.1	NA
External sector	NA	18,245.2	NA	11,039.2	NA
Total	NA	156,861.7	NA	122,138.3	NA

Source The Fed's flow of funds accounts for the first quarter of 2012 (see the Federal Reserve System 2012)

GDP in the same period), but under the influence of the subprime lending wave, the size of assets shrank severely. For example, the total assets decreased by $12.8 trillion (nearly 90% of the GDP) in 2008 over the previous year (the real estate market value alone decreased by $3.6 trillion). Second, in terms of components of assets, the proportion of financial assets in the total assets increased from 60 to 68% during 1980–2011, indicating the growing "financialization" trend of assets of the household sector. However, as shown in Fig. 18.2, compared to other sectors, the accumulation of financial assets in the household sector was at a relatively slow pace, resulting in a decrease of its share in total financial assets of all sectors in the United States from 47 to 32%. Finally, in the same study period, the asset-liability

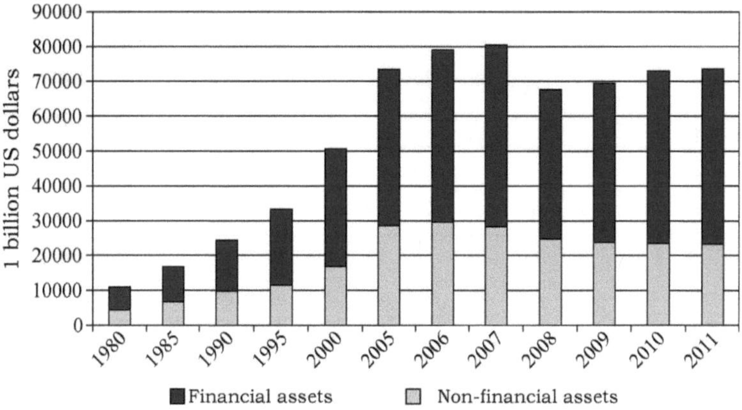

Fig. 18.1 Size of assets of households and nonprofit institutions of the United States (unit: $1 billion). *Source* The Fed's flow of funds accounts for the first quarter of 2012 (see The Federal Reserve System 2012)

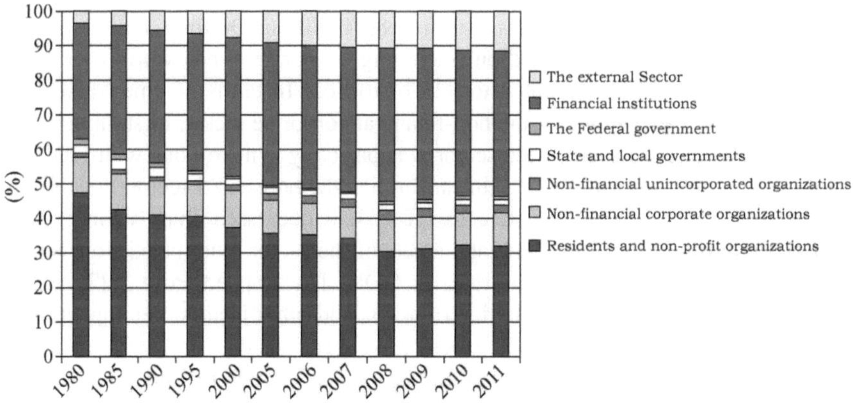

Fig. 18.2 Subsectors constitute US financial assets. *Source* The Fed's flow of funds accounts for the first quarter of 2012 (see the Federal Reserve System 2012)

ratio (i.e. debt/total asset ratio) of the household sector of the United States rose from 13 to 18% and once reached the highest point of 21% in 2008 and later experienced a slow deleveraging process (see Fig. 18.3). This indicates that over more than 30 years, the US household sector's financial risk was showing an upward trend on the whole and closely related to the macroeconomic trends.

Secondly, the non-financial corporate sector (including non-financial incorporated and unincorporated businesses).[5] In 2011, the total assets of all sectors was

[5]Among them, the former category mainly refers to mid- and large-size enterprises and the latter mainly refers to small-sized enterprises.

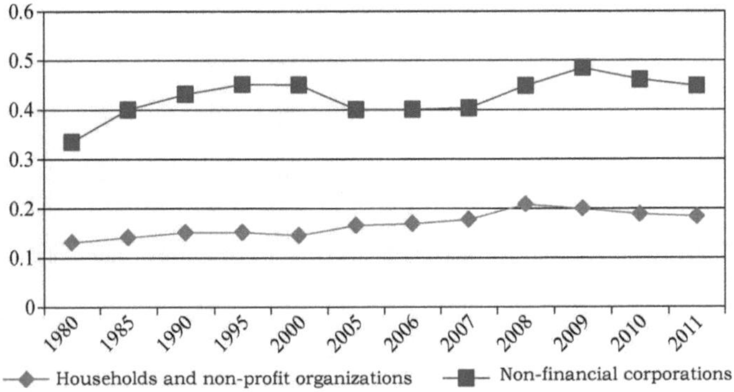

Fig. 18.3 The debt to assets ratio of households and non-financial corporation in the US. *Source* The Fed's flow of funds accounts for the first quarter of 2012 (see the Federal Reserve System 2012)

$43.04 trillion, or about 2.9 times of the US GDP. Among them, 57% were non-financial assets, worth $24.5 trillion (including nearly 71% of real estate assets); 43% were financial assets, worth $18.54 trillion. On the liability side, the liabilities amounted to $19.3 trillion (including corporate bonds worth over $5.08 trillion). The net assets amounted to $23.74 trillion. In terms of time trend, three points need to be explained for the non-financial corporate sector. First, in the study period, the asset expansion of the sector was basically synchronous with GDP, the ratio between the two was about 3 times. But like the household sector, the absolute and relative size of assets (relative to GDP) had decreased sharply since 2007. Especially during 2007–2009, the total assets of the sector plummeted from $45.19 trillion to $38.33 trillion, and its ratio to GDP also dropped from 3.22 to 2.75. Therefore, due to the price revaluation of assets and other factors, the impact of the financial crisis on assets (i.e. wealth stock) was far serious than on GDP (i.e. income flow) in the short term. Second, in terms of asset structure, the proportion of financial assets of non-financial corporations in the total assets of this sector rose from 20% in 1980 to 43% in 2011, but the proportion of the assets in the total financial assets of all sectors remained at about 10%. This shows that non-financial corporations experienced the process of asset financialization basically synchronously with other sectors. Finally, not only the horizontal value was far higher than the household sector, but also the asset-liability ratio of the non-financial corporate sector was also showing a rising trend: from 34% in 1980 to 45% in 2011. As shown in Fig. 18.3, before and after the subprime mortgage crisis, the ratio had experienced a sharp change. In fact, during 2005–2007, this rate remained at the low level of 40% (below the level in the 1990s), but rapidly rose in 2008 and 2009 to reach the historic high of 49%. After the crisis, enterprises had also embarked on the deleveraging process.

Thirdly, the information on the financial sector (including the Federal Reserve Bank) in the stock of funds accounts shows that, in 2011, its total financial assets amounted to $65.97 trillion (including $13.05 trillion worth of real estate mortgages, $7.13 trillion worth of corporate and foreign bonds, $6.02 trillion worth of Agency- and GSE-Backed Securities, and $11.05 trillion worth of corporate equities), while its liabilities amounted to $62.34 trillion, and its net financial assets amounted to $3.63 trillion. Based on the trend shown in Fig. 18.2, the size of the financial assets of the US financial institutions expanded rapidly compared with other sectors. In 1980, its proportion in the total financial assets of all sectors was only 34%, but rose to up to 40% in 1995 and later exceeded the household sector and became the largest holder of financial assets in the United States. But it should be emphasized that this crisis interrupted the momentum of expansion of financial assets in the sector. The relevant data show that, the above-mentioned proportion fell for three consecutive years after reaching a record high of 44% in 2008.

Fourthly, the government sector. The absolute and relative size of financial assets of the government sector was relatively small. In 2011, the federal government's financial assets were only $1.35 trillion (including $0.42 trillion worth of consumer loans, $0.11 trillion worth of real estate mortgages and $0.18 trillion worth of other loans), accounting for 0.9% of the total sector, but the debt of this sector was as high as $12.26 trillion (including $1.52 trillion worth of treasury bills and $8.72 trillion worth of other treasury securities), accounting for 10% of the total debts of other sectors. The financial positions and the state and local governments were better, and their financial assets amounted to $2.52 trillion (including $0.44 trillion worth of treasury securities, $0.39 trillion worth of Agency- and GSE-Backed Securities and $0.17 trillion worth of real estate mortgages), accounting for 1.6% of the total financial assets of the sector, and their liabilities amounted to 3.72 trillion (including 2.94 trillion worth of long-term municipal bonds), accounting for 3% of the total liabilities of the sector. The historical data show that the US governments at all levels have long been in a state of "insolvency". In addition, compared with other sectors, the size of government financial assets had slightly declined, while the size of its debt was on the rise (especially since 2007). This is largely attributed to the cumulative result of the deteriorating financial position of the United States in recent years. In fact, according to the data of IMF, during 2001–2011 alone, the structural deficit of the United States soared from $73 billion to $ 1.14 trillion. The sum of the deficits of all years during this period was up to $6.83 trillion (see Fig. 18.4). Of course, it should also be noted that the "small government" and "poor government" phenomena in United States were closely related to its high levels of economic and social development. Based on the general experience of the developed economies, in such context, the main functions of governments have shifted from organizing production and construction to providing public services, and the resources under their direct control are reducing, but the public responsibilities taken by them are expanding. Thus, the above US government's fiscal dilemma is to a certain extent inevitable and even reasonable.

Finally, since the flow of funds accounts failed to reflect the external non-financial assets held by the United States, the following analysis of the external sector is based on the IIP released by the Bureau of Economic Analysis. In 2011, the external assets held by the United States amounted to $21.13 trillion (of which

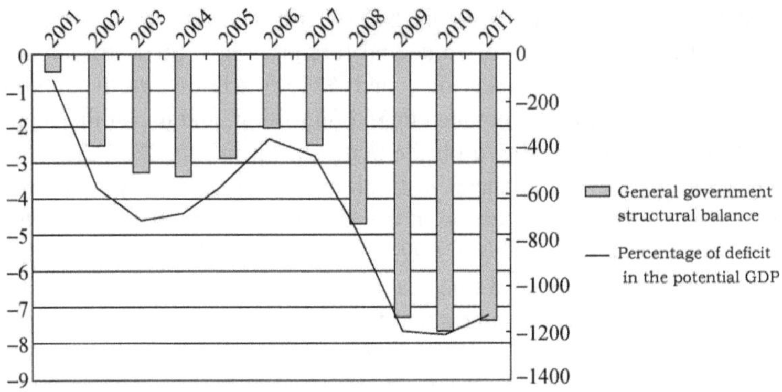

Fig. 18.4 The financial position of the US government in recent years. *Note* 1. The data are from IMF, World Economic Outlook Database, April 2012. 2. The *right axis* in the figure represents the structural deficit (General government structural balance) (unit: $1 billion); the *left axis* represents the percentage of deficit in the potential GDP

official reserves were only $536 billion, and direct investments and securities held by the private sector were 4.68 trillion, 5.92 trillion), while the US assets held by foreign holdings amounted to $25.16 trillion (including $4.28 trillion of all types of the US government bonds, $3.06 trillion of shares, $2.91 trillion of corporate bonds and $2.91 trillion of direct investment, which are officially held by foreign countries), and the net position as the difference between the two items is −4.03 trillion US dollars, accounting for 27% of the GDP that year. Based on the trend as shown in Fig. 18.5, the mid-1980s to present, the net foreign investment position of the United States has always been negative, and the size is growing (its size relative to GDP is also expanding). The main cause for the above external imbalance is on the one hand in the US dollar-dominated international monetary system, the United States is the main provider of international security assets (including official reserves), and this is the direct cause that a huge amount of US assets are held by other countries. On the other hand, the economy of the United States characterized by long-term low domestic savings and high consumption has improved the United States' dependence on foreign capital inflows and thus exacerbated the international investment deficit. Here it should be emphasized that the above external imbalance is unsustainable in the long term. This is not only because of the existence of intertemporal budget constraint but also because as revealed by the famous "Triffin dilemma" (Triffin 1961), the United States' continuous external imbalance would eventually endanger the international status of the US dollar and reverse revenues and expenditures. In addition, the external assets held by the United States as shown in Fig. 18.6 show that like the domestic sector, the external wealth of the United States is still mainly owned by the private sector, and this characteristic has an increasingly enhancing trend. In addition, it should also be noted that, as the country grasping the currency hegemony, the United States actually does not need to maintain a huge amount of official reserves.

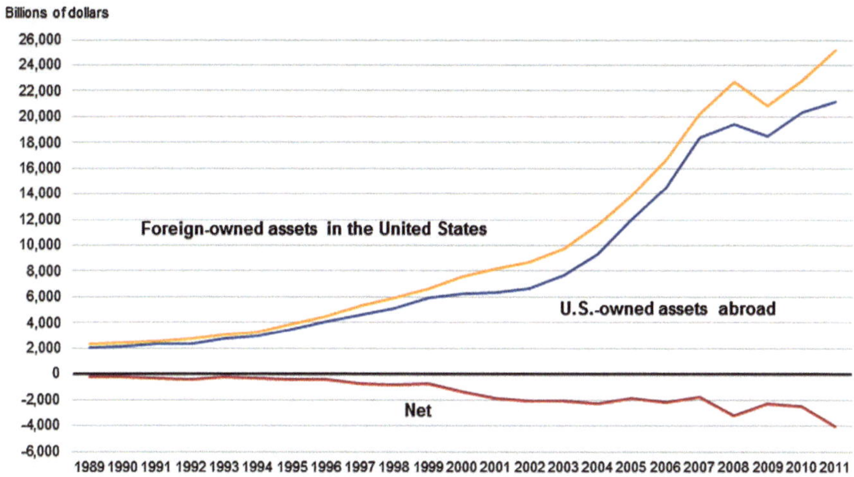

Fig. 18.5 The external investment position of the US in recent years. *Note* 1. The chart is from the US Bureau of Economic Analysis. 2. From *top* to *bottom* in the figure, the *yellow line* represents the US assets held by the US, the *blue line* represents the foreign assets held by the US, and the *red line* represents the net position (i.e. the difference between the first two items) (unit: $1 billion). 3. The data for 2011 are forecasts

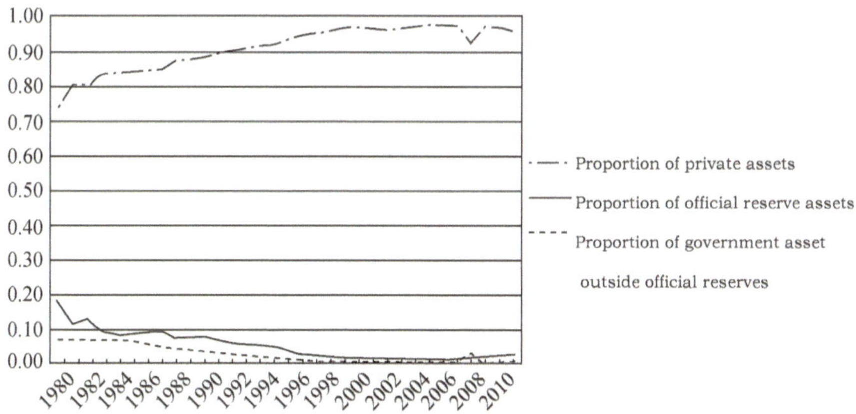

Fig. 18.6 The foreign assets held by the US. *Note* 1. The data are from US Bureau of Economic Analysis. 2. The above assets exclude financial derivative assets. 3. The data for 2011 are forecasts

18.3 Japan's Experience

Based on the SNA93 and SNA08 statistical frameworks, the Economic and Social Research Institute of the Cabinet Office has estimated the national asset and liability stocks for various years and published them in the Annual Report on National accounts (see The Government of Japan 2012). According to the latest data, Table 18.2 presents the 2010 national balance sheet of Japan.

Table 18.2 National balance sheet of Japan for 2010 (unit: 1 billion yen)

Main asset item	Households	Non-financial corporations	Financial corporations	General government	Private non-profit organizations	Totals of all sectors
Non-financial assets	1,080,905	1,036,719	36,941	579,339	50,811	2,784,715
Produced assets	359,726	740,252	14,813	454,128	9391	1,578,310
Inventories	7717	59,958	–	1730	–	69,405
Fixed assets	352,009	680,294	14,813	452,398	9391	1,508,905
Non-produced tangible assets	721,179	296,467	22,128	125,211	41,420	1,206,405
Land	720,835	295,269	22,128	125,211	41,420	1,204,863
Fisheries	344	–	–	–	–	344
Minerals	–	1198	–	–	–	1198
Others	344	1198	–	–	–	1542
Financial assets	1,506,970	830,555	2,836,942	493,873	46,968	5,715,308
Cash and deposits	819,704	210,069	202,251	79,216	21,103	1,332,343
Loans	–	44,146	1,197,303	31,844	1397	1,274,690
Securities (excluding stocks)	92,698	42,652	912,562	127,875	23,152	1,198,939
Stocks and other capital	109,365	147,997	128,915	114,099	111	500,487
Financial derivatives	505	1360	54,906	–	–	56,771
Insurance and pensions	419,361	–	–	–	–	419,361
Other financial assets	65,337	384,331	341,006	140,839	1206	932,719
Total assets	2,587,875	1,867,273	2,873,883	1,073,212	97,778	8,500,021
Liabilities	360,860	1,226,682	2,823,065	1,037,243	15,963	5,463,813
Cash and deposits	–	–	1,329,811	–	–	1,329,811
Loans	297,885	399,278	418,954	165,920	13,373	1,295,410

(continued)

Table 18.2 (continued)

Main asset item	Households	Non-financial corporations	Financial corporations	General government	Private non-profit organizations	Totals of all sectors
Securities (excluding stocks)	–	89,557	358,292	819,598	–	1,267,447
Stocks and other capital	–	454,141	133,430	22,854	–	610,425
Financial derivatives	627	5816	56,044	47	–	62,534
Insurance and pensions	–	–	419,361	–	–	419,361
Other liabilities	62348	277,890	107,173	28,825	2590	478,826
Net liabilities	2,227,015	640,592	50,818	35,969	81,816	3,036,210
Total liabilities and net liabilities	2,587,875	1,867,273	2,873,883	1,073,212	97,778	8,500,021

1. The data are from the Economic and Social Research Institute of the Cabinet Office (Government of Japan 2012), and the statistical standard method used was revised in 2005
2. The non-financial assets were calculated based on the market prices
3. The "household" sector includes households and private unincorporated enterprises; "financial corporations" include the monetary authority; the "general government" sector includes the central government, local governments and social security funds

First, on the whole, as shown in Table 18.2, the total assets of all sectors of Japan amounted to 8500 trillion yen, about 17.6 times of the GDP that year, in which financial assets and non-financial assets amounted to 5715 trillion yen and 2785 trillion yen and the financial interrelations ratio was 2.05. The main items of assets include "Fixed Assets", "Cash and Deposits", "Loans", "Land" and "Securities (excluding Stocks)", together accounting for 77% of total assets. The total liabilities amounted to 5464 trillion yen, accounting for 64 and 96% of total assets and financial assets respectively. The constituent items include "Cash and Deposits", "Loans", and "Securities (excluding Stocks)", together accounting for 71% of total liabilities. The difference between assets and liabilities, i.e. net assets, amounted to 3036 trillion yen, about 6.3 times of the GDP. This indicator reflects the real national wealth.

The assets and liabilities by sector. First, the households of Japan were the largest sector holding non-financial assets, in which the value of land was 721 trillion yen, accounting for nearly 60% of the total land held by all sectors; "Fixed Assets" amounted to 352 trillion Yen, mainly composed of housings; the financial assets of households mainly came in the form of "Cash and Deposits" and "Insurance and pensions". Household liabilities only amounted to 361 trillion yen (mainly composed of loans), and the corresponding liabilities/assets ratio of 14%. Because of this balance sheet structure, the households of Japan also became the largest holders of net assets, reaching 2227 trillion yen, accounting for 73% of total assets. Second, the non-financial assets held by the non-financial corporate sector reached 1037 trillion yen, second only to the household sector, mainly composed of "Fixed Assets" and "Land"; the financial assets of the sector totaled 831 trillion yen, mainly composed of "Other Financial Assets", "Cash Deposits" and "Stocks and Other Capital". The liabilities of the sector totaled 1227 trillion yen, accounting for 66% of its total assets, mainly composed of "Stocks and Other Capital", "Loans" and "Other Liabilities". The net assets of the sector totaled 641 trillion yen, second in size only to the household sector. Third, the non-financial assets of the financial corporate sector were only 37 trillion yen, composed of the two items of "Land" and "Fixed Assets"; the financial assets of the sector amounted to 2837 trillion yen, about half of total assets of all sectors, mainly composed of "Loans", "Securities (excluding Stocks)" and so on. The liabilities of financial corporations amounted to 2823 trillion yen, accounting for 52% of total liabilities, ranking the first among all sectors. The main items included "Cash and Deposits" "Insurance and Pensions", "Loans" and so on. The size of net assets of the sector was smaller and amounted to 51 trillion yen. The corresponding liabilities/assets ratio was 98%, also higher than other sectors, in line with the essential characteristics of leverage operations of the financial sector. Fourth, the non-financial assets of the general government sector amounted to 579 trillion yen, mainly composed of "Fixed Assets" and "Land";[6] the financial assets of the sector amounted to 494 trillion yen, of which 43, 15, and 42% were held by the central government, local governments and social security funds

[6]In the "Land" item, the share of the central government, local governments and the social security funds was 20, 79 and 1% respectively.

respectively. The liabilities of the sector amounted to 1037 trillion yen, of which 81, 18, and 1% were owed by the central government, local governments and social security funds respectively. The net assets of the sector were less than other sectors and amounted to 36 trillion yen. The corresponding liabilities/assets ratio was 97%, second only to the financial corporations. Fifth, the assets and liabilities of private non-profit organization were smallest in size and amounted to 98 trillion yen and 16 trillion yen respectively. However, the financial structure of the sector was sound, its asset/liability ratio was 16%, and its net assets were up to 82 trillion yen.

Finally, from a dynamic perspective, Fig. 18.7 presents the changing trends of some important ratios in Japan's national assets and liabilities during 2001–2010 (totals of all sectors). First, as shown in the figure, compared with GDP, Japan's assets, liabilities and net assets showed a slight upward trend, but there is a clear trend of reverse, especially for the first two ratios which reached a local high in 2005 and later continuously declined and began to rise only after the international financial crisis. Second, the debt to capital ratio reflecting the financial risks basically remained stable in a narrow range of 63–67%, and comparing with the two nodes in 2001 and 2010, the ratio rose slightly from only 63 to 64%. Third, during this period, the financial interrelations ratio reflecting the financial structure also edged up in fluctuations, showing the Japanese financial deepening process had not stalled.

Figure 18.8 presents the changes in the constituent sectors of the balance sheet of Japan during the same period again with net assets that measure the national wealth as an example. The figure shows that the household sector has always been the largest holder of net assets, accounting for more than 70% over the years; the proportion of net assets of the non-financial and financial sectors increased in the period, but fluctuated violently. Both were changing at a rang of 12.4–21.3 and 0.5–1.7% respectively; the proportion of net assets held by general government

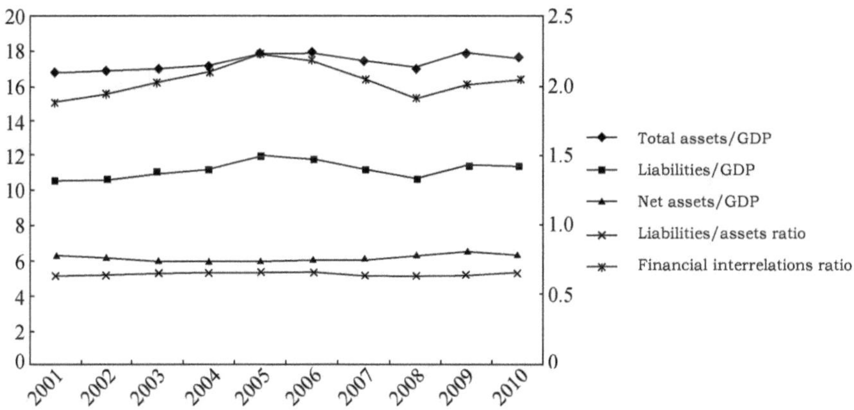

Fig. 18.7 The changing trends of some important ratios in Japan's national assets and liabilities during 2001–2010 (totals of all sectors). *Note* 1. The data are from the Economic and Social Research Institute of the Cabinet Office. 2. The total assets/GDP, liabilities/GDP, and net assets/GDP are expressed by the *left axis*; the liabilities/assets ratio and the financial interrelations ratio are expressed by the *right axis*

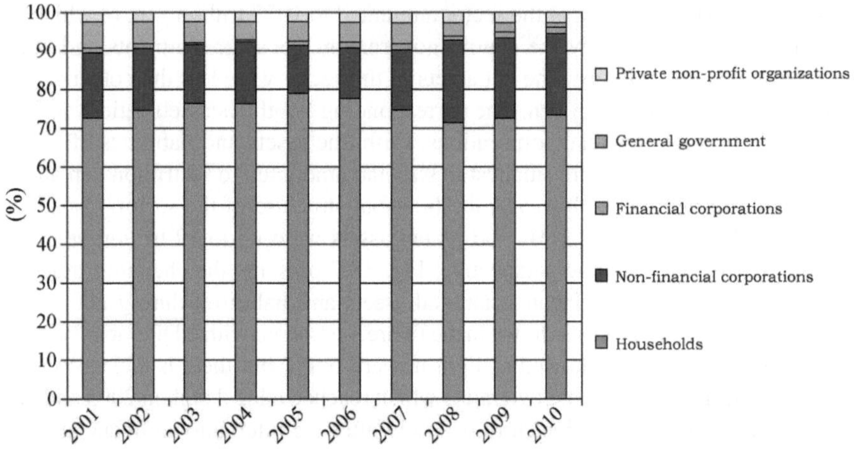

Fig. 18.8 The sectors of Japan with national net assets (2001–2010). *Source* The Economic and Social Research Institute of the Cabinet Office

showed a downward trend and declined from 6.8% at the beginning of the period to 1.2% at the end of the period; the net assets of private non-profit organizations rose steadily in size and exceeded the general government in 2009.

18.4 Germany's Experience

Based on the ESA95 framework (European System of Accounts 1995), the German Federal Statistical Office (Federal Statistical Office 2012) prepared the overall and sectoral balance sheets of Germany and published the relevant data in September 2012. Also as an example, Table 18.3 presents the balance sheet of the German economy in 2011.

German national balance sheet table list 1,832,011 (unit: one billion euros).

First, on the whole, the total assets of all sectors in Germany amounted to €29.2 trillion in 2011, 11.3 times of the GDP, among which financial assets and non-financial assets amounted to €18.2 trillion and €11 trillion respectively and the f financial interrelations ratio was 1.65. The asset items are mainly composed by size "Housings and Buildings", "Negotiable Securities", "Cash and Deposits", "Monetary Gold, SDRs and Other Claims" and so on. On the liability and net asset side, the total liabilities amounted to €17.7 trillion, and its ratio to total assets and financial assets was 61 and 97% respectively. The net assets amounted to €11.6 trillion, and its ratio to the GDP that year was 4.5.

The assets and liabilities by sector. First, the households and non-profit household service organizations (the household sector) in Germany were the largest non-financial asset holding sector. The non-financial assets of the sector are mainly composed of "Residential Housings" and "Land for Construction", worth €3.7 billion and €1.9 trillion respectively; the financial assets amounted to €4.7 trillion,

Table 18.3 National balance sheet of Germany in 2011 (unit: 1 billion euros)

Main asset item	Households and non-profit household service organizations	Non-financial corporations	Financial corporations	General government	Total of all sectors
Non-financial assets	6139.4	3315.4	212.2	1345.5	11,012.5
Tangible assets	4277	2767.7	168.8	1121.4	8334.9
Farming assets	–	–	–	–	–
Machinery equipments	130.5	950	11.1	33	1124.6
Housings and buildings	4140.4	1813.7	157.7	1088.4	7200.2
Incl.: residential housings	3736.7	557.4	26.8	32.7	4353.7
Intangible assets	8.3	52.9	3.8	4.8	69.8
Land for construction	1854.1	494.8	39.6	219.3	2607.8
Financial assets	4714.5	2386.6	10,220.3	903.6	18,225
Cash and deposits	1927.5	460.5	1946.8	257.4	4592.2
Negotiable securities	1065.9	1408.4	3740.2	420.6	6635.1
Insurance reserves, pensions and other claims	1721.1	–	–	–	1721.1
Insurance reserves, loans and other claims	–	517.7	–	225.5	743.2
Monetary gold, SDRs and other claims	–	–	4533.3	–	4533.3
Total assets	10,853.9	5702	10,432.5	2249.1	29,237.5
Total liabilities and net assets	10,853.9	5702	10,432.5	2249.1	29,237.5
Liabilities	1549.5	3742.5	10124.6	2237.7	17,654.3
Loans and other liabilities	1549.5	–	–	–	1549.5

(continued)

Table 18.3 (continued)

Main asset item	Households and non-profit household service organizations	Non-financial corporations	Financial corporations	General government	Total of all sectors
Borrowed money	–	1912.1	8543	2237.7	12,692.8
Stocks and other equities		1830.4	1581.6	–	3412
Net assets	9304.4	1959.5	307.9	11.4	11,583.2

1. The data on non-financial assets are from the Federal Statistical Office (2012) and the values are calculated at market prices; the data on financial assets and liabilities are from Bundesbank
2. According to ESA95, general government includes central government, state governments, local governments and social security funds; financial corporations include the central bank
3. Due to repeated accounting and omissions among various sectors, the totals of all sectors are not equal to the data of total economy defined by the German Federal Statistical Office

second in size only to financial corporations, mainly composed of "Cash and Deposits", "Insurance Reserves, Pensions and Other Claims" and "Negotiable Securities". The liabilities of the household sector were only €1.5 trillion, less than the other sectors, and the corresponding liabilities/assets ratio was 14.3%. The net assets of the household sector amounted to €9.3 trillion, accounting for 80.3% of total net assets of all sectors. Second, non-financial assets held non-financial corporations amounted to €3.3 trillion, second only to the household sector, mainly composed of "Housings and Buildings", "Machinery Equipments" and "Land for Construction"; the financial assets of the sector totaled €2.4 trillion, mainly composed of "Negotiable Securities", "Insurance Reserves, Loans and Other Claims" and "Cash and Deposits". The liabilities of the sector reached €3.7 trillion, mainly composed of "Borrowed Money" and "Stocks and Other Equities", and the liabilities/assets ratio was 65.6%. The net assets of the sector were nearly €2 trillion, only second to the household sectors, accounting for 16.9% of total net assets of all sectors. Third, the non-financial assets of the financial sector amounted to €212.2 billion, less than the other sectors, mainly composed of "Housings and Buildings"; the financial assets amounted to €10.2 trillion, accounting for about 56.1% total assets of all sectors, mainly composed of "Monetary Gold, SDRs and Other Claims", "Negotiable Securities" and "Cash and Deposits". The liabilities of the financial sector amounted to €10.1 trillion, mainly composed of "Borrowed Money" and "Stocks and Other Equities", and the corresponding assets/liabilities ratio was 97%. The net assets of the sector amounted to €307.9 billion, accounting for 2.7% of total net assets of all sectors. The leverage degree was lower than that of the United Kingdom and close to that of Japan. Fourth, due to unavailability of data, it is impossible to analyze constituent subsectors of the general government sector in Germany. On the whole, its total assets and liabilities amounted to €2249.1 and €2237.7 billion respectively, which were smaller compared to other sectors, accounting for 7.7 and 12.7% respectively. The amounts of assets and liabilities

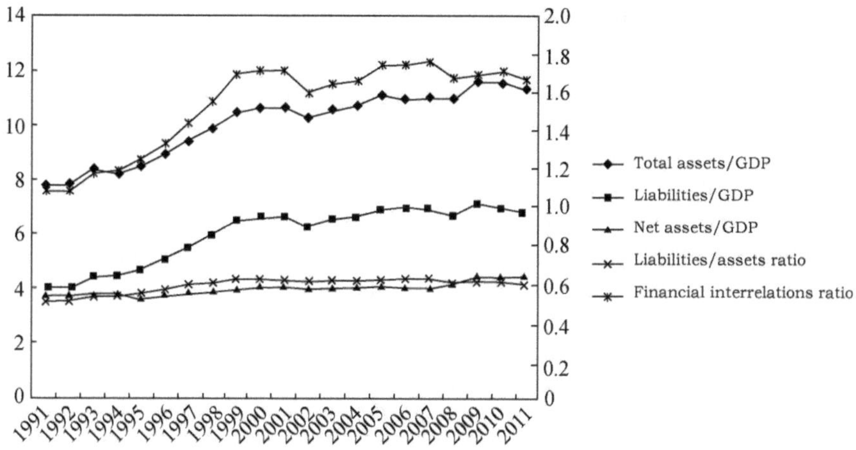

Fig. 18.9 Some important ratios in Germany's national assets and liabilities (1991–2011). *Note* 1. The data are from the German Federal Statistical Office. 2. The total assets/GDP, liabilities/GDP, and net assets/GDP are expressed by the *left axis*; the liabilities/assets ratio and the financial interrelations ratio are expressed by the *right axis*

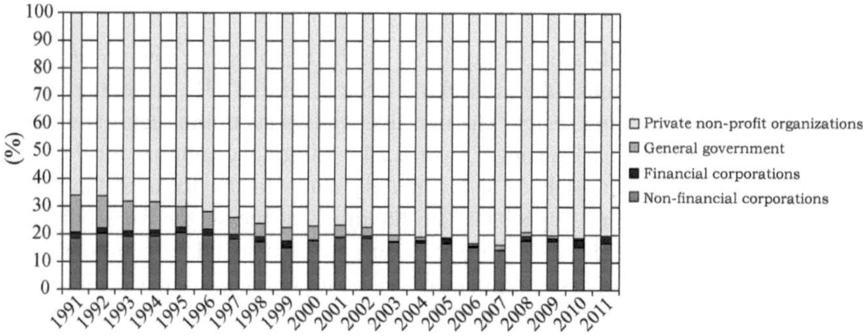

Fig. 18.10 The sectors of Germany with national net assets (1991–2011). *Source* The German Federal Statistical Office

were basically the same, but the former was slightly more than the latter, the net assets amounted to €11.4 billion, and the liabilities/assets ratio was 99.5%.

From a dynamic perspective, Fig. 18.9 below presents the changing trends of some important ratios in Germany's national assets and liabilities during 1991–2011 (totals of all sectors). First, as show in the figure, compared with GDP, Germany's assets, liabilities, and net assets showed an obvious upward trend, but there was obvious replication in trend during 2002 and 2008. Second, the debt-to-capital ratio reflecting the overall financial risk rose from 0.51 in 1991 to 0.60 in 2011, showing a gradually enhancing reliance of the German economy on debt financing in the 20 years and more, but the level was still weaker than that of Japan. Third, like Japan, Germany's financial interrelations ratio also fluctuated and increased slightly during the investigation period, and the financial deepening was continuously strengthened (Fig. 18.10).

18.5 The UK's Experience

In the UK, Revell tentatively compiled he national balance sheet for 1957–1961 years (see Revell 1966). Since 1975, the balance sheet was officially included in the official statistics (see Holder 1998). According to the related data in the Blue Book on national accounts published by the Office for National Statistics (ONS) (see ONS 2012), we will give a survey of the balance sheet of the United Kingdom for recent years. Also, as an example, Table 18.4 presents the main information (year-end values) of the 2011 National Balance Sheet of the UK.

First, on the whole, the total assets of the UK amounted to £36.0 trillion in 2011, 24 times of the GDP, in which financial assets and non-financial assets were £29 trillion and £7.0 trillion respectively, and the financial interrelations ratio was 4.14. The main asset items include "Securities and Other Equities", "Cash and Deposits", "Loans", "Residential Housings" and "Stocks and Other Capital", together accounting for 85% of total assets. The liabilities totaled £29.2 trillion, and its ratio to total assets and financial assets was 81 and 100% respectively. Its main liability items were similar to those of Japan, including "Securities and Other Equities", "Cash and Deposits" and "Loans", together accounting for 78% of total liabilities. The net assets amounted to £6.8 trillion, 4.5 times of the GDP that year. It is equal to that of England.

The assets and liabilities by sector. First, the households and non-profit household service organizations (the household sector) in the UK were the largest non-financial asset holding sector. The non-financial assets of the sector are mainly composed of "Residential Housings", worth £4.1 trillion, accounting for 94%; the financial assets of the household sector mainly came in the form of "Insurance Reserves" and "Cash and Deposits". The liabilities of the sector were only £1.5 trillion (in which loans accounted for 94%), and the corresponding liabilities/assets ratio was 17.5%. The net assets amounted to £7 trillion, ranking first in all sectors, even exceeding the total of all sectors. Second, the non-financial assets held by the non-financial corporate sector was second only to the household sector and reached £1.8 trillion, mainly composed of "Other Buildings Facilities" and "Machinery and Equipments"; the financial assets of the sector totaled £2.2 trillion, main composed of "Equities and Other Capital", "Cash and Deposits" and "Loans". The liabilities of the sector were large higher and reached £3.9 trillion, accounting for 98% of its total assets. The liability items mainly include "Stocks and Other Capital", "Loans" and "Securities and Other Equity". The net assets of the sector were only £76.2 billion. Third, the non-financial assets of the financial corporate sector amounted to £141.8 billion, less than other sectors; the financial assets amounted to £21.9 trillion, about 76% of total assets of all sectors, mainly composed of "Securities and Other Equities", "Cash and Deposits", "Loans" and so on. The liabilities of financial corporations amounted to £22.1 trillion, accounting for 76% of total liabilities of all sectors, mainly composed of "Securities and Other Equities", "Cash and Deposits" and so on. The net assets were—£24.8 billion, and thus the liabilities/assets ratio was more than 100%, with the degree of leverage more than those of Japan and

Table 18.4 Survey of the balance sheet of the United Kingdom for 2011 (unit: 1 billion pounds)

Main asset item	Households and non-profit household service organizations	Non-financial corporations	Financial corporations	Central government	Local governments	Total of all sectors
Non-financial assets	4302.1	1819.1	141.8	335.1	434.9	7033.0
Residential housings	4064.8	202.0	4.1	9.3	0	4280.1
Other construction facilities	61.4	792.0	113.7	281.3	422.9	1671.3
Machinery and equipments	112.0	537.0	15.6	22.2	9.8	696.5
Agricultural equipments	45.4	3.5	0.8	0.1	1.8	51.7
Intangible fixed assets	1.0	50.4	7.6	0.1	0.4	59.5
Inventories	17.6	234.2	0	0.2	0	252.0
Non-produced Intangible assets	0	0	0	21.9	0	21.9
Financial assets	4283.7	2175.5	21,945.8	400.4	153.0	28,958.4
Monetary gold and SDRs	0	0	0	19.3	0	19.3
Cash and deposits	1251.9	732.7	4626.4	70.2	27.6	6708.8
Securities and other equities	67.4	93.1	11,073.6	45.5	2.5	11,282.0
Loans	18.4	309.0	3874.2	106.9	5.7	4314.3
Stocks and other capital	603.4	895.1	2302.2	77.8	116.2	3994.7
Insurance reserves	2209.9	10.6	1.1	0	0.7	2222.3
Other receivables	132.8	134.9	68.2	80.7	0.4	417.1
Total assets	8585.8	3994.6	22,087.6	735.5	587.9	35,991.4

(continued)

Table 18.4 (continued)

Main asset item	Households and non-profit household service organizations	Non-financial corporations	Financial corporations	Central government	Local governments	Total of all sectors
Financial debts	1541.3	3918.4	22,112.4	1498.4	84.4	29,154.9
Cash and deposits	0	0	6808.1	133.6	0	6941.7
Securities and other equities	8.5	474.1	9611.5	1319.9	1.6	11,415.7
Loans	1446.3	1172.7	1811.7	9.0	71.6	4511.3
Stocks and other capital	0	2105.5	1535.8	0	0	3641.3
Insurance reserves	0	0	2230.9	0	0	2230.9
Other receivables	86.5	166.1	114.3	36.0	11.2	414.0
Total net assets	7044.5	76.2	−24.8	−762.9	503.6	6836.6

1. The data are from ONS (2012)
2. Non-financial assets were calculated based on the market prices
3. “Financial corporations” include the monetary authority
4. Due to statistical errors, the sums of all sub-items are not equal to the totals

Germany. Fourth, the non-financial assets held by the central government and local governments amounted to £335.1 and £434.9 billion respectively, mainly composed of "Other Building Facilities"; the financial assets of the two sectors amounted to £400.4 and £153 billion respectively, of which the assets of the central government were large "Loans", while the assets of local governments were largely "Equities and Other Capital". The liabilities of the two sectors were £1498.4 and £84.4 billion respectively. It is particularly worth noting that the liabilities of the central government in the item of "Securities and Other Equities" alone were up to £1319.9 billion. The net assets of the two sectors were—£762.9 and £503.6 billion respectively, and the corresponding liabilities/assets ratio was 204 and 14% respectively. Thus, regardless of the absolute or relative size, the financial position of the British central government was significantly worse than that of local governments.

Finally, from the dynamic perspective, Fig. 18.11 presents the changing trends of some important ratios in the UK's national assets and liabilities during 2002–2011. First, in the study period, the total national assets and liabilities of the UK expanded much faster than its GDP, and their ratios to GDP almost doubled, rising from 14 times and 10 times in 2002 to 24 times and 19 times in 2011 respectively. However, as both were changing almost synchronously, there was little change in the size of net assets relative to GDP, which only edged up from 4.3 to 4.5 times. Second, the liabilities/assets ratio in the same period rose from 70 to 81%, showing an increase in the UK's overall financial risk. Especially in the 2008 crisis, the ratio jumped from 77% in the previous year to 82%. Despite a slight decline thereafter, it remained at a high level of more than 80%, so the impact of the crisis has not yet been eliminated. Third, the financial interrelations ratio increased from 2.2 in 2002

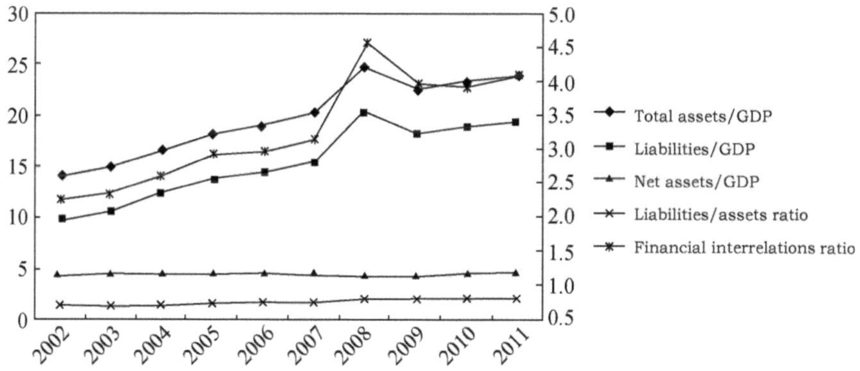

Fig. 18.11 Some important ratios in the UK's national assets and liabilities (2002–2011). *Note* 1. The data are from ONS (2012). 2. The total assets/GDP, liabilities/GDP, and net assets/GDP are expressed by the *left axis*; the liabilities/assets ratio and the financial interrelations ratio are expressed by the *right axis*

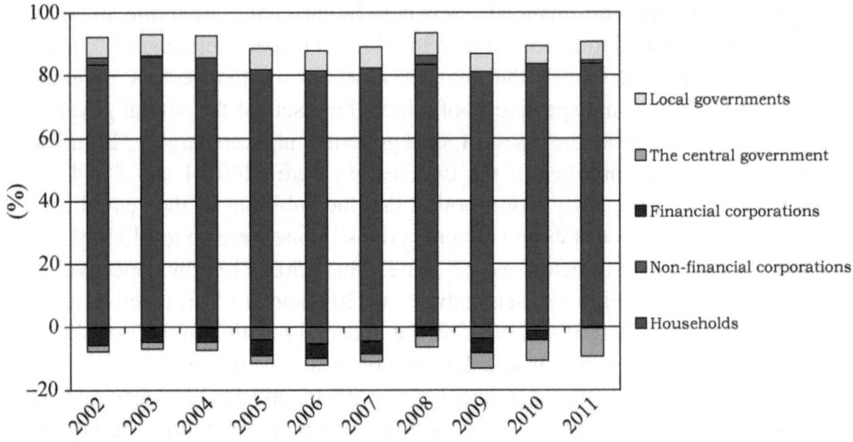

Fig. 18.12 The sectors of the UK with national net assets (2002–2011). *Source* ONS (2012)

to 4.1 in 2011, reflecting the rapid expansion of the British financial sector during this period. Of course, this process was also significantly affected by the crisis. For example, in 2008, this ratio jumped from 3.1 to 4.6 and later dropped to 3.9 in 2009. This was probably because non-financial assets (such as real estate) shrank earlier when the crisis occurred and later financial assets were affected.

Figure 18.12 presents the sectors of the UK with net assets during 2002–2011. As shown in the figure, the vast majority of net assets were held by the household sector, accounting for more than 95% and even more than 100% in most of the years. But it is worth noting that this proportion fell from 105 to 96% in 2008. This was probably because the most important part of the assets held by households—housing assets—were seriously shrank in the crisis; the proportion f net assets of non-financial corporations fluctuated violently between the range of −7 to 3%; the net assets of financial corporations were always negative in the study period, reflecting that the overall risk level of the UK financial sector continued to remain at a high level, even indicating an excessive deleveraging tendency in the sector; the net assets of the central government were once below zero and still deteriorating. Especially since the financial crisis, the proportion had plummeted from −3% in 2007 to −11% in 2011; the financial position of local governments was much better than that of the central government, and its net assets were basically changing at the same pace with other sectors in the period, and the proportion maintained at a level of 7–8%.

Table 18.5 Canada's national balance sheet for 2011 (unit: 1 billion Canadian dollars)

Main asset item	Individuals and non-corporate businesses	Non-financial corporations	Financial corporations	Federal government	Provincial and local governments	Total of all sectors
Non-financial assets	3621	2341	93	62	713	6830
Residential housings	1655	235	–	–	16	1906
Non-residential buildings	36	1045	51	40	510	1681
Machinery and equipments	13	369	27	11	32	451
Durable consumer goods	441	–	–	–	–	441
Inventories	22	220	–	–	–	242
land	1454	473	15	12	155	2108
Financial assets	4338	1988	7490	262	624	14,895
Official reserves	–	–	64	–	–	64
Cash and deposits	1028	368	230	3	34	1663
Consumer credit	–	1	451	–	–	452
Loans	–	22	516	19	32	589
Real estate mortgages	9	7	1234	1	11	1261
Bonds	84	28	1365	6	145	1667
Equities	1461	25	860	–	70	2425
Corporate claims	–	662	1352	–	–	2043
Government claims	–	18	1	205	130	389
Life insurance and pensions	1579	–	–	–	–	1579

(continued)

Table 18.5 (continued)

Main asset item	Individuals and non-corporate businesses	Non-financial corporations	Financial corporations	Federal government	Provincial and local governments	Total of all sectors
Other financial assets	177	857	1417	28	202	2764
Total assets	7959	4329	7582	324	1336	21,725
Total liabilities and net assets	7959	4329	7582	324	1336	21,725
Liabilities	1617	3969	7546	923	1072	15,132
Cash and deposits	–	–	1687	5	–	1692
Consumer credit	452	–	–	–	–	452
Real estate mortgages	1027	215	–	–	2	1261
Bonds	–	422	785	518	613	2338
Equities	–	2151	1877	–	–	4028
Life insurance and pensions	–	–	1353	151	75	1579
Other liabilities	138	1181	1844	249	382	3782
Net assets	6342	361	36	−599	264	6593

1. The data are from Statistics Canada
2. "Financial corporations" include the monetary authority
3. Due to accounting omissions for the assets and liabilities of the federal government and provincial and local governments, the sums of all sub-items are not equal to the totals

18.6 Canada's Experience

Canada officially published the national balance sheet for the first time in 1985 and estimated part of the data for several years earlier (see Statistics Canada 2010).[7] Since 1990, Canada begun to prepare its quarterly national balance sheet with data calculated at book and market values. As market values could better reflect the current real worth of assets and liabilities, the following expositions are based on market values (the data above are basically based on market values). As an example, Table 18.5 lists the primary information of the Canadian national balance sheet for 2011.

First, on the whole, the total national assets of Canada reached 21.7 trillion Canadian dollars in 2011, 12.6 times of the GDP, in which financial assets and non-financial assets were 14.9 and 6.8 trillion Canadian dollars respectively, and the finance interrelations ratio was 2.18. The asset items mainly included "Other Financial Assets", "Equities", "Land", "Corporate Claims" and "Residential Housings", together accounting for 52% of total assets. The total liabilities were 15.1 trillion Canadian dollars, and its ratio to total assets and financial assets was 70 and 102% respectively. The liability items mainly included "Equities", "Other Liabilities" and "Bonds", together accounting for 67% of total liabilities. The net assets were 6.6 trillion Canadian dollars, and its ratio to GDP that year was 3.8.

The assets and liabilities by sector. First, the individual and non-corporate business sector (the household sector) is the largest holder of non-financial assets, and the asset items mainly included "Residential Housings" and "Land", worth 1.7 and 1.5 trillion Canadian dollars respectively; the financial assets of households mainly came in the form of "Life Insurance and Pensions", "Equities" and "Cash and Deposits". The liabilities of households were only 1.6 trillion Canadian dollars (including real estate mortgages, accounting for 64%), and the corresponding assets/liabilities ratio was 20.3%. The net assets of households were 6.3 trillion Canadian dollars, accounting for 96% of total assets of all sectors. Second, the non-financial assets held by non-financial corporations reached 2.3 trillion Canadian dollars, second only to the household sector, mainly composed of "Non-residential Buildings", "Land", "Machinery and Equipments and so on; The financial assets of the sector totaled 2 trillion Canadian dollars, mainly composed of "Other Financial Assets", "Corporate Claims" and "Cash and Deposits". The liabilities of the sector reached 4.0 trillion Canadian dollars, accounting for 92% of

---

[7]It should be noted that the balance sheets in the Canadian statistical system are expressed in three methods: first, the total (all sectors) is the total assets and liabilities of all domestic sectors and foreign sectors. In such case, the financial assets and financial liabilities stay balanced by definition; second, the national balance sheet lists the total assets and liabilities of all domestic sectors. In such as case, the difference between financial assets and financial liabilities is the net external claim or debt of Canada; third, the consolidated national balance sheet is the statement listing national net assets, including the difference between domestic financial assets and financial liabilities and non-financial assets (see Statistics Canada 2010). Unless otherwise stated, in this study, we are discussing the expression second, namely the national balance sheet.

total assets, mainly composed of "Equities" and "Other Liabilities". The net assets of the sector were 361 billion Canadian dollars, still only less than the household sector. Third, the non-financial assets of the financial corporate sector were 93 billion Canadian dollars; the financial assets were 7.5 trillion Canadian dollars, about 50% of total assets of all sectors, mainly composed of "Other Financial Assets", "Bonds", "Corporate Claims" and "Real Estate Mortgages". The liabilities of financial corporations were 7.5 trillion Canadian dollars, mainly composed of "Equities", "Other Liabilities" and "Cash and Deposits". The net assets of the sector were 36 billion Canadian dollars, and the corresponding assets/liabilities ratio was nearly 100%. Fourth, the non-financial assets held by the federal government (the central government) and provincial and local governments (local governments) were 62 and 713 billion Canadian dollars respectively, mainly composed of "Non-residential Buildings" and "Land" (primarily held by local governments); the financial assets of the two sectors were 262 and 624 billion Canadian dollars respectively, of which the asset items of the central government included "Central Claims", while the asset items of local governments were dispersed. The liabilities of the sectors were 923 and 1072 billion Canadian dollars respectively. The main items included "Bonds", "Other Liabilities" and "Life Insurance and Pensions". The net assets of the two sectors were—599 million and 264 billion Canadian dollars respectively, and the corresponding liabilities/assets ratio was 285 and 80% respectively. This phenomenon is the basically same as the situations in Japan and the UK. That is, the financial position of the central government was significantly worse than that of local governments.

Finally, from a dynamic perspective, Fig. 18.13 presents the changing trends of some important ratios in Canada's national assets and liabilities during 2002–2011). As shown in the figure, first, in the period, the growth of total assets and liabilities of Canada outpaced its GDP, but like Japan, at a modest rate: their ratio to GDP rose from 10.5 times and 7.3 times in 2002 to 12.6 times and 8.8 times in 2011 of respectively. As the growth of assets slightly outpaced liabilities, the size of net assets relative to GDP edged up from 3.3 to 3.8 times. Second, the liabilities/assets ratio in the same period remained stable with a changing range of 68% (2008)–70% (2010). Third, the financial interrelations ratio was also relatively stable in the study period and only edged up from 2.07 at the beginning of the period to 2.18 at the end of the period. Of course, this rate fluctuated violently in the crisis. For example, the financial interrelations ratio was 2.19, 2.07 and 2.18 respectively during 2007–2009. This shows that the decline rate of financial assets and non-financial assets varied with the time in this period.

Figure 18.14 presents the sectors of Canada with net assets during 2002–2011. As shown in the figure, the vast majority of net assets were held by the household sector, accounting for more than 90% and even more than 100% in most of the years. But in the financial crisis, the net assets of households fluctuated violently. For example, its proportion was 105, 92 and 98% respectively during 2007–2009. Similar to the case of the United Kingdom, this was also probably attributed to the changes in the value of residential housing assets; the net assets of non-financial corporations in the period remained positive, but its proportion changed greatly and

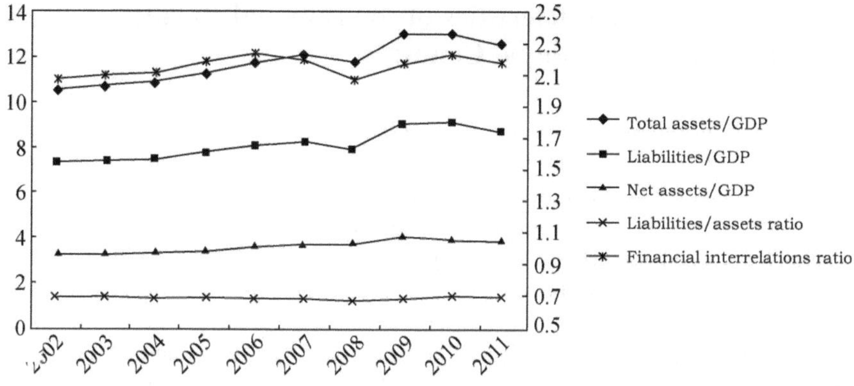

Fig. 18.13 Some important ratios in Canada's national assets and liabilities (2002–2011). *Note* 1. The data are from Statistics Canada. 2. The total assets/GDP, liabilities/GDP, and net assets/GDP are expressed by the *left axis*; the liabilities/assets ratio and the financial interrelations ratio are expressed by the *right axis*

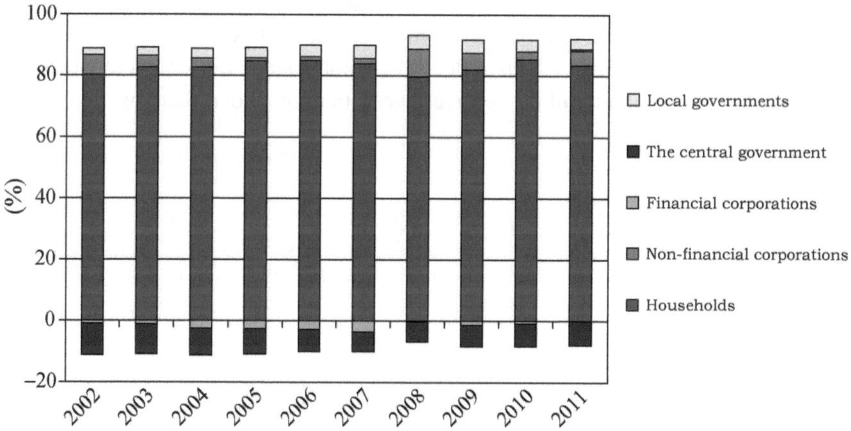

Fig. 18.14 The sectors of Canada with national net assets (2002–2011). *Source* Statistics Canada

jumped from 2.2 to 10.4% and then dropped to 6.5% during 2007–2009; the net assets of financial corporations were negative in most years and only positive in 2011, accounting for 0.6%. Although the level of risk of Canada's financial sector was still high measured by this, it should be noted that since 2008, the relative size of net assets has increased. Although in the study period the relative size of net assets of the central government increased on the whole, its value was always negative and has been deteriorating since 2008. The financial position of the Canadian local governments was much better than that of the central government, and the accumulation of net asset outpaced other sectors in the period.

18.7 Common Characteristics of the National Balance Sheets of the Sample Countries

The accounting frameworks for the national balance sheets of the sample countries are different and the values are not fully comparable, but based on the experience of the United States and other developed countries, we can come to the following conclusions: first, the expansion of national balance sheets in the study period generally outpaced the GDPs, especially the growth of financial assets generally outpaced non-financial assets, showing the accelerated financial deepening trend during this period. Second, the household sector held the largest amount of non-financial assets (mainly residential housings) and net assets, and the net assets held by the household sector often exceeded 100% of total net assets of all sectors. Third, the non-financial corporate sector held a comparatively larger amount of non-financial assets, and its net assets were generally positive, but the proportion fluctuated violently. Fourth, the financial corporate sector held the largest amount of financial assets, but its liabilities were also large in size, and the liabilities/assets ration was high and even sometimes more than 100%, so the net assets were generally negative. This is in line with the characteristics of deleveraging of the financial sector. Fifth, the central government's financial position was worse than that of local governments, which reflects to some extent the characteristics that social security and other public services were mainly undertaken by the central government.

Chapter 19
Balance Sheet Methods and the Financial Crisis: A Research Application

In our daily life, we should spend based on our earnings. Apart from daily consumer spending, we still need to prepare for spending on some major items, such as medical care, pension and shopping and gift for friends and contacts. Apart from savings, we may also borrow money from relatives and friends or banks. Such is also the case for a country. If a government or an enterprise, a household or a bank only owns assets and does not carry any debt, this is not a good thing because this mechanism does not make full use of resources, especially for a country with adequate overall savings but imbalanced savings among various sectors. However, if an economy has inadequate savings or borrows too much, it will ultimately get stuck in a debt crisis due to difficulties in debt repayment; if an economy carries some debt but holds more assets, part of the assets are cashable at any time, the cashed value can offset the debt, then it will be economically and financially stable. A national balance sheet aims to study of this kind of issues. In this section, we will introduce the research applications and policy revelations of national balance sheets based on the international experience and lessons, especially the lessons from the global financial crisis that began in 2007.

The basic conclusion of this section is: the US subprime crisis and the European sovereign debt crisis indicate again that in the face of a financial crisis, no country is indestructible and no powerful government is always the "savior". A sovereign government should not only pay for its own explicit debt, but also for its debt as a result of policy failures in the time of a crisis, especially for the debt of the private sector covering households, enterprises and financial institutions. In an era with increasingly close financial links at home and abroad, no country or sector can be an exception: the crisis of a country can be quickly transmitted to other countries, and the risk of a sector can be quickly transmitted to other sectors. One of the main factors that a country can resist the contagion of a crisis from another country is the healthiness of the country's national balance sheet.

Y. Li and X. Zhang, *China's National Balance Sheet*, China Insights,
DOI 10.1007/978-981-10-4385-7_19

19.1 National Balance Sheet and Its Analysis Method: The International Perspective

19.1.1 Internal Logic of National Balance Sheet

As mentioned above, a national balance sheet can reflect the vulnerability stock of assets and liabilities of various sub-sectors of a national economy and their transmission mechanism. Preparation and understanding of the relationship between assets and liabilities of various sectors can help policy-makers to reduce the economic vulnerability and formulate the best policy to cope with the crisis in advance. Given that the US has a relatively developed financial system and has prepared the national balance sheets for many years, we introduced the basic structure, inter-sectoral relationship and risk mechanism of national balance sheet with the United States as an example.

The US national balance sheet consists of four parts: the public sector (the central bank, the central government, state and local governments, and government non-financial corporations), the financial sector (other depositary corporations and other financial corporations), the non-financial private sector (non-financial businesses and residents) and the world (non-household sector). All the sectors have close contacts in claims and debt. An example is the relationship between the Fed and the federal government: the federal government had $289 billion worth of claims on the Fed and owed $1016 billion worth of debt to the Fed, so the federal government's net debt to the Fed was $727 billion; accordingly, the Fed had $1016 billion worth of claims on the federal government and owed $289 billion worth of debt to the federal government, so the Fed's net claims on the federal government was $727 billion. Obviously, the federal government's claims and debt correspond respectively to the Fed's claims and debt.

Another example is the relationship between the Fed and other depositary corporations: other depositary corporations had $1028 billion worth of claims on the Fed and owed $45 billion worth of debt to the Fed, so the net claims of other depositary corporations was $983 billion; the Fed had $45 billion worth of claims on other depositary corporations and owed $1028 billion worth of debt to other depositary corporations, so the Fed's net claims on other depositary corporations was $983 billion.

The above two examples show that through the national balance sheet, we can straighten out the complicated debtor–creditor relationships among various sectors of the national economy in a year. Straightening out these relationships has played a major role for the United States to cope with this global financial crisis. We can clearly see the reflection of the crisis-response policy in the national balance sheet. For example, the Fed held a net worth of $727 billion treasury securities of the federal government in 2010, which was a reflection of the result of the quantitative easing policy adopted by the Fed during the crisis.

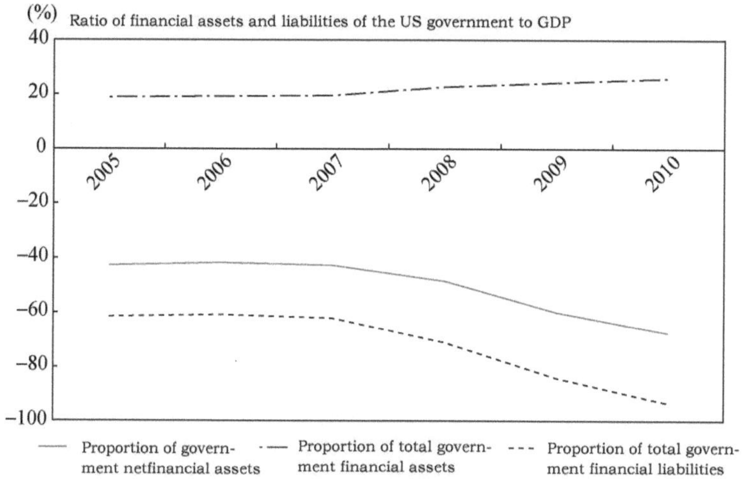

Source: the IMF (the US Article IV Consultation Report), 2011.
Explanation: Government net financial assets are the difference between total government financial assets and total government financial liabilities.

Fig. 19.1 Ratio of financial assets and liabilities to GDP of the US government (%)

Figure 19.1 illustrates the cases that the US government borrowed too much: The US government's net financial assets had been negative, and its proportion of GDP rose from 43% in 2005 to 68% in 2010.

In addition to the relationships among various domestic sectors, a country also has economic, trade and financial contacts with the international community. IIP is an important indicator reflecting such contacts. IIP reflects the size of a country's net assets in foreign countries and its external payment capacity and its ability to respond to an external crisis. Figure 19.2 shows that the US's IIP started to turn from positive to negative in 1980 and declined all the way and reached −239.6 billion US dollars in 2010; Japan's IIP started to surge in the mid 1990s and has currently reached $286 billion, ranking first in the world. China's IIP is also growing rapidly and has reached $151.1 billion currently, ranking second in the world.

19.1.2 Contingent Liabilities and Balance Sheet Risks

Contingent liability is a concept related to the national balance sheet. A contingent liability is a concept in general sense, and it usually refers to a debt repayment obligation whose timing and magnitude depend on the occurrence of some uncertain future event outside the control of Government. This definition highlights

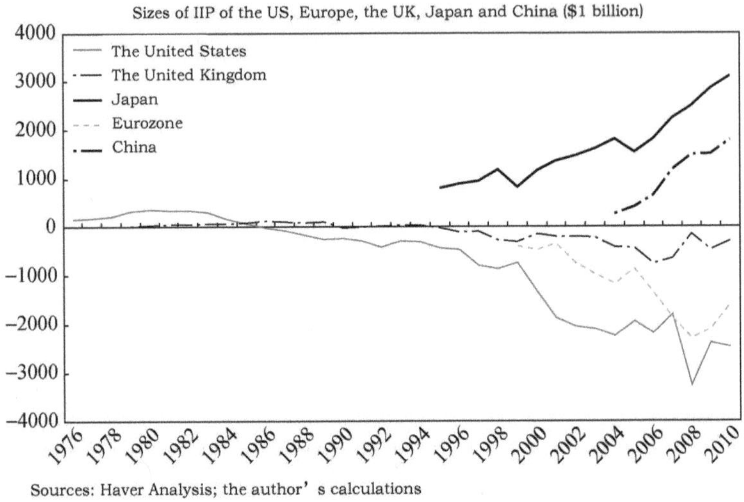

Fig. 19.2 Sizes of IIP of the US, Europe, the UK, Japan and China ($1 billion)

uncertainty with regard to timing and magnitude of the payment, and includes the possibility of the payment not coming due at all. This definition is deferent from the definition in the field of statistics: the IMF's *2001 Government Finance Statistics Manual* (GFSM) defines contingent liabilities as including, in addition to guarantees, the net present value of the accrued obligations of social security schemes. Such liabilities are implicit liabilities. Thus, according to different national conditions of different countries, the meaning of contingent liabilities may differ. In some countries, only uncertain liabilities outside the control of government are treated as contingent liabilities, in some countries, implicit liabilities inside the control of government are also treated as contingent liabilities, while I some countries, liabilities inside or outside the control of government are treated contingent liabilities.

In the United States, the best examples for contingent liabilities are two Government-sponsored enterprises engaged in housing mortgage business—Freddie Mac and Fannie Mae. Their important role was to provide financial support for housing mortgage loans. They bought mortgage loans from the banks and package the loans into mortgage-backed securities (MBS) and sold them to investors. They also provided guarantee for potential loss from default of mortgage-backed securities or issued bonds and bought and held mortgage-backed securities.

Prior to the 2007 subprime debt crisis, Freddie Mac and Fannie Mae were not supported by the federal government, and their businesses were not reflected in the federal budget. However, the market generally believes that the government had provided implicit guarantees to Freddie Mac and Fannie Mae. In 2008, Freddie Mac and Fannie Mae were taken over by the federal government, and the implicit guarantee became explicit guarantee. The US Department of the Treasury provided sufficient capital to ensure that their net assets were zero, and the US Department of the Treasury received their preferred stocks and warrants. In the meanwhile, Freddie Mac and Fannie Mae gradually reduced the size of securities assets held by them to reduce the losses of taxpayers. Nevertheless, the two companies brought a huge size of contingent liabilities about 35% of the GDP in 2008, and the decline of housing prices forced the US Department of the Treasury to inject the money about 1.25% of the GDP.

From a global perspective, the time when a financial crisis breaks out is often the time contingent liabilities grow "explosively". Liabilities to households, non-financial corporations, financial institutions and even to other countries may all come out. Apart from treasury securities that the government should be responsible for repayment, some other liabilities will eventually become the liabilities of the country where a crisis occurs through government's injection of capital into banks, writing off household housing mortgage loans and non-performing corporate loans, tax breaks and other ways.

In particular, the central bank's balance sheet is an important part of the national balance sheet and an important source of contingent liabilities. This is because the central bank itself is a sector that has assets, liabilities and capital, and more importantly, the central bank is a sector that is able to create unlimited liabilities (issuing currency). As the final lender, especially during a financial crisis, the central bank not only can hold assets, but also can purchase a large amount of non-performing financial assets of financial institutions and corporations no one is interested in the market through expanding the monetary base and even adopting the quantitative easing policy. During this global financial crisis, the central banks of the United States, Europe, Britain, Japan and China "giftedly" implemented this strategy unexceptionally. Figure 19.3 illustrates the expansion of the balance sheets of the US, Japan, Britain and Europe. The Fed's assets rose rapidly from less than $1 trillion in 2008 to nearly $3 trillion currently. The balance sheet of the euro zone also rose from $1.9 trillion in 2006 to nearly $2.6 trillion currently. The balance sheet the People's Bank of China expanded much faster from $1.4 trillion in 2006 to nearly $4.4 trillion currently. The People's Bank of China has become the world's largest central bank.

Apart from the total sizes, the debt structures of the central banks have also undergone major changes. In late 2007, nearly 90% of the liabilities of the Fed were currencies in circulation, and since September 2008, the deposit reserves of financial institutions and the amount of Treasury Supplementary Financing Accounts have increased rapidly. The former was mainly due to the Fed's policy of paying interest on deposit reserves, and the latter is the fiscal appropriation granted by the government to avoid issuing more money. Despite the different approaches, the purpose of expanding the two types of accounts is to provide liquidity support to the market[1] (Fig. 19.4).

---

[1]In fact, the drastic changes in the structure of liabilities of the Federal Reserve had triggered the discussions on monetary policy instruments (See Curdia and Woodford 2011).

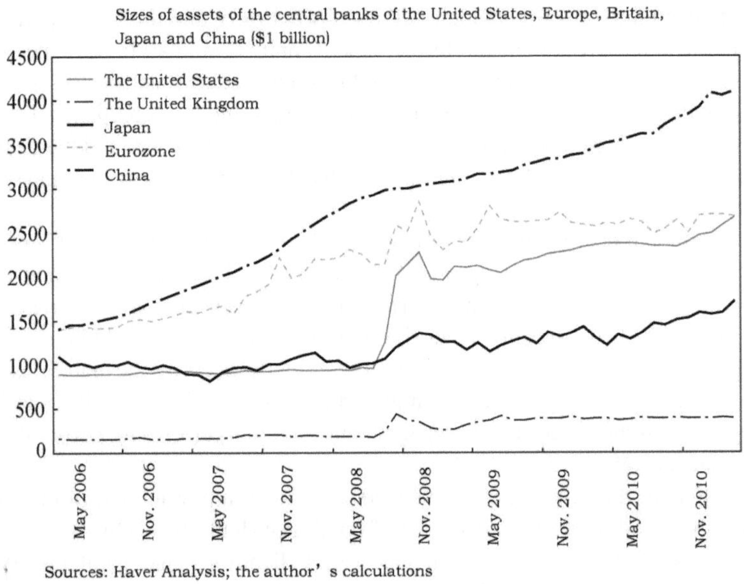

Fig. 19.3 Sizes of assets of the central banks of the United States, Europe, Britain, Japan and China ($1 billion)

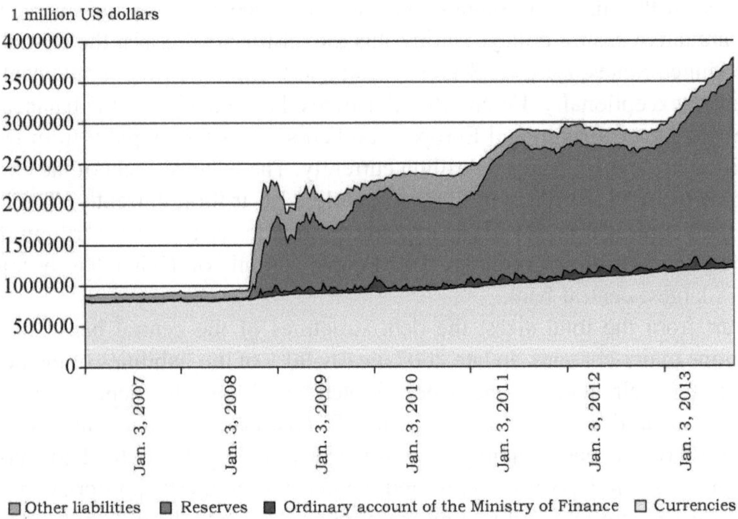

Fig. 19.4 Changes in the Fed's debt structure before and after the crisis. *Note* 1. The data are from the website of the Federal Reserve. 2. The unit is one million US dollars

Meanwhile, the euro zone's reserves rose from $290.6 billion at the beginning of 2008 to nearly $3.2 trillion currently. The reserves of the People's Bank of China also rose from $950.4 billion at the beginning of 2008 to more than 2 trillion currently. In addition, the crisis intervention measures of the central banks include not only the expansion of balance sheets, but also the extension of the term of assets, such as the term of liquidity support instruments and the term of treasury securities and other long-term assets purchased. By comparison, although the central banks of many countries absorbed and injected liquidity the toxic assets of the private sector through a variety of policy instruments, the European Central Bank and the Bank of England tended to use the traditional facilities (see Table 19.1) to stabilize financial markets such as loan extension and expansion of the scope of collaterals.[2] Therefore, there were relatively smaller changes in the structures of their balance sheets, and there were more long-term and illiquid assets (see Bagus and Howden 2009).

The changes in the balance sheets of the central banks during the crisis tended to lead to increase in risk assets and contingent liabilities. For example, the central banks of the United States, Britain Japan and Europe were mainly exposed to interest rate and credit risks. The global financial crisis has changed the asset structure of the four central banks, and the value of treasury securities and collaterals held by them are particularly sensitive to interest rate and credit risks because the rise in interest rates and credit default losses will lead to the decline in value of collaterals and asset losses. For example, the money the Fed used to bought $1.5 trillion worth of treasury securities was bank reserves rather than newly issued money, bonds produced high yields, while the interest rates for reserves were low, which ensures that the Fed locked up profits. In 2010, the Fed earned $81.7 billion, nearly equivalent to the total profits of all commercial banks and savings banks in the US. However, if interest rates rise, then the prices of treasury securities and mortgage-backed securities held by the Fed will decline. It is estimated that if the long-term interest rates increases by every one percentage point, the market value of the assets held by the Fed will fall by $100 billion, then the profits in 2010 will be all gone.

The European Central Bank. To support the countries affected by the crisis, the European Central Bank bought treasury securities and bank collaterals, which brought risks at two levels: first, the risk of default of €210 billion worth of collaterals of the banks in Greece, Ireland and Portugal; second, the interest rate and default risks of €75 billion worth of treasury securities of Greece, Ireland and Portugal. Obviously, if these countries undergo debt restructuring or if the interest rates in the euro zone increase and thus the prices of treasury securities and collaterals held by the ECB decline by 20%, then the ECB's capital will be completely obliterated. In addition, the Bank of England and the Bank of Japan were also exposed to the interest rate risk. The Bank of Japan was also exposed to the stock market volatility risk due to holding a portion of the shares of financial institutions.

[2]As of the beginning of 2011, the asset-backed securities (ABS) held by the European Central Bank had reached 480 billion euros, while ABS is one of the culprits triggering the US subprime mortgage crisis.

Table 19.1 Main financial instruments used by the Fed and the Bank of England in a crisis

The Fed	The Bank of England
1. Term Auction Facility (TAF): the Fed provided loans to the banks and accepted the high-risk collaterals provided by banks (such as real estate mortgage-backed securities (MBS) 2. Commercial Paper Funding Facility (CPFF): the Fed bought illiquid commercial paper from financial institutions 3. Term Securities Lending Facility (TSLF): the Fed lent treasury securities to primary dealers and accepted the high-risk collateral provided by the banks 4. Term Asset-Backed Securities Loan Facility (TALF): the Fed and the Treasury jointly provided loans to individual consumers and small businesses with eligible collaterals 5. Primary Dealer Credit Facility: the Fed provided loans to primary dealers and accepted low-quality assets as mortgages 6. Central bank liquidity swaps: the Fed provided dollar liquidity to the central banks of other countries 7. Maiden Lane (I, II, III): the special funds used by the Fed to absorb the non-performing assets of Bear Stearns and AIG	1. Intra-day repo 2. The reserve policy 3. Open market operations 4. Overnight operational standing facilities 5. Long-term repo 6. Discount window

The introduction to the financial instruments of the Bank of England was based on Tucker (2009)

The People's Bank of China (PBC). Due to the current exchange rate mechanism and export mode, the foreign exchange reserves of the PBC become the main channel for the supply of the monetary base in China, so the PBC is exposed to the exchange rate and inflation risks. First of all, the PBC is exposed to exchange rate risk arising from currency mismatch (its assets are mostly denominated in foreign currencies while its liabilities are mostly denominated in the local currency): if the foreign currencies depreciate (the RMB appreciates), the value of assets denominated in foreign currencies will decline. Second, the assets denominated in foreign currencies of the PBC will also shrink due to global inflation. Third, the PBC also is exposed to the risk arising from rising inflationary pressures. Apart from the interest costs of central bank bill and reserves that will fuel the inflation pressures, the 13.6 trillion yuan of reserves constitute the source of the monetary base, so the monetary expansion potential and potential inflationary pressure are high.

In short, the policies of the government and the central bank are often an important factor affecting the national balance sheet. For example, during the crisis, the governments of many countries adopted the intervention policy, which increased the size of their explicit and implicit liabilities. For example, to provide liquidity support, the central bank expanded the collateral base and extended the term of liquidity facilities; to strengthen the confidence of depositors, the central bank expanded the scope of deposit guarantee; to promote the flow of credit, the central bank implemented asset swap arrangements and asset purchase programs.

To solve insufficient liquidity of banks, the central banks have launched the bank recapitalization program. Table 19.2 summarizes the impact of the bailout measures of various countries during the crisis on their national balance sheets.

Table 19.2 Impact of the bailout measures of various countries during the crisis on their national balance sheets

Type of bailout measures	Assets	Liabilities
Liquidity injection	Repurchased bonds (+)	Cash in circulation (±)
	Unsecured loans (+)	Bank reserves (+)
	Central bank foreign exchange swap transactions (+)	Central bank swap transactions (+)
	Other swap transactions (+)	Other swap transactions (+)
	Foreign currency loans (+)	
	Foreign exchange reserves (−)	
Capital injection	Preferred/ordinary stocks (+)	The US treasury bonds (short-term/long-term) (+)
	Warrants (+)	
	Convertible bonds (+)	
	Subprime loans (+)	
Asset acquisition	Non-performing assets (+)	The US treasury bonds (short-term/long-term) (+)
	Corporate bonds/commercial paper/other fixed-income securities (+)	
	Other financial assets (+)	
Mortgages	Guarantee fund (+)	
Other intervention measures	Assets held by sovereign wealth funds (−)	
		Contingent claims (++)

19.2 Balance Sheet Risk Contagion: A Case Study of the Financial Crisis

When analyzing the national balance sheets, we should take into consideration the balance sheets of enterprises, financial institutions and the government sector. The impact from the market—interest rates, exchange rates or the market sentiment volatility—will lead to a decline in the value of assets and net assets of these sectors. If the net assets drop to negative, this will lead to large-scale contagion of losses and risks in the entire balance sheet. Therefore, to develop a method for discovering and assessing the vulnerability of balance sheet is the basis to minimize risks and ensure financial stability.

A risk may be transmitted in a "bottom-up" manner: from enterprises to banks and then to the national balance sheet. Such is the case for the Asian financial crisis and the US subprime crisis. It may also be transmitted in a "top-down" manner: from a sovereign power to banks and then to the balance sheets of enterprises. Such is the case for the Latin American debt crisis and the European sovereign debt crisis. In the following paragraphs, we will introduce the "bottom-up" and "top-down" risks contagion paths by taking the subprime crisis as an example. (For China, top-down contagion is more likely to occur because the state assume too much. This is decided by the characteristics of the government-led regime).

First, the contagion of debt risk of households to the financial institutions in the US. After the US subprime crisis occurred, the US institutions suffered losses worth of $370 billion in 2008 alone due to subprime loans and asset-backed securities (IMF 2007). First, these losses first offset the banks' profits and wrote-off the capital, and later the government had to recapitalize the banks.

Second, the contagion of risk from the US financial institutions to the US government. During 2008–2009, the US government injected capitol to a number of large financial institutions through the TARP program. The ratio of treasury securities to GDP increased accordingly. For example, the Federal Deposit Insurance Corporation (FDIC) launched the Temporary Liquidity Guarantee Program (TLGP) to provide guarantees for the unsecured debt of financial institutions, and the US Department of the Treasury provided guarantees for the money market funds. These are modern version of deposit insurance. In addition, the debt of Freddie Mac and Fannie Mae in the US was not directly included in the federal debt, but constituted the contingent liabilities of the US, and it accounted for 35% of the GDP (around the debt of Freddie Mac and Fannie Mae accounting for 8.25% of the GDP was held by the US Department of the Treasury and the Federal Reserve).

Third, the contagion of the risks from the Bank of America to the European financial institutions and investors. As European investors hold a large amount of mortgage securities products issued by the US financial institutions, the decline in the prices of these products led to the losses of the assets of the European investors, the decline of capital and tight liquidity. To achieve the capital adequacy requirements, the European banks had to sell assets, leading to continued decline in the prices of their financial assets, forming a vicious cycle.

Fourth, the contagion of risks from the European financial institutions to the governments of the European countries. During this global financial crisis, to prevent the collapse of financial institutions and the proliferation of liquidity risk, the United States and the European countries provides a huge amount of financial support to financial institutions. Figure 19.5 shows that the costs for the bailout of the financial sector in some countries accounted for an average of 5% of their GDPs, and the total amount of the bailout funds reached $1.27 trillion.

Fifth, the contagion of the risks of the European sovereign debt crisis to the European financial institutions. The losses from treasury bonds in some European countries were transmitted as the losses of assets of the European banks. The demand of domestic and foreign investors for the treasury bonds issued by the countries most seriously hit the EU sovereign debt crisis (the five PIIGS countries) decreased, leading to further decline of the prices of these bonds, so the Eurozone banks holding these bonds suffered losses. For example, the decline in the prices of the Greek treasury bonds led to the losses of €60 billion to the European banking system; if coupled with the losses of Ireland and Portugal, the losses reached €80 billion; if coupled with the losses of Belgium, Spain and Italy, the losses reached

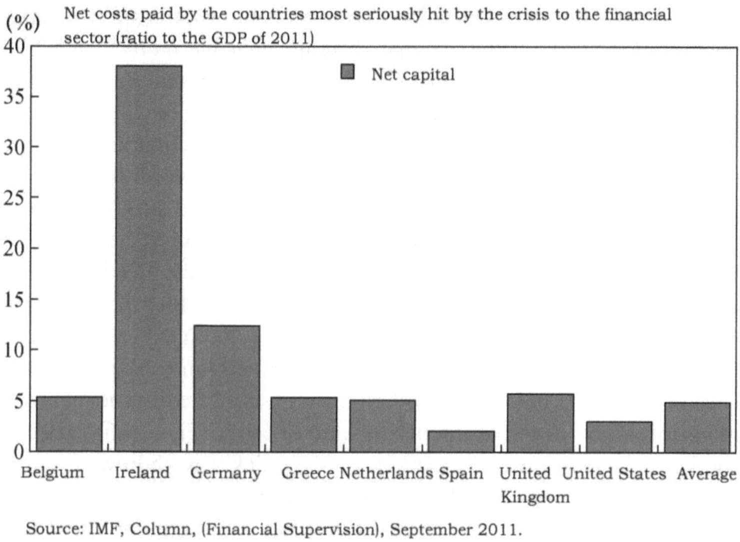

Fig. 19.5 Net costs paid by the countries most seriously hit by the crisis to the financial sector (ratio to the GDP of 2011)

€200 billion. In addition, in the treasury bonds worth of €450 billion held by the 24 largest banks in Europe, only €50 billion were from Greece, Ireland and Portugal and €400 billion were from other countries. This shows that, once the sovereign debt crisis is spread to more countries, the European banks will suffer greater losses. These concerns are reflected directly in the decline in the stock market: since the beginning of 2010, the prices of the stocks of the banks that hold the treasury bonds of the countries mostly seriously hit by the crisis have plummeted, and the market capitalization has dropped by more than 40%. Domestic and foreign investors reduced their holdings of stocks and bonds of the European banks, forcing the banks to sell their assets (exacerbating the asset losses of the banks) or seek the liquidity support from the ECB (increasing the ECB's pressure to buy bonds and its potential loss), which led to the credit crunch and the weak economic recovery.

Sixth, the contagion of the European sovereign debt crisis to the US financial institutions. The worsening of the European debt crisis and the banking crisis has not only fermented and cycled inside Europe but also spread to the financial institutions in the US. For example, the French banks hold both Greek treasury bonds and French treasury bonds, while the banks in the US have plenty of businesses with the French banks. In other words, the losses on Greek treasury bonds will influence first the French banks and then the US banks. Such contagion has changed to some extent the trading rules of the stock markets. Before the European debt crisis broke out, the concept deciding the trading in the stock market was whether today was an "adventuring" day or a "hedging" day, i.e. to buy or sell. Now, it is whether today is a "contagious" day (contagion from the European debt crisis) or "non-contagious" day (no contagion from the European debt crisis).

Another channel through which the European debt crisis is spread to the US is the money market funds in the US that currently manage more than $2.7 trillion worth of assets, among which the Prime Money Market Mutual Fund that invests in high-quality, short-term credit products (such as large-denomination certificates of deposits, repurchase, commercial paper, asset-backed commercial paper and short-term corporate notes etc.) has a total of $1.6 trillion worth of assets under its management. Due to the subprime crisis, the size of the products that can be invested by the money market funds in the US declined from $12 trillion in 2008 to $9.1 trillion present. Thus, the money market funds in the US had to invest in similar financial products on the European money markets after the subprime crisis, such as the US dollar-denominated European bonds and Yankee bonds issued by foreign institutions in the US. By June 2011, the Prime Money Market Mutual Fund had invested up to 675 billion US dollars in short-term credit products in Europe, accounting for 41.2% of the assets of this kind of funds (Fig. 19.6). After the debt crisis broke out, these money market funds quickly withdrew from Europe, resulting in a more serious liquidity crunch in the European financial institutions.

Seventh, the contagion of the US and European sovereign debt risks to the US and European central banks. The troubled finances forced the US and European governments to rely on the central banks to meet the liquidity and even solvency demands of financial institutions and finances, and the central banks bought a large amount of bonds of financial institutions and treasury bonds. For example, the Fed had, through its quantitative easing policy, bought the treasury securities accounting for 7.5% of the GDP, representing that 12% of the entire treasury securities were held by the public. The central bank of Japan bought the treasury bonds accounting

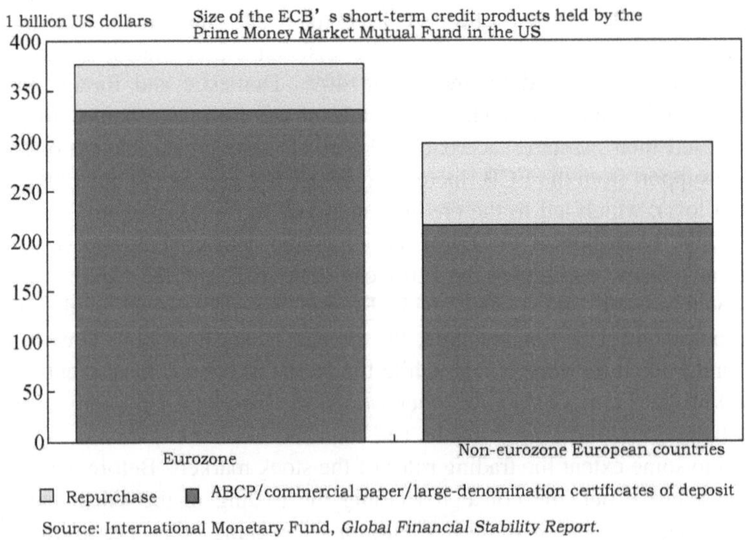

Fig. 19.6 Size of the ECB's short-term credit products held by the Prime Money Market Mutual Fund in the US

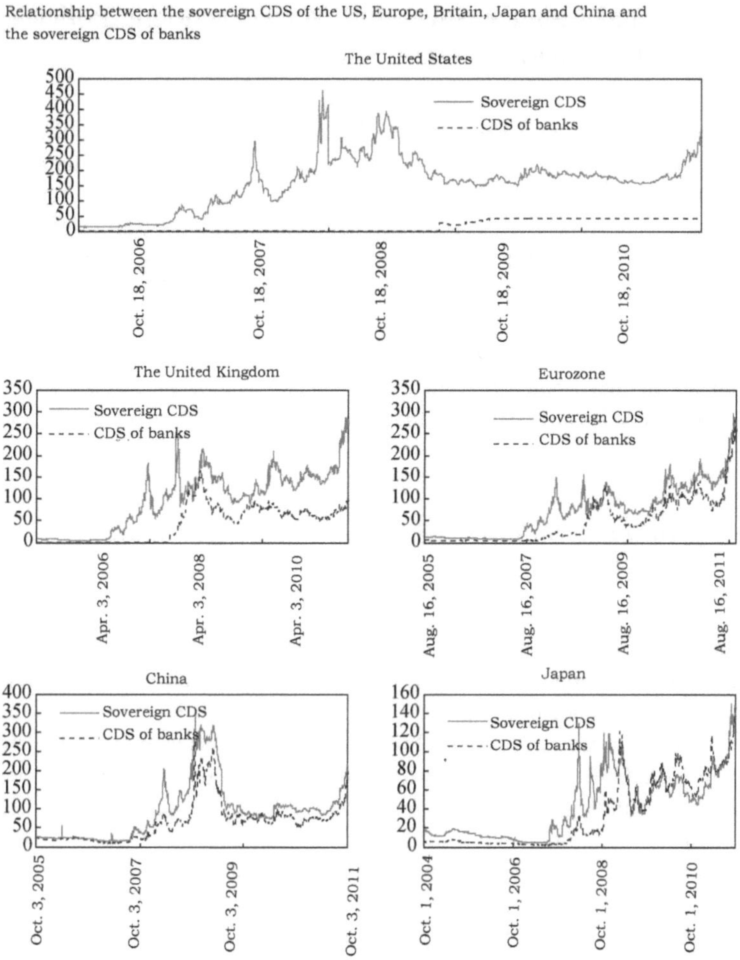

Fig. 19.7 Relationship between the sovereign CDS of the US, Europe, Britain, Japan and China and the sovereign CDS of banks

for 1% of the GDP (if including the bonds purchased through the monetary policy operations, then the proportion of treasury bonds held by the Bank of Japan was up to 17%). The Bank of England bought the treasury bonds accounting for 11.5% of the GDP through the asset purchase program.

Eighth, the bidirectional contagion of the sovereign debt risks and bank risks. As the banks in some countries hold a large amount of treasury bonds of the countries mostly seriously hit by the crisis, the sovereign risks were translated into bank risks. In the meanwhile, the bailout and support to the banks by the governments were translated into sovereign risks. Figure 19.7 illustrates the close relationship between sovereign CDS and banks' CDS.

19.3 National Balance Sheet and Macroeconomic Policies and Their Revelations

When discussing the macroeconomic policies, the traditional textbooks are often based on various combinations of the expansionary (tightening) monetary and fiscal policies in different economic cycles. For example, when a country is caught in the debt crisis, the tightening fiscal policy is adopted to limit the fiscal deficit and the expansionary monetary policy is adopted to promote economic growth. When the economy is overheating, the tightening monetary policy is adopted to control inflation and the tightening fiscal policy is adopted to prevent the economy from growing too fast. These policies are important basis for decision making. However, the analysis of these policies from the perspective of balance sheet can help us improve the effectiveness of the policies.

19.3.1 National Balance Sheets and Macroeconomic Policies

The bursting of a country's asset price bubbles is usually a factor triggering the balance sheet recession. The bursting of an asset-price bubble is usually attributed to excessive confidence of the private sector in the future economic growth. Japan was intoxicated in the world's lavishing praise on its management mode since the late 1980s; the United States and the world were overconfident as deluded by the information technology revolution in the late 1990s. The final result of the two is the bursting of price bubbles.

The bursting of asset price bubbles is in turn usually induced by the tightening monetary policy. To prevent the overheating of the economy and asset price bubbles, a country may adopt the tightening monetary policy to let the asset price bubbles burst. Of course, the bursting of some asset price bubbles is a natural adjustment after they have risen too much. The decline of asset prices will directly hit the balance sheet of the private sector, forcing the companies to repay their debts and reduce their financing needs.

In the balance sheet recession stage, the effectiveness of monetary policy will decline because enterprises are busy repaying their debts and have insufficient demand for funds. For example, after the 1929 crisis, the interest rates in the US took 30 years to return to the average level (4.1%) in the 1920s, showing a long time period during which enterprise avoid borrowing debts. Only after the companies in the private sector have repaired their balance sheets and start to borrow money, the effectiveness of monetary policy can be seen.

The fiscal policies—government borrowing and spending—have greater effect in preventing a crunch in economic and monetary supply. The government is unable to prevent enterprises from stopping repairing their balance sheets, but it can borrow money and use the private sector's accumulated savings to promote household savings and corporate debt repayment process. On the contrary, if the government does nothing, then the "invisible hand" will work, thus the economy will enter a deflationary vicious circle and the private sector will be increasingly poor and unable to save money. For example, Japan reduced the budget deficit by raising taxes and reducing spending in 1997. However, this led to falling instead of rising tax revenues and a substantial increase in the budget deficit. For another example, Germany expected to improve the financial or economic growth by reducing the budget deficit and promoting the results of reforms during 2000–2005, but the fiscal austerity also failed to achieve the purpose of improving the financial conditions and promoting economic growth. After the support from the fiscal policy for a long time, the problem of balance sheet can be addressed to some extent. Even so, many enterprises might be still repaying their debts, the economic recession continues, and enterprises are still reluctant to borrow. Therefore, it generally will take a longer time for enterprises to restart to borrow than the time needed for balance sheet repair.

In this financial crisis, the United States, Britain, Japan, Europe and other countries that were most seriously hit were in the balance sheet recession stage. Its main characteristics is that households, enterprises and governments had a large amount of debts after the bursting of asset price bubbles, so the main objective of the sectors was to reduce their debts (i.e. deleveraging). Particularly for enterprises, their primary goal was to reduce debts as quickly as possible rather than maximize profits so as to improve their balance sheets. In addition, the European banks had insufficient own capital, and the sovereign countries were unable to repay their debts, which indicated they were facing the risk of insolvency as a whole. These basic characteristics determined that these countries' economic recovery was weak and highly sensitive to various negative impacts at home and abroad. The turmoil in the financial markets caused by Standard & Poor's lowering the US debt rating is an example.

19.3.2 External Debt is a Key Factor in Increasing the Risk of Conduction

It is noteworthy that, despite facing the impact of similar risks, the markets reacted differently in different countries. The countries that heavily relied on foreign investors and had high net external debts were those mostly seriously hit, which was reflected as the soaring of sovereign CDS and yields of these countries during the crisis. Specifically, before the crisis, not every country hit by the European debt crisis had a large amount of fiscal deficit. Indeed, Greece and Italy had large fiscal deficits, but Ireland and Spain had no fiscal deficit and instead had a fiscal surplus, and their net treasury bonds to GDP ratios were only 12 and 31% in 2006, far lower than 53 and 60% of Germany and France. Why, then, Ireland and Spain that had better financial positions before the crisis were so vulnerable and suddenly faced

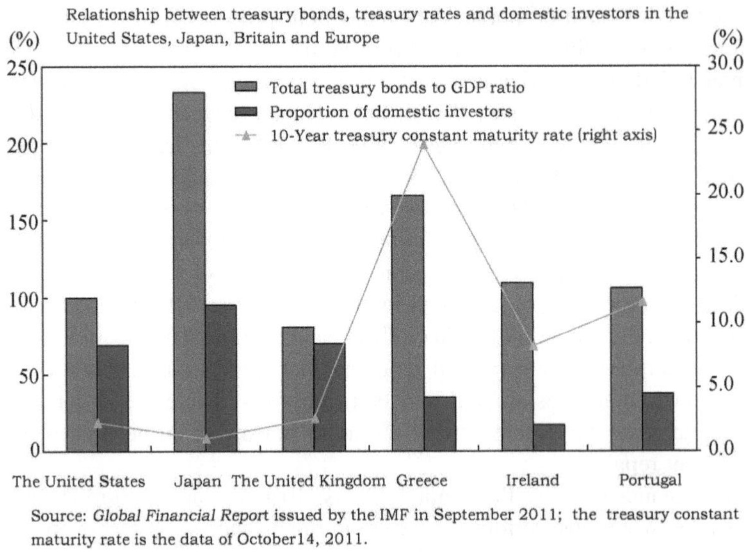

Fig. 19.8 Relationship between treasury bonds, treasury rates and domestic investors in the United States, Japan, Britain and Europe

with high financing costs and CDS? There are two main factors: first, there were too much contingent liabilities; second, foreign investors accounted for a high proportion of treasury bond investment. Therefore, when foreign investment fell, these countries got immediately into a debt crisis. Moreover, even though they were able to raise money, the interest rates were relatively high. Figure 19.8 shows that the treasury bonds to GDP ratios of the United States, Japan and the UK were high, but as domestic investors accounted for more than 60% in these countries, especially up to 95% in Japan, the treasury rates in the United States, Japan and Britain were low.

The above reality is also consistent with the history of the debt crisis. If a country's debt is mainly denominated in foreign currencies, then it is at greater risk of default directly. Apart from the factor that foreign investors account for a lower proportion, the international reserve currency status and the developed financial markets of the United States, Britain and Japan also made it possible for them to realize financing for treasury bonds at low costs: by relying on their international reserve currency status, these countries can reap income by seigniorage and some liquidity may flow to other countries to reduce the upward pressure on domestic inflation; by relying on their well-developed financial markets, the reserve currency issuing countries can not only retain a portion of liquidity and capital at home, but also can attract the out-flowed currency and capital to return and even attract the savings of other countries (such as foreign exchange reserves) to their financial markets.

19.3.3 Policy Revelations

A major revelation of this crisis is that: we should view financial risks from a country's overall balance sheet. This is because the liabilities of households, enterprises or a country will rapidly be translated into the sovereign risk of a country in the time of a crisis. On such occasion, the most important thing is that the government has the resources—capital and credibility—to stabilize the market confidence. Based on the international experience, contingent liabilities are an important factor in the crisis. Therefore, we need to establish a crisis response mechanism at the national level, and the preparation of the national balance sheet is an important part of it.

First, establishing the concept of national balance sheet.

On the asset side, how much assets a country owns determines how much resources it can use in the face of a financial crisis. To prevent and grapple with a financial crisis, we should certainly depend on confidence, but confidence is based on strength. After 30 years and more of economic growth, we need to count our real properties: how much assets we have indeed.

On the liability side, the size of China's overall liabilities is rising, and the government's explicit external debt and the debts of state-owned enterprises, banks and households are growing. In particular, many contingent liabilities are also growing, such as non-formal financing of SMEs, the debt of LGFPs, pension debts and incremental liabilities brought by longevity risk.[3] These debts are not worth worrying about in the time of rapid economic growth, but once the economy turns down, inter-contagion is inevitable, and the overall level of a country's debt will increase sharply, just like the European debt crisis, and the government will turn into a big debtor overnight and be highly sensitive to the markets, or have to issue bonds at high costs or is simply unable to issue bonds.

Second, rapidly preparing the national balance sheet. Being aware of the importance of national balance sheets, many countries in the world are sparing no effort to prepare their national balance sheets. According to the IMF's statistics, apart from the United States, already more than 40 countries have completed the preparation of their national balance sheets, among which many are developing and emerging market countries. The Chinese Ministry of Finance and other departments have also been preparing the national balance sheets for several years. As the local governments in China play an important role in promoting investment and economic growth and have borrowed huge debts in the form of government financing platform in recent years, so it is critical to prepare the balance sheet assets of local governments.

Third, minimizing the sources of contingent liabilities through market-oriented approaches. The purpose of preparation of the national balance sheet is to understand the overall situation of China's assets and liabilities, analyze the causes for

[3]Longevity risk refers to the extension of life expectancy as a result of technical breakthroughs medical care, which will virtually increase the future pension payment liabilities.

accumulation of assets and liabilities, strengthen and improve the accumulation and reduce unnecessary debt, especially contingent liabilities. For example, the government has certainly achieved some short-term policy goals in its intervention and regulation of some industries, but at the same time it has accumulated explicit and implicit liabilities. For another example, we have only emphasized that China's treasury to GDP ratio is within the international safety line and often neglected various kinds of implicit liabilities accumulated and their various sources. The pattern of the national economy intervened by the state and dominated by state-owned enterprises is bound to have brought China more implicit liabilities than the United States and Europe. Therefore, from a national balance perspective, it is absolutely urgent and necessary to reduce state intervention and convert implicit contingent liabilities into direct explicit liabilities.

Finally, we need to consider introducing a number of policies to cope with the shocks of liability risk in the future. For example, we can consider establishing China's financial stability fund. The European sovereign debt crisis reveals that the best mechanism is the European sovereign debt fund, which played a crucial role in stabilizing the financial markets.[4] More importantly, in response to the risks of interest rates, exchange rates and capital accounts and the risks appearing in the reform of financial institutions, the government needs adequate capital reserves.[5] Likewise, we can also consider make use of the favorable conditions such as good financial position, enormous capital flows and increase in land prices to launch China's financial stabilization fund by issuing bonds, capital injection by the government and income from land allocation. We may also consider using the existing platform of CIC.

[4]The European stabilization fund provides financial support to the member countries, and the assets under its management have increased from the initial 250 to 440 billion euros and to more than 700 billion euros recently. The fund has played a crucial role in maintaining confidence in financial markets.

[5]Competing for market shares and excessive competition will make banks relax their lending standards, capital inflows will lead to more loans, and the liquidity created by low interest rate policy will quickly reverse when interest rates rise. These may lead to the need for a stabilization fund.

References

References in Chinese

艾慧、张阳、杨长昱、吴延东 (2012),《中国养老保险统筹账户的财务可持续性研究——基于开放系统的测算》,《财经研究》, 02, 91–101页.

曹远征、马骏 (2012),《问计国家资产负债表》,《财经》2012 年 6 月.

曾令波 (2006),《投资回报率与中国养老体系的基金制改革》,《社会保障问题研究》, 294–311 页.

陈杰 (2012), 再论中国居民资产之谜,FT中文网,10月12日.

程永宏 (2005),《现收现付制与人口老龄化关系定量分析》,《经济研究》, 03, 57–68页.

樊纲 (1999),《论"国家综合负债"—兼论如何处理银行不良资产》,《经济研究》第5期.

Hui, Ai, Zhang Yang, Yang Changyu, and Wu Yandong. 2012. Study of financial sustainability of China's pension insurance accounts—Estimates based on the open systems. *The Study of Finance and Economics* 02: 91–101.

Cao Yuanzheng and Ma Jun. 2012. Asking advice for the national balance sheet. Finance, June 2012.

Zeng Lingbo. 2006. Return on investment and reform of the old-age insurance system in China. *Studies of Social Security Issues* 294–311.

Chen Jie. 2012. Re-discussion on the mystery of chinese households' assets. FT Chinese network, October 12.

Cheng Yonghong. 2005. Quantitative analysis of the relationship between the PAYG system and the population aging. *Economic Research* 03:57–68.

Fan Gang. 1999. On the national integrated liabilities—How to deal with the bad assets of banks. *Economic Research* Issue 5.

封进 (2004),《中国养老保险体系改革的福利经济学分析》,《经济研究》, 02, 55–63页。Feng Jin. 2004. Analysis of welfare economics of the reform of China's old-age insurance system. *Economic Research* 02:55–63.

郭永斌 (2012),《中国养老保险隐性债务的可持续性研究》,《南方金融》, 11, 70–76页。Guo Yongbin. 2012. Study of the sustainability of Chinese implicit pension debt. *South China Finance* 11:70–76.

国家统计局 (1997、2007),《中国资产负债表编制方法》,中国统计出版社。The National Bureau of Statistics (1997, 2007), *Method for Preparation of China's Balance Sheet*, China Statistics Press.

国家统计局(历年),《中国统计年鉴》,中国统计出版社。The National Bureau of Statistics (the previous years), *Statistical Yearbook China*, China Statistics Press.

国家统计局国民经济核算司 (2003), 中国国民经济核算,中国统计出版社。Department of National Accounts, NBS (2003), *China National Accounting*, China Statistics Press.

Y. Li and X. Zhang, *China's National Balance Sheet*, China Insights,
DOI 10.1007/978-981-10-4385-7

国家统计局国民经济核算司 (2007),中国资产负债表编制方法,中国统计出版社。Department of National Accounts, NBS. 2007. *Method for Preparation of China's Balance Sheet*, China Statistics Press.

国家统计局国民经济综合统计司 (2005),《新中国55年统计资料汇编》,中国统计出版社。Department of Comprehensive Statistics, NBS. 2005. *China Compendium of Statistics 1949–2004*, China Statistics Press.

韩燕, 曾令波 (2007),《资本市场投资回报率与我国养老金体系改革》,《证券市场导报》, 09, 23–29页.

Han Yan and Zeng Lingbo. 2007. Return on investment in the capital market and reform of the old-age insurance system in China. *Securities Market Herald* 09:23–29. 何平 (2001),《我国社会保障体系构架研究》,《中国劳动》, 05:8–10页.

He Ping. 2001. Study of the architecture of China's social security system. *China Labor* 05:8–10.

侯杰 (2006), 国家资本结构与新兴市场国家金融危机[博士学位论文].中国人民大学。 Hou Jie. 2006. The National Capital Structure and the Financial Crisis of the Emerging Market Countries [PhD thesis]. China People's University.

贾康等 (2007),《关于中国养老金隐性债务的研究》,《财贸经济》, 09, 15-21页。Jia Kang et al. 2007. Study of China's implicit pension debt. *Finance and Trade Economics* 09:15–21.

克莱德.斯蒂克尼、罗蔓.威尔 (2010), 财务会计:概念、方法与应用,机械工业出版社。Clyde P. Stickney and Roman L. Weil. 2010. *Financial accounting: An Introduction to Concepts, Methods and Uses*, China Machine Press.

课题组 (2010), 资本化扩张与赶超型经济的技术进步,《经济研究》第5期。The research group. 2010. Capitalization expansion and technological progress of catching-up economy. *Economic Research*, Issue 5.

莱因哈特、罗格夫 (2010),《这次不一样:八百年金融危机史》,机械工业出版社。李实、魏众、古斯塔夫森B. (2000), 中国城镇居民的财产分配,《经济研究》,第3期,16–23页。Reinhart and Rogoff. 2010. *This Time is Different: A Panoramic View of Eight Centuries of Financial Crises*, China Machin Press.

Li Shi, Wei Zhong and Gustafson B. 2000. Distribution of properties of China's urban residents. *Economic Research* 3:16–23.

李扬 (2009),《要从资产负债表来控制资产泡沫》,2009年夏季达沃斯论坛发言。http://money.163.com/09/0910/15/5IS2VHQJ00253NDC.html. Li Yang. 2009. Control of asset bubbles from the balance sheet. Speech at the 2009 Summer Davos Forum. http://money.163.com/09/0910/15/5IS2VHQJ00253NDC.html

梁运文、霍震、刘凯 (2010), 中国城乡居民财产分布的实证研究,《经济研究》,第10期,33–47页。 Liang Yunwen, Huo Zhen and Liu Kai. 2010. Empirical research on distribution of properties of urban and rural residents in China. *Economic Research* 10:33–47.

林永春 (2008),《基本养老保险基金资金缺口问题的对策研究》,《浙江金融》, 08, 50–59页。 Lin Yongchun. 2008. Research on countermeasures for the basic pension insurance funding gap problem. *Zhejiang Finance* 08:50–59.

刘儒婷 (2012),《人口老龄化背景下中国城镇养老金支付能力研究》, 东北财经大学。 Liu Ruting. 2012. *Research on China's Pension Payment Capacity for Urban Residents and Worker under the Background of Population Aging*, Dongbei University of Finance and Economics.

刘尚希 (2003),《财政风险:一个分析框架》,《经济研究》第5期。 Liu Shangxi. 2003. Financial risk: An analytical framework. *Economic Research* Section 5.

刘尚希 (2005),《财政风险:从经济总量角度的分析》,《管理世界》第7期。 Liu Shangxi. 2005. Financial RISKS: Analysis from the perspective of total economic output. *Management World*, Issue 7.

刘尚希、赵全厚 (2002),《政府债务:风险状况的初步分析》,《管理世界》第5期。 Liu Shangxi and Zhao Quanhou. 2002. Government debt: Preliminary analysis of risk profile. *Management World* Issue 5.

刘向耘、牛慕鸿、杨娉 (2009), 中国居民资产负债表分析,《金融研究》,第10期,107–117页。 Liu Xiangyun, Niu Muhong and Yang Ping. 2009. Analysis of China's household balance sheet. *Journal of Financial Research* 10:107–117.

路甬祥等 (2007),中国可持续发展总纲,科学出版社。 Lu Yongxiang et al. 2007. Pandect on *the Sustainable Development of China*, Science Press.

骆正清、陈周燕、陆安 (2010),《人口因素对我国基本养老保险基金收支平衡的影响研究》,《预测》, 02, 42–46页。 Luo Zhengqing, Chen Zhouyan and Lu Ann. 2010. Research on the impact of demographic factors on China's basic old-age insurance fund balance. *Forecasting* 02:42–46.

马骏、张晓蓉、李治国等 (2012),《中国国家资产负债表研究》,社会科学文献出版社。 Ma Jun, Zhang Xiaorong and Li Zhiguo et al. 2012. *Research on China's National Balance Sheet*, Social Sciences Academic Press.

.钱雪亚,王秋实,伊立夫 (2009), 中国人力资本和物质资本存量:基于总资本框架的估算,《商业经济与管理》第3期。 Qian Xueya, Wang Qiushi and Yi Lifu. 2009. China's human capital and material capital stock: Estimates based on the total capital framework. *Business Economics and Management*, Issue 3.

人民银行 (2012),《中国金融稳定报告 2012》,中国金融出版社。 The People's Bank of China. 2012. *China Financial Stability Report 2012*. China Financial Publishing House.

沈君霞 (2009),《中国基本养老保险基金收支平衡研究》,天津财经大学。 Shen Junxia. 2009. *Research on China's Basic Old-Age Insurance Fund Balance*, Tianjin University of Finance and Economics.

沈毅 (2011),《基于统筹账户的城镇老年人口养老金收支预测分析》,《党政干部学刊》, 05:60–63+15页。 Shen Yi. 2011. Forecasting and analysis of pension payments for the urban elderly population pooling based on the pooling accounts. *Journal for Party and Administrative Cadres* 05:60–63+15.

斯密,亚当 (1996),《国民财富的性质和原因的研究》,(郭大力、王亚南译),商务印书馆。 Adam Smith. 1996. Inquiry into the nature and causes of the wealth of nations. (translated by Guo Dali and Wang Yanan, the Commercial Press.

宋晓梧等 (2000),《中国养老保险隐性债务》,研究报告。 Song Xiaowu et al. 2000. China's implicit pension debt. the Researchers Report.

孙祁祥 (2001),《"空账"与转轨成本——中国养老保险体制改革的效应分析》,《经济研究》, 05, 20-27页。 Sun Qixiang. 2001. Empty accounts and transition costs—Analysis of the effects of China's pension reform. *Economic research* 05:20–27.

孙涛 (2011),《人民银行意外夺魁全球最有影响力央行力压美联储》,《新世纪》7月18日。 Sun Tao. 2011. The people's bank of China unexpectedly beat the federal reserve and won the world's most influential Central Bank. The New Century, July 18.

汤铎铎 (2013), 非金融企业资产负债表的初步研究,内部工作论文。 Tang Duoduo. 2013. *Preliminary Study of Non-financial Corporate Balance Sheet*, The Internal Work Thesis.

汪泽英、何平 (2008),《我国社会保障制度改革30年成就与发展》。 Wang Zeying and He Ping. 2008. Achievements of the reform of the social security system in China in the past 30 years and its development.

王德文 (2006),《中日养老金筹措及其可持续性分析》, 《经济社会体制比较》, 03, 55–60页。 Wang Dewen. 2006. Analysis of the sustainability of pension financing in China and Japan. *Comparative Economic and Social Systems* 03:55–60.

王国刚, 2010:《基于资产负债表的央行调控能力分析》,《金融评论》,第 01 期,1–16。 Wang Guogang. 2010. Analysis of the Central Bank's regulation capacity base on the balance sheet. *Chinese Review of Financial Studies* 1:1–16.

王国刚, 2012:《中国货币政策调控工具的操作机理:2001—2010》,《中国社会科学》,第 04 期,62–82。 Wang Guogang. 2012. Operation mechanism of Chinese monetary regulation policy tools: 2001–2010. *Social Sciences in China* 04:62–82.

王晓军、任文东 (2013),《我国养老保险的财务可持续性研究》,《保险研究》, 04, 118–127页。Wang Xiaojun and Ren Wendong. 2013. Study of financial sustainability of the old-age insurance in China. *Insurance Studies* 04:118–127.

王燕、徐滇庆、王直、翟凡 (2001),《中国养老金隐性债务、转轨成本、改革方式及其影响——可计算一般均衡分析》,《经济研究》, 05, 3–12页。 Wang Yan, Xu Dianqing, Wang Zhi and Zhai Fan. 2001. China's implicit pension debt, transition costs, reform mode and its influence—Computable general equilibrium analysis. *Economic Research* 05:3–12.

肖立晟、王博 (2011),《全球失衡与中国对外净资产:金融发展视角的分析》,《世界经济》,02 Xiao Lisheng and Wang Bo. 2011. Global imbalances and China's net external assets: Analysis from the perspective of financial development. *The Journal of World Economy* 02.

徐建炜、姚洋 (2010),《国际分工新形态、金融市场发展与全球失衡》,《世界经济》第3期。 Xu Jianwei and Yao Yang. 2010. A new form of international division of labor, financial market development and global imbalances. *The Journal of World Economy* Issue 3.

徐梅、邱长溶 (2006),《不同群体对中国养老保险体系选择的经济学分析》,《数量经济技术经济研究》, 04, 22–29页。 Xu Mei and Qiu Changrong. 2006. Economic analysis of selection of China's old-age insurance systems by different groups. the *Journal of Quantitative and Technical Economics* 04:22–29.

叶永刚、刘春霞 (2008), 我国非金融企业部门信用风险评估:基于宏观金融工程分析框架,《武汉大学学报(哲学社会科学版)》,第3期。 Ye Yonggang and Liu Chunxia. 2008. Credit risk assessment for China's non-financial corporate sector: A analysis framework based on the macro-financial engineering. Wuhan University Journal (Philosophy and Social Sciences), Issue 3.

易纲 (2008),《中国能够经受住金融危机的考验》,《求是》杂志22期。 Yi Gang. 2008. China can withstand the test of the financial crisis. *Seeking Truth*, Issue 22.

余永定 (2000),《财政稳定问题研究的一个理论框架》,《世界经济》第6期。 Yu Yongding. 2000. A theoretical framework for the study of financial stability. *The Journal of World Economy* on page 6.

袁飞、陶然、徐志刚、刘明兴 (2008),《财政集权过程中的转移支付和财政供养人口规模膨胀》,《经济研究》第5期。 Fei Yuan, Tao Ran, Xu Zhigang and Liu Mingxing. 2008. Transfer payments and expansion of population supported by finance in the fiscal centralization process. *Economic research* Issue 5.

袁志刚 (2001),《中国养老保险体系选择的经济学分析》,《经济研究》, 05, 13–19页。 Yuan Zhigang. 2001. Economic analysis of selection of China's old-age insurance systems. *Economic Research* 05:13–19.

岳希明、李实 (2013), 我们更应该相信谁的基尼系数,《华尔街日报》中文网1月24日。 Yue Ximing and Li Shi. 2013. Who's gini coefficient should we believe. *The Chinese website of the Wall Street Journal* Jan. 24.

张春霖 (2000),《如何评估我国政府债务的可持续性?》,《经济研究》第2期。 Zhang Chunlin. 2000. How to assess the sustainability of China's government debt? *Economic Research* Issue 2.

张帆 (2000), 中国的物质资本和人力资本估算,《经济研究》第8期。 Zhang Fan. 2000. Estimation of China's material and human capital. *Economic Research* Issue 8.

张国生 (2006),《改进我国政府资产负债表的思考》,《财经论丛》第3期。 Zhang Guosheng. 2006. Reflection on improving the preparation of the government balance sheet. *Collected Essays on Finance and Economics* Issue 3.

张军,吴桂英,张吉鹏 (2004), 中国省际物质资本存量估算:1952–2001,《经济研究》第10期。 Zhang Jun, Wu Guiying and Zhangji Peng. 2004. Estimation of provincial capital stock in China: 1952–2001. *Economic Research* Issue 10.

赵俊康 (2006),《我国养老保险转轨成本研究》,《社会保障问题研究》, 66–78页。 Zhaojun Kang. 2006. Study of transition costs of China's old-age insurance. *Studies of Social Security Issues*, 66–78.

赵人伟 (2007), 我国居民收入分配和财产分布问题分析,《当代财经》,第7期,5–11页。 Zhao Renwei. 2007. Analysis of residents' income distribution and wealth distribution in China. *Contemporary Finance and Economics* 7:5–11.

中国家庭金融调查与研究中心 (2012),《中国家庭金融调查报告》,西南财经大学。 China Household Finance and Survey. 2012. *Report on the China Household Finance Survey*, Southwestern University of Finance and Economics.
周小川 (2004),《央行行长周小川谈银行改革和金融改革》,2004年北京国际金融论坛发言。见:http://www.people.com.cn/GB/jingji/1040/2507904.html Zhou Xiaochuan. 2004. Central Bank Governor Zhou Xiaochuan on Banking and Financial Reform, Speech at Beijing International Financial Forum 2004. See: http://www.people.com.cn/GB/jingji/1040/2507904.html.
周志凯 (2006),《国外养老保险个人账户管理模式比较——以智利、新加坡、瑞典为对象》,《社会保障问题研究》,420–437页。 Zhou Zhikai. 2006. Comparison of foreign old-age insurance personal account management models—The models of Chile, Singapore and Sweden. *Study of Social Security Issues* 420–437.
朱孟楠,赵茜 (2012): 《人民币汇率、外汇占款变动对通货膨胀的影响》,《经济学动态》, 01, 76–81页。 Zhu Mengnan and Zhao Qian. 2012. Impact of fluctuations in RMB exchange rate and the position for forex purchase on inflation. *Economic Perspectives* 01:76–81.

References in English

Allen, Mark, Rosenberg, Christoph, Keller, Christian, Setser, Brad, and Roubini, Nouriel. 2002. A balance sheet approach to financial crisis, *IMF Working Paper*, WP/02/210.
Arpaia, Alfonso, Perez, Esther, and Pichelmann, Karl. 2009. Understanding labour income share dynamics in Europe, *European Communities, Economic Papers* 379.
Arrow, K., Dasgupta, P., Goulder, L., Mumford, K., and Oleson, K. 2007. China, the U.S., and sustainability: Perspectives based on comprehensive wealth, *Stanford Center for International Development Working Paper* No. 313.
Arrow, K., Dasgupta, P., Goulder, L., Mumford, K., and Oleson, K. 2010. Sustainability and the measurement of wealth, *NBER Working Paper* No. 16599.
Asian Development Bank. 2011. *Asia 2050: Realizing the Asian Century*, Asian Development Bank.
Bagus, Philipp, and David Howden. 2009. The federal reserve and eurosystem's balance sheet policies during the financial crisis: A comparative analysis. *Romanian Economic and Business Review* 4 (3): 165–185.
Carlson, Keith M. 1991. The U.S. balance sheet: What is it and what does it tell us? *Federal Reserve Bank of St. Louis Review*, September/ October, 3–18.
Calvo, G. 1990. The Perils of Sterilization, Imf Working Paper No. 90/13.
Cecchetti, Stephen G., Mohanty, M. S. and Zampolli, Fabrizio. 2011. The real effects of debt, *BIS working paper* No. 352.
Chinn, Menzie D., and Hiro Ito. 2008. A new measure of financial openness. *Journal of Comparative Policy Analysis* 10 (3): 309–322.
Christensen, J. 2004. *Capital Inflows, Sterilization, and Commercial Bank Speculation: The Case of the Czech Republic in the Mid-1990s*, IMF Working Paper No. 04/218.
Citibank. 2011. *Global Growth Generators: Moving Beyond Emerging Markets and Bric.*
Curdia, Vasco, and Michael Woodford. 2011. The central-bank balance sheet as an instrument of monetary policy. *Journal of Monetary Economics* 58: 54–78.
Dickinson, Frank, and Eakin, Franzy. 1936. *A Balance Sheet of The Nation's Economy*. University of Illinois.
Federal Reserve System. 1991. *Balance Sheets for the U.S. Economy: 1945–90*, Board of Governors of the Federal Reserve System, Washington DC.
Federal Reserve System. 2012. *Flow of Funds Accounts of the United States: Flows and Outstandings, First Quarter 2012*. Washington DC: Board of Governors of the Federal Reserve System.

Federal Statistical Office. 2012. *Balance Sheets for Institutional Sectors and the Total Economy: 1991–2011*, Statistisches Bundesamt.

Frankel, Jeffrey and Saravelos, George. 2011. Can leading indicators assess country vulnerability? Evidence from the 2008–09 global financial crisis, *HKS Faculty Research Working Paper Series*, RWP11-024, June.

Goldsmith, R., W. 1966. The uses of national balance sheet. *Review of Income and wealth* 12 (2):95–133.

Goldsmith, Raymond W. 1982. *The National Balance Sheet of the United States, 1953–1980*, The University of Chicago Press.

Goldsmith, R. W. 1985. *Comparative National Balance Sheets, A Study of Twenty Countries, 1688–1978*. Chicago, London: University of Chicago University Press.

Goldsmith, R., W., and Lipsey, R. E. 1963. *Studies in the National Balance Sheet of the United States*. Princeton University Press.

Government of Japan. 2012. *Annual Report on National Accounts of 2012*, Economic and Social Research Institute, Cabinet Office.

Gramlich, Edward. 1969. State and local governments and their budget constraint. *International Economic Review*, 10:163–182.

Gramlich, Edward. 1977. Intergovernmental grants: A review of the empirical literature, in W.E. Oates (ed.), *The Political Economy of Federalism*, Lexington, MA: Lexington Books, 219–240.

Gray, Dale F., Merton, Robert C., and Bodie, Zvi. 2007. New framework for measuring and managing macrofinancial risk and financial stability, *NBER Working Paper*, No. 13607.

Haim, Yair, and Levy, Roee. 2007. Using the balance sheet approach in financial stability surveillance: Analyzing the Israeli economy's resilience to exchange rate risk, No. 1/07, Bank of Israel.

Hana, Polackova Brixi. 1998. Contingent government liabilities: A hidden risk for fiscal stabilities, *World Bank Policy Research Working Paper*, No. 1989.

He, Zhiguo, Khang, In Gu, and Krishnamurthy, Arvind. 2010. Balance sheet adjustments in the 2008 crisis, *NBER Working Paper*, No. 15919.

Henderson, James. 1968. Local government expenditures: A social welfare analysis. *Review of Economics and Statistics* 50 (May): 156–163.

Hinz, R., A. Zviniene, S. Biletsky, and T. Bogomolova. 2009. *The impact of the financial crisis on public pension systems: Stress testing models of mandatory pension systems in middle income and developing countries, Social Protection and Labor Department*. Washington, DC: World Bank. Mimeo.

Holder, Andrew. 1998. Developing the public-sector balance sheet. *Economic Trends* 540:31–40.

Holzmann, R., Robalino, D., and Takayama, N. 2009. Closing the coverage gap: The role of social pensions and other retirement income transfers, World Bank-free PDF.

IMF. 2009a. *Government Finance Statistics Yearbook 2008*. Washington, DC: International Monetary Fund.

IMF. 2009b. Crisis-related measures in the financial system and sovereign balance sheet risks, International Monetary Fund, Fiscal Affairs and Monetary and Capital Markets Departments.

IMF. 2011. *Public sector debt statistics: guide for compilers and users*. Washington, DC: International Monetary Fund.

Inman, Robert P. 1988. Federal assistance and local services in the United States: The evolution of a new federalist fiscal order. In *Fiscal Federalism: Quantitative Studies*, ed. Harvey S. Rosen, 33–74. Chicago: University of Chicago Press.

Kennedy, Jim. 2012. Overview of Flow of Funds Accounts, unpublished paper, Board of Governors of the Federal Reserve System.

Kiyotaki, Nobuhiro, and Moore, John. 2002. Balance-sheet contagion, *American Economic Review, Papers and Proceedings*, May, 46–50.

Klenow, P.J., and A. Rodríguez-Clare. 2005. Externalities and growth. In *Handbook of Economic Growth*, ed. P. Aghion, and S. Durlauf. Amsterdam: North Holland.

Lane, Philip, and, Milesi-Ferretti, Gian Maria. 2007. The external wealth of nations mark II.
Revised and extended estimates of foreign assets and liabilities, 1970–2004. *Journal of International Economics* 73:223–250.

Lane,Philip, and Milesi-Ferretti,Gian Maria. 2008. The Drivers of financial globalization, *American Economic Review* 98(2):327–32.

Lima, Juan Manuel, Montes, Enrique, Varela, Carlos, and Wiegand, Johannes. 2006. Sectoral balance sheet mismatches and macroeconomic vulnerabilities in Colombia, 1996–2003, *IMF Working Paper*, WP/06/5.

Madigan, Brian F. 2009. Bagehot's dictum in practice: Formulating and implementing policies to combat the financial crisis, Speech at the Federal Reserve Bank of Kansas City's Annual Economic Symposium, August 21, http://www.federalreserve.gov/newsevents/speech/madigan20090821a.htm.

Mathisen, Johan, and Pellechio, Anthony. 2006. Using the balance sheet approach in surveillance: Framework, data sources, and data availability, *IMF Working Paper*, WP/06/100.

McKinsey Global Institute (MGI). 2009. Global capital markets: Entering a new era, www.mckinsey.com.

McKinsey Global Institute (MGI). 2010. Debt and deleveraging: The global credit bubble and its economic consequences, www.mckinsey.com

McKinsey Global Institute (MGI). 2012. Debt and deleveraging: Uneven progress on the path to growth, www.mckinsey.com

Obstfeld, Rogoff. 2009. Global imbalances and the financial crisis: Products of common causes, *CEPR Discussion Paper*, No. DP7606.

OECD. 2013. *OECD Factbook 2013: Economic*. Organisation for Economic Co-operation and Development: Environmental and Social Statistics.

Office for National Statistics. 2012. United Kingdom National Accounts: The Blue Book. Oi, Jean (1992), Fiscal reform and the economic foundations of local state corporatism in China, *World Politics*, Vol. 45, No. 1.

Oksanen, H. 2010. The Chinese pension system: First results on assessing the reform options, Directorate General Economic and Monetary Affairs (DG ECFIN), European Commission.

Economics, P.W.C. 2013. *World in 2050: The Brics and Beyond: Prospects*. Challenges and Opportunities: PWC Publishing.

Reinhart,Carmen M., and Rogoff,Kenneth S. 2008. Is the 2007 U.S. subprime crisis so different? An international historical comparison, *American Economic Review* 98(2):339–344.

Reinhart, Carmen M., and Rogoff, Kenneth S. 2010. From financial crash to debt crisis, *NBER working paper*, No. 15795.

Reinhart, Carmen M., and Sbrancia, M. Belen. 2011. The liquidation of government debt, *NBER Working Paper*, No. 16893.

Revell, Jack. 1966. The National Balance Sheet of the United Kingdom. *Review of Income and wealth* 12 (4): 281–310.

Rosenberg, Christoph, Halikias, Ioannis, House, Brett, Keller, Christian, Nystedt, Jens, Pitt, Alexander, and Setser, Brad. 2005. Debt-related vulnerabilities and financial crises: An application of the balance sheet approach to emerging market countries, IMF, *Occasional Paper*, No. 240

Rutledge, John. 2009. Total Assets of the U.S. Economy $188 Trillion, 13.4xGDP, http://rutledgecapital.com/2009/05/24/total-assets-of-the-us-economy-188-trillion-134xgdp/

Sin, Y. 2005. Pension liabilities and reform options for old age insurance, *World Bank working paper*.

Statistics Canada. 2010. *A User Guide to the Canadian System of National Accounts: Chapter 5, Financial Flows and Balance Sheets*, Statistics Canada.

Triffin, Robert. 1961. *Gold and the Dollar Crisis: The Future of Convertibility*, Yale University Press, Revised Edition.

Tucker, Paul. 2009. The repertoire of official sector interventions in the financial system: Last resort lending, market-making, and capital, Speech at the Bank of Japan 2009 International Conference, May 27–28. http://www.bankofengland.co.uk/publications/speeches/2009/speech390.pdf

Turner, J.A. 2012. Closing the Coverage gap: The role of social pensions and other retirement income transfers. *Journal of Pension Economics and Finance* 01: 141–143.

UNU-IHDP and UNEP. 2012. *Inclusive Wealth Report 2012: Measuring Progress toward Sustainability*. Cambridge: Cambridge University Press.

World Bank. 1994. *World Development Report 1994: Infrastructure for Development*. Washington D.C: World Bank.

World Bank. 2006. *Where is the wealth of nations? measuring capital for the 21st century*. World Bank: Washington D.C.

World Bank. 2011. *The Changing Wealth of Nations: Measuring Sustainable Development in the New Millennium*. Washington D.C: World Bank.

Zeng. Y. 2006. Estimating the impacts of demographic and policy changes on pension deficit: A simple method and application to China, *SCAPE Working Paper Series*.

MIX
Papier aus verantwortungsvollen Quellen
Paper from responsible sources
FSC® C105338

If you have any concerns about our products,
you can contact us on
ProductSafety@springernature.com

In case Publisher is established outside the EU,
the EU authorized representative is:
Springer Nature Customer Service Center GmbH
Europaplatz 3, 69115 Heidelberg, Germany

Printed by Libri Plureos GmbH
in Hamburg, Germany